CW00347904

1,000,000 Books

are available to read at

Forgotten Books

—◆—

www.ForgottenBooks.com

—◆—

Read online
Download PDF
Purchase in print

ISBN 978-1-5277-3249-0
PIBN 10885427

English
Français
Deutsche
Italiano
Español
Português

www.forgottenbooks.com

Mythology Photography **Fiction**
Fishing Christianity **Art** Cooking
Essays Buddhism Freemasonry
Medicine **Biology** Music **Ancient
Egypt** Evolution Carpentry Physics
Dance Geology **Mathematics** Fitness
Shakespeare **Folklore** Yoga Marketing
Confidence Immortality Biographies
Poetry **Psychology** Witchcraft
Electronics Chemistry History **Law**
Accounting **Philosophy** Anthropology
Alchemy Drama Quantum Mechanics
Atheism Sexual Health **Ancient History**
Entrepreneurship Languages Sport
Paleontology Needlework Islam
Metaphysics Investment Archaeology
Parenting Statistics Criminology
Motivational

IN THE XXVIII EDWARD I. A. D. MCCC;

WITH

WHO WERE PRESENT ON THE OCCASION;

WITH

A TRANSLATION, A HISTORY OF THE CASTLE,

AND

MEMOIRS OF THE PERSONAGES COMMEMORATED BY THE POET.

BY

NICHOLAS HARRIS NICOLAS, Esq.

OF THE INNER TEMPLE, BARRISTER AT LAW.

LONDON:

J. B. NICHOLS AND SON.

MDCCCXXVIII.

TO THE

KINGS, HERALDS, AND PURSUIVANTS,

OF THE

College of Arms.

GENTLEMEN,

I do myself the honour of inscribing this volume to you, in testimony of my high respect for your profession, and of my gratitude for the liberal manner in which you have for many years been pleased to allow me access to your invaluable archives.

By those individuals of your Corporation, with whom I have long lived on terms of uninterrupted intimacy, I hope this dedication will also be received as evidence that I admire their talents as much as I value their friendship.

I have the honour to subscribe myself,

Gentlemen,

Your very faithful and obliged humble Servant,

NICHOLAS HARRIS NICOLAS.

February 10*th,* 1828.

a

PREFACE.

THE claims of the following Poem to attention are great and unquestionable : instead, therefore, of a feeling of surprise being excited at its present appearance, it is extraordinary that it should not long since have been given to the world in an accurate and satisfactory manner.

For the Historian—the Poem minutely details the siege of a celebrated fortress in Scotland, by King Edward the First, in July, 1300, of which no other account is to be found, excepting in one line of Peter de Langtoft's rhyming Chronicle, and in a few words of the inedited Chronicle of Lanercost Abbey.

For the Antiquary—it abounds in descriptions of considerable interest, chiefly respecting the mode in which a siege was conducted, and the appearance and equipment of an army, at the end of the thirteenth century.

By the Bibliographer—its value must be at once admitted, since its antiquity is undoubted. When compared with other poems of the time, its merits as a composition are at least equal if not superior to most of those which are extant, and, from the subject of which it principally treats, it is unique.

It is by the lover of Heraldry, however, (if, which it is difficult to believe, such an individual can exist, who is not to a greater or less extent an antiquary,) that this Poem will be the most eagerly perused and the most attentively studied. It contains the accurate blazon of above one hundred Knights or Bannerets of the reign of Edward the First, among whom were the King, the Prince of Wales, and the greater part of the Peers of the realm. At the same time that this production may, perhaps, be considered the earliest blazon of arms which is known, it

affords evidence of the perfect state of the science of Heraldry at that
early period, and from which it is manifest that it was reduced to a science,
when it is generally considered to have been but in its infancy.

Valuable as the " Siege of Carlaverock" is to Historians and Antiquaries, it is difficult to believe that the raciness of the author's descriptions,
his quaint notices of the characters of the different personages, and the
occasional beauty of his passages, will not possess a charm for far more
general readers.

The merits of the Poem having been pointed out, it is necessary that the
proofs of its authenticity should be briefly noticed. It is sufficient to
state the fact that a *contemporary* copy at this moment exists in the British
Museum;[a] and, irrefragable as that evidence is, the internal proofs, to
which various allusions are made in the biographical memoirs, are no less
satisfactory.

Although the name of the author has not been decidedly ascertained,
there is one line which affords strong presumptive proof of his identity.
When speaking of the Earl of Warwick, he says he has alluded to him in
his " rhyme of Guy :"

De Warwik le Count Guy
Coment ken ma rime de Guy.

It may therefore be presumed that the author of the " Siege of Carlaverock" was Walter of Exeter, a Franciscan friar, who " is said on good
authority to have written the romantic history of Guy Earl of Warwick
about the year 1292."[b] Bale asserts that the said Walter wrote " Vitam
Guidonis," and which, Warton observes, " seems to imply a prose history."[c] An imperfect but contemporary copy of the romance in question
is thus described in the Harleian Catalogue, " Historia Feliciæ filiæ Comitis Warwicensis, et Guidonis filii Seguarti dispensatoris ejus, aliter dicti
Guido Warwicensis, versibus Gallicis :"[d] and a few extracts from it will

---

[a] In the Cottonian MSS. Caligula, A. xviii.

[b] Warton's History of English Poetry, ed. 1774, vol. I. p. 87, apparently on the authority of Bale
and Carew. Bishop Nicolson and some other writers state, however, that it was written in 1301, about
the same time as the " Siege of Carlaverock."

[c] Warton's History of English Poetry, p. 87, note.   [d] Harleian MSS. 3775, art. 2.

be found among the notes at the end of this volume. A copy also occurs in the College of Arms,[d] in the collection of MSS. presented to that body by Henry, Duke of Norfolk, in 1678; and perhaps other transcripts exist. Two reasons, besides the lines which have been just extracted, render it probable that the author of the following Poem wrote the one in question; the date which has been assigned to it, 1292, and its having been written in the same language.

Of Walter of Exeter very few particulars are known. Carew considered him to have been born in Cornwall, and says he was " a Franciscan friar of Carocus[e] in that county, and that at the request of Baldwin of Exeter he formed the History of Guy of Warwick;" but Prince claims him, with more probability, as a native of Devon, " as his name plainly demonstrates the place to which he owed his nativity, Exeter in Devon."[f] The biographical facts of him mentioned by that writer, are so few that they will be here inserted. He was, he informs us, a religious man professed, but of what order is not known. Bale thought he was a Dominican, Carew that he was a Franciscan friar, and Izaac that he was a monk of the order of St. Bennet. The greater part of his time was passed in a little cell in Cornwall near St. Caroke, a short distance from Lostwithiel, in study and devotion; but his chief pursuit was history: " for his knowledge therein he hath obtained this character, ' Quòd in historiarum cognitione non fuit ultimus,' and the part of history he was most skilled in was the lives of the saints and other great men, which induced Baldwin, his fellow citizen, to put him upon writing the life of Guy of Warwick." " What more things he wrote," Prince adds, " he does not find, but, dying as is probable in his cell, he lieth interred near that place."

The studies for which that monk was distinguished peculiarly fitted him for the task of composing a poem of so historical and biographical a nature

---

d Now numbered 27.

e Tonkin supposes Carew to have meant Carantocus, Crantock, in Cornwall.

f Survey of Cornwall, with Tonkin's notes, published by Lord de Dunstanville in 1811, p. 159.

g Worthies of Devon, ed. 1810, p. 345.

as the " Siege of Carlaverock ;"₁ and heraldry and genealogy, of which the
writer displays a profound knowledge, were, it is probable, then deemed
to form no trifling part of the necessary acquirements of an historian. That
it was the production of a priest may be inferred from the laboured eulogium of the Bishop of Durham, though Warton supposes that it was undoubtedly written by a herald :ʰ but in this instance his opinion is not
to be relied on, for he could never have examined the Poem with attention,
as in the extract which he has given from it, though consisting of only four
lines, the most important words, " D'ermine," are printed " Determinee,"
nor was the banner to which it relates that of John Duke of Brittany, but
of his nephew, John of Brittany.

.Whether it be considered that the Poem was written by Walter of
Exeter or not, the probability is sufficiently great to justify what has been
said on the subject.

The text has been formed from a MS. copy of the Poem in the auto-
graph of Glover, the celebrated herald, preserved in the Library of the
College of Arms,ⁱ in consequence of the following certificate that it was
transcribed from the original :

Exemplar verissimum vetusti eundem reverendæ antiquitatis monumenti, religiosè admodum
transcripti, renovati, et ab injuria temporis vindicati. Eundem fideliter cum prototipo sive ori-
ginali in omnibus concordare testatur Robert' Gloverus, Somersett' fecialis regius, Armorum regi
cui Norroy nomen inditum, Mariscallus designatus. Qui veritati testimonium perhibere pulchrum
ducens, tam hic in fronte, quam etiam in calce, manu propria nomen suum subscripsit, tertio nonas
Februarij. Anno Christi Salvatoris M. D. lxxxvijⁿ Regni vero Sermᵃᵉ Reginæ Elizabethæ tricesimo.

                                        GLOVER SOMERSETT,
                                Mareschal au Norroy Roy d'Armcs.

          The signature at the end of the Poem is,
              R. GLOVER SOMERSETT,
                Mareschal au Norroy Roy d'Armes.

It has also been most carefully collated with the *contemporary* copy in the
Museum, and every variation is inserted in the notes.

ʰ History of English Poetry, vol. I. p. 335.

ⁱ Following the Poem in that volume is a catalogue of the names and arms of the Princes and Noblemen and Knights who were with King Edward the First at Calais, with their arms illuminated in the
margin. This catalogue has been printed more than once.

Another transcript is deposited in the office of Ulster King of Arms at Dublin, to which a similar certificate by Glover is affixed ;[k] and modern copies are in the possession of various individuals.

In 1779 the Poem was printed in the "Antiquarian Repertory," professedly from the contemporary copy just alluded to, and with a translation; the text there given is, however, as corrupt as the translation is unfortunate. For the former there is no apology; but of the mistakes in the latter no person is disposed to speak more tenderly than he who now submits one which he is sensible requires but little less indulgence. Perhaps few tasks are more difficult, and certainly none more laborious, than to translate an early French poem. The sacrifice of sense to rhyme, not only in the transposition of words, but in the substitution of one which in some cases almost bears the mark of being coined for the occasion; the quaint conceits with which these productions abound ; the errors or abbreviations of transcribers ; the allusion to things or events of which no trace remains ; combine to form a host of difficulties which no sagacity can surmount, and which can only be understood by those who have encountered them. As the translation was so unsatisfactory to himself, the Editor was induced to solicit a gentleman of the highest reputation for his acquaintance with the French of the period, and indeed with every thing else which is connected with English history, to favour him with his remarks. These will be found in the notes; and they merit the reader's attention as much as the readiness and kindness with which they were written claim his acknowledgments. It is also just to the learned individual by whom they were contributed to add, that he is also indebted to him for the important suggestion that the author of the poem had previously written a romance " of Guy."

With the view of rendering the volume as complete as possible, a topographical and general history of Carlaverock Castle has been prefixed to the poem ; and memoirs of every individual who is noticed by the Poet have been added to it.

---

[k] From the information of Sir William Betham, Ulster King of Arms.

The description of the banner of each Knight is illustrated by a woodcut, which has been taken from the illuminations in the margin of the copy of the Poem by Glover, in the College of Arms.

The materials for these memoirs, which might almost be entitled " Biographical Notices of the Baronage of England in 1300," since there are but few of them who were not present at the siege, have been chiefly derived from the invaluable labours of Sir William Dugdale, a writer whose fame can derive no lustre from any praise which it is in the power of the Editor to bestow, but who may at least be permitted to express the surprise and regret with which he has lately seen that indefatigable antiquary designated as a mere " plodding and laborious collector of records and dates," by a gentleman who ought to be able to form a more just opinion of productions which tend in so important a degree to illustrate the history of this country.[1]

In many instances, however, several facts have been introduced into the account of the Peers who were at Carlaverock which escaped that distinguished Herald, whilst of such persons as it was not the object of his work to notice, very considerable trouble has been taken to collect all the information possible : hence it is presumed that this volume may be useful from the biography which it contains.

To apologize for the errors which may be found in a work of this description would be impertinent. Those who can best estimate the time and research which it has consumed, will be sensible that it could not be wholly free from mistakes or omissions.

To his friend Charles George Young, Esq. York Herald, F. S. A., Michael Jones, Esq. F. S. A., Dr. Meyrick, F. S. A., Frederick Madden, Esq. F.S.A., for their assistance and suggestions, and to William Constable Maxwell, Esq. the proprietor of Carlaverock Castle, for the account of the present state of his family, the Editor begs to offer his sincere thanks.

---

[1] Preface to Godwin's " History of the Commonwealth."

HISTORY

OF

CARLAVEROCK CASTLE.

THE Castle of Carlaverock, which is said to have been the Carbantorigum of Ptolemy,[a] stood in the parish of that name, in the county, and about nine miles south of the town, of Dumfries, on the north shore of Solway Frith, at the confluence of the rivers Nith and Locher.

Tradition states that it was founded in the sixth century by Lewarch Og, son of Lewarch Hen, a celebrated British poet; and that it derived its name from his own, Caer Lewarch Ogg, which in the Gaelic language signified the city or fortress of Lewarch Ogg, and which was afterwards corrupted to Caerlaverock.[b] Mr. Grose, however, doubts this etymology; and it would be a waste of time to speculate upon its correctness.

Carlaverock Castle was, according to a MS. pedigree cited by that writer, the principal seat of the family of Maxwell as early as the time of Malcolm Canmore; but Sir Robert Douglas informs us in his Peerage, that Sir John Macuswell acquired the Barony of Carlaverock about the year 1220.

It is impossible to give any other account of the original Castle than the Poet's description of it. He says, " Carlaverock was so strong a Castle that it did not fear a siege, therefore the King came himself, because it would not consent to surrender; but it was always furnished for its defence, whenever it was required, with men, engines, and provisions.

---

a Gough's Camden, vol. III. p. 327.   b Grose's Antiquities of Scotland, vol. I. p. 159.

c

Its shape was like that of a shield,[c] for it had only three sides, all round, with a tower on each angle; but one of them was a double one, so high, so long, and so large, that under it was the gate with the drawbridge, well made and strong; and a sufficiency of other defences. It had good walls, and good ditches filled to the edge with water; and I believe there never was seen a Castle more beautifully situated; for at once could be seen the Irish Sea towards the west; and to the north a fine country, surrounded by an arm of the sea, so that no creature born could approach it on two sides, without putting himself in danger of the sea. Towards the south it was not easy, because there were numerous dangerous defiles of wood and marshes, ditches where the sea is on each side of it, and where the river reaches it; and therefore it was necessary for the host to approach it towards the east, where the hill slopes."[d] Mr. Grose informs us that the site and foundation of the original castle were very conspicuous and easy to be traced, in a wood about three hundred yards to the south of the present building; that it appears to have been rather smaller than the second castle, but of a similar form; and that it was surrounded by a double ditch.

Such was the fortress which Edward the First, on his invasion of Scotland in June, 1300, found it necessary to reduce. By writs tested on the 29th December, 28 Edw. I. 1299, all who owed military service to the crown were ordered to attend at Carlisle on the feast of the Nativity of St. John the Baptist next ensuing, to serve against the Scots.[e] The command was punctually obeyed; and about the first of July the English army quitted Carlisle. The Poet's description of it is very interesting. " They were habited," he says, " not in coats and surcoats, but were mounted on powerful and costly chargers, and, that they might not be taken by surprize, they were well and securely armed. There were many rich caparisons embroidered on silks and satins; many a beautiful pennon fixed to a lance; and many a banner displayed. And afar off was heard the neighing of horses: hills and vallies were every where covered with

---

[c] Shields in the thirteenth century were nearly triangular.   [d] Pages 62, 63.
[e] Palgrave's " Parliamentary Writs," and the Poem, p. 2.

sumpter horses and waggons with provisions, and sacks of tents and pavilions. And the days were long and fine : they proceeded by easy journies, arranged in four squadrons."[f]

He then notices the arms, and, in many cases, personal merits or appearance of each of the Bannerets and some of the Knights who were present, among whom were the King, his eldest son the Prince of Wales, and the most illustrious peers of the realm, to the number of " eighty-seven,"[g] but he describes the banners of eighty-eight individuals. The men at arms amounted to three thousand,[f] and " quite filled the roads to Carlaverock."[g] If any reliance can be placed upon his statement, it must be inferred that a summons was sent to the Castle before the King determined to besiege it, and that it was in consequence of the refusal to surrender, for it " was not to be taken like a chess-rook,"[g] that his Majesty appeared before it in person.[h]

The exact time of the siege cannot be ascertained, but it undoubtedly took place between the 6th and 12th of July, 1300, for on the former day Edward was at Carlisle,[h] and on the latter at Carlaverock ;[i] but as he was at Dumfries on the 10th,[j] it may be concluded that the Castle was taken either on the 10th or 11th of that month.

The investiture and siege are minutely described in the Poem. As soon as the English army appeared before the place, it was quartered by the Marshal ; and the soldiers proceeded to erect huts for their accommodation, the account of which is very picturesque.[k] Soon afterwards the military engines and provisions were brought by the fleet, and the foot-men immediately marched against the Castle.[k] A sharp skirmish took place, which lasted about an hour, in which time several were killed and wounded.[k] The loss sustained by the infantry caused the men at arms to hasten to their assistance ; or, as the Poet has expressed it, many of them " ran there, many leaped there, and many used such haste to go that they did not deign to speak to any one."[k] It would be difficult to find more appropriate words to detail what ensued than his own : " Then might

---

f Pages 4-5.   g Page 59.   h Liber Quoditianus Garderobæ, aᵒ 28 Edw. 1. p. 72.
i Ibid. p. 41.   j Ibid.   k Page 65.

there be seen such kind of stones thrown as if they would beat hats and
helms to powder, and break shields and targets in pieces, for to kill and
wound was the game at which they played. Great shouts were among
them when they perceived that any mischief occurred."[1] He then notices
some Knights who particularly distinguished themselves in the assault;
and proceeds to state that the first body was formed of Bretons, and the
second of Lorains, who rivalled each other in zeal and prowess,[m] and
that those engaged in the attack " did not act like discreet people, nor as
men enlightened by understanding, but as if they had been inflamed and
blinded by pride and despair, for they made their way right forwards to
the very brink of the ditch."[n] At that moment the followers of Sir Thomas de Richmont passed close up to the draw-bridge, and demanded
admission, but they received no other answer to the summons " than
ponderous stones and cornues."[n] Sir Robert de Willoughby was
wounded in his breast by a stone ; and the valour of Sir John Fitz-Marmaduke,[n] Sir Robert Hamsart, " from whose shield fragments might often
be seen to fly in the air,"[n] Sir Ralph de Gorges,[o] Sir Robert de Tony,[o] and
especially of the Baron of Wigton, " who received such blows that it was
the astonishment of all that he was not stunned," is especially commemorated.[o]

The party engaged was reinforced by the followers of the Prince of
Wales :[p] the walls were mined with considerable effect by Sir Adam de la
Forde :[o] and Sir Richard de Kirkbride assailed the gate of the Castle in so
vigorous a manner, " that never did smith with his hammer strike his iron
as he and his did there."[q] Nor was the bravery of the besieged less conspicuous. They showered such huge stones, quarrels, and arrows upon
their enemies, that the foremost among them became so much hurt and
bruised that it was with great difficulty they could retreat.[q] At that junc-
ture Robert Lord Clifford sent his banner and many of his retinue, with
Sir Bartholomew de Badlesmere and Sir John de Cromwell, to supply
their places,[r] though they were not permitted to remain there long ; and on

[1] Page 65.　　[m] Page 69.　　[n] Page 71.　　[o] Page 75. .
[p] Page 73.　　[q] Page 77.　　[r] Page 79.

their retiring, Sir Robert la Warde and Sir John de Grey renewed the attack, but the besieged were prepared for their reception, and " bent their bows and cross-bows, and kept their espringalls in readiness both to throw and to hurl." The retinue of the Earl of Brittany, " fierce and daring as the lions of the mountain," recommenced the assault, and soon covered the entrance to the Castle : they were supported by the followers of Lord Hastings, one of whom, John de Cretings, is said to have nearly lost his horse on the occasion.t

   The courage of the little garrison was not yet subdued. As one of them became fatigued another supplied his place, and they gallantly defended the fortress the whole of one day and night, and the next day until about nine o'clock in the morning." But the numerous stones which were thrown from the Robinet depressed their spirits ; and it was impossible to resist the effect of three ponderous battering engines on the opposite side, every stroke of which, by " piercing, rending, and overturning the stones, caused the pieces to fall in such a manner that neither an iron hat nor wooden target " could protect them, and many were consequently killed.v Finding resistance to be hopeless, they requested a parley, and in token thereof hung out a pennon ; but the unfortunate soldier who displayed it was shot through his hand into his face by an arrow,ʷ when the others demanded quarter, surrendered the Castle to the King of England, and threw themselves upon his mercy.x

   The Marshal and Constable of the army immediately commanded that all hostilities should cease, and took possession of the place. The English were excessively surprised to find that the whole number of the garrison amounted only to sixty men, who were, the Poet says, " beheld with much astonishment," y and were securely guarded until the King ordered that life and limb should be granted to them, and bestowed on each a new robe ;y but this account of the treatment of the prisoners differs entirely from that in the Chronicle of Lanercost, where it is said that many of them were hung.

ˢ Pages 80, 81.   t Page 81.   u Page 83.   v Page 85.   w Page 86.
x Page 87.   y Page 87.

As soon as the Castle fell into Edward's hands, he caused his banner, and that of St. George and St. Edward, to be displayed on its battlements, to which were added the banner of Sir John Segrave the Marshal, and of the Earl of Hereford the Constable, of the army; together with that of Lord Clifford, who was appointed its Governor.[y]

Only two contemporary chroniclers notice the event, and their statements are excessively brief. Peter of Langtoft says the rain

> ....ran down on the mountayns and drenkled the playnes,
> Sir Edward sauh tho paynes, and tok the gate agayn,
> The more he forsoke, the fotemen ilk a flok,
> A pouere hamlete toke, the castelle Karelaverok:

The Chronicle of Lanercost gives a much more accurate account of the circumstance, though it is scarcely less concise:

A° MCCC. Eodem [anno] circa festum Sancti Johannis Baptistæ, Dominus Edwardus Rex Angliæ cum proceribus et magnatibus Angliæ venit apud Karleolum, cum quo venit Dominus Hugo de Veer, et fecit moram apud Lanercost. Et inde transivit Rex in partes Galwithiæ usque ad aquam de Grithe, cepitque castrum de Carlaverok, quod dedit Domino Roberto de Clifforde, et fecit plures intùs castrum inventos suspendi, fuitque tunc annus Jubilei anno pontificatus Bonifacii Papæ vj°.[z]

The capture of the Castle is also noticed by Robert Winchelsey, who was then Archbishop of Canterbury, in a letter to the Pope, dated on the 8 id. October, 1300, in which he says that in obedience to his Holiness's commands to present a certain Bull to the King, he proceeded to his Majesty, " versus castrum de Carlandrok quod prius ceperat."[a]

The " Liber Quotidianus Garderobæ" of that year, contains numerous notices of Carlaverock, the first of which proves that Edward was there on the 12th of July, as on that day an oblation of seven shillings was offered in honour of St. Thomas in his majesty's chapel at that place:

xij die Julij in obl' Regis ad altare in capella sua apud Karlaverok, in honore Sancti Thome vij s.[b]

---

y Page 87.   z Cotton. MSS. Claudius, D. vii. f. 209.
a Leib. Cod. Jur. gent. vol. II. p. 280.   b Liber Quotidianus Garderobæ, page 41.

But the most important are those which relate to the siege of the Castle, and which will therefore be extracted at length:

Magistro Ricardo de Abyndon, [pro vyndag' vini, &c. et] pro vadiis diversorum operarior' fabrorum et carpentar' missorum de Karliol' usque Carlaverok, pro ingen' Reg', per manus Domini Henr' de Sandwyco capellani Domini Job'is de Drokenesford, liberant' eidem denariis apud Karliol', mense Julij, ij *li.* iiij *s.* xj *d.* c

Magistro Ricardo de Abyndon, Clerico, pro vad' carpentar' fabrorum et aliorum operariorum diversorum retentorum ad vadia Regis, per preceptum Regis per literam Thes' de scaccario ad unum catum, unum multonem, et unum berfrarium, et alia ingenia facienda, per visum et ordinacionem D'ni Joh'is de la Dolive, Militis, ad insultum faciend' castro de Karlaverok in adventu Regis et exercitus sui ibidem anno presenti, et ad cariend' cum Rege in eadem guerra ad diversa loca Scocie inter xx diem Nov' anno predicto incipien' ad xxiiij diem Julij anno eodem, una cum diversis cariag' conductis pro maeremio et aliis diversis pro predictis negociis necessariis cariand' ad loca diversa infra idem comp', sicut patet per comp' predictum, xlvj *li* .xiij *s.* j *d. ob.* d

D'no Joh'i de la Dolyve, Const' castri de Dunfres, pro expensis quorumdam hominum eund' circa victualia pro municione dicti castri querenda, expens' quorumdam nunc' defer' literas per diversas vices, ciphis, ligneis, platell', et discis emp' per eundem, calciatura quorumdam balistar' commoranc' in municione predicta, ac expen' suis et quorumdam hominum euncium per preceptum Regis, pro ingeniis querendo de Carliolo usque Carlaverok pro captione ejusdem castri, infra tempus predictum [a ix° die Marcij anno presenti xxviij° usque xxx diem Julij anno eodem] iij *li.* xix *s.* ix *d. ob.* e

Magistro Ade Glasham, carpentar' retento eodem modo ad vadia Regis pro ingenio venienc' de Loghmaban ad obsidionem castri de Carlaverok, pro vadiis suis, et vij sociorum suorum carpentar', a x die Jul' usque xx diem ejusdem mensis, utroque comp' per xj dies, predicto Ade per diem vj *d.* et cuilibet alio carpentar' per diem iiij *d.* j *li.* xj *s.* ij *d.* f

And other carpenters, masons, &c. were retained for the same period. g

Roberto de Wodehous, pro den' per ipsum solutis Petro de Preston et ix sociis suis const' cum equis coopertis, pro vadiis suis vj CLx sag' ped' ven' usque Karliolum de com' Lanc', per ij dies, veniendo de Karliolo usque Karlaverok ad Regem vilj die Jul' pro primo comp' xij *li.* xj *s.*; eidem, pro vadiis ij balist' et xlij sag' de municione castri de Roukesburgh, unius balist' et xj sag' peditum de municione castri de Geddeworth, per eosdem ij dies, veniendo eodem modo ad Regem j *li.* ij *s.* vilj *d.*; eidem, pro vadiis v hobelar' de municione de Rokesburgh, per idem tempus, sic veniendo, v *s.*; eidem, pro vadiis iv carpentar' et v fossator' per unum diem, videlt, viij diem Jul', veniendo ut supra, ij *s.* ij *d.* Summa, xiv *li.* x *d.* h

Steph'o Banyng, mag'ro navis • • • • • • • • • et x sociis suis nautis ejusdem navis, car' in pre-

---

c Liber Quotidianus Garderobæ, page 67.   d Ibid. page 140.   e Ibid. page 153.
Ibid. page 258.   g Ibid. page 259.   h Ibid.

dicta navi sua quoddam ingen' de Skynburnesse usque Karlaverok, pro vadiis suis, per duos dies, x die Julij, pro primo comp', mag'ro percip' per diem vj d. et quol't alio nauta per diem iij d. vj s.[i]

Several entries occur which tend to prove that the King was at Carlaverock on the 13th[k] and 14th of July;[l] on the 29th of August, when seven shillings were paid in the King's chapel there in alms,[m] and on the 30th of that month;[n] and again on the 3rd of November, on which day the same sum was offered at the altar in his Majesty's chapel there.[o]

It appears that Edward left Carlaverock Castle in the custody of Lord Clifford a few days after it surrendered, for on the 17th of July he was at Loghroieton;[p] that he proceeded to Kirkcudbright, Twynham, Flete, and Suthesk, and returned to it on the 29th of August; that he quitted it for Holmcoltram before the 2nd of September, whence he went to Rose Castle, Carlisle, and Dumfries; and that he came for the last time to Carlaverock on the 3rd of November, where he perhaps remained until the 10th of that month, as on the 11th he is stated to have been at Carlisle.[p]

The Castle evidently continued in the possession of the English for several years. On the 12th May, 2 Edw. II. 1309, the Sheriffs of Somerset and Dorset were ordered to purchase, and send to Skinburness, 150 quarters of corn and the same quantity of malt, for the munition of the castles of Dumfries and Carlaverock;[q] and on the 15th of December following Robert Lord Clifford was commanded to furnish the castles of Carlaverock, Dumfries, Dalswynton, and Thybres, with men and provisions, and all other necessaries for their defence; and the Constables of them were respectively enjoined to defend them against the King's rebels and enemies, without any truce or sufferance whatever.[r] In 1312 Sir

---

[i] Liber Quotidianus Garderobæ, page 272. [k] Ibid. pages 64, 248.

[l] Ibid. pages 79, 102. In the month of July the following entry occurs: " Ciphus argenti pond' iij marc' di' x st. precij xx *li.* ix *s.* vij *d.* Datur per Dominum J. de Drokenesford, nomine Regis, D'no Salvo de Parma venienti ad Regem apud Karlaverok cum certificatione super creacione cujusdam Cardinalis, mense Julij." Page 339. [m] Ibid. pages 41, 68, 70, 174. [n] Ibid. page 138.

[o] Ibid. page 42. Other notices of Carlaverock will be found in pages 72, 82, 127.

[p] Ibid. page lxviij. By a reference to page 42 of that work, it will be seen that, in this abstract, the King is *erroneously* said to have been at Carlaverock on the 1st of November.

[q] Rot. Scot. vol. I. [r] Ibid.

Eustace de Maxwell appears from the following document to have joined
the English interest :

Pro Eustathio de Maxwelle et securitate castri sui de Carlaverok.

R. dilecto clerico suo Willielmo de Bevercotes, cancellarlo suo Scotie, salutem. Ut dilectus
nobis Eustauthius de Maxwelle, majorem et securiorem custodiam in castro suo de Carlaverok
contra insidias Scotorum inimicorum nostrorum apponat, concessimus ei illas viginti et duas libras
annuas quas nobis debet singulis annis ad scaccariam nostram Berewyci, de alba firma pro custodia ,
castri sui predicti in ejus subsidium, ad securam custodiam castri sui supradicti, ad voluntatem nostram. Et ideo vobis mandamus quod eidem Eustathio brevia nostra sibi super hoc sufficientia sine
dilatione habere faciatis. T. R. apud Novum Castrum super Tynam xxx die Aprilis [1312].
Per ipsum Regem.[s]

It is uncertain how long Sir Eustace de Maxwell supported the invaders of
his country, but it is unquestionable that he soon afterwards distinguished
himself in the service of Robert Brus. The castle being again besieged
by the English, he defended it for several weeks, and obliged them to
retire, when, fearing, that it might ultimately fall into their hands,
he demolished all its fortifications, for which generous sacrifice King
Robert compensated him by the grant of an annual rent, " pro fractione
castri de Carlaverok,"[t] and moreover released him from the payment of
£32 sterling due to the crown from his lands.[u] Sir Eustace died between
1340 and 1347, and his son, Sir Herbert Maxwell, in September in the
year last mentioned, consented to swear fealty to Edward the Third;
about which time he received letters of safe conduct to attend a treaty at
London with William de Bohun Earl of Northampton,[x] the result of which
is shown by the annexed document. It is also manifest from it, either
that Sir Eustace Maxwell did not completely destroy Carlaverock Castle,
or that his son had rebuilt it.

[s] Rot. Scot. vol. I. p. 110.
[t] Wood's Douglas's " Peerage of Scotland," and Robertson's " Index of Records and Charters from
1309 to 1413," p. 15.
[u] Robertson's " Index," p. 12. Grose says the sum remitted him and his heirs was *ten* pounds yearly.
[x] Rot. Scot. vol. I. p. 703.

Protectio pro Herberto Maxwell, Anglicato, et pro castro suo Carlaverok.

R. omnibus ballivis et fidelibus suis tam in Anglia quam in Scotia ad quos, &c. salutem. Sciatis quòd, cùm Herbertus de Maxwell nuper per amicabilem tractatum inter dilectum consanguineum et fidelem nostrum Willielmum de Bohun, comitem Northampton', et ipsum Herbertum de mandato nostro habitum, idem Herbertus ad obedientiam et ligeantiam nostras gratis venit et certos obsides sufficientes ad castrum de Carlaverok quod in custodia sua existit in manus nostras reddendum prefato comiti liberaverit: Nos providè volentes securitati ipsius Herberti providere, suscepimus ipsum Herbertum, ac omnes homines secum in munitione castri predicti existentes, ac dictum castrum, cum armaturis et victualibus ac aliis bonis et catallis in eodem existentibus, in protectionem et defensionem nostram speciales. Et ideo vobis mandamus quòd ipsum Herbertum ac homines suos predictos manuteneatis protegatis et defendatis, non inferentes eis vel inferri permittentes injuriam molestiam dampnum aut gravamen. Et si quid eis forisfactum fuerit id eis sine dilacione faciatis emendari. Nolumus enim quòd de armaturis victualibus ac bonis et catallis in castro predicto existentibus, seu de bladis feni, equis, carectis, cariagiis, victualibus, aut aliis bonis et catallis ipsius Herberti, aut hominum suorum predictorum, per ballivos seu ministros nostros aut alios quoscumque de Marchia Angliæ, aut aliunde de obedientia nostra existentes, contra voluntatem ipsius Herberti aut hominum suorum predictorum ad opus nostrum aut aliorum quicquam capiatur. In cujus, &c. per unum annum duratur. T. custode apud Glouces' quinto die Septembris [21 Edw. III. 1347].y

In 1355 the Castle is said to have been taken by Roger Kirkpatrick, and levelled with the ground; z and on the death of Sir Herbert Maxwell without issue, the baronial lands of Carlaverock devolved, on his first cousin, Sir John Maxwell, and of which he was possessed in 1371 : a his son, Sir Robert, is presumed to have erected the present castle. From the said Sir Robert Maxwell it has descended to its present possessor, William Constable Maxwell, of Everingham in Yorkshire, Esq. and which is shown by the following pedigree of the ancient family of Maxwell.

---

y Rot. Scot. vol. I. p. 704 b.

z " Illic Donaldus Macdowel in ecclesia de Cummok fidelitatem Regi jurat; et Rogerus Kirkpatricius totam terram de Niddisdale ad idem induxit: arces de Dalswynton et Carlaverok de adversariorum ma‐ nibus eripuit, quas solo æquavit." Historia Majoris Britanniæ tam Angliæ quam Scotiæ. Per Joannem Majorem, p. 248.

a Wood's Douglas's Peerage. See the pedigree.

PEDIGREE OF THE ANCIENT FAMILY OF MAXWELL,

Lords Maxwell, Herries, Eskdale, and Carleile, and Earls of Nithsdale; Lords of the Castle and Barony of Carlaverock.

[From Douglas's Peerage of Scotland, edit. Wood, vol. II. pp. 311-13, excepting where other authorities are cited.]

Maccus, son of Unwin, attached himself to Earl David, and obtained lands from that Prince on the banks of the Tweed, which acquired from him the appellation of Macusville : he was one of the witnesses to the " Inquisitio Davidis," and to the charter of the foundation of the monastery of Selkirk by King David.

Hugo de Maccusville, eldest son: was a witness to a donation from David I. to the monastery of Newbottle.	Edmund, 2nd son, witness to a perambulation and division of the lands of Mella.	" Liulph filius Maccus," 3rd son, witness to a charter of Malcolm IV. to the abbacy of Kelso, 1159.

Herbert de Maccusville, flourished under Malcolm IV. and William I.: was sheriff of the county of Roxburgh: ob. circa 1200.

Sir John Macuswell, eldest son, was Sheriff of Roxburgh, and witnessed agreements of the Abbot and Convent of Kelso, 1203 and 1207: was one of the guarantees of the marriage treaty of Alexander II. and Joan of England, 15 June, 1220, and was present at their marriage at York, 18 June, 1221 : ACQUIRED THE BARONY OF CARLAVEROCK: he was constituted Great Chamberlain of Scotland 1231 : ob. 1241. — Robert de Macuswell.

Eumerus de Macuswell, of Carlaverock: was a witness to divers charters in 1232, 1235, and 1239, Chamberlain of Scotland 1258, by which title he is designated in the agreement that Scotland should not make a separate peace with England without the consent of the Welsh; and was Justiciary of Galloway. He was removed from the councils of Alexander III. by the King of England in 1255. — Mary, daughter and heiress of Roland de Mearns: she brought to her husband the barony and castle of Mearns in Renfrewshire.

Sir Herbert de Maxeswell, eldest son, ob. ante 1300.a	Sir John de Makeswell, 2nd son: he obtained from his father the barony of Nether Pollock in Renfrewshire, with other lands, and was ancestor of the Maxwells of Pollock; of Calderwood; and of Cardoness, Baronets; of the Earls of Farnham in Ireland; of the Maxwells of Park-hill, Newark, and of other families of that name.

a

* Sir Herbert de Maxwell sat in the parliament of Scone, 5th February, 1283-4, when the nobles agreed to receive Margaret of Norway as their sovereign in the event of the death of Alexander III. ; was present in the assembly at Brigham, 12 March, 1289-90, when the marriage of Queen Margaret with Prince Edward was proposed ; was one of the nominees on the part of Robert Bruce, in his competition for the crown of Scotland in 1292 ; swore fealty to Edward the First in 1296 ; and he and a John de Maxwell received letters of credence concerning military service to be performed in parts beyond the sea, in July, 1297. (Palgrave's " Parliamentary Writs," Digest, p. 733.)

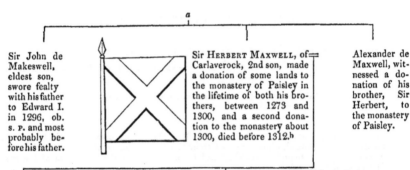

a

Sir John de Makeswell, eldest son, swore fealty with his father to Edward I. in 1296, ob. s. p. and most probably before his father.

Sir HERBERT MAXWELL, of Carlaverock, 2nd son, made a donation of some lands to the monastery of Paisley in the lifetime of both his brothers, between 1273 and 1300, and a second donation to the monastery about 1300, died before 1312.[h]

Alexander de Maxwell, witnessed a donation of his brother, Sir Herbert, to the monastery of Paisley.

Sir EUSTACE MAX-=HELEN MAXWELL, WELL, of Carlaverock, eldest son,[c] died before September, 1347.[d] of the house of Maxwell of Pollok; she survived her husband.

JOHN DE MAXWELL, 2nd son: he is supposed to have succeeded his nephew, Herbert de Maxwell, as his next heir. He possessed the estate of Pencaitland, and granted an annuity out of it to the monks of Dryburgh. Was one of the prisoners taken at the battle of Durham, 17 October, 1346, and died soon afterwards.

HERBERT DE MAXWELL, of Carlaverock, probably his son: he is considered to have died s. p.[e]

Sir JOHN MAXWELL, of Maxwell=CHRIS-and Carlaverock, died soon after November, 1373.[f] TIAN.

Eustace Maxwell, ob. v.p.; his brother John became his heir.

Sir ROBERT DE MAXWELL, of Carlaverock, died= about 1420.[g]

Agnes, married Robert Pollock, of Pollock.

b

---

[b] Rot. Scot. p. 110. His arms were, Argent, a saltire, Sable.

[c] The castle of Carlaverock having been besieged by the English, Sir Eustace Maxwell defended it for some weeks, and forced them to retire, but fearing that it might afterwards fall into their hands he dismantled and threw it down, in recompense of which service, "pro fractione castri de Caerlaverok," he obtained a grant of an annual rent from King Robert. He signed the letter to the Pope, asserting the independency of Scotland, on the 6th April, 1320; in which year he was tried for being concerned in the conspiracy of the Countess of Strathern against King Robert, but was acquitted. He received 300 marks out of a payment from Edward III. to Edward Baliol, King of Scots, 24 March, 1336; and was a witness to a charter of Edward Baliol in 1340.

[d] Rot. Scot. vol. I. p. 704 b.

[e] Herbert de Maxwell obtained from David II. a charter of discharge of the duty of Carlaverock, and in September, 21 Edw. III. 1347, he received letters of protection for himself and his castle of Carlaverock. (Rot. Scot. vol. I. p. 704 b.) His rebellion was punished by David II. who granted to Herbert Murray some lands in Lanarkshire which were forfeited by him.

[f] Sir John Maxwell confirmed a grant of his father to the abbacy of Dryburgh, in which he calls himself, "son of the late John de Maxwell, and heir of Eustace Maxwell his brother." He sat in the parliament at Edinburgh, 26 September, 1357, and received a safe conduct to go into England in 1365. Granted some lands, &c. to the monastery of Kilwinning for the health of his soul, and the soul of Christian his wife, which was confirmed by King David II. in 1367; and obtained a grant of some forfeited lands, 11th November, 1373.

[g] Sir Robert de Maxwell received letters of safe conduct to go into England, with six horses in his retinue, 5th December, 1363; again to visit the shrine of St. Thomas of Canterbury, 8th June, 1364; and to go abroad, 16th October, 1365. Obtained from Robert II. a charter dated 19 Sept. 1371, by the description of "Robert de Maxwell, son and heir of John de Maxwell, of Carlaverock, Knt." of all the lands which the said Sir John held of the King in capite, and which he had resigned into his Majesty's hands on the preceding day, reserving the life-rent of the same to himself, and the terce to Christian his wife if she survived him. Gave lands to the monks of Dryburgh for the welfare of his soul and the soul of Herbert his son and heir. He was one of the Ambassadors to England in 1418.

b

Sir HERBERT=MARGARET, dau. and heiress of Sir John MAXWELL, of de Cragy, of Cragy in Linlithgow, Carlaverock, widow of Sir John Stewart. Charter from eldest son.ᵍ Robert Duke of Albany, 25th Oct. 1407.		Amerus de Maxwell, 2nd son; called "frater Herberti," in a royal charter 1424-5.	Margaret, married Sir John de Mont-gomery, of Eglis-ham.

ROBERT MAXWELL, of Car-=JANET, dau. of Sir laverock, eldest son; ac- John Forrester, of cording to a pedigree cited Costorphin, Cham-by Grose he was slain at Ban- berlain of Scot-nockburn in 1448.ʰ land.		Eustace Maxwell, of Tealing, in Forfarshire, which lands he ac-quired by his marriage with Mary, 3rd sister and coheiress of Hugh Gifford, of Yester.	Janet, married William Dou-glas, of Drum-lanrig.

...... dau. of sir=HERBERT MAXWELL, of Car-=KATHERINE, eldest dau. of Sir William Seton, of
Herbert Herries, | laverock. He is considered | Seton, and widow of Sir Alan Stewart, of Darnley,
of Terregles; 1st | to have been the first Lord | who was killed in 1439, by whom she was mother of
wife. | Maxwell.ⁱ | John 1st Earl of Lennox; 2nd wife.ᵏ

ROBERT, 2nd Lord Max-=JANET, dau. of George Crich-well, eldest son, was ton, Earl of Caithness. The served heir of his father, great seal register, however, Herbert Lord Maxwell, contains a charter, dated 25 4th February, 1453; was May, 1460, of lands to George guarantee of a truce with Maxwell on the resignation England, on the 11th June, of his mother "Janet, dau. 1457; again, 12th Sep- of the deceased George Earl tember, 1459; sat in par- of Caithness, wife of John liament as a peer 14th Maxwell." October, 1467.				Sir Edward Maxwell, of Tinwald: obtained a charter of the ba-rony of Monreith, 15thJan.1481-2. An-cestor of the Max-wells of Monreith, Baronets. Katherine, married Gilbert Lord Ken-nedy; they had a charter in 1450.		George Maxwell, ancestor of the Maxwells of Garnsalloch. David. Adam Maxwell, ancestor of the Maxwells of Southbar. John Maxwell. William Maxwell. Janet. Mariot.	

c

ᵍ Sir Herbert Maxwell was appointed Steward of Annandale by his kinsman, Archibald Earl of Douglas, 5th February, 1409-10; was granted lands in the Barony of Dalswinton by Murdoc Duke of Albany, 28th October, 1420; obtained letters of safe conduct to go to Durham to James I. 13 Dec. 1423; was arrested with the Duke of Albany, 1425; Warden of the West Marches, 1430 and 1438; by the description of "Herbertus Dominus de Carlaverok," was one of the conservators of the truce with England, 20th March, 1438.

ʰ Robert Maxwell obtained a charter of the lands of Libertoun, in the Barony of Carnwath, from his cousin Thomas de Somer-ville, by the description of "Roberto de Maxwell, filio et heredi Domini Herberti de Maxwell, Militis, Domini de Carlaverock, et Jonetæ, filiæ Joannis Forstare, Domini de Corstorphin," and to the heirs male of their bodies; failing which, to Herbert, and the heirs male of his body; failing which, to Amerus de Maxwell, brother of Herbert, 13th Jan. 1424-5.

ⁱ Herbert Maxwell was one of the guarantees of a treaty with the English, 15 Dec. 1430, when he was styled "Herbertus, Do-minus de Maxwell," and again in November, 1449; was one of the conservators of a truce, with England, 14th August, 1451; again, 23 May, 1453, although according to the first edition of Douglas's Peerage he is said to have died in October, 1452. Captain Rid-dell's MS. in the possession of Mr. Nichols, which will be again noticed, gives the following copy of this nobleman's accounts with the King's Exchequer for the Stewartry of Annandale in 1452:

"Computum Dn. Herberti Domini Maxwell Seuescal. Vallis Annandiæ, redditum apud Stryvilin per Herbertum Maxwell, scil. die 25th mensis Novembris an Dom. 1452, de omnibus debitis suis et expensis per firmas et exitu; Vallis suæ, a die 26 mensis Junii an. Dom. 1449, usque in diem presentem, per tres annos integros ad terminos beati Martini ut infra computum. Imprimis, idem onerat se de xxxvs. de primitiis terrarum dominicarum de Lowchmaben de dictis septem terminis infra computum Regi debitis, quia dictæ terræ se extendunt annuatim ad decem libras; et de xxxvs. de firmis terrarum de Hetea et de Smalhame per dictum imprimis computum debitis, quia de dictis terris debentur d'no Regi annuatim decem libræ, et de xxxvs. de firmis piscariæ de Annand d'no Regi, per tempus computi de dictis septem terminis, quia dicta piscaria annuatim valet decem libr."

ᵏ The marriage of Katherine Seton with Herbert Maxwell, and her issue by him, are proved by a charter of lands in Dumfriesshire, dated 20th March, 1475-6.

f

c

JOHN, 3rd Lord Max-=AGNES, dau. of Sir well : slain at Flodden Field, 9th September, 1513.[1]	Alexander Stewart, of Garlies, living February, 1492.	George Maxwell [query?]. Thomas Maxwell, ances- tor of the Maxwells of Kirkconnel.[m]	Janet, wife of John 1st Lord Carlyle of Tortherwald.

JANET, dau.=ROBERT,=AGNES, natural dau. of James of Sir Wil-|4th Lord liam Dou-|Maxwell, glas, of |died 9th Drumlanrig,|July, died before|1546.[n] September, 1529.	Earl of Buchan, widow of Adam, 2nd Earl of Bothwell. She had a charter of half of Carlaverock and Mernes from her husband Lord Max- well, 13th Nov. 1545, mar- ried before September, 1529: 2nd wife.	Herbert Maxwell, 2nd son, ancestor of the Maxwells of Clowdon. Edward Maxwell, 3rd son, was taken prisoner at Solway in 1542, and released in the next year on the payment of a ransom of £100.	1. Mary, married Sir John John- ston, of Johnston. 2. Agnes, married Robert Charteris, of Amisfield. 3. Elizabeth, mar- ried .. Jardine, of Applegirth.

d

[1] This nobleman, on the resignation of his father, received a charter dated 14 Feb. 1477-8, to John Maxwell, son and heir appa-
rent of Robert Lord Maxwell, of the barony of Maxwell in Roxburghshire, Carlaverock in the county of Dumfries, and Mernys in
Renfrewshire; he is mentioned in the records of parliament, 12 Dec. 1482, as the son and heir apparent of Robert Lord Maxwell ;
Steward of Annandale, and was one of the Commissioners appointed to settle border differences by the treaty of Nottingham, 23rd
September, 1484 ; was one of the Conservators of a truce for the West Marches, 3rd July, 1486 ; obtained a charter of lands in
Wodden to him and to Agnes Stewart his wife, 20th Feb. 1491-2 ; was one of the Commissioners to treat with England, 29th July,
1494 ; received grants of divers lands, 5th June, 1507, and 2nd March, 1507-8, from the King.
 The following copy of an agreement of man-rent from the Murrays of Cockpool to this nobleman, is of some interest as a specimen
of those curious deeds :
 " Be it kende till all men be this p'nt l'res, us Shyr Adam of Murraye, Thomas of Murraye son ande apperande ayr to Cuthbert of
Murraye of Cockpool, Charlyss of Murrye and Cuthbert of Murrye young[r] sones to y[e] said Cuthbert off Murrye off Cockpuil, to be
bundyne and oblyst ande be thir p'nt l'res ande y[e] faith and treuth in our bodies lelelye and treuly bynds and obless us men ande
servands in manrent and service to ane nobill and mychtie Lorde, John Lorde Maxwell, bay[t] in peace ande wyer. Ande we sal be till
him leill ande trew and neyde req[r] his skay[t] nor see it bot wee sal let it at all oure gudlye power, and gif wee mayen not latt it wee sal
wayrne hyme in all possibill best. Ande gif he schawiss us his counsaill, or any ane off us, wee sall consult it, ande gif he asks at us
any consale wee sall gif hyme the best at we can. Ande at wee sall tak an afauld upry[t] part wy[t] hyme in all his leffull and honest
actionis causes and querilliss wy[t] or kyne men and freynds at all or gudly pouer forst befor and againe all y[t] ciess or dee may als oft ass
wee salbe chargit be y[e] saide Lorde or be ony uther in his name exerpe ande o[t] allegienss till o[r] Sovrane Lorde the King allandlye for
all y[e] dais oft oure life but fraude or guile. In witness heyr off to yis or bande oft maurent ande service lelely and trewlyle to be kepit
in all poynts ande articles above exprimit. Becauss we had na seyll proper present of yer auyn saide Shyr Adam Thomas of Murraye
Cherlyss ande Cuthbert hass wy[t] the seill oft ane honourabell man Cuthbert Murraye of Cockpule brither to y[e] saide Shyr Adam
and fadyr to y[e] saide Thomas Charlyss ande Cuthbrt to y's p'nt bonde of manrent and service for us to be affixit at Carlaverock ye
XXVII daye of the monet of August y[e] zer of Gode a thousande CCCCLXXXVII zers befor yir witness Jamess Lyndessayne of Fairgirth,
Thomas of Carruthers of y[e] Holmains, Thomas of Cairns of Orchertoane, Gavind of Murraylwaite, Styne Scott, Herbert of Johnstone,
and Adam of Jonestone, wy[t] uthers many diverss."

 [m] Nisbet, in his Heraldry, vol. I. p. 446, says that Kirkconnell of that Ilk ended about 1421 in an heiress, Janet de Kirkconnell,
who married Homer Maxwell, a second son of Herbert Lord Maxwell.

 [n] Robert Lord Maxwell obtained a charter of lands in Dumfriesshire, 29th Nov. 1510; knighted and was constituted Steward of Annandale on his father's resignation, 10th June, 1513; obtained divers forfeited lauds in 1516, 1526, 1528; to him and to Agnes Stewart,
Countess of Bothwell, his wife, 29th Sept. 1529; 1532; to him and his said wife, 31st July, 1534; of the Barony of Maxwell, Carlaverock, and others, 28th July, 1534; to him and his said wife, 10th June, 1535; 1536; to him and his said wife,
12 June, 1541; was guardian of the West Marches, 7th Oct. 1517, and in June, 1540; was appointed a Commissioner of Regency,
29th August, 1536; sent as ambassador to France to negociate the marriage of James V. with Mary of Lorraine, in December, 1537;
a charter passed the great seal 6th June, 1540, of the lands and baronies of Maxwell, Carlaverock, &c. to him for life, remainder
to Robert, Master of Maxwell, his son and heir apparent; John, his second son; Edward Maxwell, of Tynwall; Edward Maxwell, of
Lochruton; John Maxwell, of Cowhill; Herbert Maxwell, brother german of the said Lord Maxwell; and Edward Maxwell, likewise his brother german; and the heirs male of their bodies respectively. Was constituted one of the extraordinary Lords of Session,
2nd July, 1541; taken prisoner at Solway in Nov. 1542, and ransomed 1st July, 1543, for 1000 marks.

d

ROBERT, 5th Lord Maxwell, was served heir of his father, 5th August, 1550; was one of the Commissioners to treat with the English, 8 May, 1551; died 14 September, 1552.	=BEATRIX, 2nd dau. of James, 3rd Earl of Morton, mar. about, but after the 25th July, 1530.	Margaret, married, first, 9 April, 1543, Archibald Earl of Angus; secondly, Sir William Baillie, of Lamington.	Sir JOHN MAXWELL, 5th Lord Herries, died before May, 1594.º	=AGNES, eldest daughter and coheiress of William, 4th Lord Herries, of Terregles.

JOHN, 6th Lord Maxwell, a posthumous son, slain December 7th, 1593.P	=ELIZABETH, 2nd dau. of David Douglas, 7th Earl of Angus, mar. in 1572. She mar. secondly, John Wallace, of Craigie, as appears by a charter dated 5th Aug. 1598, and died at Edinburgh, in Feb. 1637; bur. at Lincluden.	WILLIAM MAX-WELL, 6th Lord Herries, was infeft as heir of his father in May, 1594, and died 10th October, 1604.	=KATHE-RINE, sister of Mark Kerr, first Earl of Lothian.	James Maxwell, of Brachinside, 2nd son. For his issue see Wood's Douglas's Peerage, vol. II. p. 319. 1. Elizabeth, married in 1563 Sir John Gordon, of Lochinvar. 2. Margaret, married Mark, first Earl of Lothian. 3. Mary, married William, 6th Lord Hay of Yester. She had a charter from him 24th Feb. 1590-1. 4. Grizel, mar. Sir Thomas Maclellan, of Bombie, and was mother of the first Lord Kirkcudbright.

e   *f*

---

* Sir John Maxwell, by the description of " John Master of Maxwell," he being then presumptive heir of Robert fifth Lord Maxwell, obtained a charter dated 1st February, 1549-50, to himself and Agnes his wife, one of the three daughters and coheirs of William Lord Herries, of one-third of Terregles and other lands. Whilst guardian of the West Marches he was one of the Commissioners to treat of peace with the English, 9 Dec. 1552; was one of the ambassadors sent from the Lords of the Congregation in Feb. 1560, to arrange a treaty with the Duke of Norfolk, and concluded another treaty with the English, 23 Sept. 1563; obtained charters of various lands to himself and his said wife, 22 May, 1561; the barony of Terregles and others were erected of new into a lordship and barony, and granted to him and Agnes his wife by royal charter, 8th May, 1566; sat in parliament as Lord Herries, 13th April, 1567, on which day the Queen of Scotland, in reward of his services for twenty-two years as Warden of the West Marches, confirmed to him and Agnes Herries his wife, a charter and infeftment of the baronies of Terregles and Kirkgunzean of the 8th May, 1566, to them and the heirs male of their bodies, failing which to his nearest and lawful heirs male whatsoever. He was at the battle of Langside on the part of the Queen in May, 1568; and was forfeited in parliament, 19 August, 1568, but sentence was deferred; he was one of the Commissioners nominated on the part of Mary in September, 1568; and in April, 1569, was committed a prisoner to Edinburgh castle, but was soon afterwards released, and continued an active adherent to the Queen; obtained a charter of lands in Kirkcudbright, 1st October, 1572; was sent to require Morton to resign the regency in March, 1578.

In Captain Riddell's MS. the subjoined copy is inserted of a speech delivered by this nobleman " in the presence of Elizabeth Queen of England," and transcribed " from the original preserved in the archives of the family of Nithsdale:"

" Madam,—The Queen my mistress, who is nothing subject to you, but by misfortune, doth desire you to consider that it is an work of an evil example and most pernicious consequence to give way that her rebellious subjects should be heard against her, who being not able to destroy her by arms, do promise themselves to assassinate her, even in your own breast, under colour of justice. Madam, consider the estate of worldly affairs, and bear some compassion to the calamities of your poor suppliant, after the most horried attempt on the King her husband, the murder of his servants, the cruel designings on her sacred person, after so many prisons and chains, the subjects are heard against their Queen, the rebels against their lawfull mistris, the guilty against the innocent, and the felons against their judge. Where are we, or what do we do? Though Nature hath planted us in the farthest parts and the extremities of all the earth, yet she hath not taken the sense of humanity from us. Consider she is your own blood, your nearest kinswoman, she is one of the best of Queens in the world, for whom your Majesty is preparing bloody scaffolds in a place where she was promised and expected greatest favours. I want words to express so barbarous a deed, but I am ready to come to the effects, and to justify the innocence of my Queen by witnesses unreproachable, and by papers written and subscribed by the hands of the accusers. If this will not suffice, I offer myself, by your Majesty's permission, to fight hand to hand, for the honour of my Queen, against the most hardy and most resolut of those who are her accusers. In this I do assure myself of your equity, that you will not deny that favour unto her who acknowledge herself obliged to your bounty."

ʸ John Lord Maxwell was served heir of his father, 24 May, 1569; with consent of his curators granted a charter of the lands of Menzies, Carlaverock, &c. 4th Feb. 1571-9, to Elizabeth, sister of Archibald Douglas, Earl of Angus, in her virginity, for the

e   f

| JOHN, 7th Lord Max-well, eldest son, was served heir male of his father, 11th Apr. 1601, 13 Sept. 1603, and 19 Sept. 1604; married Margaret, only dau. of John, first Marquess of Hamilton: he killed Sir James Johnston, 6th April, 1608, in a feud, for which he was tried, and beheaded at the cross of Edinburgh, 21 May, 1613, died s. p. | ROBERT, 8th Lord Max-well, died in May, 1646.q | ELIZABETH, daughter of Sir Francis Beaumont, and a near relation of George Vil-liers, Duke of Bucking-ham. | 2. Agnes, married William Douglas, of Pen-zie. 3. Marga-ret, mar-ried Hugh Wallace, of Crai-gie. | 1. ELI-ZA-BETH, eldest daugh-ter. | JOHN MAX-WELL, 7th Lord Her-ries, only son, died about 1627.r | 1. Sarah, married, first, Sir James Johnston, of Johnston, who was kill-ed by Lord Maxwell in 1608 ; 2ndly, John, 1st Earl of Wigton ; 3rdly, Hugh Montgo-mery, Viscount of Airds in Ireland ; buried 29th March, 1636. 2. Margaret, married Robert Glendonwyn, of Glendonwyn : mar-riage contract dated 14 Jan. 1605. |

g   h

matrimony to be contracted between them ; obtained charters of various lands in 1573, 1574, and 1581 ; on the execution and attainder of the Regent Morton, he, as representative of his mother, obtained a charter of the earldom, barony, and regality of Morton, of new erected into the Earldom of Morton, 5th June, 1581, and which was ratified with consent of parliament, 19th Nov. 1581, but the attainder being rescinded, he was deprived of that title in January, 1585 ; was guardian of the West Marches, but being deprived of it, a feud commenced between him and the Laird of Johnston to whom it was granted, and though restored to that office the ani-mosity continued, and he was killed in an engagement with the Johnstons on the 7th Dec. 1593, "when, being a tall man, and heavy with armour, he was struck from his horse and dispatched ;" buried at Lincluden. The following account of this affair occurs in Captain Riddell's MS.

"The Laird of Johnstone, Warden of the West Marches, opposed Lord Maxwell in his being re-elected Provost of Dumfries ; but Lord Maxwell, with his numerous and armed friends, preoccupying the town on the day of election, had himself continued Provost of Dumfries. Upon this, complaint being lodged against Lord Maxwell at court, where he was out of favour, and being in vain commanded to present some of the Armstrongs for whom he was bound, he was denounced a rebel, and the Laird of Johnstone had orders to pursue him, some soldiers, well officered, being sent to his assistance ; but these ere they joined him were defeated by Lord Maxwell's bastard brother. To revenge this, Johnstone carried fire and sword into the territories of the Maxwells, which they repaying, a destructive war was carried on by the two clans, until the Laird of Johnstone was taken ; risoner, when he soon died of grief for his disaster. Lord Maxwell fled to Spain to let the storm blow over. When he returned, the King determined to march against him, for Lord Maxwell had many alliances on the West Border, and the broken men of the Border had repaired to him in such numbers that the Warden [then the Lord Herries] was unable to contend with him. Upon the King's approach Lord Max-well fled to Galloway, and the houses of Langholm, Thrieve, and Carlaverock surrendered to his Majesty. Lochmaben only re-sisted till a train of artillery was brought from Cumberland, when the garrison capitulated for life, from which the Governor was excepted. His name was Maxwell ; he having refused to deliver the castle to the King in person, he was shown no mercy. Castle Milk and Morton Castle James ordered to be burned, and he ordered Sir William Stewart to bring him Maxwell dead or alive, who pursued Lord Maxwell from Kirkcudbright to the Isle of Sky, and from thence to Carrick ; he seized him in a cave near the Abbey of Coxersqwel, and carried him to the King at Edinburgh, who afterwards pardoned him on his giving bond not to disturb the esta-blished religion on pain of £100,000 sterling. He was again appointed Warden ; for some of the name of Johnstone having, in July, 1590, committed great depredations in the barony of Sanquhar and Drumlanrig, and killed many who pursued to recover the booty, Lord Maxwell, the Warden, was commissioned to pursue the plunderers with the utmost hostility. But not long before the

Laird

---

q Robert Lord Maxwell was restored to the title and estates. of his family by letter under the great seal, 13 Oct. 1618, and was served heir of his brother 13 July, 1619. Created Earl of Nithsdale, Lord Maxwell, Eskdale, and Carlyle, by patent, dated at Farnham, 20th August, 1620. to him, " euosque hæredes masculos," with precedency from the 29th October, 1581, the date of the charter of the earldom of Morton to his father. Was appointed a Commissioner to obtain an unconditional surrender of tithes by Charles I. in 1625 ; was, on the 11th May, 1630, served heir in general of John Lord Maxwell, abavi, and Robert Lord Maxwell proavi. He joined Montrose in 1644, for which he was excommunicated by the general assembly.

r John Maxwell, 7th Lord Herries, was served heir of his father, 26th Jan. and 26 Dec. 1604 ; and of his grandfather, John Lord Herries, 25th Jan. 1609. and 28th Oct. 1617; obtained a charter of Trailtrow, 31st May, 1610 ; and of Craigley 5th Jan. 1611.

g

h

ROBERT, 2nd Earl of Nithsdale, and 9th Lord Maxwell, only son, died unm. in October, 1667. ⁸

Elizabeth Maxwell, died unmarried in 1623, at Dumfries, when the plague was in that town.

JOHN MAXWELL, 8th=ELIZABETH, eldest dau. Lord Herries, only son, t succeeded as third Earl of Niths-dale 1667, ob. .....

of Sir Robert Gordon, of Lochinvar, Bart. sis-ter of the first Viscount Kenmure.

Elizabeth, married George, 2nd Earl of Win-toun. ✝

ROBERT MAXWELL, fourth=LUCY, 8th dau. of Wil-Earl of Nithsdale, &c. eldest son, died in March, 1695.

liam, first Marquess of Douglas.

John Maxwell, 2nd son, and William Max-well, 3rd son, both of whom appear to have died issueless.

WILLIAM MAXWELL, fifth Earl of Nithsdale, &c.=WINIFRED, youngest dau. of William Herbert, first only son, died at Rome, 20th March, 1744.ᵘ   Marquess of Powis; she died at Rome in 1749.ˣ

Laird of Johnstone had contracted an intimate friendship with his Lordship, and had exchanged bonds of man-rent for their mutual defence. Lord Sanquhar and Drumlanrig, knowing how ambitious Lord Maxwell was of being followed, offered him their services, which he eagerly accepted, as he thought this an opportunity not to be omitted for rendering all Nithsdale dependent on him. Ac-cordingly a mutual obligation was signed by them and many in their friendship. This, however, was not kept so secret as it ought to have been. One Johnstone, who served the Warden, carried it to his chief, who, although he was startled with this double dealing of Lord Maxwell, resolved to dissemble his knowledge of it, and only to ask the Warden if the report of his entering into such an engagement was true. Lord Maxwell at first denied; but missing the bond, he excused the matter, as he was obliged to obey the King, and to do as he was directed. Johnstone now knowing what he had to expect, associated with the Scotts of Tiviotdale, and the Elliots and Grahams of the Esk; and, hearing that Lord Maxwell had levied a considerable force, part of which he had garrisoned Lochmaben with, till he himself could come there, he resolved to prevent him, and cut them off. This he executed with a bar-barous precipitation. The Lord Maxwell, to repair this disgrace, entered Annandale with banners displayed, as the King's Lieute-nant, followed by two thousand desperadoes, resolving to raze the houses of Lockwood and Lockerby. Johnstone being inferior in numbers, kept aloof, and detached some prickers only, in the Border way, to watch opportunities. These performed their orders so effectually that they forced back a party who came to attack them with such precipitancy that they even broke their main body. This Johnstone observing, completed their confusion by a furious onset; and in the flight, the Warden, being a heavy man and loaded with armour, was struck from his horse, and unmercifully murdered. This happened in Dec. 1593."

    ˢ Robert second Earl of Nithsdale was excommunicated by the General Assembly, 26th April, 1644, and was in the same year taken prisoner when Newcastle was stormed by the Scot-tish army. On the 3rd February an act was passed restoring him against his father's forfeiture. He was commonly called the Philosopher.

    ᵗ John Maxwell, eighth Lord Herries, was excommunicated by the General Assembly, 26th April, 1644, for joining Montrose; and was proposed to be excepted from pardon by the articles of Westminster in July, 1646. He succeeded to the titles of Earl of Nithsdale and Lord Maxwell, &c and to the family estates, on the death of his kinsman, Robert Earl of Nithsdale, &c. in October, 1667, to whom he was served heir male and of entail, 6th April, 1670, " proavi fratris immediatè senioris," in his estates in several counties.

    ᵘ William Maxwell, fifth Earl of Nithsdale, &c. was served heir male and of line and entail of his father, 26 May, 1696; and heir male and of entail of Robert Earl of Nithsdale, " vulgo nuucupat' le Philosopher, pronepotis quondam Roberti Domini Maxwell, fratris immediatè senioris quondam Joannis Domini Herries, proavi quondam Joannis Domini Herries postea Comes de Nithsdale, qui fuit frater nuper Roberti Comitis de Nithsdale patris Willielmi, nunc Comitis de Nithsdale pronepotis fratris tritavi," 19th May, 1698. Having engaged in the rebellion in 1715, he was taken at Preston on the 14th Nov. in that year, and sent to the Tower of London; was tried and found guilty in January, 1716, and was sentenced to be ex-ecuted, with the Earl of Derwentwater and Viscount Kenmure, on the 24th Feb. 1716: by the heroism of his wife he, however, effected his escape. By his attainder all his honours became forfeited; but, having disponed his estates to his son in Nov. 1712, they were preserved from forfeiture. The arms of this nobleman were, Argent, an eagle displayed Sable, beaked and membered Gules, surmounted by an escutcheon of the First, charged with a saltire of the Second, and surcharged in the centre with a hedgehog Or. His crest: a stag Proper, attired Argent, couchant before a holly-bush Proper. His supporters; two stags Proper, attired Argent: and his motto; " Reviresco."

i

JOHN MAXWELL, son and heir, succeeded to=KATHERINE, fourth dau. of | Anne, married John
his father's estates on his death in 1744, and | Charles Stewart, 4th Earl of | Lord Bellew, of Ire-
assumed the title of Earl of Nithsdale. He died | Traquair. She died at Lon- | land, at Rome in De-
at London, 4th August, 1776. | don, 6th March, 1773. | cember, 1731.

MARY MAXWELL, | WINIFRED MAXWELL, 2nd dau.=WILLIAM HAGGERSTON CONSTABLE, of Ever-
eldest dau. and | and eventually sole heiress, suc- | ingham Park, second son of Sir Carnaby Hag-
coheiress, died at | ceeded to all her father's estates, | gerston, of Haggerston, in the Bishopric of
Terregles, unmar- | including CARLAVEROCK; mar. | Durham, Bart. He assumed the name and
ried, 31 December, | at Terregles, 17 Oct. 1758; died | arms of MAXWELL, and died at Terregles, 20th
1747, æt. 15. | at Terregles, 13 July, 1801, æt.66. | June, 1797.

MARMADUKE WIL-=THERESA | Charles Haggerston Constable, 3rd and | William =Clara
LIAM HAGGERSTON | APPOLO- | youngest son, assumed the name and | Hagger- | Louisa,
MAXWELL CONSTA- | NIA, dau. of | arms of Stanley only, of Ackham; mar- | ston Con- | only dau.
BLE, born 2nd Jan. | Edmund | ried, first, in Sept. 1793, Elizabeth, | stable,2nd | of William
1760, assumed the | Wakeman, | sister and heiress of Sir William Stan- | son, assu- | Grace,
name of MAXWELL, | Esq. bro- | ley, of Hooton in Cheshire, who died in | med the | Esq. and
and succeeded to | ther of | 1792, died at London, 23 June, 1797; | name of | aunt of
CARLAVEROCK and | William | 2ndly, Miss Macdonald, mar. at York, | MIDDEL- | the pre-
the other estates of | Wakeman, | 24 Feb. 1800. | TON, of | sent Sir
that family, married | of Beckford | Mary, mar. 24 June, 1794, John Webb | Stockeld | William .
26th Nov. 1800, died | Place, in | Weston, of Sutton Place in Surrey, Esq. | Park, in | Grace,
30th June, 1819. | Worcester- | who died s. p. She living Jan. 1828. | Yorkshire, | Bart.
 | shire, Esq. | Theresa, unmarried. | Esq.

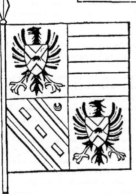

WILLIAM | 2. Marmaduke Constable | Peter Middelton, of
CONSTA- | Maxwell, of Terregles, | Stockeld Park, in
BLEMAX- | co. Dumfries, Esq. born 1 | Yorkshire, Esq. eld-
WELL, of | Jan. 1806. | est son; married
Evering- | 3. Peter Constable Max- | Hon.Juliana,daugh-
ham Park | well, born 7th Feb. 1807. | ter of Charles, 16th
in York- | 4. Henry Constable Max- | Lord Stourton.
shire, | well,of Milnhead,co.Dum- | Francis Middelton,
Esq. | fries,born 28th Dec.1810. | Esq. 2nd son; mar-
Present | 5. Joseph Constable Max- | ried Alice, daughter
LORD OF | well, born 27th Oct. 1811. | and coheiress of
CARLA- | Mary, married, 1st May, | James Taylor, of
VEROCK, | 1821, Hon. Chas. Lang- | the county of Lan-
eldest son, | dale, 4th son of Charles, | caster, Esq.
born 25th | 16th Lord Stourton. | Ann, died unmarried,
August, | Theresa, m. Jan. 15, 1822, | 30th Dec. 1826.
1804.y | Hon. Chas. Clifford, 2nd | Barbara Clara Mid-
 | son of Charles, 7th Lord | delton.
 | Clifford of Chudleigh.
 | Ann, born 17th March,
 | 1808,died15thJune,1811.

* A circumstantial and most interesting narrative of the escape of the Earl of Nithsdale, from the pen of his Countess, in a letter
to her sister Lady Lucy Herbert, was printed in the first Volume of the Transactions of the Society of Antiquaries of Scotland, and
some other publications. It has lately been beautifully printed, from a MS. in the possession of Lord Arundel, with illustrative notes
and a pedigree, by Sheffield Grace, of Lincoln's Inn, Esq. brother of Sir William Grace, Bart.

ʸ The arms of this gentleman are, 1st and 4th, Argent, an eagle displayed Sable, beaked and membered Gules, surmounted by an
escutcheon of the First charged with a saltire of the Second, and surcharged in the centre with a hedgehog Or: MAXWELL. 2nd,
Barry of six Or and Azure: CONSTABLE. 3rd, Azure, on a bend cotised Argent three billets Sable, a crescent for difference :
HAGGERSTON.

The little which is known of the history of the Castle after the reign of Edward the Third is detailed in the following narrative of Grose :

" This Castle again experienced the miseries of war,[z] being, according to Camden, in his Annals, in the month of August, 1570, ruined by the Earl of Sussex, who was sent with an English army to support King James VI. after the murder of the Regent. The same author, in his Britannia, written about 1607, calls it a weak house of the Barons of Maxwell, whence it is probable that only the fortifications of this Castle were demolished by Sussex ; or that, if the whole was destroyed, only the mansion was rebuilt.

" The fortifications of this place were, it is said, once more reinstated by Robert, the first Earl of Nithsdale, in the year 1638 ; and, during the troubles under Charles I., its owner nobly supported the cause of royalty, in which he expended his whole fortune ; nor did he lay down his arms till he, in 1640, received the King's letters, directing and authorizing him to deliver up the castles of Thrieve and Carlaverock upon the best conditions he could obtain ; in both which castles the Earl maintained considerable garrisons at his own expense ; namely, in Carlaverock an hundred, and in Thrieve eighty men, besides officers. The ordnance, arms, ammunition, and victuals, were also provided at his cost.

" The following particulars respecting the articles of capitulation, and furniture left in this castle, are copied from a curious manuscript in the possession of Captain Riddell.

---

[z] In a letter from the Earl of Hertford to Lord Wharton and Sir Robert Bowes, April 1544, the Earl desires them to send " Patie Grayme or other trustie and wise felowe, under colour of some other message, for to view the castles of Lowmaban, Tress, Carlavroke, and Langholme, being within the rule and custodie of Robert Maxwell," as the King wished " to knowe the strength and scituations" of them, " whether the same, or any of them, stonde in such sorte, and be of such strength, as, if they were in the King's Majesties hands, they might be kept and holden aynenst the enemyes." In case either of them was tenable, the said messenger was to " ernestly travaile with Robert Maxwell for the delyverie of the same into his Majestie's hands, if with money and rewarde, or other large offers, the same may be obtayned ;" and Lord Wharton and Mr. Bowes were further instructed, as opportunities might be given them, " to feale the mynde and inclination of the said Robert Maxwell in the same." Hayne's Burleigh Papers, pp. 27-8.

" *Copy of the Capitulation between the Earl of Nithsdale and Colonel Home, at Dumfries, the 1st day of October,* 1640.

" The q'lk day, p'ns of the Committee of Nithsdale, residing at Dumfries, compeared Lieutenant-Colonel Home, and gave in and produced the articles of capitulation past betwixt Robert Earl of Nithsdale and the said Lieutenant-Colonel, at the Castle of Carlaverock, the 26th day of September last by past, and desired the said articles to be insert and registrate in the bukes of the said Committee, and that the extract y^{r}of might be patent to any party havand interest, and the principal articles re-delivered to him, q'lk the said Committee thought reasonable; of the q'lk articles the tenor follows, viz.

" Articles condescended upon betwixt the Earl of Nithsdale and Lieutenant-Colonel Home, the 26th day of September, 1640, at the Castle of Carlaverock.

" For the first article it is condescended on that for my Lord, his friends, and followers, $_{t}$ha$_{t}$ there shall no other course be taken with him and them in their religion, than with others of his and their professions.

" Wheras it is desired be my Lord, that he, his friends, and followers, be no farther trouble in their persons, houses, and estates, house guides therein, then according to the common course of the Kingdom; it is agreed unto, that no other course shall be taken with him and his foresaids, then with others of his and their professions.

" Wheras it is desired he and they may sorte out with bag and baggage; it is agreed, that he, his friends, and followers, and soldiers, with each of them their arms and shotte, with all their bag and baggage, trunks, household stuff, belonging on their honour and credit to his Lordship and them, w^t safe conduct to Langholm, or any other place within Nithsdale, is granted.

" Wheras it is desired be my Lord, that guides intromitt with, belonging to his Lordship's friends and followers, restitution thereof be made; it is agreed to, what course shall be taken with others of his and y^r condition, shall be taken with him and them.

" It is condescended upon be my Lord, takened the burden on him for himself, his friends, and followers, that he nor they sall not in any time coming, tack arms in prejudice of this kingdom, nor shall have any intelligence with any prejudice thereof, upon their honour and credit.

" It is condescended on be my Lord, and his friends, and followers, that they sall contribute and do every thing lying incumbent on them, according to the general course of the kingdom.

" Lastly, it is condescended on be my Lord, his friends, and followers, that he and they sall deliver up the house and fortalice of Carlaverock to Lieutenant-Colonel Home, w^t the cannon, superplus of ammunition, and other provisions; and that he shall remove himself, officers, and whole garrison and followers, out of the said castle and fortalice.

" And this his Lordship obliest himself and his to perform upon his honour and credit, betwixt this and the 29th day of September instant, 1640.

(Sic subscribitur,)   NITHSDALE.
Jo'N HOME.

" This is the just copy of the said articles of capitulation, extract forth of the Books of the said Committee, by me, Mr. Cuthbert Cunninghame, notter clerk y^{r}of undescribing.

(Signed,)   CUTHBERT CUNNINGHAME, Clerk.

" Imprimis, in the wine sellar, 4 barrels of seake. Item, in the other seller, 3 hogsheads of French wine, and an iron grate. Item, more, 30 bolls of meal. Item, in the end of the kitchen, 2 barrels of herring. Item, in the high wardrop, 1 locked trunk, and three timber beds, and 1 iron window. Mare, 1 stoller, 1 old katell, and 2 picks and a moald. Item, up high, four cubards and a crucifix. Mare, in the warehouse, an crokpin. Item, in chamber, a cubard. In my Lord Maxwell's chamber, two beds and a cubard, and a locked chest, and another chest. The outer room, two trunks and a bed, and a great tow. Mare, in the musket chamber, a bed and a belows : in the turnpike a cupbord. Mare, in the new wardrope, 3 beds. Item, in the master's chamber a bed and a cupbord. Mare, in the damask bed chamber, a bed, and a cupbord, and a targe, and a fire chuvell. Item, in the kitchen, a chimney and grate, and a pair of long raxes. In the new ball, a leid, and a masken fatt, and a study, and a pair of bellies. Item, in the long hall, 6 cases of windows, with 22 pikes, 13 lancies, and 2 sakes of white stules. Item, mare in Sander's chamber, 4 beds. Mare, in my Lord's hall, 2 burds and 6 turkies-fowls. Item, mare in the round chamber, without my Lord's chamber, 5 feder beds, 9 bolsters, 4 cods, 5 pair of blankets, and 4 rugs, 6 pieces of buckram, with my Lord's arms, and 2 . . . . . and another bed with black fring and a painted brods, a cuburd, 9 stooles covered with cloth of silver, 2 great chairs of silver cloth ; mare, a green caniby bed ; mare, a sumber cloth ; mare, 3 great and little . . . . . , and 4 stoles, and a long coussin, all of black and white stuff ; mare, 4 stooles and 2 chairs, coveret with brune cloth passementet yealow ; mare, a great locke and a wauroke net ; mare, there is one great chair, 4 stules coveret reid with black passment ; mare, 22 curtain rods, a trunk locked full, and 2 of virginals ; mare, in the drawing room, a brace of iron and canaby bed, with a fender, bed, and a bolster, and 3 tronks locket, a Turky stule, and a rich work stule, and ane old chair, with a cod nailed on ; mare, a frame of a chair. Item, in fire house, is 7 covers of Turkey work for stules, and a coffer, 2 chests, 15 chamber pots, 5 pots for easements, a mortar and a pistol, a brazen pot, a brazen ladle, a bed pan, 4 wine sellers, a little chopin pot, and my Lord and my Ladies pictures ; mare, a chest, with some glasses, and 5 fedder beds, 5 bolsters, 3 char pots, 2 red window curtings ; mare, there is in the dining room before my Lady's chamber, a burd, and a falling bed, 2 Turkey stooles, a blue . . . . . on the case of the knock ; mare, in my Lord's chamber there is a bed furnished of damask, and lead our with gold lace ; mare, there is 2 chairs, and 3 stools of damask, and a cuburd, and a carpet, and a chair coveret with brune cloth, and a chamber all hanged, a water pot, a tongs and bellies, 1 knoke, 28 muskets, 28 bandlers, and 2 2-banded swords, and 9 collers for deggers ; mare, in Conheathe's chamber, a bed, and cuburd, and sundries ; mare, in the ould house, 38 spades of iron.

" This is the true inventory of the goods left in Carlaverock, taken there be Arthur M'Machan and William Sleath ; there was one locked trunk in the high wardrop, which was full of men's cloaths ; and in that great trunk which was mentioned to be in the round chamber, there was a great wrought bed, a suit of cloaths of silver, chairs and stools to be made up, and an embroidered cannabic of grey sattin to be made up too ; as for the other trunks, which were left in the open

h

rooms, it cannot be remembered in particular what was left into them; and that this is all true we underwritten can witness,

                             (Signed,)   WILLIAM WOOD, witness.

                                              WILLIAM MAXWELL, witness.

                                              THOMAS MAXWELL, witnèss.

" A note of the household stuff intromitten with by Lieutenant-colonel Home at Carlaverock.

" Imprimis. He has intromitten with five suit of hangings, there being eight pieces in every suit, the price of every suit overheid estimate threescore pounds sterling.

" Item. Has intromitten with five beddies, twa of silk and three of cloth, every bed consisting of five coverings, course rugs, three over ballens, and ane long . . . . . . , with masse silk fringes of half quarter deep, and ane counter pont of the same stuff, all laid with braid silk lace, and a small fringe about, with chairs and stools answerable, laid with lace and fringe, with feather bed and bolster, blankets and rug, pillers, and bedsteid of timber answerable; every bed estimate to be worth an hundred and ten pounds sterling.

" Item. He was intromitten with ten lesser bedies, q^{r}of four are cloth cortens, and six with stuff or ferge, every bed furnished with bottoms, vallens, and testers, fedder bed, bolster, rugge, blankets, and pillows, and bedsteid of timbèr answerable; every bed estimate to fifteen pounds sterling overheid.

" Item. He has intromitten with seventy other beds for servants, consisting of fether bed, bolster, rug, blankets, and estimate to seven pound sterling a-piece.

" Item. He has intromitten with forty carpets, estimate overheid to forty shillings sterling a-piece.

" Item. He has intromitten with the furniture of ane drawing room of cloth of silver, consisting of an entire bed . . . . . . cobbert and six stools, all with silk and silver fringe, estimate to one hundred pounds sterl.

" Item. He has intromitted with twa dozen of chairs and stools covered with red velvet, with fringes of crimson silk and guilt nails, estimate to threescore pounds sterling.

" Item. He has intromitten with five dozen of Turkey work chairs and stools, every chair estimate to fifteen shillings sterling, and every stool to nine shillings sterling.

" Item. He has intromitten with an library of books, q^{lk} stood my Lord to twa hundred pounds sterling.

" Item. He has intromitten with twa ope truncks full of Holland shirts, and pillabers, and dorock . . . . damask table cloths, and gallons, and towells, to the number of forty pair of shittes or thereby, and seventy stand of neprey, every pair of sheets consisting of 7 ells of cloth, at six shillings sterling the ell, amounts to £5. 2s. sterling the pair. Inde £704 sterling.

" Item, the stand of neprey, consisting of ane table cloth, of twa dozen napkins, twa long towells, estimate to xx pound ster.

" Item. He has intromitten with an knock that stands upon ane table, estimate to xx pound sterling.

" Item.　He has suffered his followers to spoil me ane coach . . . . of the furniture q^{lk} stood me fifty pounds sterling.

" Item.　He has intromitten with other twa trunks full of course sheets and neprie, to the number of forty pair or thereby of sheets, and twenty . . . . stand of coarse neprie or thereby; the pair of sheets and the furniture consisting of twelve ells, at half a crown an ell, amounts threttie shillings sterling the pair.　Inde VII and xx pound.

" Item.　The stand of neprie, consisting of table cloth, twa dozen of nepkins, and ane towell, estimate to . . . . . the stand.　Inde . . . . . .

" Item.　He has intromitten with an trunk full of suits of apparel, q^{r}of there was eight suits of apparell or thereby, some of velvet, some of saten, and some of cloth, every suit consisting of cloaths, bricks, and close dublets with velvet, estimate at . . . . the suit.　Inde . . . . .. ii—viij—iiij lib."

" To this and other complaints of a breach of the articles of capitulation, Col. Home, among various excuses, answered that what he did was by order of the Committee of Estates ; by whose particular directions this place was demolished, on their being informed that the Earl's officers and soldiers had broken their parole, and were then actually in arms.

" This castle, like the old one, is triangular, and surrounded by a wet ditch ; it had a large round tower on each angle ; that on the east is demolished ; that on the western angle is called Murdoc's tower, from Murdoc Duke of Albany having been confined there, as has been before mentioned.　The entrance into the castle yard lies through a gate on the northernmost angle, machicollated, and flanked by two circular towers. Over the arch of the gate is the crest of the Maxwells, with the date of the last repairs, and this motto, " I BID YE FAIR."　The residence of the family was on the east side, which measures 123 feet.　It is elegantly built, in the style of James VI.　It has three stories, the doors and window cases handsomely adorned with sculpture ; over those of the ground floor are the coats of arms and initials of the Maxwells, and the different branches of that family ; over the windows of the second story are representations of legendary tales ; and over the third, fables from Ovid's Metamorphoses ; in the front is a handsome door case leading to the great hall, which is 91 feet by 26.

" At a considerable distance towards the north-east of the area on which the castle stands, and near the farm-house, is a handsome gate of squared stone, having a circular arch."

Several views of the remains of the second castle occur in that work, and others will also be found in Pennant's " Tour in Scotland," in Cardonnel's " Picturesque Antiquities of Scotland," and in Daniell's " Voyage round Great Britain." Mr. Pennant evidently considered the castle of which he speaks as the one which was besieged in 1300.

A MS. account of Carlaverock, by Captain Riddell, in 1787, thus describes the present building.

" The present building is triangular. At two of the corners had been round towers, one of which is now demolished ; and on each side of the gateway, which forms the third angle, are two rounders. Over the arch is the crest of the Lords Maxwell, and this motto, ' I BID YE FAIR.' This castle yard is triangular ; one side, which seems to have been the family residence, is elegantly built ; has three stories, with very handsome window cases. On the pediments of the lower story are coats of arms carved, with different figures and devices. The opposite side of the court-yard is plain. In the front is a handsome door-case that leads to the great hall, which is ninety feet by twenty-six. The whole internal length of that side is 123 feet."[a]

---

[a] Now in the possession of J. B. Nichols, Esq. F. S. A.

Le Siege de Karlaverok.

El ᵃ millime ᵇ tresenteisime ᶜ an de
Grace au iour de seint John ᵈ
Tint a Carduel Edward grant courte ᵉ
E comanda q' ᶠ a terme court
Tout ᵍ si home se appareillassent
Ensemble oveoc li alassent ʰ
Sur les Escos ses enemis
Dedems ⁱ le iour que ᵏ leur ˡ fu mis
Fu preste tout le ost bame ᵐ
E li bons Roys o sa maisine ⁿ
Tantost se vint vers les Escos
Non pas en rotes et surcos ᵒ
Mais sur les gra's chevaus de pris
Por ceo q' il ne feussent surpris ᵖ
Arme bien et ᑫ seurement
La ont meinte riche garnement ˢ
Brode sur cendeaus et samis ᵗ
Meint beau penon en lance mis
Meint baniere desploie ᵘ
E loing estoit la noise oie ˣ
Des henissemens des chevaus ʸ
Par tote estoient mouns e vauls ᶻ
Pleins ᵃᵃ de sommers ᵇᵇ e de charroi

---

[a] *The copy of the poem in the Cottonian Library commences with these lines:*

A cronicles de granz moustiers
Tru et ien ke vois Edewars li ters

[b] Milem.   [c] treicentaine an
     De Grace au iour, &c.

[d] Johan.   [e] Fu a Carduel e tint grant court.   [f] Ke.   [g] tint.

In the year of Grace one thousand three hundred, on the day of Saint John, Edward held a great Court at Carlisle, and commanded that in a short time all his men should prepare, to go together with him against his enemies the Scots.

On the appointed day the whole host was ready, and the good King with his household, then set forward against the Scots, not. in coats and surcoats, but on powerful and costly chargers ; and that they might not be taken by surprise, well and securely armed.

There were many rich caparisons embroidered on silks and satins; many a beautiful penon fixed to a lance ; and many a banner displayed.

And afar off was the noise heard of the neighing of horses : mountains and vallies were every where covered with

---

h E ensemble oVec li alassent.　　i Dedens.　　k Ke.　　l iour.
m banie.　　n E li roys o sa grant maisnie.　　o e sou'cos.
p *This line is omitted in the copy in the Cottonian Library.*　　q ben e.
s guarnement.　　t Brode sur sendaus et samis.
u Meint banier deploie.　　x Se estoit la noise loign oie.
y De henissemens de chevaus.　　z Par tout estoient mons e vaus.
aa Plein.　　bb somiers.

Que ^a la bitaile et ^b la couroi

De tentes et de pavillons ^c

E li iours estoit beaus e longs

Se erroient ^d petites iournees

En quatre eschieles ^e ordinees ^f

Les ^g queles vous ^h deviserai

Que ⁱ nulle n'en ^k trespasserai

Ains ^l vous dirray ^m de ⁿ compaignons

Toutes les armes et les noms ^o

Des banieres nomement ^p

Si vous volies oier coment ^q

Henri le bon Conte de Nichole ^r.

De prowesse enbrasse e a cole ^s

E en son coer ^t le a souveraine ^u

Menans le eschiele ^x primeraine ^y

Baniere ot de un cendall saffrin ^z

O un lion ^{aa} rampant porprin ^{bb}

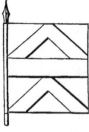

Que li Robert le fitz wautier ^{cc}

Ke bien siet de armes le mestier ^{dd}

Si ^{ee} en fesoit qanq's ^{ff} il devoit

En la iaune banier ^{gg} avoit

Fesse entre deus chevrons vermaus

---

sumpter horses and waggons with provisions, and sacks of tents and pavillions.

And the days were long and fine.   They
proceeded by easy journeys, arranged in
four squadrons; the which I will so describe
to you, that not one shall be passed over.
But first I will tell you of the names and
arms of the companions, especially of the
banners, if you will listen how.

Henry the good Earl of Lincoln, burn-
ing with valour, and which is the chief
feeling of his heart, leading the first squadron, had a banner of yellow silk with a
purple lion rampant.

With him Robert le Fitz Walter, who
well knew the use of arms, and so used
them when required.   In a yellow banner
he had a fess between two red chevrons.

---

r Enris li bons quens de Nicole.   ˢ Ki proueste enbraste e acole.
ᵗ cuer.   ᵘ soueraine   x eschele.   ʸ premeraine.
ᶻ Baner ont de un cendal saffrin.   ᵃᵃ lioun.   ᵇᵇ purprin.
ᶜᶜ O lui Robert le fiz Water.   ᵈᵈ Ke ben sont dez armes le mester.
ᵉᵉ Se.   ᶠᶠ Ranques.   ᶠˢ baner jaune.

E Guillemes [a] li Mareschaus [b]
Dont en Irelande [c] ot la baillie
La bende de or engreillie [d]
Portoit en la rouge baniere

Hue Bardoulf [e] de grant maniere
Riches homs preus e courtois [f]
En asure [g] quint fuelles [h] trois
Portoit de fin or esmere

Un grant seigneur mout honore [i]
Puis [k] ie bein [l] nom'er le cinkime
Phillipe le seigneur de Kime [m]
Qui [n] portoit rouge ove [o] un cheveron
De or croiselle tout environ [p]

Henry [q] de Grai vi ie la
Ki ben e noblement ala
Ovec son bon seigneur [r] le Conte
Banier avoit e par droit conte
De vis [s] piecis [t] la vous mesur
Barre [u] de argent e de asur

---

[a] Guillems. [b] Marescaus. [c] Irlande. [d] engreellie. [e] Bardoul.
[f] Riches homs e preus e cortois. [g] asur. [h] fullez.
[i] Une grant seignour mu'lt honnore. [k] Pus. [l] ben.

And William le Marshall, who in Ireland had the chief command. He bore a gold bend engrailed in a red banner.

Hugh Bardolf, a man of great appearance, rich, valiant, and courteous. He bore, azure, three cinquefoils of pure gold.

A great lord, much honoured, may I well name the fifth, Philip the Lord of Kyme, who bore red, with a chevron of gold surrounded by crosslets.

I saw Henry de Grey there, who well and nobly attended with his good Lord the Earl. He had a banner, and reckoned rightly you would find it barry of six pieces of silver and blue.

---

m Phelippe le seignur de Kyme. n Ki. o O.
p De or croissillie tot en viron. q Henri. r seignour. s sis.
t pecys. u Barree.

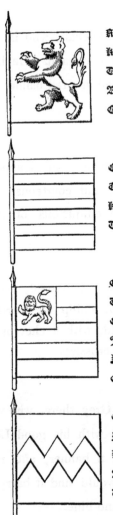

Robert de Monhaut i estoit
Ki mout haute entente i mettoit [a]
De faire a haute honeur [b] ateinte [c]
Baniere avoit en asure teinte [d]
Que un lyon rampant d'argent [e]

E compaignes a cele gent [f]
Thomas de Multons se fu
Ke [h] avoit baniere [i] e escu
De argent ove [k] treis bars [l] de goules [m]

Ces [n] armes ne furent pas soules
De siente en la parellement [o]
Car telles ou resemblement [p]
John [q] de Longaster entre meins
Mes ke en lieu de une barre meins
Quarter [r] rouge e iaune luppart [s]

E de celle mesme part [t]
Fu Guillemis [u] li Vavasours
Ki darmes nest muet ne sours [x]
Baniere [y] avoit bein [z] conoissable
De or fin oue la daunce de sable [a]

---

[a] Ky m'lt haute entent metoit.   [b] honur.   [c] atainte.
[d] *This line is omitted in the copy in the Cottonian Library.*
[e] O un lyoun rampant de arge't.   [f] Acompainiez a cel gent.
[g] Moulton.   [h] Ky.   [i] baner.   [k] O.   [l] barres.   [m] gouly's.

Robert de Montalt was there, who *highly* endeavoured to acquire *high* honor. He had a banner of a blue colour, with a lion rampant of silver.

In company with these was Thomas de Multon, who had a banner and shield of silver with three red bars.

These arms were not single, for such, or much resembling them, were in the hands of John de Lancaster; but who, in the place of a bar less, bore a red quarter with a yellow leopard.

And of this same division was William le Vavasour, who in arms is neither deaf nor dumb. He had a very distinguishable banner of fine gold with a sable dauncet.

---

[n] Ses. [o] le apparellement. [p] Kar teles ut resemblantme't. [q] Johans de Langastre. [r] Quartier. [s] lupart. [t] E le cele meispart. [u] Guillames. [x] Ky de armes ne est muet ne sours. [y] Baner. [z] ben. [aa] De or fyn o la dance de sable.

Johan de Odelston [a] ensement
Ki bien e adessement [b]
Ua darmes [c] toutes les saisons
Au Counte [d] estoit si est raisons
Ke nomes [e] soit entre [f] sa gent
Rouge portoit frette d'argent [g]

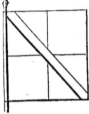

Le bon Robert le fitz Rogier [h]
Ui ie sa baniere a rengier [i]
Les [k] cele au Counte [l] en cele alee
De or et [m] de rouge esquartelee
Ove une bende taint en noier [u]

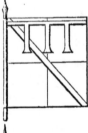

A [o] Johan son filz et P son heir [q]
Ki [r] de Clavering a surnom [s]
Nestoit [t] diverse de rien non [u]
Fors de un labell [x] vert seulement

Se estoient du retenement
Au bon Conte et au bien ame [y]
Tuit cil ke ci vous ai nome
Ses companis [z] fu li Conestables
Joefnes homes [aa] riches e metables [bb]
Ki [cc] Quens estoit de Herefort
Baniere ot [dd] de Inde cendal fort
O une blanche bende lee

---

[a] Johans de Odilstane.   [b] Ky' ben e adesscement.   [c] de armes.
[d] conte.   [e] nomez.   [f] entyr.   [g] frettéz de argent.
[h] Robert le fiz roger.   [i] arenger.   [k] **Lez.**   [l] conte.   [m] e.

Also John de Holdeston, who at all times appears well and promptly in arms. He was with the Count, which makes it proper that he should be named among his followers. He bore gules fretty of silver.

I saw the good Robert Fitz Roger's banner ranged with that of the Earl in the march: it was quarterly of gold and red with a black bend.

That of John his son and heir, who has the surname of Clavering, was not at all different, excepting only a green label.

All those whom I have named to you were the retinue of the good and well-beloved Earl. His companion was the Constable, who was Earl of Hereford, a rich and elegant young man. He had a banner of deep blue silk, with a white

---

[n] O un bende tainte en noir. [o] La. [p] e. [q] boir. [r] Ky.
[s] claveringhe a surnoun. [t] Ne estoit. [u] noun. [x] label.
[y] Le bon conte e le ben ame. [z] compaigns. [aa] homs.
[bb] mectables. [cc] Ky. [dd] ont.

De deus costices entre alee
De or fin dont au dehors assis [a]
Ot en rampant lyonceaus gis [b]

Nicholas de Segrabe o li
Ke nature avoit embeli
De corps [c] et [d] enrichi de cuer
Vaillant pere ot ki getta puer
Les garbes et [d] le lyon prist
A ses enfauns [e] ensi aprist
Les coragous a resembler
E o les nobles assembler [f]
Cils [g] ot la baniere [h] son pere
Au label rouge por son frere

Johan ke li ainsnez estoit
E ki entere la portoit
Li peres ot de la moillier
Cink filz [i] estoient chevalier [k]
Prue et [d] hardi et [d] defensable
O un lyon [l] de argent en sable
Rampant et [d] de or fin coronne [m]
Fu la baniere [h] del ainsne
Ke li Quens Mareschaus avoit
Mis el service kil [n] devoit
Por ce ke ke kil [o] ne i pooit venir
Il ne me [p] puet pas soubenir
Ke baneret i fuissent plus
Mes si le voir bous en conclus
Bons bachelers i ot bien [q] cent

---

[a] asis.   [b] *This line is omitted in the copy in the Cottonian MS.*   [c] cors.
[d] e.   [e] enfans.   [f] *This line is omitted in the copy in the College of Arms.*

bend between two cotises of fine gold, on the outside of which he had six lioncels rampant.

With him was Nicholas de Segrave, whom nature had adorned in body and enriched in heart. He had a valiant father, who wholly abandoned the garbs, and assumed the lion; and who taught his children to imitate the brave, and to associate with the nobles. Nicholas used his father's banner with a red label; by his brother John, who was the eldest, it was borne entire. The father had by his wife five sons, who were valiant, bold, and courageous knights. The banner of the eldest, whom the Earl Marshal had sent to execute his duties because he could not come, was sable with a silver lion rampant, crowned with fine gold. I cannot recollect what other Bannerets were there, but you shall see in the conclusion that he had one

---

[g] Cil. [h] baner. [i] fiz. [k] chivalier. [l] lyoun. [m] couronne. [n] Ke il. [o] li. [p] *This word is omitted in the copy in the Cottonian MS.* [q] ben.

Dont nuls en ostell [a] ne destent
Nulle [b] foiz tant ke il aient touz
Cerchies [c] les passages doutouz
O ens chevauchent chescun iour
Li mareschal li herbergour [d]
Ki livrent places a logier
A ceus ke doivent [e] herbergier [f]
Par tant ai dit de avant [g] garde
Ki sont dedeinz [h] et [s] ki la garde i

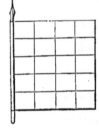

Johans li bons Quenas de Warene [k]
De lautre eschele [l] avoit la rene [m]
A iusticier et gouvorner [n]
Com [o] cil ki [p] bien scavoit [q] mener
Gen seignourie & honnouree [r]
De or et [s] de asur eschequeree [t]
Fu sa baniere noblement

Il [u] ot en son assemblement
Henri de Perci son nevou
De ki [p] sembloit ke eust fait vou
De aler les escos de rampant x
Jaune o un bleu lyon rampant
Fu sa baniere [y] bien vuable

Robert le Filz Payne [z] sievable
Ot sa baniere [y] flanc a flanc
Rouge a passans lyons de blanc
Trois de un baston [aa] bleu surgettez

---

[a] Ostel.   [b] Nule.   [c] Cerchiez.   [d] berbirgour.   [e] devent.
[f] herberger.   [g] lavant.   [h] dedenz.   [i] guarde.   [k] Warenne.
[l] chel.   [m] renne.   [n] a iustiçer e governer.   [o] cum.   [p] Ky'.

hundred good bachelors there, not one
of whom would go into lodgings or tent
until they had examined all the suspected passes, in which they rode every
day. The Marshal, the harbinger, assigned lodgings to those who were entitled to them. Thus far I have spoken of
those who are in and form the vanguard.

John the good Earl of Warren held the
reins to regulate and govern the second
squadron, as he who well knew how to
lead noble and honorable men. His banner was handsomely checquered with gold
and azure.

 He had in his company Henri de Percy
his nephew, who seemed to have made a
vow to humble the Scots. His banner
was very conspicuous, a blue lion rampant
on yellow.

Robert le Fitzpayne followed them;
he had his red banner, side by side, with
three white lions passant, surcharged with
a blue baton.

---

savoit.   Gent segnourie e bounouree.   e.   eschequere.
E.   rompant.   bauer.   Robert le fiz paien.   bastoun.

Gautiers de Monci ᵃ aioustez
Estoit en cele compaignie ᵇ
Car ᶜ tuit furent de une maisnie ᵈ
Cils ot baniere ᵉ eschequeree
De blanc et ᶠ rouge coulurec ᵍ

Le ʰ Valence Aymars li baillans
Belle ⁱ baniere i fu baillans
De argent et ᶠ de asure burlee ᵏ
O la bordure poralee
Tout entour de rouge i merolos ᵐ

Un bailliant hom et de grant los ⁿ
O lui Nichole de Karru
Dont meinte foiz orent paru
Li fait en couvert et ᶠ en lande
Sur la felloune gent dirlande ᵒ
Baniere ot iaune bien passable
O trois passans lyons de sable ᴾ

Rogier ᑫ de la Ware ovec eus
Ung chivaller sage et preus ʳ
En ˢ les armes ot vermeillectes ᵗ
O blanc lyon et croisselectes ᵘ

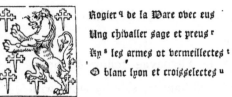

ᵃ Wautiers de Moncy'.   ᵇ compaigneye.   ᶜ Kar.   ᵈ maisine.
ᵉ Cil ot baner.   ᶠ e.   ᵍ couloure.   ʰ De.   ⁱ Bele.   ᵏ burelee.
ˡ rouges.   ᵐ merlos.   ⁿ Un vaillant home e de grant los.

Add to these Walter de Moncy, who was in this company because they were all of one household. He had his banner chequered of silver and red.

The valiant Aymer de Valence bore a beautiful banner there of silver and azure stuff, surrounded by a border of red martlets.

With him Nicholas de Carew, a valiant man of great fame, which had often been displayed both in cover and on the plains against the rebellious people of Ireland. He had a handsome yellow banner with three lions passant sable.

With them was Roger de la Ware, a wise and valiant knight, whose arms were red, with a white lion and crosslets.

---

* *This line is omitted in the copy in the Cottonian MS.*
ɪ treis lyouns passans de sable.   ꞇ Rogers.
.ꞏ Uns chevalers sagis e preus.   ꞏ * Ki.   ꞏ ꞇ vermellectis.
ꞏ O blonc lyoun e cruissellectes.

P

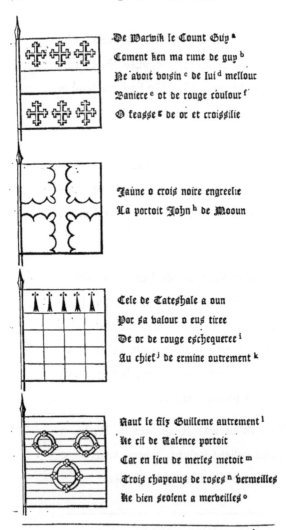

De Warwik le Count Guy [a]
Coment ken ma rime de guy [b]
Ne avoit voisin [c] de lui [d] mellour
Baniere [e] ot de rouge coulour [f]
O feasse [g] de or et croissilie

Jaune o crois noire engreelie
La portoit John [h] de Mooun

Cele de Cateshale a oun
Por sa valour o eus tiree
De or de rouge eschequeree [i]
Au chief [j] de ermine outrement [k]

Rauf le filz Guilleme autrement [l]
Ke cil de Valence portoit
Car en lieu de merles metoit [m]
Trois chapeaus de roses [n] vermeilles
Ke bien seoient a merveilles [o]

Guy Earl of Warwick, who of all that are mentioned in my rhyme had not a better neighbour than himself, bore a red banner with a fess of gold and crusilly.

John de Mohun bore there, yellow, with a black cross engrailed.

Tateshal, for valour which he had displayed with them, has one of gold and red chequered, with a chief ermine.

Ralph le Fitzwilliam bore differently from him of Valence, for instead of martlets he had three chaplets of red roses, which became him marvellously.

---

^¹ De or e de rouge eschequere.   ^j chef.   ^k outreemént.
^l *This line is omitted in the copy in the Cottonian MS.*
^m Car en lieu des merlos mettoit..   ⁿ rosis.
^o Ki bien auienent a mervelles.

Guillemes de Ros aſſemblans
I fu rouge a [a] trois bouʒ blans

. .

E la baniere Que Poinʒ
Eſtoit barre [b] de viii [c] poinʒ
De or et [d] de goules ovelment

Johans de Beauchamp proprement [e]
Portoit ſe [f] baniere de vair
Au douʒ tens et [d] au ſoveſt aier [g]

Preſtes a laſcier [h] leſ ventailleſ [i]
Enſi ſe aroutent leſ batailleſ [k]
Dont ia de deuſ oi aveſ [l]
E de la tierce oier deueſ [m]

---

[a] O.   [b] barree.   [c] viiij.   [d] e.   [e] propirment.   [f] la.
[g] ſouef far.   [h] bascier.   [i] ventailes.   [k] batalles.   [l] avez.

That which William de Ros displayed there, was red with three white bougets.

And the banner of Hugh Pointz was barry of eight pieces of gold and red.

John de Beauchamp bore handsomely, in a graceful manner, and with inspiring ardour, a banner vair.

The ventailes were soon lowered, and the battalions proceeded on their march. Of two of them you have already been told, and of the third you shall hear.

ⁿ E de la terce oir devez.

G

Edward[a] Sires de Irois
De Escoce[b] et[c] de Engleterre[d] rois
Princes Gualois Duc de Acquitaine[e]
La tierce eschile un poi loingtaine[f]
Conduit et[c] guye arreement
Si bel e si serrement[g]
Ke nuls de autre ne se i depart[h]
En sa baniere[i] trois luparte[k]
De or fin estoint[l] mis en rouge
Courant felloun fier et harouge[m]
Par tel signifiance mis
Ke ausi est vers ses enemis
Li rois fiers feloung[n] et[c] hastans[o]
Car sa morsure nest[p] tastans
Nuls ki nen[q] soit envenimez
Non porqant[r] tot[s] est ralumez
De douce debonairete
Quant[t] il requerent se amiste
Et[c] a sa pais veullent venir
Tel prince doit bien avenir
De grans gens estre cheveraigne[u].

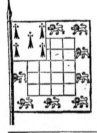

Soun nevou Johan de Britaigne[x]
Pur ce ke plus de lui est pres[y]
Doy[z] ie plus tost noumer[aa] apres
Si le avoit il bien[bb] deserbi
Com cil ki son oncle ot servi
Puis se[cc] enfance peniblement

Edward King of England and Scotland,
Lord of Ireland, Prince of Wales, and
Duke of Aquitaine, conducted the third
squadron at a little distance, and brought
up the rear so closely and ably that none
of the others were left behind. In his banner were three leopards courant of fine
gold, set on red, fierce, haughty, and cruel;
thus placed to signify that, like them,
the King is dreadful, fierce, and proud
to his enemies, for his bite is slight to
none who inflame his anger; not but his
kindness is soon rekindled towards such
as seek his friendship or submit to his
power. Such a Prince was well suited to
be the chieftain of noble personages.

I must next mention his nephew John
of Brittany, because he is nearest to
him; and this preference he has well
deserved, having assiduously served his
uncle from his infancy, and left his father

---

k lupart.   l estoient.   ▪ Courant feloun fier e harouge.
▪ felons.   ◦ haustans.   ▪ ne est.   ◦ ne en.   ◦ porquant.
▪ tost.   ◦ Kant.   ◦ De granz genz estre chievetaine.
x bretaigne.   y Pur ce ke plus est de li pres.   ◦ Doi.   ◦ nomer.
bb ben.   cc De se.

Et de guerpi [a] outreement

Son pere et [b] son autre lignage

Por demourer de son maisnage

Kant li Rois ot besoigne [c] de gens

Et [b] il ke estoit beaus et [b] gens

Baniere avoit cointe et [b] paree

De or et [b] de azur [d] eschequeree

Au [e] rouge ourle o iaunes lupars

Dermine [f] estoit la quarte [g] pars

Johan [h] de Bar iloec [i] estoit

Ken [k] la baniere [l] Inde portoit

Deus [m] bars de or et [b] fu croissillie

O la rouge ourle engreeillie [n]

Guillemes de Grant son palee

De argent et [b] de asur surealee [o]

De bende rouge o trois eigleaus

Portoit de or fin bien fais e beaus

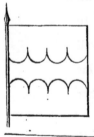

Bien doi mettre [p] en mon serventois

Ke Elis [q] de Aubigni li courtois

Baniere ot rouge ou entaillie

Ot fesse blanche engreeillie

---

[a] d. guerpi.   [b] e.   [c] bosoign.   [d] asur.   [e] a.   [f] De ermine.

and other relations to dwell in his household when the King had occasion for his
followers. He was handsome and amiable,
and had a beautiful and ornamented banner, chequered gold and azure, with a
red border and yellow leopards, and a
quarter of ermine.

John de Bar was likewise there, who, in
a blue banner, crusilly, bore two barbels
of gold, with a red border engrailed.

William de Grandison bore paly silver
and azure, surcharged with a red bend,
and thereon three beautiful eaglets of fine
gold.

Well ought I to state in my lay, that
the courteous Elias de Aubigny had a red
banner, on which appeared a white fess
engrailed.

---

g quart.　　h Johans.　　i iluec.　　k Ke en.　　l baner.
m Deuz.　　n engreellie.　　o suralee.　　p mettere.　　q Elys.

H

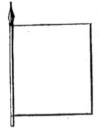

Mais Eurmenions de la Brecte[a]
La baniere eut toute rougecte[b]

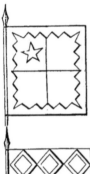

Apres eus[c] ci truis en mon conte
Hue de Uer le filz au Conte
De Oxenford[d] et[e] frere son hoir
O le ourle endente[f] de noir
Avoit baniere e long et[g] lee
De or[h] et[e] de rouge esquartelee
De bon cendal none pas de toile[i]
Se ot devant un blanche estoile[k]

Johan[l] de Rivers[m] le appareil
Ot mascle de or et de vermeil
Et[n] par tant compare le a oun[o]
Au bon Morice de Crooun[p]

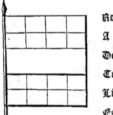

Robert le Seigneur[q] de Clifford
A ki raisons donne confort
De ses enemis encombrer[r]
Toutes les fois ke remembrer[s]
Li puet de son noble lignage
Escoce pregn a testmoignage[t]

---

[a] Mes Eumenions de la Brette.   [b] La baner ot tout rougette.
[c] ceus.   [d] Oxinfort.   [e] e.   [f] endentee.   [g] &.   [h] ore.

But Eurmenions de la Brette had a banner entirely red.

After these I find in my account Hugh de Vere, son of the Earl of Oxford, and brother to his heir. He had a long and narrow banner, not of silk but of good cloth, and quartered gold and red, with a black indented border, and in the upper part a white star.

John de Rivers had his caparisons mascally of gold and vermillion; and they were therefore similar to those of the good Maurice de Croun.

Robert, the Lord of Clifford, to whom reason gives consolation, who always remembers to overcome his enemies. He may call Scotland to bear witness of his noble lineage, that originated well and

---

ⁱ De bon cendal non pas de toyle.   ᵏ E devant une blanche estoyle.
ˡ Johans.   ᵐ Riviers.   ⁿ E.   ᵒ on.   ᵖ Croon.   ᵠ seignour.
ʳ emcombrer.   ˢ Toutes le foiz ki remembrer.   ᵗ teismoignage.

Ke bien[a] et[b] noblement comence

Com[c] cil ki est de la semence

Le Conte Mareschall[d] le noble

Ki par dela Constantinoble[e]

Al unicorne[f] se combati

Et[b] de souz luis mort le abati

De li de par mere est venus

A ki fu bien[a] pareil tenus

Li bon Rogier[h] pere son pere

Mes ne ot provesse[i] ki ne apere

Resuscitee el filz du fitz[k]

Par coi bien sai ke onques ne en fiz

Loenge dont il ne soit dignes

Car en li est ausi bon signes[l]

De estre preudom ken nul co'boie[m]

Le Roi son bon seigneur[u] convoie

Sa banier moult honnouree[o]

De or et[b] de asur eschequeree[P]

O une fesse vermellette

Si ie estoie une pucellette

Je li donroie ceur[q] et[b] cors

Tant est de lu[r] bons li recors

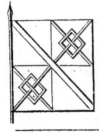

Le[s] bon Hue le Despensier

Ki vassaument sur le cursier[t]

Savoit desrompre une mellee

La baniere ot esquartellee[u]

De une noir[x] bastoun surblanc gette

Et[b] de vermeil iaune frette

[a] ben.   [b] e.   [c] cum.   [d] Mareschal.   [e] costentinoble.

[f] unicorn.   [g] li.   [h] Rogers   [i] value.   [k] Resuscitee el filz del filz.

[l] *This line, though omitted in the copy in the College of Arms, occurs in*

nobly, as he is of the race of the noble Earl Marshal, who at Constantinople fought with an unicorn, and struck him dead beneath him; from whom he is descended through his mother. The good Roger, his father's father, was considered equal to him, but he had no merit which does not appear to be revived in his grandson; for I well know there is no degree of praise of which he is not worthy, as he exhibits as many proofs of wisdom and prudence as any of those who accompany his good Lord the King. His much honoured banner was chequered with gold and azure, with a vermillion fess. If I were a young maiden, I would give him my heart and person, so great is his fame.

The good Hugh le Despenser, who loyally on his courser knows how to disperse an enemy, had a banner quarterly, with a black baton on the white, and the gules fretty yellow.

---

^m De estre preudom ke en mil ke en voie.   ⁿ seignour.
^o Sa baniere mout honouree.   ^p eschequere.   ^q quer.   ^r li.
^s Du.   ^t coursier.   ^u Fu la baniere esquartelee.   ^x noier.

I

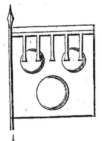

Du bon Hue de Courtenai[a]
La baniere obliee[b] ne ai[c]
De or fin o trois rouges rondeaus
Et[d] asourins[e] fu li labeaus

E le Aumari[f] de Saint Amant
Ki va prouesee[g] reclamant
De or et[d] de noir frette a[h] chief
O troi[i] rondeaus[k] de or derechief

Johan Dengaigne[l] le ot iolie
Rouge o dance de or croissilie[m]

Puis i ot Wautier de Beauchampe[n]
Sis merlos de or el rouge champe[o]
O une fesse en lieu de dance
Chivallier selon ma evidance[p]
An[q] des mellours fut[r] entre tous[s]
Se il ne fust trop fiers et[d] estous
Mes vous ne orrez parler iames
De Seneschal[t] ke[u] ne ait une mes

---

[a] Del bon Hue de Courtenay. [b] oubliee. [c] ay. [d] e.
[e] asurins. [f] Amauri. [g] prouese. [h] au. [i] trois. [k] gasteaus.
[l] Johans de Engaigne. [m] Rouge dance de or croissillie.

I have not forgotten the banner of the good Hugh de Courtenay, of fine gold with three red roundlets and a blue label.

And that of Aumary de Saint Amand, who advances, displaying his prowess, of gold and black fretty, on a chief three roundlets, also of gold.

John de Engaigne had a handsome one of red, crusilly, with a dancette of gold.

Next, Walter de Beauchamp bore there, six martlets of gold in a red field, with a fess instead of a dancette. A Knight, according to my opinion, one of the best of the whole, if he had not been too rash and daring ; but you will never hear any one speak of the Seneschal that has not a *but.*

ᵃ Watiers de beauchamp.   ᵒ champ.   ᵖ *This line is omitted in the copy in the Cottonian MS.*   ᵠ uns.   ʳ fuit.   ˢ touz.
ᵗ senescal.   ᵘ hi.

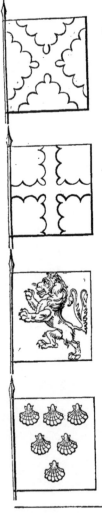

Cil ke a tout bien faire a cuer lie
Au sautour noir engreellie
Jaune ot et baniere et penoun [a]
Johan Boutourte ot a nom [b]

Baniere bel appareille [c]
Jaune a [d] crois rouge engreellie
La Eustache [e] de Hache estoit

Adam de Welles [f] la portoit
Jaune o unes [g] noire [h] lyon [i] rampant
Dont la coue en doubles [k] se espant

Robert de Scales bel et [l] gent
Le ot rouge a coquilles [m] de argent

---

[a] Jaune baniere ot e penon.   [b] Johans Boutetourte ot a noun.
[c] apparellie.   [d] o.   [e] Eustace.   [f] Adam de Welle.   [g] un.

He, who with a light heart, doing good
to all, bore a yellow banner and pennon
with a black saltire engrailed, was called
John Botetourte.

The banner of Eustace de Hache was
well ornamented : it was yellow with a
red cross engrailed.

Adam de Welles bore there, gold, a
black lion rampant, whose tail spread
itself into two.

The handsome and amiable Robert de
Scales bore red with shells of silver.

---

 noir.   ᶦ lyoun.   ᵏ double.   ᶦ Robert de Scales.   ᵐ e.
ⁿ cokilles.

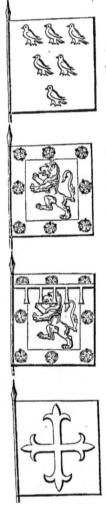

Touches chevalier de bon los[a]
Le ot vermeille o[b] iaunes merlos

Cele au Conte de Laonis[c]
Rouge o une[d] blanc lyoun connois[e]
E blanche en estoit le ouerloure[f]
O s roses del emchampeure[h]

Patrik de Dunbar filz[i] le Conte
Ne la portoit par nul aconte
Fors de une label de agure diverse[k]

Richard Sieuart[l] ke o eus converse
Noir[m] baniere ot aprestee
A[n] crois blanche a[n] bous[o] flouretee

Touches, a knight of good fame, bore red, with yellow martlets.

That of the Count of Laonis was known as red with a white lion, and a white border with roses like the field.

Patrick of Dunbar, son of the Count, bore in no way different from his father, excepting a blue label.

Richard Suwart, who was in company with them, had a black banner painted with a white cross, flowered at the ends.

---

^b a.   ^c Laonois.   ^d un.   ^e conois.   ^f ourleure.   ^g A.
^h enchampeure.   ⁱ fiz.   ^k inde.   ^l Richart Suwart.   ^m Noire.
ⁿ o.   ^o bouz.

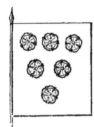

Symon Fresel de cele gent
Le ot noir[a] a rosettes de argent

Le beau Brian le filz Alepn
De courtoisie et[b] de honour[c] plepn
Si vi o baniere barree
De or et[b] de goules bien paree
Dont de chalange[d] estoit li poinz
Par entre lui[e] et[b] Hue Poinz
Ki portoit cel ne plus ne meins
Dont marveille avoit meinte & meins

Puis i fu Rogier[f] de Mortaigne
Ki se peine ke honnour a taigne
Jaune le ot o sis bleus lyons
Dont les coues doubles dions[g]

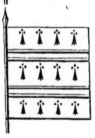

& de Hontercombe li beaux[h]
De ermine o deus rouges jumeaus

---

[a] noire.   [b] e.   [c] honnour.   [d] chalenge.   [e] li.

Simon de Fresel, of that company, bore *Zu· r*
black with roses of silver.

The handsome Brian Fitz Alan, full of
courtesy and honour, I saw with his well-
adorned banner, barry of gold and red;
which was the subject of a dispute between him and Hugh Pointz, who bore
the same, neither more nor less, at which
many and many marvelled.

Then there was Roger de Mortaigne,
who strives that he may acquire honour;
he bore yellow with six blue lions, the
tails of which we call double.

And of the handsome Huntercombe,
ermine with two red gemelles.

---

¹ Rogiers.   ᵍ dioms.   ʰ beaus.

Guilleme de Ridre i estoit
Ke en la baniere inde portoit
Les croissans de or enluminez

Obec[a] eus fu achiminez[b]
Li beau[c] Thomas de Fourneval
Ki kant[d] seoit sur le cheval
Ne sembloit home ke[e] someille
Sis merlos et[f] bende vermeille
Portoit en la baniere blanche

Johans de la Mare une manche
Portoit de argent en rouge oubree.

Johans le Estrange le ot livree
Rouge o deus[h] blancs[i] lyons passans

---

[a] Avoec. [b] acheminez. [c] beaus. [d] quant. [e] ki. [f] e.

William de Ridre was there, who in a blue banner bore crescents of brilliant gold.

With them marched the handsome Thomas de Furnival, who, when seated on horseback, does not resemble a man asleep; he bore six martlets and a red bend in a white banner.

John de la Mare bore a silver maunch worked on red.

John le Estrange had red caparisons with two white lions passant.

<hr />

<small>ᵉ Johans.　ʰ deuz.　ⁱ blans.</small>

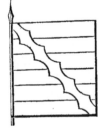

Encore i fu[a] le connoissans
Johan de Grai[b] ki viree[c]
J ot sa baniere barree
Dargent et de asur entaillie[e]
O bende rouge engreellie

E Guillemes de Cantelo
Ne se par ceste raison lo
Ke en honneur[f] a tous[g] tens vescu
Fesse vaire ot el rouge escu
De trois floures[h] de lis de or espars
Naissans de testes de lupars

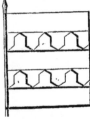

E puis Hue de Mortemer
Ke bien se scavoit[i] faire[k] amer
O deus fesses de vair levoit
La baniere ke rouge avoit

Mes a Symon de Montagu
Ke[l] avoit baniere et[d] escu
De inde au grifoun rampant de or fin
Pernoit la tiers eschiel fin[m]

[a] fiu.   [b] Gray.   [c] virree.   [d] e.   [e] De argent e de asur entallie.
[f] honnour.   [g] touz.   [h] flours.   [i] savoit.   [k] fere.   [l] Ki.

Also I· know John de Grey was there,
who I saw had his banner barry of silver
and blue, with a red bend engrailed.

And William de Cantilupe, whom I for·
this reason praise, that he has at all times
lived in honour.   He had on a red shield
a fess vair, with three fleurs de lis of
bright gold issuing from leopards' heads.

And then Hugh de Mortimer, who well
knew how to make himself loved: he bore
a red banner with two fesses vair.

But by Simon de Montagu, who had
a blue banner-and shield with a griffin
rampant of fine gold, the third squadron
was brought to a close.

---

* *This line is omitted in the copy in the Cottonian MS.*
M

La quart eschiel ou son couroy[a]
Conduit Edward[b] le filz[c] le Roy
Jouvenceaus de dix et sept ans[d]
Et[e] de nouvel armes portans
De corps[f] fu beaus et[e] aligniez
De cuer courtois et[e] enseigniez[g]
Et[e] desirans de lieu[h] trouver
Ou poust[i] sa force esprouver
Si chevauchoit merveilles bel
Et[e] portoit o un bleu labell[k]
Les armes le bon Roy[l] son pere
Or li doint dieus grace ke il pere
Ausi vaillans et[e] non pas meins
Lors porront en ses meins[m]
Tel ki nel beent faire oan

Li preus Johan[n] de Saint Johan
Fu par tout o lui assemblans
Ki sur touz ses garnemens[o] blans[p]
El chief rouge ot de or deus molettes[q]

Blanche cote et[e] blanches alettes[r]
Escu blanc et[e] baniere blanche
Avoit[s] o la vermeille manche
Robert[t] de Tony ki bien signe
Ke il est du chevalier a cigne[u]

---

[a] Il quarte eschiele o son couroi. [b] Edewars. [c] fielz.
[d] Jovencaus de dis e set ans. [e] e. [f] cors. [g] ensegniez. [h] ben.
[i] peust. [k] label. [l] roi. [m] Lors porront chair en ses meins.

The fourth squadron, with its train, was led by Edward the King's son, a youth of seventeen years of age, and bearing arms for the first time. He was of a well proportioned and handsome person, of a courteous disposition, and intelligent; and desirous of finding an occasion to display his prowess. He managed his steed wonderfully well, and bore with a blue label the arms of the good King his father. Now God give him grace that he be as valiant and no less so than his father: then may those fall into his hands who from henceforward do not act properly.

The brave John de Saint John was every where with him, who on all his white caparisons had upon a red chief two gold mullets.

A white surcoat and white alettes, a white shield and a white banner, were borne with a red maunch by Robert de Tony, who well evinces that he is a Knight of the Swan.

Baniere ot Henri li Tieis [a]
Plus blanche de un poli liois [b]
O un chievron vermeil en mi

Prouesse [c] ke avoit fait ami
De Guilleme de [d] Latimier
Ke [e] la crois patee de or mier
Portoit en rouge bien portraite [f]
Sa baniere ot cele part traite

Guillemes de Leybourne ausi
Vaillans homs sans [g] mes et [h] sans si
Baniere i ot o larges pans
Inde o sis blanc lyons rampans [i]

E puis Rogier [k] de Mortemer
Ki deça mer [l] et [h] dela mer
A porte quel part ke ait ale
Lescu barree [m] au chief pale
E les cornieres gironnees [n]
De or et [h] de asur enlumines [o]

[a] Baniere ot Henris li Tyois. [b] lyois. [c] Prouesce. [d] le. [e] Ki.
[f] pourtraite. [g] sanz. [h] e. [i] De Inde o sis blans lyouns rampans.

Henry le Tyes had a banner whiter than a smooth lily, with a red chevron in . the middle.

Prowess had made a friend of William le Latimer, who bore on this occasion a well-proportioned banner, with a gold cross patée, pourtrayed on red.

Also William de Leyburne, a valiant man, without *but* and without *if*, had there a banner and a large pennon, of blue, with six white lions rampant.

And then Roger de Mortimer, who on both sides the sea has borne, wherever he went, a shield barry, with a chief paly and the corners gyronny, emblazoned with gold and with blue, with the escutcheon

---

ᵏ Rogiers.   ˡ Ki beca mer e dela mer.   ᵐ barre.   ⁿ gyrounces.

N

O le escuchoun[a] vuidie de ermine
Ovec[b] les autres se achemine
Car il et[c] li devant nomes[d]
Au filz le Roy furent romes[e]
De son frein guiour[f] et[c] guardein
Mes coment ke ie les ordein
Li Seins[g] Johans li Latimiers
Baillie[h] li furent des premiers[i]
Ki se eschiele areer devoient
Com[k] cil ki plus de ce scavoient[l]
Car cuere[m] aillours ne seroit preus
Deus[n] plus baillans ne deux[n] plus preus
Ami lour furent et[c] voisin[o]
Deus[n] frere au filz le Roi cousin
Thomas et[c] Henry[p] les nome on
Ki furent filz mon sire Eymon
Frere le Roi le mieus ame[q].
Ke onques visse ensi nome

Thomas de Langcastre estoit contes
Si[r] est de ses armes tiels[s] li contes
De Engleterre au label de France
Et[c] ne veul plus mettre en souffrance

---

[a] escuchon.   [b] Ovoec.   [c] e.   [d] nomez.   [e] remez.
[f] Guyour.   [g] sains.   [h] Ballie.   [i] primers.   [k] Cum.   [l] savoient.

voided of ermine. He proceeded with the others, for he and the before named were appointed to conduct and guard the King's son. But how can I place them? The St. Johns, the Latimers, were leaders from the first, who ought to have been in the rear of the squadron, as those who best understood such matters, for it would not be wise to seek elsewhere two more valiant or two more prudent men.

Their friends and neighbours were two brothers, cousins to the King's son, named Thomas and Henry, who were the sons of Monsieur Edmond, the well-beloved, who was formerly so called.

Thomas was Earl of Lancaster: this is the description of his arms; those of England with a label of France, and he did not wish to display any others.

---

^m quere.   ⁿ deuz.   ^o veisin.   ^p Henri.
^q Frere le Roi mielz ame.   ^r Se.   ^s ceus.

Ke de -Henri ne vous redie
Ki touz iours toute se estudie
Mist a resembler son bon pere
Et[a] portoit les armes son frere
Au bleu bastoun sans label[b]

Guillemes de Ferieres bel
Et[a] noblement i fu remes[c]
De armes vermeilles bien[d] armes
O mascles de or du[e] champ voidies

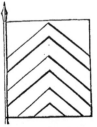

Celui[f] dont bien furent aidies
Et[a] achievees les amours
Apres grans[g] doubtes[h] et[a] cremours
Tant ke dieus [en voult[i] delivre estre
Por la Contesse de Gloucestre
Por long[k] tens souffri grans[g] maus
De or fin a trois chiobrons[l] vermaus

I ot[m] baniere seulement[n]
Si ne faisoit pas malement
Kant ses propres armes vestoit[o]
Iaunes ou le egle verde estoit
Et ot nom[p] Rauf de Monthermer

Those of Henry I do not repeat to you,
whose whole daily study was to resemble
his good father, for he bore the arms of
his brother, with a blue baton, without the
label.

William de Ferrers was finely and nobly
accoutred and well armed, in red, with
gold mascles voided of the field.

He by whom they were well supported,
acquired, after great doubts and fears
until it pleased God he should be delivered, the love of the Countess of Gloucester, for whom he a long time endured
great sufferings. He had only a banner
of fine gold with three red chevrons. He
made no bad appearance when attired in
his own arms, which were yellow with
a green eagle. His name was Ralph de
Monthermer.

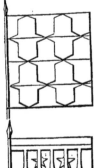

Apres lui[a] vi ie tout premier
Le vaillant Robert de la Warde
Ke bien[b] sa baniere[c] rewarde
Vairie est de blanc e de noir

Johan de St. John[d] son hoir
Lour ot baillie a compaignon
Ki de son pere avoit le noum[e]
Et[f] les armes au bleu label

Richard[g] le Conte de Aroundel[h]
Beau chivalier[i] et[f] bien ame
J vi je richement arme
En rouge au lyon rampant de or

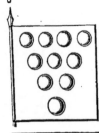

Aleyn de la Souche tresor
Signifioit[k] ke fust brisans
Sa rouge baniere a[l] besans
Car bien scai kil[m] a despendu
Tresor[n] plus ke en burce[o] pendu

---

[a] li.   [b] ben.   [c] banier.   [d] Johans de Seint Johan.   [e] uon.
[f] e.   [g] Richart.   [h] Arondel.   [i] chevalier.   [k] signefioit.

After him I saw first of all the valiant
Robert de la Warde, who guards his
banner well, which is vaire of white and
black.

The heir of John de St. John was there
a companion; he bore the name of his
father, and also his arms with a blue label.

Richard the Earl of Arundel, a handsome and well-beloved Knight, I saw
there, richly armed in red, with a gold
lion rampant.

Alan de la Zouche, to shew that riches
were perishable, bore bezants on his red
banner; for I know well that he has spent
more treasure than is suspended in his
purse.

---

¹ o.   ▪ Kar bien sai ke il.   ▪ Tresour.   ▪ bourse.

Par amour^a et^b par compagnie
O eus fu jointe la maismie^c
Le noble Evesq. de Douraume^d
Le plus vaillant clerke^e de^f roiaume
Voire voire^g de crestiente
Si vous en dirai verite
Por coy^h se entendre me volez
Sages fu et^b bien enparlez
Atempresⁱ droiturels^k et^b chastes
Ne onques riche home ne aprochastes
Ki plus bel ordenaste sa vie
Orguel couvotise^l en^b envie
Avoit il du^m tout gette puer
Non porqant hautein le cuerⁿ
Por ses droitours^o meintenier^p
Si kil ne laissoit convenier^q
Ses enemis par pacience
Car dune^r propre conscience
Si hautement se conseilloit
Ke chescuns sen esmerveilloit^s
En toutes le^t guerres^u le Roi
Avoit este de noble aroi
A grans^x gens et^b a grans coustages^y
Mes ie ne scai^z par quels^{aa} outrages
Dont uns plaiz li fu entames
En Engleterre^{bb} fu^{cc} remes

With them were joined both in company and affection, the followers of the noble Bishop of Durham, the most vigilant clerk in the kingdom, a true mirror of Christianity; so, that I may tell you the truth, I would be understood that he was wise, eloquent, temperate, just, and chaste. Never was there a great man, nor like person, who regulated his life better. He was entirely free from pride, covetousness, and envy : not, however, that he wanted spirit to defend his rights, if he could not work upon his enemies by gentle measures, for so strongly was he influenced by a just conscience, that it was the astonishment of every one. In all the King's wars he appeared in noble array, with a great and expensive retinue. He was detained in England in consequence of a treaty which was just entered into, but I know not about what wrong, so that he did not come

---

* Ke checuns se ensemerveilloit.   † les.   ᵘ guerrers.   ˣ grant.
ʸ *This line is followed by the words* Dont uns plais, *but they are dotted under, to shew that they were inserted by mistake.*   ˢ sai.
ᵃᵃ queus.   ᵇᵇ Engletere.   ᶜᶜ estoit.

P

Si ken[a] Escoce lors ne vint
Non purgant[b] si bien li saubint[c]
Du Roi ke emprise la voie[d] a
Ke de ses gens li envoia
Cent et[e] soissante[f] homes a armes
Onques Artours[g] por touz ses charmes
Si beau present ne ot de Merlin
Vermeillie[h] o un fer de molin[i]
Dermine[k] i envoia se enseigne[l]

Celuy ki tot honnour enseigne[m]
Johans[n] de Hastingues a nom[o]
La deboit conduire en son non[p]
Car il estoit o lui[q] remes[r]
Li plus prives[s] li plus ames[t]
De qanques[u] il en i aboit
Et[e] voir bien estre le deboit
Car[x] conneus estoit de tous[y]
Au fait de armes fiers et estouz[z]
En ostel douz et[e] debonnaires[aa]
Ne onques ne fu justice en aires
Plus voluntiers[bb] de droict[cc] iugier
Escu aboit fort et[e] legier
E baniere de oeure pareille[dd]
De or fin o la manche vermeille

---

[a] Li ke en.   [b] porquant.   [c] souvint.   [d] voi.   [e] e.
[f] seisante.   [g] Arturs.   [h] vermeille.   [i] molyn.   [k] De ermine.
[l] ensegne.   [m] *This line is omitted in the copy in the College of Arms.*
[n] Johan.   [o] non.

into Scotland; notwithstanding, being well informed of the King's expedition, he sent him of his people one hundred and sixty men at arms. Arthur, in former times, with all his spells, had not so fine a present from Merlin. He sent there his ensign, which was gules with a fer de moulin of ermine.

He who all honour displays, John de Hastings, was to conduct it in his name; for it was entrusted to him, as being the most intimate and the best beloved of any one he had there. And assuredly he well deserved to be so; for he was known by all to be in deeds of arms daring and reckless, but in the hostel mild and gracious; nor was there ever a Judge in Eyre more willing to judge rightly. He had a light and strong shield, and a banner of similar work of fine gold with a red maunch.

---

^v La conduit o meint compaignon, *in the copy in the College of Arms.*
^q li.   ^r remez.   ^s privez.   ^t amez.   ^u kanques.   ^x Kar.
^y touz.   ^z Au fair des armes feris e estous.   ^{aa} debonaires.
^{bb} volentris.   ^{cc} druit.   ^{dd} pareile.

Eymon[a] ses freres li baillans
Le label noir i fu cuellans
A ki pas ne devoit faillir
Honnours dont se penoit cuellir

Un bacheler iolif et[b] cointe
De amours et[b] darmes[c] bien acointe
Avoient[d] il a compaignon
Johan[e] Paignel avoit a nom[f]
Ken[g] la baniere verde tainte[h]
Portoit de or fin la manche painte[h]

Et kant li bons a Eymons Daincourt[i]
Ne pout mie venir a court[k]
Ses deus bons filz en son lieu[l] mist[k]
O[m] sa baniere o eus tramist
De inde coulour de or biletee[n]
O un[o] dance surgette

De Johan le filz Mermanduc[p]
Ke tout[q] prisoient Prince et[b] Duc
Et[m] autre ke li connoissoient[r]
La baniere rembellissoint[s]
La fesse et[b] li trois papegai
Ke a deviser[t] blancs en rouge ai

---

[a] Eymons. [b] e. [c] de armes. [d] avoint [e] Johans. [f] non. [g] Ke en. [h] peinte. [i] E q'nt li bons Eymo's deincourt. [k] *These lines are transposed in the copy in the College of Arms.* [l] leu. [m] E.

Edmond, his valiant brother, chose there
the black label. He could not fail of those
honours which he took so much pains to
acquire.

They had a handsome and accomplished
bachelor, well versed in love and arms,
named John Paignel, as a companion, who
in a green banner bore a maunch of fine
gold.

And, as the good Edmond Deincourt
could not attend himself, he sent his two
brave sons in his stead, and with them
his banner of a blue colour, billetté of
gold with a dancette over all.

Of John le Fitz Marmaduke, whom all
esteemed, Prince and Duke and others
who knew him, the banner was adorned
with a fess and three popinjays, which
were painted white on a red field.

ⁿ billetee.   ° une.   ᵖ fiz mermenduk.   ᑫ tuit.
ʳ conoissoient.   ˢ renbellissoient.   ᵗ daviser.

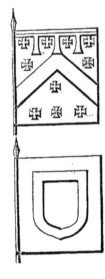

E Morices de Berkelee
Ki compaignis fu de cele alee
Baniere o vermeille cum sanc
Croissillie o un chievron blanc
Ou un label de asur avoit
Porce q' ces[a] peres vivoit

Mes Alissandres de Bailloel
Ke a tout bien fere[b] metoit[c] le oel
Jaune baniere[d] avoit el champ
Al rouge escu voidie du champ

A cestui daerain[e] nomme[f]
Ai sans[g] les doubles assome
Seissante et[h] vint et[h] set banieres
Ki tienent les voies plenieres
Au chastel de Karlaverok
Ki pas neit[i] pris de eschek de rok
Ainz i aura trait de[k] lancie
Engin[l] leve et[h] balancie
Com[m] nous vous en avisserons[n]
Kant le assaut en devisserons[o]

And Maurice de Berkeley, who was a companion in this expedition, had a banner red as blood, crusilly with a white chevron, and a blue label because his father was alive.

But Alexander de Balliol, who had his eye on doing every good, bore a banner with a yellow ground and a red escutcheon voided of the field.

To those last named, without reckoning double, were eighty-seven banners, which quite filled the roads to the castle of Carlaverock, which was not taken like a chess rook, but it will have thrusts of lances, and engines raised and poised, as we shall inform you when we describe the attack.

 ᵉ daerein.   ᶠ nome.   ᵍ sanz.   ʰ E.   ⁱ Ne pas ne ert.
ᵏ e.   ˡ Engin.   ᵐ Cum.   ⁿ aviseroms.   ᵒ deviseroms.

Le Siege de Karlaverok.

Karlaverok casteaus[a] estoit
Si fort[b] ke siege ne doubtoit[c]
Ainz ke li Rois iluec venist
Car rendre ne le convenist[d]
James mais kil[e] fust a son droit
Garniz qant[f] besoigns en vendroit
De gens de engins et[g] de vitaile
Com[h] uns escus estoit de taile
Car ne ot ke trois costez entour
Et en chescune[i] angle une tour
Mes ke le une estoit jumelee
Tant haute[k] tant longue e tant lee
Ke par desouz estoit la porte
A pont tourniz bien faite et forte[l]
Et autres defenses asses[m]
Et ot[n] bons murs et[g] bons fossez
Tretouz plains de eaue rez a rez[o]
Et[g] croi ke iames ne verres[p]
Chastel plus bel de lui seoir
Car a lun[q] puet on veoir
Devers le west la mere[r] de Irelande[s]
Et[g] vers le north la bele lande
De un bras de mere[r] environnee[t]
Si kil ne[u] est creature nee
Ki de deus[x] pars puist aprismer
Sans[y] soi mettre en peril de mer

Carlaverock was so strong a castle, that it did not fear a siege, therefore the King came himself, because it would not consent to surrender. But it was always furnished for its defence, whenever it was required, with men, engines, and provisions. Its shape was like that of a shield, for it had only three sides all round, with a tower on each angle; but one of them was a double one, so high, so long, and so large, that under it was the gate with a draw-bridge, well made and strong, and a sufficiency of other defences. It had good walls, and good ditches filled to the edge with water; and I believe there never was seen a castle more beautifully situated, for at once could be seen the Irish sea towards the west, and to the north a fine country, surrounded by an arm of the sea, so that no creature born could approach it on two sides, without putting himself in danger of the sea.

" Se avoit.   * Tres touz pleins de eawe reza rez.   ᵖ verres.
ᖋ Car al vules.   ' de Irlande.   * mer.   ᵗ avironne.
" Si ke il ne.   ˣ deuz.   ʸ Sanz.

R

Devers le su legier n'est[a] pas
Car il i a meint mauvais pas
De bois de more et[b] de trenchies
La ou[c] la mere[d] les a cerchies
Ou seult la riviere encontrer
Et[b] por ce convint lost[e] entrer
Vers le est ou pendant[f] est li mons
Et[b] iluec a li rois somons
Ses batailes arengier[g]
En trois com[h] devoit herbergier
Lors se arengierunt baneour[i]
Si veist on meint poigneour
Il loet[k] son cheval esprouver
Et[b] puest on iluec trouver
Trois[l] mil homes de armee gent
Si veist[m] on le or et[b] le argent
Et[b] de tous[n] riches colours[o]
Les plus nobles et[b] les meillours[p]
Trestout le val enluminer
Par coi bien croi ke a deviner
Cil du chastell[q] pussant[r] donques
Ken tel perell[s] ne furent onques
Dont il lour peust souvenir
Kant ensi nous virent venir
Tant com ensi fumes rengie[t]
Mareschal[u] orent herbergie

---

[a] ne est.   [b] e.   [c] Si cum.   [d] mer.   [e] le ost.
[g] Ses batailes a arengier.   [h] En trues con.   [i] ..ors se
baneour.   [k] Ilvec.   [l] Troi.   [m] vest.   [n] toutes.

Towards the south it was not easy, because there were numerous dangerous defiles of wood, and marshes, and ditches, where the sea is on each side of it, and where the river reaches it; and therefore it was necessary for the host to approach it towards the east, where the hill slopes.

And in that place by the King's commands his battalions were formed into three, as they were to be quartered; then were the banners arranged, when one might observe many a warrior there exercising his horse: and there appeared three thousand brave men at arms; then might be seen gold and silver, and the noblest and best of all rich colours, so as entirely to illuminate the valley; consequently, those of the castle, on seeing us arrive, might, as I well believe, deem that they were in greater peril than they could ever before remember. And as soon as we were thus drawn up, we were

---

[p] mellours. [q] chastel. [r] peussent. [s] Ke en tel peril.
[t] E tant cum si ſumes rengie. [u] Marescal.

Et ᵃ tout par tout places librees ᵇ

Lors veist on maisons oubrees ᶜ

Sanz ᵈ charpentiers et ᵃ sanz masons

De mult de diverses facons

De toile blanche et ᵃ toile teinte ᵉ

La ot tendue corde meinte ᶜ

Meint poisson en terre ᶠ fichie ᵍ

Meint ʰ grant arbre a terre ᶠ trenchie

Por faire ⁱ loges et ᵃ fuellies

Herbes et ᵃ flours es bois cuellies

Dont furent joinchies dedens ᵏ

Et ᵃ lors descendirent nos gens ˡ

A ki tantost si bien avint

Ke la navie a terre ᶠ vint

O les engins et ᵃ la vitaile

Et ᵃ ja comencoit la pietaile

Au devant du chastel aler

Si veist on entre eux ᵐ voler

Pieres sagettes ⁿ et ᵃ quarreaus ᵒ

Mes tant chier changent lour meraus

Cil dedenz a ceux ᵖ dehors

Ken petist heure plusoures corps ᑫ

J ot et blesciez et navrez ʳ

Et ne scai qans ˢ a mort librez

Des quant les gens ᵗ de armes perturent ᵘ

Ke li sergant tels maus recurent

ᵃ e.   ᵇ liverees.   ᶜ *This line is omitted in the copy in th*
of Arms.   ᵈ Sanz.   ᵉ tainte.   ᶠ tere.   ᵍ fiche.   ⁱ
ʲ fere.   ᵏ dedenz.   ˡ genz.   ᵐ eus.   ⁿ saiettes.   ᵒ q

quartered by the Marshal, and then might
be seen houses built without carpenters
or masons, of many different fashions, and
many a cord stretched, with white and
coloured cloth, with many pins driven into
the ground, many a large tree cut down
to make huts; and leaves, herbs, and
flowers gathered in the woods, which were
strewed within; and then our people took
up their quarters.

Soon afterwards it fortunately happened
that the navy arrived with the engines and
provisions, and then the foot-men began
to march against the castle; then might
be seen stones, arrows, and quarreaus to
fly among them; but so effectually did
those within exchange their tokens with
those without, that in one short hour there
were many persons wounded and maimed,
and I know not how many killed.

When the men at arms saw that the
foot-men had sustained such losses who

ᵖ Cil de dedenz a ceus.   ᵠ Ke en petite houre plusours cors.
ʳ l ot blesciez e navirez.   ˢ E ne sai quanz.   ᵗ Kant les genz.
ᵘ percurent.

Ki comencie orent le assaut
Meint en i court meint en i saut
Et [a] meint si haste si de aler
Ke a nul i nen daigne parler [b]
Lors i peust on reveoir
Aussi [c] espes pieres chaoir
Com [d] si on en deust poudrer
Chapeaus et heaumes effondrer [e]
Escus et targes despecier [f]
Car de tuer et de blescier
Estoit li jus [g] dont cil suoient
Ki a granz criz [h] se entre huoient
· Quant [i] mal veoient avenir

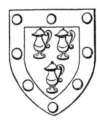

La vi je tout premier [k] benir
Le bon Bertram de Montbouchier
De goules furent trois pichier
En son escu dargent [l] luissant [m]
En le ourle noire li besant

Gerard de Goundronbile [n] o li
Bacheler legier et [a] joli
Le escu ot vair ne plus ne moins [o]
Cist ne orent pas oiseuses [p] meins
Car meinte piere [q] amont offrirent
Et [a] meinte pesant coup i souffrirent [r]

---

[a] e.   [b] Ke a nulli ne endaigne parler.   [c] ausi.   [d] Cum.
[e] E chapeaus e heames effrondrer.   [f] depescier.   [g] ju.   [h] cris

had begun the attack, many ran there, many leaped there, and many used such haste to go, that they did not deign to speak to any one. Then might there be seen such kind of stones thrown as if they would beat hats and helmets to powder, and break shields and targets in pieces; for to kill and wound was the game at which they played. Great shouts arose among them, when they perceived that any mischief occurred.

There, first of all, I saw come the good Bertram de Montbouchier, on whose shining silver shield were three red pitchers, with besants in a black border.

With him Gerard de Gondronville, an active and handsome bachelor. He had a shield neither more nor less than vaire. These were not resting idle, for they threw up many a stone, and suffered many a heavy blow.

Kant. [k] primer. [l] de argent. [m] luisant. [n] Gondronvile. meins. [p] oiseus. [q] pere. [r] coup soffrirent.

Bretouns estoit li premerains [a]

E li secons [b] fu Loherains

Dont nuls ne troeve lautre [c] lent

Ains [d] donent [e] baudour et [f] talent

As autres de se i acuellir [g]

Lors vint le chastel asailler [h]

De filz Marmaduc [i] a baniere

O un [k] grant route e pleniere

De bons bachelers esleus

Robert de Wileby veus

Il fu en or de inde frette

Robert de Haunsart [l] tout appreste [m]

Il vi venir o bel [n] gent

Rouge o trois estoiles de argent

Tenant lescu [o] par les enarmes

Henri de Graham unes armes

Avoit vermoilles come [p] saunc [q]

O une [r] sautour et [f] au chef blaunc [s]

Ou ot trois vermeilles cokilles

---

[a] primerains.   [b] secunds.   [c] le autre.   [d] ainz.   [e] donnent.
[f] e.   [g] acuellier.   [h] assaillir.   [i] Li fiz mermenduc.   [k] une.

The first body was composed of Bretons, and the second were of Lorrain, of which none found the other tardy; so that they afforded encouragement and emulation to others to resemble them. Then came to assail the castle, Fitz-Marmaduke, with a banner and a great and full troop of good and select bachelors.

Robert de Willoughby, I saw, bore gold fretty azure.

Robert de Hamsart I saw arrive, fully prepared, with fine followers, holding a red shield by the straps, containing three silver stars.

Henry de Graham had his arms red as blood, with a white saltire and chief, on which he had three red escalop shells.

---

¹ Hamsart.   ᵐ apreste.   ⁿ bele.   ⁰ le escu.   ᵖ cume.
ᑫ sanc.   ʳ un.   ˢ blanc.

Thomas de Richemond[a] ki killes
Faisoit[b] de lances de rechief,
O deus jumeaus de or et[c] au chief
Avoit vermeilles armeures
Cist ne vent com gens meures[d]
Ne com[e] gens[f] de sen alumees
Mes com[e] arses et[c] enfumees[g]
De orguel et[c] de melancolie[h]
Car droit ont leur[i] voie acoillie[k]
Juk a la rive du fosse
Et cil de Richemond[a] passe
A meintenant juques au pont
Le entrer demande oti li respont[l]
De grosses pieres et[c] cornues
Wyllebi[m] en ses avenues
Ot un[n] peire[o] en mi le pis
Dont bien devroit porter le pis
Son escu si le daignoit faire
Le filz Marmaduc[p] cel affaire
Tant entreprist a endurer
Com[e] li autre i porent durer
Car il estoit[q] com[e] une estache
Mes sa baniere ot meinte tache
Et[c] meint pertuis[r] mal a reconstre
Maunsart tant noblement si monstre[s]
Que[t] de son escu mouit souvent
Voit on voler le taint au vent

---

[a] Richmont.   [b] fesoit.   [c] e.   [d] Cist ne vont pas cum geus meures.
[e] cum.   [f] genz.   [g] enfumes.   [h] malencolie.   [i] lour.
[k] acuellie.   [l] Le entre demande on li respont.   [m] Wilebi.   [n] une.

Thomas de Richmont, who a second time collected some lances, had red armour, with a chief and two gemells of gold. These did not act like discreet people, nor as persons enlightened by understanding; but as if they had been inflamed and blinded with pride and despair, for they made their way right forwards to the very brink of the ditch.

And those of Richmont passed at this moment quite to the bridge, and demanded entry; they were answered with ponderous stones and cornues. Willoughby in his advances received a stone in the middle of his breast, which ought to have been protected by his shield, if he had deigned to use it.

Fitz Marmaduke had undertaken to endure as much in that affair as the others could bear, for he was like a post; but his banner received many stains, and many a rent difficult to mend.

Hamsart bore himself so nobly, that from his shield fragments might often be

---

° piere.　　◦ Le fiz mermenduc.　　◦ estut.　　◦ percuis.
◦ Hamsart tant noblement se i moustre.　　◦ Ke.

Car il et^a cil de Richemont
Ruent les^b pieres contrement^c
Com^d si ce fust as enviailes^e
Mes^f cil dedenz^g a deffailes
Lor^h enchargent testes et^a cous
Del encombranceⁱ de granz cous^k
Cil de Graham^l ne fu pas quites
Car ne vaudra deus promes^m quites
Sanques entierⁿ enportera
Del escu quant^o sen partira
Os^p vous la noise comencie
Ovoet eus sest^q entre lancie
Des gens le Roy un grant masse^r
Dont si ie tous^s les noms^t nomasse
Et^a recontasse^u les bons fais
Trop men serroit^x pesans li fais
Tant furent et^a tant bien li^y ferent
E non portant^z pas ne souffirent
Sans^{aa} la maisnie au filz^{bb} le Roy^{cc}
Ki moult i vint de noble aroy^{dd}
Car^{ee} meinte targe freschement
Peinte et^a guarni^{ff} richement
Meinte heaume et^a meint chapeau burni
Meint riche gamboison garni^{gg}
De soie^{hh} et^a radas et^a coton
En lour venue veist ounⁱⁱ
De diverses tailes et^a forges

---

^a e. ^b lour. ^c contremont. ^d cum. ^e enviales. ^f E.
^g dedenz. ^h Lour. ⁱ emcombrance. . . ^k cups. ^l Cil Graham, in
the copy in the College of Arms. ^m pomes. ⁿ Kanques entere.
^o k_{ant}. ^p Es. ^q se est. ^r De genz le Roi une grant masse.

seen to fly in the air ;- for he, and those of
Richmont, drove the stones upwards as
if it were rotten, whilst those within defended themselves by loading their heads
· and necks with the weight of heavy blows.

Those led by Graham did not escape,
for there were not above two who returned
unhurt, or brought back their shields entire.

Then you might hear the tumult begin.
With them were intermixed a great body
of the King's followers, all of whose names
if I were to repeat, and recount their brave
actions, the labour would be too heavy,
so many were there, and so well did they
behave. Nor would this suffice without
those of the retinue of the King's son,
great numbers of whom came there in
noble array; for many a shield newly
painted and splendidly adorned, many a
helmet and many a burnished hat, many
a rich gambezon garnished with silk, tow,
and cotton, were there to be seen of divers
forms and fashions.

ᵃ touz.	ᵗ nons.	ᵘ recontaisse.	ˣ seroit.	ʸ le.
ᶻ porquant.	ᵃᵃ Sanz.	ᵇᵇ fiz.	ᶜᶜ roi.	ᵈᵈ aroi.	ᵉᵉ Kar.
ᶠᶠ guarnie.	ᵍᵍ guarni.	ʰʰ soi.	ⁱⁱ on.	

U

Iloeques ᵃ vi ie Rauf de Gorges

Chevalier ᵇ nouvel a doube

De pieres ᶜ a terre ᵈ tumbe .

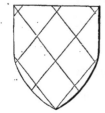

Et ᵉ de foule plus de une fois ᶠ

Car tant estoit de grant buffois ᵍ

Kil ʰ ne sen daignoit ⁱ departir

Tout son harnois et ᵉ son atir ᵏ

Avoit mascle de or et ᵉ de asur

Ceus ki estoient sur le mur

Robert de Tony moult greboit

Car en sa compaignie aboit

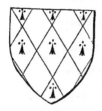

Le bon Richart de la Rokele

Ki ceus dedenz si enparkele

Ke moult soubent les fait retraire

Cil ot son escu fait portraire ˡ

Mascle de goules et ᵉ de ermine

Adam de la Forde au mur mine

En tel maniere ᵐ com ⁿ il puet

Car ausi dru com ⁿ pluie pluet

Volent ses pieres ens ᵒ et ᵉ hors

Dont moult fu defoules ᵖ li·ors

De trois lionceaus ᑫ couronnes ʳ

Kil ˢ ot rampans en inde nez

Le bon Baroun de Wygnetone ᵗ

Merveilles ᵘ est ke tout ne estone

Li fais des coupes ˣ ki ʸ il i recoit

Car ia ce ke benus i soit

ᵃ Ilveques. ᵇ Chevalier. ᶜ peres. ᵈ tere. ᵉ e. ᶠ foiz.
ᵍ bufoiz. ʰ Ke il. ⁱ deignoit. ᵏ atire. ˡ *This line is omitted*
in the copy in the College of Arms. ᵐ maner. ⁿ cum. ᵒ enz.

There I saw Ralph de Gorges, a newly dubbed Knight, fall more than once to the ground from stones and the crowd, for he was of so haughty a spirit that he would not deign to retire. He had all his harness and attire mascally of gold and azure.

Those who were on the wall Robert de Tony severely harassed; for he had in his company the good Richard de Rokeley, who so well plied those within that he frequently obliged them to retreat. He had his shield painted mascally of red and ermine.

Adam de la Forde mined the walls as well as he could, for his stones flew in and out as thick as rain, by which many were disabled. He bore, in clear blue, three gold lioncels rampant crowned.

The good Baron of Wigtown received such blows that it was the astonishment of all that he was not stunned; for, without

---

P defoulez.   q lyonceaus.   r couronnez.   s Ke il.   t Wignetone.
u Merveilleis.   x coups.   y ke.

Sanz seigneur[a] hors de retenance
Ja a[b] plus nen a la contenance
Esbahie[c] ne espoentee
Et il[d] portoit bordure endentee
O trois estoiles de or en sable
Meint[e] pesant piere et[f] quassable[g]
Cil de Kirkbride[h] i porta
Mes le escu blanche devant bota[i]

O la crois verde engreslie[k]
Si ke moult fu bien assaillie[l]
Par lui la porte[m] du chastel
Car onques feures de martel
Si sour son fer ne martela[n]
Com[o] il et[f] li sien firent la
Non porqant[p] tant i ont este
De grosses pieres tempeste
Et de quarreaus[q] et[f] de sagettes
Ke de blescures[r] et[f] plaiettes
Sont li[s] las et[f] si amorti
Ke a moult grant peine en sont parti[t]
Mes ainz kil sen[u] fussent partiz
Cil de Cliffort com[o] avertiz
E com[o] cil ki ne a eu pourpos
Ke cil bedenz aient repos
Ja a sa baniere envoie
Et[f] tant com[o] bien le ai[x] convoie

---

excepting any lord present, none shewed a more resolute or unembarrassed countenance. He bore within a bordure indented, three gold stars on sable.

Many a heavy and crushing stone did he of Kirkbride receive, but he placed before him a white shield with a green cross engrailed. So stoutly was the gate of the castle assailed by him, that never did smith with his hammer strike his iron as he and his did there. Notwithstanding, there were showered upon them such huge stones, quarrels, and arrows, that with wounds and bruises they were so hurt and exhausted, that it was with very great difficulty they were able to retire.

But as soon as they had retreated, he of Clifford, being advised of it, and like one who had no intention that those within should have repose, sent his banner there, and as many as could properly

---

De Badelesmere Bartholmieus [a]

Johans de Cromewelle au mieus

Que [b] puet i a mise se entente

Car nuls de ceus ne fait atente

De abessier et [c] pieres cuellir [d]

Et [c] de ruer et [c] de assaillir

Tant com [e] durer lour puet aleine

Mes les gens [f] a la chesteleine [g]

Ne lour leissent [h] avoir souiour

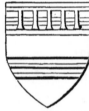

Badelsmere ki tout le iour

Iluec se contint bien et [c] bel

Portoit en blanc au bleu label

Fesse rouge entre deus [i] jumeaus

Cromewelle li preus li beaus

Ke entre le pieres va tripant

En inde ot blanc lyoun [k] rampant

Couronne de or ou [l] double coue

Mes pas ne croi [m] ke il la rescoue

Ke iluec ne li soit recoupee

Tant fut [n] de pieres estampee [o]

E broie ainz kil sen a la [p]

Apres ces deus [q] revindrent la

La Warde et [c] Johans de Grai [r]

Ki [s] de noubel ont enbai [t]

Ceus dedenz ki bien atendent

Et arcs et [u] arbalestes tendent

---

[a] De Badelsmere Bartholmieuis.   [b] Ke.   [c] e.   [d] cuellier.

[e] cum.   [f] genz.   [g] chasteleine.   [h] lessent.   [i] deuz.

[k] lyon.   [l] o.   [m] Mes ne croi pas.   [n] fu.   [o] estampe

escort it, with Bartholomew de Badlesmere, and John de Cromwell, as those
who could best perform his wishes; for
whilst their breath lasted, none of them
neglected to stoop and pick up the stones,
to throw them, and to attack.

But the people of the castle would not
permit them to remain there long.   Badlesmere, who all that day behaved himself well and bravely, bore on white with
a blue label a red fess between two gemelles.   Cromwell, the brave and handsome, who went gliding between the
stones, bore on blue a white lion rampant
double-tailed, and crowned with gold;
but think not that he brought it away,
or that it was not bruised, so much was
it battered and defaced by stones before
he retreated.

After these two, La Warde and John de
Gray returned there, and renewed the attack.   Those within, who were fully expect-
ing it, bent their bows and cross-bows,

Ebroie ainz ke il se en ala.   Apres ceus deuz.   Gray.
Ke.   envay.   E ars e.

Et ^a traient de lour espringaut

Et ^a bien se tienent paringaut

Et ^a au iecter ^b et ^a au lancier

Puis dont le assaut recomencir ^c

Les gens le seigneour de Britaigne ^d

Com ^e li lyons ^f de la montaigne

Coragiouses ^g et ^a empernans

Et ^a sont checun ^h iour apernans

Le fait de arms ⁱ et ^a le mestier

Mult tost coubrent li portier

Du chastel lour, acointement

Car autre plus folonnement ^k

Ains ^l ne les orent assailli ^m

Non porqant ⁿ ne ont mie failli

Ke ki ke pres viegne ne ait part

De lour libree ains ^l qil sen part ^o

Tant ke plus ke assez li ensemble

Apres i ceus ^p ilvec se assemble

La gent mon seignour de Hastingues ^q

Ou je vi Johan de Cretinques ^r

En peril de perdre un cheval

Kant sour ^s li un vint contre val

Esperounant au sagettes ^t

Mes pas ne semble estre feintiez ^u

Ki tant se haste au fait attaindre ^x

En son blanc escu ot fait taindre ^y

Un chievron rouge o trois molettes

---

^a e.   ^b getter.   ^c recomencier.   ^d Le gens mon segnour de Bretaigne.
^e cum.   ^f lyon.   ^g Coraiouses.   ^h chescun.   ⁱ armes.
^k felounement.   ^l Ainz.   ^m assilli.   ⁿ porquant.

and prepared their espringalls, and kept themselves quite ready both to throw and to hurl.

Then the followers of my Lord of Brittany recommenced the assault, fierce and daring as lions of the mountains, and every day improving in both the practice and use of arms. Their party soon covered the entrance of the castle, for none could have attacked it more furiously. Not, however, that it was so subdued that those who came after them would not have a share in their labours; but they left more than enough for them also.

After these, the people of my Lord of Hastings assembled there, where I saw John de Cretinques in danger of losing a horse. When upon it, one came beneath pricking it with an arrow; but he did not seem to be dissembling, he used such haste to strike him. On his white shield he had caused to be depicted a red chevron with three mullets.

---

[o] ke il se enpart. [p] E apres ceus. [q] segnour de Hastingues. [r] Cretingues. [s] sur. [t] saietiz. [u] faintuz. [x] ateindre. [y] teindre.

Cil ki porte dance et[a] billettes
De or en asur al assaut court
Johans avoit a nom[b] Daincourt
Ki tres[c] bien i fist son devoir
Ausi li[d] firent bien por voir
En recevant meinte colee
Li bon frere de Berkelee

Et li frere[e] Basset aussi[f]
Dont li aingnez portoit ensi
De ermine au chief rouge endente
De trois molettes de or ente
Li autres de cokilles trois
Chemins trouveoierent[g] estrois
Cil dedens se or se en alassent[h]

Car tousiours com[i] li un se lassent
Autre i revienent fres et[a] froit
Mes porqanques[k] on lour offroit[l]
De tels assaus ne se rendirent
Cels dedens[m] ainz se deffendirent
Et[a] se tindrent ki ke il anuit
Tout cel iour et[a] toute[n] la nuit
Et[a] lendemain[o] iuques a tierce[p]
Mes durement eus et[a] iour fierce
Entre les assaus esmaia
Frere Robert ki envoia
Meinte piere par robinet
Juq[q] au soir des le matinet

---

[a] e. [b] non. [c] m'lt. [d] le. [e] E li ij frere, *but the*
figures ij *have been subsequently added.* [f] ausi. [g] trouveroient.
[h] Cil de dedenz se or sen alassent. [i] touz iours cum. [k] porquanques.

He who bore a dancette and billets of gold on blue, John Deincourt by name, rushed to the assault, and there extremely well performed his duty.

It was also a fine sight to see the good brothers of Berkeley receiving numerous blows; and the brothers Basset likewise, of whom the eldest bore thus, ermine, a red chief indented, charged with three gold mullets; the other, with three shells; found the passages straitened. Those within continually relieved one another, for always as one became fatigued, another returned fresh and stout : and, notwithstanding such assaults were made upon them, they would not surrender, but so defended themselves, that they resisted those who attacked, all that day and night, and the next day until tierce. But their courage was considerably depressed during the attack by the brother Robert, who sent numerous stones from the robinet, without cessation from the dawn of the

---

¹ offrit.   ᵐ Cil dedenz.   ⁿ tout.   ° lendemein.
ᵖ terce.   ᵠ Juk.

Le jour devant cesse ne avoit

De autre parte[a] oncore i leboit

Trois autres enging[b] moult plus grans[c]

Et[d] il penibles et[d] engrans

Ke le chastel du tout confonde

Tent et[d] reent[e] met piere enfonde[f]

Deschoee et kangs[g] ateint fent

A ses coups rien ne se deffent

Bors bretesche[h] ne gros fus

Non porquant ne fierent[i] refus

Ainz tindrent tous[k] ses enbiaus

Cil dedens[l] tant ke en mi aus

En fu uns ferus a la mort

Mes lors checuns daus[m] se remort

De son orguel et[d] se esbachi[n]

Car ausi li combles chai[o]

Par tout par ou la piere entra

Et quant ascun[p] de eus encontra

Chapeaus de fer[q] targe de fust

Ne sauba ke blesciez[r] ne fust

E qant[s] virent ke plus durer

Ne porent[t] ne plus endurer

Pes requiterent[u] li compaignon

Et bouteront[x] hors une[y] penon

Mes celui[z] ki hors le bouta

Ne scai quels sergans sagitta[aa]

<hr/>

[a] part.   [b] enginz.   [c] granz.   [d] e.   [e] retent.   [f] en
[g] Descoche e quanques.   [h] Bors de bretesche.   [i] nen firent.   [k]
[l] Cil de dedens.   [m] de eus.   [n] esbabi.   [o] chay.   [p] E kant
[q] Nel pout quarir, *in the copy in the College of Arms.*

preceding day until the evening. Moreover, on the other side he was erecting
three other engines, very large, of great
power and very destructive, which cut
down and cleave whatever they strike.
Fortified town, citadel, nor barrier—nothing is protected from their strokes. Yet
those within did not flinch until some of
them were slain, but then each began to
repent of his obstinacy, and to be dis-
mayed. The pieces fell in such manner,
wherever the stones entered, that when
they struck either of them, neither iron
cap nor wooden target could save him
from a wound.

And when they saw that they could not
hold out any longer or endure more, the
companions begged for peace, and put
out a pennon; but he that displayed it
was shot with an arrow, by some archer,
through the hand into the face. Then he

ʳ Ke maintenant blesciez, *in the copy in the College, of Arms.*   ˢ E quant.
ᵗ porrent.   ᵘ Pas requistrent, *in the copy in the College of Arms.*
ˣ bouterent.   ʸ un.   ᶻ celuy.   ᵃᵃ Ne sai ques sergans saieta.

Z

Parmi la mein iuq[a] en la face

Lors requist qe[b] plus ne li face

Car le chastel au Roy[c] rendront

Et[d] en sa grace hors viendront[e]

Et[d] Mareschaus et[d] Conestables

Ke a des iluec furent estables

A cel mot[f] le assault[g] deffendirent

Et[d] cil le chastel lour rendirent

Lors sen issirent ce est la some

Ke de uns ke de autres seissante[h] home

A grant merveille resguarde

Mes tenu furent e[d] guarde

Tant ke li Rois en ordena

Ke[i] vie et[d] membre lour donna[k]

Et[d] a chascun[l] robe noubele

Lors fu ioieuse[m] la noubele

A toute la ost du chastel pris

Ki tant estoit de noble pris

Puis fist le Roy[n] porter amont

Sa baniere et[d] la Seint Eymont

La Seynt[o] George et[d] la Seint Edwart

Et[d] o celes par droit eswart

La Segrave et[d] la Herefort

Et[d] cele[p] au seignour de Cliffort

A ki li Chasteaus fut[q] donnes[r]

---

[a] Par mi la mien jok.   [b] com.   [c] Roi.   [d] e.   [e] vendront.
[f] moult, *in the copy in the College of Arms.*   [g] assault.   [h] seisant.
[i] Ki.   [k] dona.   [l] chescun.   [m] ioiouse.   [n] Rois.   [o] seint.
[p] tcel.   [q] fu.   [r] donnez.

begged that they would do no more to him, for they will give up the castle to the King, and throw themselves upon his mercy. And the marshal and constable, who always remained on the spot, at that notice forbad the assault, and these surrendered the castle to them.

And this is the number of those who came out of it; of persons of different sorts and ranks sixty men, who were beheld with much astonishment, but they were all kept and guarded till the King commanded that life and limb should be given them, and ordered to each of them a new garment. Then was the whole host rejoiced at the news of the conquest of the castle, which was so noble a prize.

Then the King caused them to bring up his banner, and that of St. Edmond, St. George, and St. Edward, and with them, by established right, those of Segrave and Hereford, and that of the Lord of Clifford, to whom the castle was entrusted.

Le Siege de Karlaverok.

Et[a] puis a li Rois ordenes[b]
Com cil[c] ki de guerre[d] est moult[e] sages
Tous[f] ses chemins et[a] ses passages
Coment[g] ira parmi[h] gawe
Cele forte[i] terre[k] loec.

Ici[l] finist le Siege[m] de Karlaverok.

---

[a] e. [b] ordenez. [c] Cum cils. [d] guere. [e] mut. [f] Touz.
[g] Comment. [h] mie. [i] fort. [k] tere. [l] Ci. [m] Assault,
in the copy in the College of Arms.

And then the King, who is well skilled in war, directed in what way his army should proceed.

Here ends the Siege of Carlaverock.

MEMOIRS

OF

The Peers and Knights

MENTIONED IN THE POEM.

The particulars contained in the following Memoirs are throughout taken from Sir William Dugdale's "Baronage," excepting where other authorities are cited in the notes.

BIOGRAPHICAL NOTICES.

HENRY DE LACY, EARL OF LINCOLN.

[PAGE 5.]

THIS distinguished nobleman, whose name occupies so prominent a place in the records of almost every public event of his time, was the eldest son of Edmund de Lacy, Earl of Lincoln, by Alice, the daughter of the Marquess of Saluces in Italy. He succeeded his father in the Earldom[a] in 1257, at which time he was probably about nine years of age, his parents having been married in May, 1247.[b] The first circumstance relating to the Earl after his birth, of which we have any notice, was his marriage, in 1256, to Margaret, the eldest daughter and coheiress of William de Longespee; the covenants of which are given by Dugdale. In 1269 the Earl became involved in a dispute about some lands with John Earl Warren,

---

[a] Dugdale says, vol. I. p. 103, that " Edmund de Lacy, the father of Henry, never used the title of Earl of Lincoln, nor was it ever attributed to him in any grant, though he enjoyed the *tertium denarium* of that county, as may be seen by a record of after time." The late Francis Townsend, Esq. Windsor Herald, in his valuable collections for a new edition of Dugdale's Baronage, has, however, proved that this assertion is erroneous, for he observes, " In the record referred to by Dugdale, relating to Henry his son, this Edmund is expressly described as ' Edmundus de Lacy, pater ejusdem Henrici, quondam Comitis Lincolniæ ;' and he is also so designated in the patent of safe conduct to the King and Queen of Scotland, dated 5 September, 39 Hen. III. 1255. Fœdera, tome I. p. 563." Dugdale's statement, that Henry de Lacy was " made Earl of Lincoln" at the same time that he received the honour of knighthood, does not appear to be supported by evidence, and even if he had been so created, it would not be conclusive that his father had not enjoyed the same honour. Some remarks on the descent of Earldoms at that period, connected with this remark, will be found in vol. XXI. of the Archæologia.

[b] Mr. Townsend's " MS. Collections for Dugdale's Baronage."

and each party prepared to establish his claim by force of arms, but their intention becoming known to the King, he commanded his Justices to hear and determine the cause, who decided it in favour of the Earl of Lincoln. William de Longespee, his wife's father, died in the 52 Hen. III. and soon afterwards the Countess and her husband performed homage for, and obtained livery of, all the lands which had in consequence devolved upon her. In her right he is considered to have become Earl of Salisbury, the said William de Longespee having been entitled to that dignity, though he was never allowed it, as son and heir of William de Longespee, the natural son of King Henry the Second by the well known Rosamond Clifford, who obtained the Earldom of Salisbury by his marriage with Elizabeth, the daughter and heiress of William d'Evereux. On the feast of St. Edward, 18 March, 1272, the Earl of Lincoln received the honour of knighthood, and in the same year was appointed governor of Knaresborough Castle. To follow Dugdale in his account of this Earl would not only be a useless repetition, but the limits which it is proposed to assign to each of the individuals who are mentioned in the preceding Poem would be considerably exceeded; hence the principal circumstances of his life only will be noticed, and even these must be alluded to as concisely as possible. In the 5 Edw. I. he had livery of the fee which his ancestors had usually received *nomine comitatús Lincoln'*, with all the arrears from the time he was invested by King Henry the Third with the sword of that Earldom. Upon several occasions between the 6th and 10th Edw. I. he obtained grants of fairs, markets, and free-warrens in different parts of his domains; and in the year last mentioned he accompanied the expedition then sent into Wales. Leland asserts that the Earl built the town of Denbigh, the land of which had been granted to him " from his having married into the blood of those princes, and that he walled it and erected a castle, on the front of which was a statue of him in long robes; and that anciently prayers were offered in Saint Hillary's chapel in that place for Lacy and Percy."

Dugdale considers that his surrender of the castle and barony of Pontefract to the King, with all the honours thereto belonging, in the 20th Edw. I. arose from his " having been long married, and doubting whether he should ever have issue, but upon condition as it seems," for the King by his charter, dated at Newcastle on Tyne, 28 Dec. 21 Edw. I. re-granted the same to him and to the heirs of his body, with remainder to Edmund Earl of Lancaster, the King's brother, and to the heirs of his body, failing which to the King and his heirs. In almost the next paragraph, however, that eminent writer says, "that in the 22nd Edw. I. the Earl received a grant of several manors from the King, with remainder to Thomas, the son of Edmund Earl of Lancaster, and Alice his wife, sole daughter of the Earl, and to the heirs of their two bodies lawfully begotten, and failing such issue, to the right heirs of the said Thomas," from which it would appear that at the time of the surrender by the Earl of Lincoln to the King, the said Alice was living; and which is further confirmed by his saying in a subsequent page, that she was twenty-eight years of age at the death of her father in 1312, in which case she must have been above seven at the time in question. In the 20th Edw. I. the Earl was sent as ambassador to the King of France to treat on the subject of the restraint of those pirates who robbed some French merchants; and in the 22nd year of that monarch he again attended him into Wales, and was likewise in the expedition sent into Gascony. He accompanied the Earl of Lancaster in the 24 Edw. I. into Brittany, and was present at various successes of the English forces. On the death of that nobleman he succeeded him in his command, and besieged the town of Aux with great vigour, though without success, and was forced to retreat to Bayonne; from which place he marched with John de St. John towards Bellegard, which was then besieged by the Count d'Artois. The engagement which took place in the vicinity of that town, does not, from Dugdale's relation of it, appear to have added to the reputation of the Earl, as he informs us, upon the authority of Walsingham, that " approaching a wood about three miles from Bellegard," he divided his army into two parts, whereof the van was led by John de St. John, and the rear by himself; but having past the wood where St. John, meeting the enemy, began the fight, discerning their strength, he retreated to Bayonne, leaving the rest to shift for themselves, so that St. John and many others were by reason thereof taken prisoners." Whatever stain this circumstance might have cast upon his military character, seems to have been partially removed towards the end of that year, by his having obliged the enemy to raise the siege which they had laid to St. Katherine's in Gascony; soon after which he proceeded into Flanders, and thence returned to England. In the ensuing year, 27 Edw. I. he was summoned by writ, tested 17 Sept. 27 Edw. I. 1299, to be at York with horse and arms on the morrow of the feast of St. Martin, to serve against the Scots,[c] and in the next

---

c Appendix to the First Peerage Report, p. 112.

year he is stated to have been sent to the Pope, with Sir Hugh Spencer, to com-
plain of injuries received from the Scots; and about the same time he was appointed Lieutenant of Gascony.   In the 29th Edw. I. he was made governor of
Corfe Castle, from which year, until the 31st of Edw. I. when he was joined in
commission with the Bishop of Winchester to treat of peace between England
and France, Dugdale gives no account of him.

It was, however, on the 24th June, in the 29th Edw. I. anno 1300, when the
Earl must have been above fifty years of age, that he commanded the first
division of the army which besieged Carlaverock Castle.   The only characteristic trait recorded of him by the Poet, is that of valour, which we are told
was the principal feeling that animated his heart, and in so rude an age this
attribute was perhaps the highest and most gratifying praise that could be
imagined.   His name does not afterwards occur in that production, from which
we may conclude that his services at the siege and assault were not very conspicuous.   In 1305 the Earl was again employed on a mission to the Pope, being
deputed with the Bishops of Lichfield and Worcester to attend the inauguration
of the Pontiff at Lyons, and to present him, in the name of the King, with several vessels of pure gold.   After having executed this command, it appears that
he was once more in the wars in Gascony, and in the ensuing year was similarly
employed in Scotland.   Upon the death of the King, at Burgh in Cumberland,
the Earl was one of the peers who attended him in his last moments, and received
his solemn request to be faithful to his son, and not to allow Piers de Gaveston
to return into England.   Immediately after Edward's demise, he joined some
Earls and Barons in a solemn engagement to defend the young King, his honour
and authority; and at his coronation he is recorded to have carried one of the
swords borne at that ceremony;[d] shortly after which he was appointed governor
of Skipton Castle.   His conduct seems to have secured the confidence of the
new monarch, for upon his expedition towards Scotland in the 3rd and 4th years
of his reign, the Earl of Lincoln was constituted Governor of the realm during
his absence.

The preceding account of this personage has been almost entirely taken from
Sir William Dugdale's Baronage.   The only facts which have been ascertained
relating to him, not stated in that work, are, that he was one of the Main-

---

d Fœdera, N. E. vol. II. part 1, p. 36.

pernors for the Earl of Gloucester in 1292; that he was a Receiver and Trier of Petitions in 1304; that he was present in the parliament held at Carlisle in February, 35 Edw. I. 1307; and that he was one of the Peers appointed to regulate the King's household in May, 3 Edw. II. 1309.[e]

His works of piety were proportionate to his extensive possessions, and, adopting this criterion of his religious sentiments, we may conclude that he was not behind his contemporaries in superstition or devotion. Amongst his more substantial gifts to the church was his large contribution to the "new work" at St. Paul's cathedral in London;[f] and three gilt crosses and a carbuncle, and a cup of silver gilt which was said to have belonged to St. Edmund, to the shrine of St. Edmund in the abbey of Salley.

The Earl of Lincoln closed a long and active career, in 1312, at Lincoln's Inn,[g] in the suburbs of London, being then about sixty-three or sixty-four years of age, and he is reported to have called his son-in-law, the Earl of Lancaster, to him upon his death-bed, and after representing how highly "it had pleased God to honor and enrich him above others," he told him that "he was obliged to love and honor God above all things;" and then added, "Seest thou the Church of England, heretofore honorable and free, enslaved by Romish oppressions, and the King's wicked exactions? Seest thou the common people, impoverished by tributes and taxes, and from the condition of freemen reduced to servitude? Seest thou the nobility, formerly venerable throughout Christendom, vilified by aliens in their own native country? I therefore charge thee by the name of Christ to stand up like a man for the honor of God and his church, and the redemption of thy country, associating thyself to that valiant, noble, and prudent person, Guy Earl of Warwick, when it shall be most proper to discourse of the public affairs of the kingdom, who is so judicious in counsel and mature in judgment. Fear not thy opposers who shall contest against thee in the truth, and if thou pursuest

---

[e] Rot. Parl. vol. I. pp. 75, 76, 159, 188, 443.　　　[f] Dugd. St. Paul's, ed. 1818, p. 11.

[g] This celebrated Inn of Court is recorded to have been the town residence of the Bishops of Chichester, from the reign of Henry the Third to that of Henry the Eighth. It seems, however, to have been for a short time possessed by the subject of this memoir, who, although the only Earl of Lincoln who resided there, left it the name which it has permanently retained during the five subsequent centuries. The arms of Lacy on the gate-house in Chancery-lane were erected by Sir Thomas Lovel, together with his own, in the year 1518.

this my advice, thou shalt gain eternal honor!"   This patriotic speech, which is attributed to him by Walsingham, who wrote in the fifteenth century, is worthy of attention as conveying the view taken of the affairs of the period by a monk about one hundred years afterwards; for it would require extraordinary credulity to consider that it was really uttered by the dying Earl, whose whole life does not appear to present a single action indicative of the sentiments there attributed to him.   His body was buried in the eastern part of St. Paul's cathedral in London, between the chapel of our Lady and that of St. Dunstan.

The Earl of Lincoln was twice married, first to Margaret de Longespee before mentioned, by whom he had a son, Edmond de Lacy, who was drowned in a well in a high tower, called the Red Tower, in Denbigh Castle, in his father's life-time; and a daughter, Alice, the wife of Thomas Earl of Lancaster, who was his sole heiress, and at the Earl's death was twenty-eight years of age.   His second wife was Joan, sister and heiress of William Baron Martin, who survived him, and was re-married to Nicholas Baron Audley.

Alice, Countess of Lancaster, whose romantic life has been made the subject of a popular novel, styled herself, as sole inheritrix of the extensive possessions of her father and mother, Countess of Lincoln and Salisbury.   She was thrice married; first, to the Earl of Lancaster; secondly, to Eubolo le Strange; and, thirdly, to Hugh le Frenes; but died without issue on the Thursday next after the feast of St. Michael, 22 Edw. III. i. e. 2nd October, 1348, when the representation of the powerful house of Lacy became vested in the descendants of Maud, the sister of Henry Earl of Lincoln, who married Richard de Clare Earl of Gloucester.

The arms of the Earl, on the authority of this Poem, and of a contemporary MS. in the British Museum, Cotton MSS. Caligula, A, xvij. as well as upon that of several of his seals, were, Or, a lion rampant Purpure.

ROBERT FITZ WALTER.

[PAGE 5.]

There is not one name in English history with which our political liberties are so intimately associated as with that of FITZ WALTER, from its having been borne by the illustrious individual to whom we are chiefly indebted for Magna Charta. Robert Fitz Walter, " Marshal of the army of God and the Holy Church," the inflexible leader of those Barons who extorted that palladium of the constitution of this country from King John, was the grandfather of the subject of this memoir; and although his deeds bear no comparison to those of his renowned ancestor, they were neither few nor unimportant.

Robert Fitz Walter was born in 1248, and succeeded his father Walter Fitz Walter in the Barony in 1258, being then ten years of age; and in 1274 he received the honour of knighthood. As Constable of Baynard's Castle, or, as it was then called, the Castle of London, to which office he succeeded by inheritance, he was banner-bearer of the city, and in time of war was to serve it by riding upon a light horse, with twenty men at arms, having their horses covered with cloth, into the great door of St. Paul's church, with the banner of his arms carried before him; and having arrived there, he was to be met by the Mayor, together with the Sheriffs and Aldermen of London, when several ceremonies were to be performed, which are minutely detailed by the historians of London.

He was present in the parliament which met at Westminster on the feast of St. Michael, 6 Edw. I. 1278, in which Alexander King of Scotland did homage to Edward;[f] and in the 8th Edw. I. he married his second wife, Devorguil, one of the daughters and coheirs of John de Burgh, son of Hubert Earl of Kent, from which time until the 21st Edw. I. when he was appointed Governor of the castle of de la Bere in the county of Merioneth, nothing is recorded of him excepting

---

[f] Rot. Parl. vol. I. p. 224 a.

what relates to his lands.   In 1292 he was a Mainpernor for the Earl of Gloucester,[g] and in the 22nd and 23rd Edw. I. served in the retinue of the Earl of
Lancaster in Gascony, and also in Scotland in the 25th of that monarch.   He
received a summons, tested at Berwick, 29th Dec. 28th Edw. I. 1299, to be at
Carlisle with horse and arms on the feast of the nativity of St. John next ensuing,
to serve against the Scots, in obedience to which writ he joined the King, and was
present with the forces sent to besiege Carlaverock; at which time he must have
been fifty-two years old.   Dugdale states that in the 28th Edw. I. he served in
Scotland in the retinue of the Earl of Lancaster, and in the next year in that of the
Prince of Wales, but the Poet asserts that he was in the squadron led by the Earl
of Lincoln. The merit which he attributes to him is that of expertness in the use
of arms, an expression which we may consider as synonymous with the character
of a good soldier in the most extensive meaning of the term.

In February in the following year he became a party to the letter written at
Lincoln by the Barons of England to the Pope, relative to his Holiness's claim to
the sovereignty of Scotland, to which important document his seal is still attached. He was summoned to parliament from the 23rd June, 23rd Edw. I. 1295,
to the 10th of October, 19th Edw. II. 1325, and was also summoned to serve
against the Scots in the 34th and 35th Edw. I. and in the 4th, 6th, and 8th Edw.
II. In 1304 he petitioned the King that a certain chapel, called a Jew's synagogue,
might be granted to him;[h] and in the same year he also prayed his Majesty to
institute an inquiry relative to his debt to the Crown, and that, after an allowance
was made for it out of the sum which was then due to him for his services in Gascony, the difference might be determined:[i] and a parliament having been ordered
to meet at Carlisle in the octaves of St. Hilary, 35th Edw. I. 1306, it is recorded
that " he would come with the Cardinal."[k]

This Baron was twice married, first to Eleanor, daughter of Earl Ferrers, and
secondly to Devorguil de Burgh; and died about the 19th Edw. II. 1325, leaving,
by his first wife, Robert, his son and heir; and, by his second, a daughter,
Christiana, who became heiress to her mother, and married John Baron le
Marshall. The barony of Fitz Walter continued vested in the male heirs of the
said Robert until the reign of Henry VI. when it passed to the family of Ratcliffe,
by marriage with the daughter and heiress of Walter Lord Fitz Walter, who

---

g Rot. Parl. vol. I. p. 76.   h Ibid. p. 162.   i Ibid. p. 169 a.   k Ibid. p. 288.

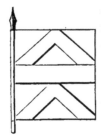

died in 1432, and from them to that of Mildmay in 1669, but fell into abeyance between the coheirs of Mary, the aunt of Benjamin Mildmay, Baron and Earl Fitz Walter, who died in 1756, s. p.

The arms of Fitz Walter were, Or, a fess between two chevronels Gules.[m]

WILLIAM LE MARSHALL.

[PAGE 6.]

William le Marshall was the son and heir of John le Marshall, a Baron in the reigns of Henry the Third and Edward the First, and was born in 1280, being three years old when he succeeded his father in the 12th Edw. I. 1283; about which time his wardship was granted to John de Bohun.[n]

Dugdale's account of this Baron, who was lineally descended from the ancestor of the Earls of Pembroke, though the latter assumed different arms, is exceedingly imperfect; as he merely states that he was in the wars of Scotland in the 34th Edw. I., that he was summoned to parliament from the 2nd to the 7th Edw. II., and that he departed this life about that time; and unfortunately there are but few materials for giving a more enlarged memoir.

The Poem informs us that he was present at the siege of Carlaverock, when he could not have been much above twenty years of age, and that he held some office of considerable importance in Ireland, though of what nature does not appear; but there is little doubt that it referred to his situation of Hereditary Marshal of Ireland, which had been granted in fee, in 1207, to his great-great-grandfather by King John; for upon his seal attached to the Barons' Letter to the Pope in 1301, are two batons, one on each side of his shield, a distinction which still belongs to the office of Marshal, but of the use of which this seal presents the earliest example.

---

m P. 5. Cotton MSS. Caligula, A. xvii. and the seal attached to the Barons' Letter, ao 1301.

n Blomefield's Norfolk, ed. 1805, vol. I. p. 434.

2 D

In February, in the 29th Edw. I. 1301, the Baron was a party to the Letter to
the Pontiff, and though that circumstance is sufficient evidence of the consideration
in which he was held, it is singular that he was never summoned to parliament
until the accession of Edward the Second, the earliest writ addressed to him being
tested on the 9th Jan. 2 Edw. II. 1309, and the last on the 26th Nov. 7 Edw. II.
1313.   No other fact connected with him appears to be recorded, excepting that
he bore two gold spurs at the coronation of Edward the Second;[n] that in the 5th
year of that monarch's reign he was involved in a personal quarrel with Nicholas
de Segrave, which will be more particularly alluded to when speaking of that
Baron;[o] that he was one of the Lords appointed in May, 1309, to regulate the
King's household;[p] and that he died in the year 1314, leaving John le Marshall his son and heir, who was never summoned to parliament, and died in
1316 without issue, when Hawyse his sister was found to be his heir, at that
time wife of Robert Baron Morley, and fifteen years of age, whose descendants
are consequently the representatives of this family.

In the Letter to the Pope, William le Marshall is described as " Lord of
Hengham," a manor in Norfolk, which, with other lands in that county, he inherited from his father.

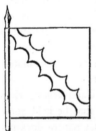
The arms of Marshall have been uniformly painted, Gules,
a bend lozengy Or, which agrees with the appearance of them
upon his seal attached to the Barons' Letter; but they are
described in the Poem, as well as in the contemporary MS.
so frequently cited, as Gules, a bend *engrailed* Or.   It has
been suggested that this discrepancy may be explained by
the resemblance which a bend lozengy would present on a
banner to a bend engrailed, that what is always considered
a bend lozengy might in fact have been a bend engrailed, and, therefore, that
the mistake has arisen from the imperfect manner in which the lines have been
marked.[q]

---

n Fœdera, N. E. vol. II part I. p. 36.   o Ibid. p. 140.   p Rot. Parl. vol. I. p. 443.
q Archæologia, vol. xxi. p. 214.

HUGH BARDOLF.

[PAGE 6.]

The particulars which have been preserved of this individual are exceedingly few and unsatisfactory. His ancestors had been possessed of baronial rank by tenure of the lordship of Bradwell in Suffolk from the reign of Henry the Second and that of Wermegay in Norfolk was acquired by the marriage of his great grandfather, Doun Bardolf, with Beatrix, the daughter and heiress of William de Warren. Upon the death of his father, William de Bardolf, in 1290,[r] those lands devolved upon him, and from his being stated to have been forty years of age at the decease of his mother Julian, daughter and heiress of Hugh de Gourney, in the 23rd Edw. I. he was probably born about the year 1255.

In June, 1294, Hugh de Bardolf was summoned to attend a great council on the affairs of the realm, and afterwards accompanied the King into Gascony. He was taken prisoner by the French at the siege of Risunce, but his captivity appears to have been of short duration, for in the 25th Edw. I. he was again in the King's service in Gascony, and in the 28th and 29th Edw. I. attended him in his expedition to Scotland, having been summoned to be present at Carlisle with horse and arms for that purpose on the feast of the nativity of St. John, in 1300. The first attempt against the Scots was the siege of Carlaverock Castle, when Bardolf was present in the division led by the Earl of Lincoln, at which time he must have been nearly forty-five years of age. The Poem states that he made a handsome appearance, and describes him to have possessed some estimable qualities.

He was summoned to parliament from the 6th February, 27th Edw. I. 1299, to the 2nd June, 35 Edw. I. 1302, and was a party to the Letter from the Barons of this country to the Pope in 1301, in which he is styled " Lord of Wirmegeye." He was again in the wars of Scotland in the 32d Edw. I. and in the same year he died. His wife was Isabel, daughter and heiress of Robert de Aquilon, who survived him, and, in 1321, petitioned the King and his council relative to a law-

---

r Esch. eod. ann.

suit respecting some tenements in Emmesworth and Warbledon, of which she, her father, and grandfather, had been peaceably seized, under the charters of Henry III. and Edward I.[s] By her Lord Bardolf left issue Thomas, his son and heir, then twenty-two years of age, and William, a younger son.

The Barony of Bardolf continued in the said Thomas and his male descccendants, until the reign of Henry IV. when it became forfeited by the attainder of Thomas, the last Baron, who left two daughters his coheirs; Anne, who married first, Sir William Clifford, and secondly Sir Reginald Cobham; and Joan, who became the wife of Sir William Philip, K. G. sometimes called Lord Bardolf.

The arms of Bardolf, according to the Poem and the seal of this Baron, as well as the contemporary MS. Caligula, A. xvii. were Azure, three cinquefoils Or.

PHILIP DE KYME.

[PAGE 6.]

Although the name of this Baron does not often appear in the records of public transactions of his time until about the 22nd Edw. I. his services subsequent to that period were frequent and laborious, and the Fœdera bears ample testimony to his zeal and activity. In that year he was summoned to attend the King at Portsmouth, with horse and arms, to accompany him into France, and from that time until his death there was scarcely an expedition in which he was not a companion, or any event connected with military service in which he was not present. It would therefore be tedious to enumerate the different occasions upon which he attended his sovereign in council or in the field, but it is pleasing to observe that his merits were ultimately appreciated, for Edward the Second, in the 10th year of his reign, in consideration of his great services in the wars in the time of King Edward the First, as well as to himself, granted him an immunity from future attendance; and in the 12th Edw. II. he obtained a discharge for a

---

[s] Rot. Parl. vol. I. p. 388 a.

debt of fifty pounds owing to the King's exchequer by a recognizance, which money had been borrowed in the time of Edward the First as a supply for the charge of his passage into Gascony.

At the siege of Carlaverock he served in the squadron which was commanded by the Earl of Lincoln, and is said to have been highly estimated by his colleagues. He was also a party to the Barons' letter to the Pope in 1301, and is stated to have been specially excused by the King from attending the parliament which met at Carlisle in the octaves of St. Hillary, 35 Edw. I.;[t] but in the parliament held at Westminster in the 9th Edw. II. he was appointed a Trier of Petitions,[u] though he was not summoned thereto.[x] Having been regularly summoned to parliament from the 23rd June, 23rd Edw. I. 1295, to the 26th Nov. 7th Edw. II. 1313, he died in the 16th Edw. II. 1322, leaving by . . . . his wife, daughter of Hugh Bigot, to whom he had been a ward, William, his son and heir, then forty years old.

There are no positive data for calculating the age of this Baron when he was at the siege of Carlaverock, but as he was a minor in 1258, and had a son born in 1282, it would appear that he was very young at the death of his brother, and hence that he was about forty-five at the period in question.

William, the son and heir of Philip de Kyme, was summoned to parliament from the 17th Edw. II. to the 9th Edw. III. and died without issue in 1338. Lucia, his sister and heiress, married Gilbert de Umfreville Earl of Angus.

The arms of Kyme were, Gules, semée of cross crosslets, a chevron Or.[y]

---

[t] Rot. Parl. vol. I. p. 188 a.   [u] Ibid. p. 350 b.   [x] Appendix to the First Peerage Report.
[y] Page 6. Cotton MSS. Caligula, A xvii. and the seal of Philip de Kyme, aº 1301.

HENRY DE GREY.

[PAGE 6.]

This individual was born in the year 1254, and succeeded his father, John de
Grey, in the lordship of Codnor. in 1271, being then seventeen years of age.
His life scarcely presents a single occurrence to distinguish it from that of his
contemporaries of similar rank; and it consequently does not afford any materials
for biography. beyond a few isolated facts, which are too remote, however, in
their occurrence to be enlivened either by personal anecdote, or by historical or
local description.

Henry de Grey was in the royal army in Wales in the 10th of Edw. I. and had
scutage from all his tenants in the counties of Norfolk, Suffolk, Kent, Essex,
Leicester, Nottingham, and Derby, that held of him by military service. In the
22nd Edw. I. he was summoned to a great council to be held on the affairs of
the realm, and likewise in September following to attend the King in his expedition into Gascony, where he served in the 23rd and 25th of Edw. I. In the
29th and 31st Edw. I. he was in the wars of Scotland, and in the retinue of the
Prince of Wales; and also in the 34th Edw. I., but he was then in the retinue
of Aymer de Valence. The "Siege of Carlaverock" states, however, that he
attended his good Lord the Earl of Lincoln on that occasion; when, it may be
added, he was about forty-six years of age.

In 1301 he was a party to the Letter from the Barons to the Pontiff, and in the
1st Edw. II. he joined several Earls and Barons in declaring their resolution to
adhere to the King with their lives and estates in defence of his crown and dignity, and upon the coronation of that monarch and his Queen, this Baron and his
wife were specially summoned to attend the ceremony, by writ tested on the 8th
Feb. 1308.ᶻ He was summoned to parliament on the 6th Feb. and 10th April,
27 Edw. I. 1299, on the 10th March, 1 Edw. II. 1308, and on the 6th Aug.
2 Edw. II. 1308; and died in 1308.

ᶻ Fœdera, N. E. vol. II. part I. p. 131.

The name of his wife has not been ascertained, but he left issue two sons, Richard, the inheritor of the dignity, and Nicholas, to whom he gave the manor of Barton in Ridale in Yorkshire. The Barony of Grey of Codnor continued for six generations in the male descendants of the said Henry de Grey, and fell into abeyance, on the death of Henry Lord Grey in 1496, between the three aunts of that nobleman, or their children.

The arms of Grey of Codnor are, barry of six, Argent and Azure.[a]

ROBERT DE MONTALT.

[PAGE 6.]

Robert de Montalt, or Monhaut, whose name has afforded the writer of the preceding Poem such an admirable opportunity for that love of iteration, or rather of punning, which, in the fourteenth century, seems to have been deemed a peculiar beauty in poetical composition, was born about 1270, and succeeded his brother in his lands in 1297, being then twenty-seven years of age.

Dugdale says that this Robert was in the expedition into Gascony in the same year that he inherited the property of his ancestors, that he was in the wars in the 26th, 29th, and 31st Edw. I. and again in the 1st, 4th, 7th, 8th, and 10th, and in Gascony in the 19th, of Edw. II.

He was present at the siege of Carlaverock in the squadron commanded by the Earl of Lincoln, but the description given of him in the Poem, though it merely implies that he was zealous to distinguish himself, so evidently appears to have been suggested by his name, that perhaps no reliance can be placed upon it as evidence of his personal merits.

---

[a] P. 6. Cotton MSS. Caligula, A xvii. and the seal of Henry de Grey, a⁰ 1301.

Lord Montalt was a party to the letter to Pope Boniface in 1301, in which he is described as Lord of Hawardyn, and on the 22nd January, 1 Edw. II. he was summoned to attend at Dover to receive the King and Queen on their return from France, and to escort them to London.[b] In the 8th Edw. II. 1314, he petitioned the King to be allowed the lands of which his father Robert died seised in Enlowe, and which belonged to the castle of Hawardyn, in the county of Chester, and which, after the death of the said Robert, fell into the King's hands on account of the minority of Roger, his son and heir, the which lands and tenements Joan, the wife of the said Robert, held in dower; that the said Roger had received two parts of the lands in question when he became of age, and likewise the third part on the death of the said Joan; that Sir Reginald de Grey, then Justice of Chester, without award or judgment, had ousted the said Roger, who petitioned the King to be restored to them, but before it could be determined he died, in consequence of which, he, the petitioner, as brother and heir of Roger, had sued for them from time to time, and from parliament to parliament; but that by reason of the war in Scotland, and other affairs in which the King had been engaged, his suit had been delayed and impeded: he therefore prayed the King graciously to consider his right, and that he would remember that he had formerly promised him, when he was with his Majesty in his service in Scotland, that he would restore him his lands.[c] In the same year Robert de Montalt prayed pourparty as one of the heirs of Hugh Daubeney, late Earl of Arundel,[d] to whom he was related in the following manner:

William de Albini, 3rd Earl of Arundel.=Isabel, dau. of William Earl of Warren.

| William de Albini, 4th Earl of Arundel, ob. 1233. s. p. | Hugh de Albini, 5th Earl of Arundel, ob. 1243, s. p. | Cicely, 2d sister and coheir.=Roger de Montalt. |

| John de Montalt, s. and h. ob. s. p. | Robert de Montalt, brother and heir.= |

| Roger de Montalt, s. and h. ob. 1297, s. p. | Robert de Montalt, the claimant as coheir of the Earl of Arundel in 1314. |

and in 1320 he was one of the Mainpernors of Henry le Tyes, Constable of Caris-brook Castle, in a cause with Ralph de Gorges.[e]

Having no issue, in the 1 Edw. III. he settled all his manors and other landed

[b] Fœdera, N. E. vol. II. part I. p. 31.
[c] Rot. Parl. vol. I. p. 294 a.   [d] Ibid. p. 325.   [e] Ibid. p. 385.

possessions, failing issue male by Emma his wife, upon Isabel Queen of England for life, with remainder to John of Eltham, the King's brother, and his heirs for ever. He was summoned to parliament from 6th Feb. 27 Edw. I. 1299, to the 13th June, 13 Edw. III. 1329, and died in 1329 without issue male, when the barony became extinct.

The arms of Montalt were, Azure, a lion rampant Argent.[f]

THOMAS DE MULTON.

[PAGE 8.]

Thomas de Multon succeeeded his father Thomas in the lordship of Egremont in Cumberland in 1294, and on the 26th January, 25 Edw. I. 1297, he was summoned among other Barons of the realm to attend a parliament, or rather perhaps a great council, at Salisbury, on Monday the feast of St. Matthew next following. In the same year, and in the 26th, 28th, and 29th Edw. I. he was commanded to attend the King with horse and arms in his wars in Scotland, and it appears was at the siege of Carlaverock, at which time he must have been about thirty-seven years of age, as he was above thirty in the 21st Edw. I. ;[g] but the Poet takes no other notice of him than to describe his banner. In 1301 he was a party to the Barons' Letter to the Pope, in which he is described as " Lord of Egremond," and in the 1st Edw. II. he was ordered to equip himself to assist John Baron of Wygeton and Richard le Brun in defence of the counties of Lancaster, Cumberland, and Westmoreland, against Robert le Brus, and in the 4th and 8th years of that monarch he was again engaged in the Scottish wars.

This Baron, jointly with Thomas de Lucy, petitioned the King in the 9th year of his reign to be allowed certain manors which had been held by Aveline

---

f P. 8. Cotton MSS. Caligula, A. xvii. and the seal of the Baron, aº 1301.   g Esch. eod. ann.

Countess of Albemarle, they being the coheirs of that personage, as is shewn by the following pedigree, which occurs on the rolls of parliament,[h] where the proceedings on the question are recorded.

William Fitz Duncan.══Alicia, his wife.

William, s. p.	Alicia, s. p.	Amabilla. ══	Cecilia. ══
Richard. ══	Reginald, s. p.	William, s. p.	Hawyse. ══
Alicia. ══	Amabilla. ══	Alicia, s. p.	William. ══
Thomas. ══	Thomas. ══		William. ══

| Thomas, s. p. | ANTHONY DE LUCY, the Claimant. | Thomas ══ THOMAS DE MULTON, the Claimant. | 1. John, s. p. 2. Thomas, s. p. 3. William, s. p. 4. Avicia, s. p. | 5. AVELINA, who died seised in the reign of Edward the First. |

On the 25th May, 10th Edw. II. 1317, he entered into covenants with the King, that John de Multon, his son and heir, should marry Joan, daughter of Piers de Gaveston, late Earl of Cornwall, provided the children on attaining a proper age should consent. The King gave £1000 for her portion, to be paid to Thomas de Multon in the following manner; 500 marks in hand, 500 at the feast of the Nativity of St. John the Baptist next following, and 500 at the ensuing feast of St. Michael; and it was agreed that the said Joan should receive 400 marks per annum for her jointure.[i]

This transaction is deserving of more attention than at a first view it would appear to merit; for, whilst it affords evidence that Edward's regard for his favourite did not die with him, it exhibits the virtues of that young monarch's heart in a striking manner, by providing for the orphan child of the unfortunate object of his attachment. The marriage did not however, Dugdale informs us, take effect, though he does not state from what cause; but as nothing more seems to be known of this lady, she probably died in her childhood.

In the 14th Edw. II. Thomas de Multon was one of the Mainpernors of Henry le Tyes in his dispute with Ralph de Gorges;[j] and having been summoned to parliament from the 6th February, 27 Edw. I. 1299, to the 15th May, 14 Edw. II.

---

h Vol. I. p. 348-9. John de Multon, the son of this Baron, and Ade Lucy, also petitioned on the same subject in the 1st Edw. III. Ibid. vol. II. p. 434.

i Fœdera, N. E. vol. II. p. 331.   j Rot. Parl. vol. I. p. 385.

1320, died in 1322, leaving Eleanor his wife surviving, and John, his son and heir, then a minor; and three daughters, namely, Joan, who married Robert Fitz Walter; Elizabeth, who was first the wife of Walter de Bermicham, and secondly of Robert de Harrington; and Margaret, who married Thomas de Lucy, of Cockermouth.

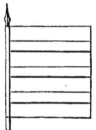

John de Multon, the second Baron, on becoming of age, was summoned to parliament, and continued to receive similar writs until his death, in 1334, without issue, when his sisters became his heirs.

The arms of Multon of Egremond were, Argent, three bars Gules.[k]

JOHN DE LANCASTER.

[PAGE 8.]

The surname of this individual is conjectured to have been derived from his ancestor having been governor of Lancaster castle in the reign of Henry the Second. Roger de Lancaster, his father, died in the 19th Edw. I. leaving him of full age; and in the 22nd of Edw. I. he was summoned to attend the King with horse and arms into France. Dugdale's account of this Baron is so very short that it is here given verbatim:

" In the 25th Edw. I. he was in that expedition then made into Scotland, being of the retinue of Brian Fitz Alan of Bedale in Yorkshire. In 34 Edw. I. he was again in the wars of Scotland. So likewise in 3, 4, and 8 Edw. II. Moreover in 11 Edw. II. he was employed in guarding the marches of Scotland; and having been summoned to parliament from [26 January] 25 Edw. I. [1296]

k Page 8. Cotton MSS. Caligula, A. xvii. and the seal of Thomas de Multon in 1301.

until [22 Dec.] 3 Edw. II. [1309] inclusive, departed this life in 8 Edw. III.
then seised (inter alia) of the manor of Rydale in Westmoreland, and of divers
other lordships in that county, as also in the counties of Northumberland and
Essex; leaving Richard, the son of Richard de Plaitz, his next heir, then twelve
years of age."

To this very little can be added.   He was present at Carlaverock in 1300, and
was a party to the Letter to the Pontiff in the following year,[l] in which he is
styled "Lord of Grisdale;" and in the 8th Edw. II. he was involved in a suit
with John de Yeland.[m]   It appears also that in the 18th Edw. II. he was warden
of certain forfeited lands in Lancashire; that he had been forcibly disseised of
some manors in that county in the early part of the reign of Edw. III.;[n] that about
the same time he petitioned the King and his council, representing that he was
one of his "serjeants" in the counties of Chester and Flint for Mons[r]. Richard
Damory, late Justice of Chester, and had taken as his wages two robes and xl*s.*
for one year, but that three years wages, namely six robes and £vi., were then
due to him, of which he prayed payment.[o]

Upon his death without issue, in 1334, his barony became extinct, and though Dugdale states that Richard de
Plaitz was his heir, other authorities[p] affirm that his nephew,
John de Lancaster, son of his brother William, was his next
heir male.

The arms of Lancaster were, Argent, two bars Gules;
on a quarter of the Second a lion passant guardant Or.[q]

---

[l] Appendix to the First Peerage Report.   [m] Rot. Parl. vol. I. p. 344.   Ibid. p. 424.
[n] Ibid. vol. II. p 380.   [o] Ibid p. 392.
[p] Burn and Nicolson's History of Cumberland and Westmoreland, vol. I. p. 64.
[q] P. 8.   Cotton MSS. Caligula, A. xvii. and the seal of the Baron a[o] 1301.

WILLIAM LE VAVASOUR.

[PAGE 8.]

William le Vavasour, though the first individual of his name who obtained
baronial honors, was descended from a family of scarcely inferior rank in
Yorkshire.

Like many of his colleagues in arms, his deeds are rather to be inferred from
the frequency with which he was summoned to the field than from any express
memorial of them; and notwithstanding that the praise bestowed upon him by
the poetical historian of the Siege of Carlaverock is of a negative description, it
was doubtlessly intended to convey the highest eulogium upon his prowess.

It is said that he succeeded his father John[r] le Vavasour, but in what year does
not appear; hence there is no positive information as to the time of his birth.
In the 18th Edw. I. he obtained a license from the King to make a castle of his
manor house of Heselwode in Yorkshire, and in the 22nd Edw. I. accompanied
the expedition into Gascony. In the 27th, 29th, and 32nd Edw. I. and 4th
Edw. II. he was in the wars in Scotland, and at the siege of Carlaverock he
served in the squadron commanded by the Earl of Lincoln, when we are assured
that in arms he was neither " deaf nor dumb." On the 6th April, 33 Edw. I.
he was appointed one of the Judges of Trailbaston,[s] and is so described in the
list of Peers who were summoned to attend a parliament at Lincoln in the octaves
of St. Hillary, 33 Edw. I.[t] From the 6th Feb. 27 Edw. I. 1299, to the 7th Jan.
6 Edw. II. 1313, he was regularly summoned to parliament, after which time
nothing is known of him.

He married Nichola, daughter of Sir Stephen le Walais, and by her had issue
three sons, 1st, Sir Robert,[u] who Kimber says was summoned to parliament in the
7th Edw. II., though the writ, tested on the 26th July in that year, was ad-

[r] Harl. MSS. 245. f. 132. containing Glover's Collections, but *William* in Kimber's Baronetage.
[s] Fœdera, N. E. vol. I. p. 970.   [t] Rot. Parl. vol. I. p. 188 b.   [u] Harl. MSS. 245.

2 G

dressed to Walter le Vavasour,[x] and died s. p. m. leaving
two daughters and coheirs, Elizabeth, wife to Sir Robert
Strelley, and Anne;[y] 2nd, Sir Henry, ancestor of the late
Baronet of Haselwood; and 3rd, William, from whom the
Vavasours of Deneby in Yorkshire are descended.[z]

The arms of Vavasour are, Or, a fesse dauncette
Sable.[a]

JOHN DE HODELSTON.

[PAGE 10.]

For the little information which we possess relative to this individual, we are
indebted to a recent work,[b] professedly treating of persons who in almost every
other respect appear to have enjoyed the rank of a Baron of the realm in the
reign of Edward the First, excepting that they are not recorded to have been
summoned to parliament.

John de Hodelston was the son and heir of the John de Hodelston, who, in
the 35th Hen. III., obtained a charter for a market and fair at his lordship of
Milburn in the county of Cumberland. In the 24th Edw. I. he was summoned to
attend a great council at Newcastle upon Tyne, and on the 26th of September,
26 Edw. I. was ordered to attend the King at Carlisle with horse and arms, in
the record of which he is called a Baron.[x] From the preceding Poem it is
manifest that he attended the Earl of Lincoln at the siege of Carlaverock, but
no particular description is there given of his person or merits. He was a party

---

x Appendix to the First Peerage Report.   y Harl. MSS. 245.

z Kimber's Baronetage, vol. I. p. 335.

a P.'8; Cotton MSS. Caligula, A. xvii.; and several drawings of seals in Harl. MSS. 245, passim.

b Banks' Stemmata Anglicana, under the division of " Barones Rejecti."

to the Letter from the Barons to Pope Boniface in 1301, in which he is styled " Lord of Aneys," which was in the lordship of Milburn before mentioned. In the 30th Edw. I. he obtained a license for a free warren in his demesnes at Milburn, and at Whittington and Holme in Lancashire, about which time he probably died, without issue.

The arms of Hodelston were, Gules, fretty Argent.d

ROBERT FITZ ROGER.

[PAGE 10.]

This Baron succeeded his father, Roger Fitz John, in his barony about Whitsuntide in 1249, at which time he was very young. He was committed to the wardship of William de Valence, the King's uterine brother, notwithstanding that Ada de Baillol, his mother, offered one thousand two hundred marks to be allowed the custody of him, a circumstance which affords ample proof of the great extent of his possessions.

Nothing further appears to be known of him until the 6th Edw. I. 1277, when he entered into covenants with Robert de Tibetot, that John, his son and heir, should marry Hawise, the daughter of the said Robert, before the quindesme of St. Martin in the same year; and that he would endow her upon her wedding day at the church door with lands to the value of £100 per annum, her portion being 600 marks. In the 19th Edw. I. he obtained a grant of several markets and fairs in his different manors. In the 22nd Edw. I. he was summoned to attend the King into Gascony, and in the 24th, 25th, and 26th Edw. I. was ordered to serve in the wars of Scotland. In the year last mentioned, he was present at the battle of Falkirk, being then in the retinue of Roger Bigot, Earl of Norfolk.

---

d P. 8; Cotton MSS. Caligula, A. xvii.; and the seal of the Baron in 1301.

By writ tested on the 30th Dec. 25 Edw. I. this Baron was commanded to
attend the marriage of the Count of Holland with Elizabeth, the King's daughter,
at Ipswich on Monday in the morrow of the Epiphany next following,[f] and
in the 27th Edw. I. he was joined in a commission with other northern
Barons to fortify the King's castles in Scotland, and also for the defence
of the Marches, in consequence of which services he had respite for the
payment of such debts as he owed to the King.   In the 28th, 29th, and 34th
Edw. I. he was also engaged in the Scottish war, and, to use Dugdale's own
words, " This Robert likewise, and John his son (called John de Clavering by
the appointment of King Edward the First), were at that notable siege of Kaer-
laverock in Scotland;" but though his name and arms are noticed by the Poet,
no particular circumstance relating to him is stated.   He was at that time about
fifty years of age, and in the following year was a party to the Letter from the
Barons to the Pope, in which he is styled " Lord of Clavering," but he does
not appear to have affixed his seal to that important document.[g]

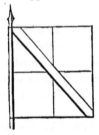

Robert Fitz Roger was summoned to parliament from the
2nd Nov. 23 Edw. I. 1295, to the 16th June, 4 Edw. II. 1311,
about which year he died; leaving, by his wife, Margery le
Zouche, John his son and heir, then aged forty-four years,
who will form the subject of the next article.

The arms of Fitz Roger were, quarterly, Or and Gules, a
bend Sable.[h]

---

f Fœdera, N. E. vol. I. part ii. p. 850.   g Appendix to the First Peerage Report.
h P. 8; and Caligula, A. xvii.

JOHN DE CLAVERING.

[PAGE 10.]

The most remarkable circumstance connected with this individual was, that he and his brothers abandoned the mode by which their ancestors distinguished themselves, according to which they would have been called " Fitz Roger," and adopted the distinct surname of " Clavering," which was evidently derived from their father's principal lordship in Essex. This assumption Dugdale, upon the authority of some ancient rolls which belonged to Sir William le Neve, asserts was made by the appointment of the King.

At the time of his father's death he was, as has just been stated, forty-four years of age, and had been summoned to parliament from the year 1299. In consideration of the services which he had rendered the King, he obtained a pardon in the 25th Edw. I. " for all his debts due unto the Exchequer, as also for the scutage then due from himself." He was in Gascony in the 22nd, and in the wars of Scotland in the 26th, 28th, 31st, and 34th Edw. I. and in the 4th and 6th Edw. II., and, as the Poet informs us, was present at the siege of Carlaverock, in the first squadron commanded by the Earl of Lincoln, being then about thirty-three years old. In the 6th Edw. II. he was taken prisoner at the battle of Strivelyn, or Stirling, but he was released very soon afterwards, for in the 8th Edw. II. he was excused from attending parliament, being ordered to serve with horse and arms against the Scots,[i] and in the 9th and 12th of Edw. II. he was again engaged in the wars of Scotland. He is recorded in the 8th Edw. II. to have held view of frank pledge in the manors of Thurgerton and Warton,[k] and to have been appointed, on the 19th January, 14 Edw. II. with several other peers, to treat for peace with Robert de Brus.[l] By writ tested on the 30th April in the same year, he was commanded to furnish his castle of Werk with men at arms, victuals, and all other necessaries for its defence against the Scots,[m]

---

i Fœdera, N. E. vol. II. p. 260.
l Fœdera, N. E. vol. II. p. 441.

k Rot. Parl. vol. I. p. 299.
m Ibid. p. 627.

2 H

which castle, it appears from a petition of Henry Percy in 1331, he held for his life.[n]   In the 4th Edw. III. 1330, he exhibited a petition, complaining that John Payne of Dunwich, and others of that place, had carried away five ships, a boat, and goods and chattels belonging to him at Walderswyke to the value of £300, and that they had assaulted his men and servants, and beaten, wounded, and imprisoned them, through which he had been deprived of their services for a long time, at a loss to him of £1000, which "horrible trespass" he prayed that certain justices might be appointed to hear and determine.[o]   It seems that John de Clavering was frequently involved in some dispute with the inhabitants of Dunwich, for in that year they petitioned parliament against his bill to establish a market at Blisburgh, which was not above two leagues from Dunwich, in prejudice of their franchise, and to the impoverishment of the said town.[p]   He also petitioned the same parliament to be restored to the possession of certain manors, which were held of him by Robert Thorp, by knight's service.[q]

The active and useful life of this Baron then drew near its close. Towards the latter part of the reign of Edward the First, being without male issue, he conveyed the greater part of his lands to Stephen de Trafford, with the intention that he should reconvey some part of them to him for life, with remainder to that monarch and his heirs, and the other part to him and his wife Hawyse during their respective lives, in consideration of which grant the King settled several manors upon him for his life.

He was summoned to parliament from the 10th April, 28 Edw. I. 1299, to the 20th November, 5 Edw. III. 1331; and died in the following year, aged about sixty-four, and was buried in the quire of the conventual church of Langley.   By his wife Hawyse, daughter of Robert de Tibetot, to whom, as is stated in the account of his father, he was married in 1278, he left issue Eve, his daughter and heiress, who was born about the year 1305, and married, first, Thomas de Audley, who died s. P. 1 Edw. II. 1307; secondly, on the 9th March, 1309, Ralph de Ufford; and, thirdly, Robert Benhale, whose wife she was in 1342.   She died 43 Edw. III. 1369, and from the inquisitiones post mortem held on her decease, it would appear that she had no issue.[r]

---

[n] Rot. Parl. vol. III. p. 63 a.   [o] Ibid. vol. II. p. 33.   [p] Ibid. p. 44.   [q] Ibid. p, 59.
[r] Mr. Townsend's MS. Collections for Dugdale's Baronage.

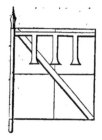

The male line of Clavering still exists in the person of Sir Thomas John Clavering, Bart. who is said to be lineally descended from Sir Alan Clavering, a younger brother of the subject of this notice.

The arms borne by this Baron in his father's life-time were, quarterly, Or and Gules, a bend Sable, with a label Vert;* but after his father's death he probably omitted the label.

HUMPHREY DE BOHUN,

EARL OF HEREFORD AND ESSEX, AND CONSTABLE OF ENGLAND.

[PAGE 10.]

By birth, titles, possessions, and alliance, this nobleman was perhaps the most distinguished of his age; to which advantages he united, at the period when the Poet commemorates him, and which he particularly notices, that of youth, being then not more than twenty-five years of age.

, He succeeded his father Humphrey, Earl of Hereford and Essex, and Constable of England, in his honors in 1298, and being of full age, did homage and obtained livery of his lands. Excepting that he was included in the usual writs to parliament, and to attend the King in his wars, the first circumstance recorded of him, after his accession to his father's earldoms, was his presence at the siege of Carlaverock, on which occasion he executed his hereditary office of Constable, and when he is described as being " young, rich, and elegant." In the following year he was a party to the Letter from the Barons to the Pontiff; and in the 30th Edw. I. it was determined that he should marry Elizabeth Plantagenet, widow of the Count of Holland, and seventh daughter of the King, for on the 4th August, 1302, the Pope granted a dispensation for their union, they being related within

---

* Page 8, and Caligula, A. xvii..

the third and fourth degrees of consanguinity. The grounds for this alliance, as stated in that document, were, that there had been great dissention between the King and the Earl's father, and that by the proposed marriage the peace and tranquillity of the realm would be effected.[t] Soon after that event took place, the Earl surrendered his earldoms, together with his office of Constable of England, and all his lordships, into the King's hands, which were regranted to him and the heirs of his body lawfully begotten; failing which, after the death of himself and his wife, it was covenanted that certain lordships, with the Constableship of England, should remain to the King and his heirs for ever, and that the manors therein mentioned should revert to his right heirs.

In the 33rd Edw. I. the Earl of Hereford was appointed to treat on the affairs of Scotland,[u] and in the ensuing year the King granted to him and his wife Elizabeth, in tail, the whole territory of Annandale in Scotland; but in the 35th Edw. I. he incurred the royal displeasure for having left the Scottish wars without license, and only obtained a pardon by the solicitations of the Queen, his mother-in-law.

Upon the accession of Edward the Second, he joined several Earls and Barons in an agreement, dated at Bologne, 31st January, 1 Edw. II. 1308, to defend the King's person and the rights of his crown; and by writ tested on the 22nd of January in that year, the Countess his consort was commanded to attend at Dover to receive the King and Queen upon their return from France.[x] At the coronation of that monarch the Earl of Hereford carried the sceptre which had a cross on the top;[y] and in the next year he was in the expedition into Scotland, and was one of the peers who conspired with the Earl of Lancaster to destroy Piers de Gaveston. To Dugdale's account of the Earl from this time until the 8th Edw. II. nothing can be added, and that eminent writer's words are therefore given verbatim:

" In 3 Edw. II. he was the principal person sent by the King from York with a sufficient strength for guarding the Marches of Scotland; and in 5 Edw. II. had restitution of the Constableship of England, which the King had for some reasons seized into his own hands. Furthermore in 6 Edw. II. he was the chief person in a commission to continue a treaty begun at Markgate, with Lodovick

t Fœdera, N. E. vol. I. p. 941.   u Rot. Parl. vol. I. p. 267 a.
x Fœdera, N. E. vol. II. p. 31.   y Ibid. p. 36.

Earl of Evreux, the Bishop of Poitou, and others, concerning certain matters of great moment touching the King himself and some of the great noblemen of England, which treaty was to continue at London, but neither the commissioners nor their retinue were to lodge in the city. But after this, in 7 Edw. II., being in that fatal battle of Strivling in Scotland, and the English army routed, he was taken prisoner in the flight near to the castle of Botheville, yet had his liberty soon after by exchange for the wife of Robert de Brus, who had been long captive in England. In 8 Edw. II. he was with the Earl of Lancaster and others of his party at the beheading of Piers Gaveston near Warwick. In 9 Edw. II. he was again in Scotland."

At the parliament which met at Lancaster in the quindecim of St. Hillary, in the 8th Edw. II. 1315, he delivered the King's answer to the petition of the Bishops,[z] and was one of the Peers appointed in that year to regulate the King's household;[a] and in 1322 he was charged by Amice, widow of Sir Richard Fitz Simond, with champarty, in behalf of Simond, the son of Richard, valet to the Earl.[b] The other circumstances recorded of this personage are not of much importance, excepting that he was in the wars of Scotland in the 12th and 13th Edw. II.; that on the 19th Jan. 14 Edw. II. he was joined in a commission with several other peers to negotiate on the subject of a peace with Robert Bruce;[c] and that in the same year the King having been informed that he was levying forces against Hugh le Spencer the younger, sent him a peremptory command to forbear. This he not only disobeyed, but joined the Earl of Lancaster in his rebellion, to whom he most faithfully adhered, and having forced the King to assent to their wishes, Hereford published the edict for the banishment of the Despencers in Westminster Hall.

In the reverse of fortune which soon attended the Earl of Lancaster's party, the Earl of Hereford lost his life. He was slain at the battle of Borough-bridge in Yorkshire on the 16th March, 1322, in the attempt to pass over the bridge, by a soldier who was beneath it running a lance through his body, and thus escaped the disgraceful fate which awaited his treasonable conduct.

This powerful nobleman, who at the time of his death was scarcely above

z Fœdera, N. E. vol. II. p. 350.   a Ibid. p. 443.   b bid. p. 398.
c Fœdera, N. E. vol. II. p. 441.

forty-five years of age, was buried in the Friars Preachers at York. By the Princess Elizabeth, daughter of King Edward the First, he had issue six sons and four daughters; Humphrey, who died young; John, his son and heir, and the inheritor of his dignities; Humphrey, who succeeded his brother in all his honors; Edward, who obtained a grant of several lordships from Edward the Third in 1331; William, afterwards created Earl of Northampton; and Æneas, of whom nothing is known. The daughters were, Margaret, who died young;

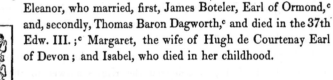

Eleanor, who married, first, James Boteler, Earl of Ormond,[c] and, secondly, Thomas Baron Dagworth,[c] and died in the 37th Edw. III.;[c] Margaret, the wife of Hugh de Courtenay Earl of Devon; and Isabel, who died in her childhood.

The arms of Bohun Earls of Hereford were, Azure, a bend Argent, cotised Or, between six lions rampant of the Second.[d]

NICHOLAS DE SEGRAVE.

[PAGE 12.]

The large space which is appropriated by the Poet to Nicholas de Segrave and his elder brother John, is not more than commensurate with that which they fill in the history of their times, and there are consequently ample materials· for their biography : but a minute account of their actions would be little short of a chronicle of the greater part of the reigns in which they lived, for almost every thing like individual character is lost, and though we may know that they filled certain offices, or were present on particular occasions, none· of those interesting facts are recorded which afford, to personal history its greatest, if not its only, interest.

---

c Esch. 37 Edw. III. No. 24.   d P. 10. Caligula, A. xvii. and the Earl's seal, aͦ 1301.

Nicholas de Segrave, the father of these Barons, died in the 23rd Edw. I., leaving, as the Poem truly states, five sons; John, the eldest, who was then thirty-nine years of age, will be spoken of hereafter; Simon, who for "diverse trespasses and offences" was in prison in the 35th Edw. I.; Nicholas, the subject of this article; Henry, and Geoffrey, both of whom were living and of full age in the 35th Edw. I.[e]

. In the 22nd Edw. I. Nicholas de Segrave was in the King's service in Gascony; and in the 26th and following years he was in the wars of Scotland, and was present at the battle of Falkirk. At the siege of Carlaverock, in June, 1300, he served in the squadron led by the Earl of Lincoln, at which time he must have been above thirty years of age, and when, we are informed, the qualities of his heart were only equalled by the beauty of his person. In the following year, by the description of "Lord of Stowe," he was a party to the Letter to the Pope, though his seal was not attached to that document; and in the 33rd Edw. I. this Baron, whom Matthew of Westminster calls one of the most worthy knights in the realm, being accused by Sir John de Cromwell of treason, he, in accordance with the manners of the age, challenged his defamer to personal combat. This affair occupies several pages of the Rolls of Parliament,[f] but the brief narrative of the contemporary writer just cited, together with a few facts from those records, will afford a sufficient account of the transaction. Not being allowed to fight his accuser in England, Segrave quitted the realm without license to pursue him, and attempted to embark at Dover, but being prevented by Robert de Burghersh, the Constable of that Castle, he proceeded to another sea-port, from which he crossed the sea. His departure gave great offence to the King, and upon his return shortly afterwards, he was arrested at Dover, and brought to trial. He submitted himself to Edward's mercy, and whilst the Judges were deliberating upon his sentence he was committed to the Tower. "After three days consultation," according to the Chronicler, "the Judges declared that he deserved death, and that all his goods should be forfeited, yet that in consideration of his noble descent, and also because he did not go out of England from any offence to the King, but to be revenged on his adversary, they thought that his Majesty would do well to pardon him; to whom the King answered, 'It is in my power to extend mercy as I please. Who hath ever submitted to my

---

[e] Mr. Townsend's MS. Collections for Dugdale.   [f] Vol. I. pp. 172 to 174.

clemency and suffered for it? Let your sentence be recorded in writing and it shall stand for law.' Whereupon he was committed to prison for a terror to other offenders in the like kind, but after a few days, divers of the nobility interceding for him, and thirty of his peers also, girt with swords, offering to be bound body and goods that he should be forthcoming whensoever the King should require, he was set at liberty and restored to his possessions." The account on the Rolls of Parliament differs but slightly in effect from this narrative, for it states that the King, moved by pity, and preferring the life to the death of those who submitted to his mercy, granted him life and limb, and ordered him to find seven good sureties that he would surrender himself to prison at the King's commands, and give up all his goods whenever his Majesty should require them. In the 34th Edw. I: he was again summoned to attend the King, with horse and arms, against Robert Brus; and after the accession of Edward the Second he advanced rapidly in honors, for in the 1st year of that monarch's reign he was appointed governor of the castle of Northampton, and on the 12th of March in the same year was constituted Marshal of England.

That appointment gave offence to William le Marshall, who considered himself possessed of an hereditary claim to the office, and the dispute between Segrave and himself was of so serious a description, and was to have been attended with so much violence, that four years afterwards the King was obliged to issue a precept to Segrave, dated on the 20th of July, 1312, in which, after stating that he had been informed of a quarrel between Marshall and himself, and that he intended to come to the next parliament with armed followers, he commanded him not to attend with weapons or in any other manner than had been usual in the time of King Edward the First.[g]

This Baron was summoned to parliament from the 24th June, 23 Edw. I. 1295, to the 25th May, 14 Edw. II: 1321, and died in 1322, leaving by Alice, daughter of Geoffrey de Armenters, who survived him, and married, secondly, Sir Gerard Lisle,[h] Maud, his daughter and heiress, then the wife of Edmund de Bohun, and thirty years of age.

The arms of Nicholas de Segrave are not described in the Poem in a sufficiently explicit manner, and Glover's construction of that account of them seems slightly erroneous; for, in the Cottonian MS. so frequently cited, they

---

g Fœdera, N. E. vol. II. p. 140.   h Baker's History of Northamptonshire.

are thus blazoned, " De Sable, a un lion rampant de Argent, *corone de Or*, a un label dè Goules." The fact mentioned in the Poem, of his father having relinquished the garbs and adopted the lion, is particularly curious, for it establishes a point which hitherto only rested on conjecture; and still more, because it shows the great accuracy òf the Poet's statements. In some remarks on the seals attached to the Barons' Letter to the Pope, in the Archæologia,[i] the following passage occurs on the seal of John de Segrave, which is introduced here rather than in the account of that Baron, to prevent a recurrence to the subject. " The arms on the seal of John de Segrave, are a lion rampant, crowned; and on each side of the shield is a garb. This circumstance requires attention, because Burton in his History of Leicestershire, in which he has been followed by a late writer,[k] states that the ancient arms of Segrave were, Sable, three garbs Argent, banded Gules; but that they afterwards assumed, Sable, a lion rampant Argent,' crowned Or. It is manifest from the seal of this Baron that Burton's statement was not entirely without foundation, though, unless by the words ' *ancient* arms' he meant anterior to the reign of Edward the First, it is certain that the arms of that family were what they afterwards bore, but that the garb was introduced on their seals, possibly as an ornament or device. From this and similar devices

it is very likely that the subsequent usage of cognizances owed its source." The notice in the Roll of Carlaverock of the garbs and the lion is then alluded to; and it may now be added, that the placing charges on the exterior of the shield on seals approached much nearer to the subsequent system of quartering arms, and seems often to have been adopted from a similar principle, namely, of perpetuating a descent from the family of a maternal ancestor.

---

[i] Vol. XXI. p. 211.   [k] Banks' Dormant and Extinct Peerage.

JOHN DE SEGRAVE.

[Page 13.]

As is stated in the preceding article, this eminent Baron, who for nearly half a · century was constantly in his country's service, and occasionally filled the highest and most important stations, was the eldest son of Nicholas Baron Segrave; and at his father's death in the 23rd Edw. I. was thirty-nine years of age. In the 54th Hen. III. he married Christian, daughter of Hugh de Plessets, Knight, and at the same time his sister Amabil became the wife of his brother-in-law, Sir John de Plessets. Soon after the accession of Edward the First he was engaged in the wars of Scotland, and in the 13th Edw. I. he attended the King in his expedition into Wales. In the 19th Edw. I. he was with his father in the Scottish wars, and in the 24th Edw. I. executed the office of Constable of the English army.

Dugdale asserts that in the 25th Edw. I. John de Segrave was by indenture retained to serve Roger le Bigot, Earl of Norfolk, the Earl Marshal, with six Knights, including himself, as well in peace as war, for the term of his whole life, in England, Wales, and Scotland, with the following retinue: in time of peace with six horses, so long as the Earl should think fit, taking *bouche of court* for himself and six knights; and for his esquires hay and oats, together with livery for six more horses, and wages for six grooms and their horses; he was also to receive two robes for himself, as for a Banneret, yearly, as well in peace as in war, with the same robes for each of his five knights, and two robes annually for his other bachelors: in war he was bound to bring with him his five knights and twenty horses, in consideration of which he was to receive for himself and his company, with all the said horses, xls. per diem; but if he should bring no more than six horses, then xxijs. per diem. It was further agreed that the horses should be valued, in order that proper allowance might be made in case any of them should happen to be lost in the service; and for the performance of this agreement he had a grant from the Earl of the manor of Lodene in Norfolk.

The preceding document has been cited nearly in Dugdale's own words, because at the same time that it affords much information with respect to the retinue by which Segrave was attended to the field, it proves that he was intimately connected with the Earl Marshal, which tends to explain his having in the same year, namely on the 12th August, 25 Edw. I. 1297, been appointed by the Earl to appear in his name before the King, in obedience to a precept directed to him and the Constable, commanding them to attend him on the subject of a body of armed men which had assembled in London. The record states that on the appointed day the Earl of Hereford as Constable, and " Monsr John de Segrave, qui excusa le Comte Mareschal par maladie," came accordingly.[1] In the 25th Edw. I. this Baron was also summoned to accompany the King beyond the sea, and afterwards at Newcastle upon Tyne, with horse and arms; and in the next year was present when the English army gained the victory of Falkirk. In the 28th Edw. I. he was again summoned to serve in the wars of Scotland, in which year, when he must have been about forty-five years old, he was at the siege of Carlaverock. The account given of him by the Poet, that he performed the Earl Marshal's duties upon that occasion, because that nobleman was prevented from attending, is not only strongly corroborated by the preceding statement of his having acted as deputy of the Earl Marshal in the year 1297, but also by the following extract from Peter de Langtoft's Chronicle, when speaking of the expedition into Scotland in 1300 :

> After Midesomer's tide, thorgh comon ordinance,
> No lenger suld thei bide, bot forth and stand to chance,
> Norreis and Surreis, that serbice auht the King,
> With hors and harneis at Carlele mad samnyng ;
> The Erle Marschalle Rogere no hele that tyme mot habe,
> He went with his banere Sir Jon the Segrabe,
> To do alle the serbice that longed the office tille,
> And mayntend alle the prise, ther he sauh lawe and skille.[m]

After Carlaverock Castle surrendered, Segrave's banner, from his having acted as Marshal during the siege, was displayed on its battlements, together with those of the King, of St. Edward, and St. Edmund, of the Earl of Hereford as Constable, and of Robert de Clifford, apparently because he was appointed governor of it, a fact which will be more fully alluded to in the notes; but, excepting an

---

1 Fœdera N. E. vol. I. p. 872.   m P. 309.

occasional notice that "" the Marshal" had performed the usual duties incidental to that office, Segrave is not again spoken of in the Poem. In the 30th of Edw. I. he was a party to the Letter from the Barons to the Pope, in which he is styled "John Lord of Segrave;"[n] and about that time was appointed Governor of Berwick, and Warden of Scotland. In the same year, whilst riding out of Berwick with a small escort, he was surprised by an ambuscade of the Scots, wounded, and taken prisoner; which event is thus noticed by Langtoft:

> Our men in Scotland with sautes sodeynly
>
> The Segrave might not stand, Sir Jon tok the gayn stie;
>
> His sonne and his brother of bedde als thei woke,
>
> And sixteene knyghtes other the Scottes alle them toke.[o]

His captivity was however, it appears, of short duration, for on Edward's return to England, Segrave was left as his Lieutenant of Scotland. At different periods during the reign of ʼEdward ʼthe First he obtained grants of free warren and other privileges in several of his manors, and possessed that elevated place in his sovereign's confidence and esteem which his long and zealous services so justly merited. Nor was he less distinguished by his successor, for soon after the accession of Edward the Second he was constituted Governor of Nottingham Castle, which had belonged to Piers de Gaveston, and was likewise appointed to his situation of Justice of the Forests beyond the Trent, and Keeper of all the rolls thereto belonging;[p] but he resigned these offices in the following year, when they were conferred upon Henry de Percy.[q] In the 2nd Edw. II. he was again appointed Warden of Scotland; in the 6th Edw. II. he was taken prisoner at the battle of Bannockburn, and about twelve months afterwards Thomas de Moram and several other Scots, then prisoners in the Tower of London, were delivered to Stephen de Segrave, son and heir of the Baron, to be exchanged for him. In the 8th Edw. II. commissioners were appointed to hear and determine all disputes relative to the taking up of carriages by him or his agent, in consequence of his offices of Keeper of the Forests beyond the

---

[n] Appendix to the First Peerage Report.   [o] P. 319.

[p] Fœdera, N. E. vol. II. p. 116, 117, aº 4 Edw. II. but Dugdale says he was appointed to these offices as early as the *first* Edw. II.

[q] Ibid. p. 163.

Trent, and of the Castles of Nottingham and Derby.[r] He was summoned upon several occasions to serve in the Scottish wars during the early part of the reign of Edw. II., and to parliament from the 26th Aug. 4 Edw. I. 1296, to the 6th May, 18 Edw. II. 1325. In the 10th Edw. II. in recompense of his great services, and of his imprisonment in Scotland, he received a grant of £1000, but what was then due to the crown for money received by him from the time of his appointment of Warden of the Forests beyond the Trent and Governor of Nottingham Castle, was to be deducted from that sum.[s]

The tide of royal favour at last turned, and he accidentally fell a victim to the displeasure of his sovereign. Having, in 1325, excited Edward's anger by the escape of Roger Lord Mortimer from the Tower, he sent Segrave and the Earl of Kent into Gascony, under the pretence of defending that province, where he was attacked with a disease then prevalent there, of which he shortly afterwards died, aged about seventy years, leaving John de Segrave, his grandson, son of his eldest son Stephen, who died in his life-time, his heir.

The preceding unadorned narrative of John de Segrave's services forms a splendid monument of his fame: for, whilst the impossibility of colouring the biography of his contemporaries with meretricious ornaments of language is strongly felt when their actions are few or obscure, the absence of such assistance tends to the advantage of those who need no other eulogy than the simple record of the occasions upon which they were present in the field, or were selected to execute high and important duties.

John de Segrave, the next Baron, added to the honors of his ancestors in an unprecedented manner, by marrying Margaret, the daughter and heiress of Thomas de Brotherton, Marshal of England, younger son of King Edward the First.

---

[r] Rot. Parl. vol. I. p. 325 a.

[s] Dugdale appears to have fallen into an error with respect to this grant, for he says that the same sum, and with precisely the same object, was given to this Baron both in the 9th Edw. I. and 10th Edw. II. which is not only unlikely, but is rendered still more improbable by his stating, upon the authority of Glover's Collections, that he was also Constable of Nottingham Castle and Warden of the Forests beyond the Trent in the 9th Edw. I. both of which offices, it is certain, were conferred upon Segrave after the disgrace of Piers de Gaveston. The mistake probably arose from the accidental insertion of 9 Edw. I. for 9 Edw. II. and under this impression all which is said by that eminent writer to have taken place on the subject in the former, is asserted in the text to have occurred in the latter, of those years.

Through the marriage of Elizabeth, their daughter and heiress, with John Lord Mowbray, that family attained the Mar-
shalship of England. The present representatives of John
Baron Segrave, the subject of this article, are the Lords
Stourton and Petre, and the Earl of Berkeley.

The arms of John de Segrave were, Sable, a lion rampant
Argent, crowned Or.[t]

JOHN EARL WARREN.

[PAGE 14.]

To do justice to the services of this powerful nobleman and distinguished
soldier, would require a volume instead of the short space which can be allowed
to·each of the individuals mentioned in the Poem; and consequently only the
most important events in his long career can be noticed.[u]

John Earl of Warren and Surrey, was the son of William Earl of Warren and
Surrey, by his second wife, Maud, widow of Hugh Bigot, Earl of Norfolk, and
sister and coheiress of Anselm Marshal, Earl of Pembroke.   In 1240, being then
five years of age,[v] he succeeded his father in his dignities; in 1247 he married
Alice, daughter of Hugh le Brun, Count of March, and uterine sister of King
Henry the Third; and in the following year, though he could not have been
above thirteen years of age, he is said to have attended the parliament which
met at London in the octaves of the Purification.   During the reign of Henry
the Third he is stated to have filled those stations which from his high rank
naturally devolved upon him, and at the battle of Lewes he served in the van of
the royal army with Prince Edward; but, together with the Earl of Pembroke,

---

[t] P. 10; Caligula, A. xvii; and the seal of this Baron, a⁰ 1301.   See the preceding article.
[u] A memoir of greater length will be found in Horsfield's Hist. of Lewes, 4to. 1824, pp. 126-132.
[v] Watson's History of the Earls of Warren and Surrey.

disgracefully deserted him at the commencement of the action, and fled first to Pevensey Castle, and from thence to France. Their flight is thus quaintly alluded to by Peter de Langtoft : [x]

> Ʈħe €rle of Ɯarenne, Ʒ ɯote, ħe ſcapeð ober tħe ſe,
> Anð Ᵹir Ɋugħ Ʒigote alſ ɯitħ tħe €rle fleð ħe.

In May following he returned, and claimed the restitution of his possessions, which, notwithstanding his treachery to the Prince, the rebellious Barons had declared to have been forfeited. The refusal of his demand induced him once more to change sides, and he confederated with the Earl of Gloucester for the restoration of the King's power, and was present with the royal forces at the battle of Evesham. Thus his interest rather than his honor seems to have been his sole rule of action, and unfortunately such conduct was then far too general to entail upon those who adopted it either punishment or reproach. In 1268 he had a dispute with Henry Earl of Lincoln, which has been already noticed in the account of that personage, and about the same time became involved in a serious affray with Alan Lord Zouche relative to some lands. This affair was attended with great violence, for, finding that he must submit to the judgment of a court of law, he abused his adversary and his son in the strongest terms, and then assaulted them in such an outrageous manner in Westminster Hall, that he nearly killed the Baron, and severely wounded his son. Neither his power nor influence could save the Earl from the vengeance of the laws he had so flagrantly violated, and, though he retired to his castle at Ryegate, he was closely pursued by Prince Edward with a strong force, and finding that opposition would be useless, he met the Prince on foot, and implored the royal clemency with great humility. For his offence he was fined ten thousand marks; but this sum was afterwards reduced to eight thousand four hundred, and he was permitted to pay it by annual instalments of two hundred marks each. Of this transaction Robert of Gloucester[y] gives the following curious account, but he erroneously states that it occurred in 1270, and that Lord le Zouche was slain by the Earl:

> Ᵹutħtħe tħer ɯaſ at ℒonðone a lute ðeſtance, icħ ɯene,
> Ʒn ᵹer of Ɓrace tuelf ħunðreð anð ſiᵹti anð tene,

So that the Erl of Wareine slou atte verste touche,
Bivore the Justises atte benche, Sir Alein de la Souche.
The king was ther of anuid vor the grete wou
The Erle hadde so gret help that he of scapede wel inou
Nor the Sonendai after Lamasse bivore the king he com
At Winchestre, as him was iset, to avonge is dom,
Wid him vive and tuenti knightes thun of suore ther
That he ne dude it vor non vuel ne malice bispete er,
He in no despit of the king; and vor this trespas
He pef the king tuelf hundred marc, and ipaised was.

Immediately after the solemnization of the funeral of Henry the Third at Westminster, the Earl of Warren and the Earl of Gloucester proceeded to the high altar, and swore fealty to his son and successor King Edward the First. In the 3rd Edw I. he received that monarch at his castle of Ryegate in so honorable a manner upon his return from Gascony, that Edward was induced to remit him one thousand marks of the sum which he had been fined for the affair with Lord le Zouche.

The next circumstance recorded of the Earl is one in which that proud and sturdy spirit for which he was celebrated, was displayed in a manner so consonant to the feelings of the present day, that this nobleman has always been a favourite character in English biography, and the pencil was on one occasion successfully employed to perpetuate his independent conduct. After the enactment of the statute of *quo warranto,* the Earl of Warren was, under its provisions, questioned by what title he held his lands; to which inquiry, first unsheathing an old sword, he is said to have replied, " Behold, my Lords, here is my warranty; my ancestors coming into this land with William the Bastard did obtain their lands by the sword, and with the sword I am resolved to defend them against whomsoever that shall endeavour to dispossess me. For that King did not himself conquer the land and subdue it, but our progenitors were sharers and assistants therein."

In the 23rd Edw. I. the castle of Bamburgh was entrusted to his custody, and in the 24th Edw. I. he commanded the forces sent to reduce Dunbar Castle, which, after a siege of three days, surrendered to him; and having met the Scotch army which came to its relief, he defeated them on Friday, the 27th

April, and pursued them several miles from the field of battle, when the enemy sustained a loss of above 10,000 men.[z] Soon after this event the Earl was appointed Regent of Scotland, and in the following year was constituted General of all the English forces north of the Trent. But his previous good fortune now deserted him, and his army sustained a signal overthrow at the battle of Stirling, in September, 1297. Of that event one of the Chroniclers before cited gives the following account:

> Whan Sir Jon of Warenne the soth understode,
> That the Waleis gan brenne, an oste he gadred gode,
> And went to Stribelpne agayn Waleis William,
> Bot the Erle with mykelle pyne disconfite away nam.
> And that was his folie, so long in his bed gan ligge,
> Until the Waleis partie had umbilaid the brigge.
> With gavelokes and dartes guilk ore was non sene,
> Myght no man tham departe, ne ride ne go bituene.
> Thore first tham tauht, how thei did fawe kirke.
> Alle gate the brigge he rauht, of nouht our men were irke.
> Whan the Erle herd say, the brigge how William toke,
> He douted to die that day, that bataile he forsoke.
> The Inglis were alle slayn, the Scottis bar them wele,
> The Waleis had the wayn, als maistere of that eschele.
> At that ilk stoure was slayn on our side
> God men of honour that wald to the bataile bide.[a]

His misfortune did not however lessen him in Edward's esteem, for he was immediately afterwards re-appointed to the command of the English forces, and in the 28th Edw. I. was made Governor of Hope Castle in the county of Derby. In that year also he commanded the second squadron at the siege of Carlaverock, at which time he must have been about sixty-five years of age, but the Poet merely says of him that he was well suited to be the leader of honorable men. In the 29th Edw. I. the Earl was appointed, jointly with the Earl of Warwick

---

[z] MS. printed in the Archæologia, vol. XXI. p. 494.

[a] Peter of Langtoft, ed. Hearne, vol. II. p. 297.

and others, to treat with the agents of the King of France relative to a peace between England and Scotland; and in the same year he was a party to the Letter from the Barons to Pope Boniface VIII., in which he is only styled " Comes Warenne," though on his seal he is also properly called Earl of Surrey.[b] On the 5th calends of October, 32 Edw. I. i. e. 27 September, 1304, being then, according to Peter de Langtoft,[c] employed in Scotland, he died.

> The moneth of September yolden was Stribelyn,
> Edward may remembre the travaille and the pyn.
> With many grete encumbre of in hard stoure
> At Brustwick opon Humbre there he mad sojoure.
> Sir Jon of Warenne that ilk tyme gan deie,
> His body was redy then in grabe for to leie.
> After the enterment the king tok his way,
> To the South, &c.

But according to the registry of the Priory of Lewes, the Earl died on that day at Kennington, having, says Dugdale, been Earl of Surrey no less than fifty-four years, though, as he succeeded his father in 1240, it is evident that he must have borne that title sixty-four years. He was buried in the midst of the pavement in the quire of the abbey of Lewes before the high altar, and the following epitaph was engraved upon his tomb:

> Uous qe passez ob bouche close
> Priez pur cely ke cy repose :
> En bie come bous estis jadis fu,
> Et bous tiel serretz come je su.
>
> Sire Johan Count de Gareyn gyst yey,
> Dieu de sa alme eit mercy :
> Ky pur sa aime priera,
> Troiz mill jours de pardon abera.

---

[b] See some remarks upon the titles and surname of this Earl in the Archæologia, vol. XXI. pp. 195, 196.   [c] P. 327.

Of the subject of this article, but little that is favorable to his memory can be said; though his faults, or more properly his vices, were those of the age in which he lived. His treachery at the battle of Lewes has, to apply the beautiful expression of a distinguished statesman of the present day, " left indelible stains upon his character which all the laurels of" Dunbar " cannot cover, nor its blood wash away;" whilst his subsequent conduct was invariably marked by a turbulent and intractable spirit. Not only was he frequently embroiled in disputes both with his compeers and his sovereign, but, with almost unparalleled hardihood, he dared in a court of justice to use personal violence towards a baron of the realm. That he should acquire renown in the field, and consequently become possessed of the King's esteem, is perfectly consistent with that impetuous temper for which he is celebrated. Bravery is, however, but one redeeming trait in a picture where all besides is dark and repulsive; and even the bold answer relative to his right to his lands, when properly considered, affords no room for praise, for the same resolute opposition to such an inquiry, would, there is no doubt, have been as readily evinced to defend any part of his property, if it had been acquired by the most flagrant injustice on his part, instead of on that of his ancestors.

A proof of the estimation in which the Earl was held by Edward the First is afforded, in Dugdale's opinion, by the fact that the King issued precepts directed to the Bishops of Canterbury and London, and to several Abbots, commanding them to cause masses to be said for his soul; but this testimony of the royal consideration might have arisen from the near connection between the Earl and his Majesty, as is shown by the annexed table:

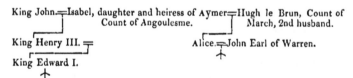

King John.⹀Isabel, daughter and heiress of Aymer⹀Hugh le Brun, Count of
Count of Angoulesme. March, 2nd husband.

King Henry III. ⹀ Alice.⹀John Earl of Warren.

King Edward I.

By the said Alice le Brun, who died on the 9th Feb. 1291, the Earl of Warren had issue, William, who died in his father's life-time, leaving his wife enceint with

John, his son and heir, who succeeded his grandfather in his honors; Alianor, who married, first, Henry Lord Percy, by whom she had Henry Lord Percy, spoken of in the Poem as the Earl's "nevou," and, secondly, the son of a Scotch Baron; and Isabel, wife of John Balliol, King of Scotland.

The arms of Warren were, checky Or and Azure.[d]

HENRY DE PERCY.

[PAGE 14.]

If the biographer of an ancient warrior is in any degree influenced by that enthusiasm which deeds of chivalrous courage are calculated to excite, it is only by more than ordinary restraint upon his feelings that he is enabled to relate them in the sober and chastened language suitable to historical truth; and perhaps in no instance is that caution so necessary as when any member of the house of Percy is the subject of his pen. In the age to which Henry de Percy belonged, as well as in a few succeeding centuries, that name was synonymous with almost uncontrolable power, impetuous valour, and all those stern military virtues which characterized the time; and the difficulty of successfully detailing the career of an individual is considerably increased, when, as in the case of this Baron, the merits of his descendants have been sung, not only by rude contemporary bards, but have been immortalized by the greatest dramatic genius that ever existed.

Henry de Percy was the third son of Henry Lord Percy, by Eleanor, daughter of John Earl Warren and Earl of Surrey, and succeeded to the barony upon the death of his brother John de Percy, who died under age soon after the year 1272, at which time he appears to have been very young. The first circumstance

---

d Page 14; Cotton MSS. Caligula, A. xvii; and the seals of this Earl.

recorded of him is, that, in the 15th Edw. I., being then in ward, on the King's expedition into Wales, he was acquitted of £120 required from him for. scutage. In the 22nd Edw. I. 1294, he made proof of his age, obtained livery of his lands, and was summoned to attend the King into Gascony; and in March, 1296, having accompanied Edward in his invasion of Scotland, he received the honor of knighthood before Berwick. He was present at the battle of Dunbar, and was soon afterwards appointed Governor of Galloway and Aire in Scotland; and in 1297, being with Robert Lord Clifford, commander for the King of England in the eastern parts of Scotland, they were appointed to receive Margery, daughter of Robert Brus Earl of Carrick, as an hostage for his fidelity to Edward. About the same time he was sent by the Earl Warren, then General of all the English army beyond the Trent, with the forces at Carlisle into Scotland, and having entered Annandale with 300 men at arms and 40,000 foot about the 10th of August, he proceeded to Aire, where he endeavoured to persuade the inhabitants of Galloway to submit. Finding that a party of Scots were on their route to oppose him he marched towards them, but from the inferiority of their numbers they surrendered upon condition of being pardoned. It would exceed the prescribed limits of these sketches to follow the biographers of this Baron in the minute details which they have recorded of his military career; and it will therefore only be remarked that he was constantly engaged in the King's wars, and appears to have enjoyed his sovereign's fullest confidence and esteem, whilst the annexed brief summary of his services, from Dugdale and Collins' account of him, will amply shew their nature and extent.

In the 26th Edw. I. Lord Percy was again in the wars of Scotland, in which year he obtained a grant of the lands forfeited by Ingelram de Umfreville; and in the following year was present at the siege of Carlaverock, a fact unnoticed by either of the writers just mentioned, when he must have been about forty-two years of age. The Poet alludes to his determined hostility against the Scots, which feeling appears to have been inherited by his descendants, and describes him as the "nevou" of the Earl Warren, which, like the word " nepos," seems to have been used for grandson as well as nephew, he being the son of Eleanor, the daughter of that nobleman. In February, 28 Edw. I. 1301, he was a party to the Letter from the Barons to Pope Boniface, wherein he is styled " Lord of Topclive," and in the 34th Edw. I. was again sent into Scotland to oppose Robert Bruce,

2 N

against whom he valiantly defended Kenteir. In the 35th Edw. I. he was a party
to the treaty of peace with Scotland.[e]

On the accession of Edward the Second, he was, in common with the other
peers of the realm, summoned to attend that monarch's coronation, and in the
3rd Edw. II. he purchased the celebrated Castle of Alnwick, which is now possessed by his representative the Duke of Northumberland. In the 5th Edw. II.
he succeeded John de Segrave as Constable of Nottingham Castle and Justice. of
the Forests beyond the Trent,[f] and about the same period was constituted Go-
nernor of Scarborough and Bamburgh Castles. From a writ tested on the 14th
September, 1309, it appears that he was then Constable of the Castle of York,
and in that and the preceding years he was again in the wars of Scotland.

Lord Percy distinguished himself by his enmity to Piers de Gaveston, and it
is perhaps just to consider that his hostility arose from patriotic motives; but
there is a suspicion attached to his behaviour towards the unhappy favorite, which
the biassed historian of the house of Percy has rather increased than lessened by
his laboured attempt to remove. It appears that Gaveston was besieged in
Scarborough Castle by the Earl of Pembroke, that he surrendered upon condition that his life and person should be secured, and that both the Earl and
Percy solemnly pledged themselves to that effect. Through a false reliance
however on the Earl's honor, by Percy, as Collins relates it, the promise was
speedily broken, and Gaveston perished on the scaffold at Warwick Castle.
This is a version of the tale which so partial a biographer as that writer uniformly shews himself[g] would naturally give; but, although the impossibility of

---

[e] Fœdera, N. E. vol. I. p. 212.   [f] Fœdera, N. E. vol. II. p. 163.

[g] The servile praise bestowed by Collins upon every individual of whom he speaks, called down
the following censure from Mr. Burke, which, however well-merited in that particular instance,
was ill applied to the College of Heralds of his time, and happily would be far less appropriate to
those of the present day. " These historians, recorders, and blazoners of virtues and arms, differ
wholly from that other description of historians who never assign any act of politicians to a good
motive. These gentle historians, on the contrary, dip their pens in nothing but the milk of human
kindness. They seek no further for merit than the preamble of a patent, or the inscription on a
tomb. With them, every man created a peer is first a hero ready made. They judge of every
man's capacity for office by the offices he has filled, and the more offices the more ability. Every
general officer with them is a Marlborough, every statesman a Burleigh, every judge a Murray or
a Yorke. They who, alive, were laughed at or pitied by all their acquaintance, make as good a
figure as the best of them in the pages of Guillim, Edmondson, and Collins "

ascertaining the real merits of the case render it unjust to pass a positive censure upon Percy's conduct, it is at least equally unfair to conclude that the whole shame of the transaction belongs to his colleague, and that his only error arose from a misplaced confidence. Certain, however, it is, that the King considered him guilty of Gaveston's death, for he issued special precepts, tested on the 30th and 31st July, 1312, for his apprehension, and for the seizure of all his lands, tenements, and chattels. Towards the end of that year, however, Percy was included in the treaty between the King and the Barons, and on making his submission his offence was pardoned and his lands restored to him. The acquittance of the King to Thomas Earl of Lancaster, Guy Earl of Warwick, Robert de Clifford, and this Baron, of the jewels and horses that belonged to Gaveston, dated on the 6th February, 1313, 6 Edw. II. by which he acknowledges to have received from them the articles therein-mentioned, by the hands of Humphrey Earl of Hereford, is still preserved. The document is highly curious; and, with the hope of relieving the dulness of this memoir, the following interesting extracts from it are introduced:

Un anel d'or, où un saphir, lequel seint Dunstan forga de ses mapns.

Une boiste d'argent en d'orrez pur porter eynz un anel entour le col de un homme.

Une grant rubi hors d'or, que fust trobe sur sire Piers de Gabaston quant il fust pris; le pris de mille libres.

Trois granz rubis en aneaur, une amiraude, un diamaund de grant pris, en une boiste d'argent enamille, que fust trobe sur le dit Pierres quant il fust pris.

Deur seaur un grant e un petit; e un petit seal une clief pendaunte, un esterling plie, et un calcedopne; les queur furent trobez en la burse quant il fuit pris.

En un cofre, lie de feer, une mirour d'argent enamaille; un pigne; un priket, que fust done au Roi par la Countesse de Bar a Gant.

Un coronal d'or où diverse perie, pris de cent mars.

Un chapelet d'argent garnis de diverse perie, pris de doze soutz.

En un autre cofre, un grant pot d'argent où trois peiz pur chaufer eawe, que poise sis libres quinze soutz dis deners.

Trois plates d'argent por especierie, e poisent quatre libres.

Deur plates d'argent pur fruit, des armes de roy d'Engleterre, que poisent sessant dis oit souz, quatre deners.

Une burse de drap d'or ove deur pierres de Jerlm' dedenz.

Un mors d'argent od quatre botons d'orrez, od deux lions pur chaq'e de cuir.

Un veil seal entaille, e un pere de Calcedoine.

Trois turchesces d'argent pur mangier poires.

Une ceinture de fil de argent blank.

Une chapelet de Paris, pris de sis souz oit deners.

Divers garnementz des armes le dit Pieres, ovek les alettes garniz et frettez de perles.

En un sak un bacenet burny od surcils.

En autre saak une peire de treppes des armes de dit Pieres.

Deux cotes de velvet pur plates coverir.

Une Pouche pur palefrei, des armes du Roy.

Quatre chemises et trois brais de Gascoigne orfresez.

Une veille banere des armes le dit Piers.

Quarant un destres et coucers e un palefrei.

Poef Somers.

Duze chibaus charetters.

Deux charettes od tut le herneis.[h]

Great part of Gaveston's plate was marked with an eagle, and several articles of jewellery were in that form; his arms being, Vert, six eagles displayed Or.

The little that remains to be said of this Baron may be related in a very few words. In 1313 he received letters of safe conduct from the King for all his dominions; in June, in the following year, he was present at the fatal battle of Bannockburn; and was regularly summoned to parliament from the 6th February, 27 Edw. I. 1299, to the 29th July, 8 Edw. II. 1314. He died in 1315, and was buried in the abbey of Fountains in Yorkshire; and by Eleanor his wife, daughter of John Earl of Arundel, who survived him, he left issue, Henry, his eldest son, then aged sixteen years; and William, who was made a Knight of the Bath 20 Edw. II. and died in 1355.

From the subject of this article sprung a line of peers which flourished in increased honor as Earls of Northumberland for several centuries; and from the deeds of the celebrated Hotspur having been described by Shakspeare, the name of PERCY is as well known to the world in general as to the genealogist and his-

---

h Fœdera, N. E. vol. II. p 203.

torian; nor will it cease to be associated with every thing that is chivalrous and brave, until the works of the immortal bard and the annals of England are alike forgotten. Thus, then, its renown stands upon an imperishable basis; and though those turbulent times which produced actions that dazzle the imagination have long since past, its ancient fame is not impaired by the conduct and character of its present illustrious representative.

The arms borne by Henry Lord Percy were those of Louvaine, Or, a lion rampant Azure;[i] his ancestor, Josceline de Louvaine, a younger son of the ducal house of Brabant, having retained his paternal coat, notwithstanding that he assumed the name of Percy upon his marriage with the heiress of William Baron Percy in the reign of Henry the Second.

---

[i] P 14; Caligula, A. xvii.; and the seal of the Baron aᵒ 1301. It has been suggested that the arms, crest, and name of Percy, admit of one of the most appropriate " canting" mottoes that has ever been devised—*Per se nobilis*,—for whether applied to that *noble* animal the lion, or to the *noble* conduct of those who for ages have borne it as part of their heraldic honors, its truth is unquestionable.

ROBERT FITZ PAYNE.

[Page 14.]

Robert Fitz Payne, of whose life very few circumstances are known, was the eldest son of a Baron of the same names, whom he succeeded in the 9th Edw. I. at which time he was seventeen years of age; but notwithstanding his minority, Dugdale states that he immediately did homage and had livery of his lands, and in the following year obtained a charter for a market and fair at his manor of Ockford Nicholl (also called from this family Ockford Fitzpayne, the name it now retains) in Dorsetshire, with a grant of free warren in all his demesne lands there; and in the 10th Edw. I. he was commanded to attend the expedition into Wales. He was summoned to the wars of Scotland in December, 1299, and was present at the surrender of Carlaverock in the June following, at which time he was about thirty-six years old; but nothing is recorded of his person or character by the Poet of that event. In February, 1301, he was a party to the Letter from the Barons of England to Pope Boniface the Eighth, and is described as " Lord of Lammer," and was again in the Scottish wars in the 31st Edw. I. Fitz Payne was appointed Governor of Corfe Castle in the 33rd Edw. I.[j] and in the 34th Edw. I. was made a Knight of the Bath[k] with Prince Edward, soon after which he accompanied him into Scotland, and in the same year that the Prince ascended the throne he was constituted Governor of the Castle of Winchester. In the 2nd of Edw. II. being then Steward of the King's household, he was sent with Otho de Grandison upon a mission to the Pope, and on the 17th May, 1309, was joined in a commission with several other peers for the reformation of the Royal household.[l] In the 8th Edw. II. he was again summoned to the wars of Scotland, and in that year was ordered to hold an assize in the county of Wilts.[m] This Baron was summoned to parliament from the 26th January, 25 Edw. I. 1297, to the 23rd October, 8 Edw. II. 1314, and died in 1315. By Isabell his wife, daughter and at length sole heiress of Sir John Clifford, of

---

[j] See also Rot. Parl. vol. I. p. 305 a.

[k] Dugdale, but no notice of the circumstance occurs in Anstis's Order of the Bath.

[l] Rot. Parl. vol. I. p. 433 b.   [m] Ibid. p. 333.

Frampton in Gloucestershire,[n] he left issue Robert his son and heir, then about twenty-eight years of age, who succeeded his father in his honors, and was summoned to parliament. It would, however, appear that Fitz Payne either married a former wife or was affianced to one, for among the ancient charters in the British Museum, is an agreement, dated in the 19th Edw. I., between Bartholomew de Badlesmere and Robert Fitz Payne, that the said Robert should marry Mary, daughter of the said Bartholomew.

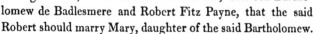

The present representatives of Robert Lord Fitz Payne are Everard Lord Arundel of Wardour, Eleanor-Mary Lady Clifford, and William Lord Stourton.

The arms of Fitz Payne are, Gules, three lions passant Argent, a bend Azure.[o]

WALTER DE MOUNCY.

[PAGE 16.]

This individual, though unquestionably a Baron of the realm, has escaped the notice of Dugdale, and such of the following particulars of him, for which other authorities are not cited, are extracted from Mr. Banks's "Stemmata Anglicana." Of his parentage nothing is positively known, and perhaps the earliest record of him extant, is that of the writ by which he was commanded to be at Carlisle with horse and arms to serve against the Scots, in the 26th Edw. I.[p] In the following year he obtained a grant of free warren in his demesne lands of Thornton juxta Skipton, Everley, and Kelebroke, in Yorkshire; and on the 6th May, 27th Edw. I. he was again ordered to attend the Scottish wars.[q] At the siege

n Mr. Townsend's MS. Collections for Dugdale's Baronage. In the 13th Edw. II. she described herself as Isabella de Fitz Payne, Lady of Frampton, formerly wife of Robert Fitz Payne, and gave to her cousin, William de Clifford of Frampton, certain lands.

o P. 14; Caligula, A. xvii.; and the seal of the Baron, a⁰ 1301.

p Appendix to the First Peerage Report, p. 100.   q Ibid. p. 107.

of Carlaverock he was in the squadron led by the Earl of Lincoln, to whose retinue or household he appears to have been attached; and in the 29th Edw. I. he was a party to the Letter from the Barons to the Pope relative to his Holiness's claim to the sovereignty of Scotland, in which document he is described as " Lord of Thornton."[r] With the exception of his name being frequently mentioned in writs of service and to parliament, the only facts concerning him which have been ascertained, are, that the lands of Thomas de Belhous were committed to his custody;[s] that he was present in the parliament which met at Carlisle in the octaves of St. Hillary in the 33rd Edw. I.;[t] and that in the 1st Edw. II. he was Custos of the Castle of Framlyngham.

Walter de Mouncy was summoned to parliament from the 6th February, 27 Edw. I. 1299, to the 22nd February, 35 Edw. I. 1307, and died in the 2nd Edw. II. for in that year the King's Escheator was ordered to take into his hands the lands of which he was seised at his demise. His heir is supposed to have been a female, who married —— Grashall, and by him was mother of two daughters and coheirs, namely, Isabel, wife of Durand Bard; and Margaret, who married, first, —— Despenser, by whom she had a son, Philip Despenser, and, secondly, John de Roos, younger son of William Lord Roos: but he died s. p. in the 12th Edw. III. and his widow in the 22nd Edw. III.

The arms of Mouncy were, checky Argent and Gules,[u] and from the seal of this Baron attached to the Barons' Letter it would seem that his crest was a fox, the helmet being surmounted by an animal resembling one, and engraved as if dead or asleep.

---

[r] Appendix to the Fourth Peerage Report, pp. 97, 98.
[s] Rot. Parl. vol. I. p. 169 a.   [t] Ibid. y. 188.
[u] P. 16; Cotton MSS. Caligula, A. xvii.; and the seal of this Baron, a° 1301.

145

AYMER DE VALENCE, EARL OF PEMBROKE.

[PAGE 16.]

There is something pleasing in the reflection that the ravages of time have not entirely swept away the memorials of those who in past ages occupied prominent parts in the drama of public life; that there is yet contemporary and splendid evidence of their wealth and importance, which alike claims the admiration and challenges the criticism of the most fastidious taste; and that a name which once filled England with respect, is not remembered alone by the dull antiquary or patient historian. These observations are suggested by that beautiful monument of Aymer de Valence in Westminster Abbey, which still renders his name familiar to those who either pity or despise the pursuits by which a knowledge of his deeds and character are alone to be acquired. The following attempt, however, to present a slight account of this celebrated Earl, is rendered the less necessary by the biographical notice which accompanies a recent engraving of his tomb, and whilst the subject affords an almost unrivalled specimen of one branch of the arts in the fourteenth century, that plate is perhaps a no less extraordinary example of them in another department in the present age.x

Aymer de Valence was the third son of William de Valence, who was created Earl of Pembroke by his uterine brother King Henry the Third. He was born about 1280,y and succeeded his father in his honors on the 13th of June, 1296; both of his elder brothers having previously died without issue. The earliest notice of him which is recorded, is, that on the 26th January, 25 Edw. I. 1297, he was summoned to parliament as a Baron,z though, according to modern opinions on the subject, he was fully entitled to the earldom of Pembroke, nor was the title ever attributed to him in public records until the 6th November,

---

x Blore's Monumental Remains, part IV. A more elaborate and equally beautiful representation of this tomb is given in Stothard's "Monumental Effigies," a work which need only be seen to excite the gratitude and respect of every real antiquary, accompanied by feelings of sincere regret at the early fate of its indefatigable author.

y Esch. 1 Edw. II. and 3 Edw. II. z Appendix to the First Peerage Report, p. 77.

2 P

1 Edw. II. 1307;[a] and the first writ to parliament addressed to him as " Earl of Pembroke," was tested on the 18th of the following January.[b] Upon this remarkable circumstance some observations have recently been made;[c] but it is wholly impossible to explain the cause of the anomaly in a satisfactory manner. Although never styled " Earl of Pembroke" until the accession of Edward the Second, it is manifest that from the death of his father he ranked above all Barons, excepting Henry of Lancaster, who, being of the blood royal, is uniformly mentioned next to Earls; hence it appears that, notwithstanding his claim was not positively acknowledged, he was considered to be entitled to a higher degree of precedency than belonged to the baronial dignity. In the 25th Edw. I. he was in the expedition into Flanders, and in the same year was appointed a commissioner to ratify an agreement between the King and Florence Count of Holland, relative to some auxiliaries from the Count in that war, and was likewise one of the ambassadors sent by Edward to treat for a truce between England and France. In the 26th and 27th Edw. I. he was in the Scottish wars, and in June, in the 28th Edw. I. 1300, was present at the siege of Carlaverock, when he must have been about twenty-one years of age; but the Poet pays him no other compliment than what a pun upon his name suggested,

Le Valence Apmars li Vaillans.

In the following year he was a party to the Barons' Letter to the Pope, in which, though his name occurs immediately after that of the Earl of Arundel, and before Henry de Lancaster's, he is only styled " Lord of Montiniac." Shortly afterwards he was appointed to treat with the ambassadors of the King of France on the subject of peace. In the 31st Edw. I. he was again in the wars of Scotland, and in the same year received permission to leave the realm upon his own affairs. He obtained a grant in 1305 of the castles of Selkirk and Traquair, and of the borough of Peebles in Scotland, to hold by the service of one knight's fee, together with other possessions in that kingdom; and in the 34th Edw. I. was constituted Guardian of the Marches of Scotland towards Berwick, when he was entrusted with the sole command of the English forces which had been levied against Robert Bruce. In the instrument by which he

---

a Fœdera, N. E. vol. II. part I. p. 11.   b Appendix to the First Peerage Report, p. 176.
c Archæologia, vol. XXI. p. 204.

was appointed to that important duty, as well as in most others, he is styled, " Dilectum consanguineum et fidelum nostrum." The appellation of " cousin" was not then a mere title of honor when addressed to a peer, but was used in its most literal sense, and Aymer de Valence's claim to it is shown by the following slight pedigree:

Hugh le Brun, Count of the Marches=Isabel, dau. and heiress of Aymer=King John, ob. 1216,
   of Acquitaine, 2nd husband.   Count of Angoulesme.   1st husband.

William de Valence, created Earl of Pembroke, ob. 1296.=   King Henry the Third, ob. 1272. =

AYMER DE VALENCE, EARL OF   KING EDWARD THE FIRST, ob. 1307.=
   PEMBROKE, ob. 1323.

              KING EDWARD THE SECOND.

The successes which attended this nobleman against Robert Bruce are thus described by a contemporary chronicler:

" Now gos the Brus about, werre he thinkis to hold,
The Inglis the katched out, to the king the told.
Edward than he toke folk with his banere,
The Erle went of Pembroke, his name was Sir Eymere.
And other men fulle gode, barons and barons pere,
At tyme well thei stode, and did there debere.
The date was a thousand three hundred mo bi ser,
Whan the werre of Scotland thorgh the Brus eft wer."

" Sire Eymere of Ualence lay at Saynt Jon toun,
In his alience with many erle and baroun,
Of Scotland the best were than in his feith
Ther thei gan alle rest, tille thei herd other greith.
Sir Robert the Brus sent to Sir Eymere,
And bad he suld refus that him had forsaken ilk a pantenere,
The traytours of hise that him had forsaken,
Thei suld to the Jewise, whan thei the town had taken;
The tother day on the morn com the Brus Roberd,
The town wist it beforn, thorugh spies that thei herd:
Sir Eymere wild haf gon out, Sir Ingram Umfrepvile
Preid him for to sout, tille it were none that while."

" Ȝif we now out wende and leve þe toun alone
Þei get þe faired ende, and we be slayn ilkone ;
Bot do crie þorgh þe toun, þat non for wele no wo,
In strete walk up and down bot to þer.innes go."

*   *   *   *   *   *

" On saynt Margarete day Sir Ingram and Sir Eymere
Com on þam þer þei lay alle dight to þe dynere :
Þer baumward was gone dight, our Inglis had mervaile,
Þei were so gone at þe fight, and redy to assaile ;
Þe Inglis þorgh þam ran and had þe fairer side,
Þe Scottis ilk a man þe lordes durst not bide.
Here now a contrevore þorgh Roberdes abis,
Abowen þer armore did serkis and surplis.
Alle þei fledde on rowe, in lynen white as milke,
For non suld þam knowe, þer armes whilk were whilk.
Our men þat wild haf dede, bar þem forþe fulle stoute,
Sir Eymer had no drede, he serchid þam alle oute ;
At þe first compyng he slouth Sir Eymere stede
Þat did Robert þe kyng, and turned bak and yede ;
Sir Eymer had inowe, þat horsid him agayn,
Robertes men þei slowe, þe numbre uncerteyn ;
Þan bigan þe chace, and drof þe kyng Robyn,
To reste had he no space, long to duelle þerin." [d]

Valence, after the contest, pursued Bruce, and presuming that he would take refuge in Kildrummie Castle, he gained possession of that place, but finding only Nigel de Bruce, brother of Robert, there, he caused him and all who were with him to be immediately hung. This action has given rise to some pertinent remarks by the able biographer of the Earl in the beautiful work before noticed,[e] who has satisfactorily shown that Nigel was not put to death by him, but that at least the forms of law were observed on the occasion. On the death-bed of Edward the First, Pembroke, with some other personages, received the King's dying injunctions to afford his son their counsel and support, and not to permit

---

[d] Peter of Langtoft, pp. 331. 333. 335.   [e] Blore's Monumental Remains.

Piers de Gaveston to return into England. His strict adherence to this command naturally excited the favourite's displeasure; and he is said, in derision of
his tall stature and pallid complexion, to have termed him "Joseph the Jew."
In the first year of the young monarch's reign, Valence was, as has been before
observed, allowed and summoned to parliament by his proper title of Earl of
Pembroke; and at the coronation of that monarch he carried the King's left
boot,[f] but the spur belonging to it was borne by the Earl of Cornwall. In the
same year, after performing homage upon the death of his mother for her lands,
he was joined with Otho de Grandison in an embassy to the Pope; and in the
3rd Edw. II. was found heir to his sister Agnes, or more probably Anne.[g] It
has been considered from the circumstance of the Earl being a witness[h] to the
instrument by which the King recalled Gaveston, and bestowed the possessions
of the Earl of Cornwall upon him, that he approved of, or at least consented
to, those acts: but this idea rests upon far too uncertain evidence to be relied
upon; and if he ever changed his opinion it was of short duration, for in the
3rd Edw. II. he joined the Earl of Lancaster against Gaveston, and when he
was banished the realm in 1311, the Earl of Pembroke was one of the persons
deputed to petition the King that he should be rendered incapable of ever holding
any office. As in the notice of Henry de Percy the manner in which Pembroke
was concerned in the death of the noxious favourite was alluded to, it is unnecessary to recur to the subject.

In the 6th Edw. II. he was again sent on a mission to Rome, and in the same
year obtained a grant of lands in London, in which was included the New Temple.
In the 7th Edw. II. he was appointed Custos and Lieutenant of Scotland until the
arrival of the King, and was present at the fatal battle of Bannockbourn. Two
inedited MSS. cited in the "Monumental Remains," allude to the Earl's conduct upon that occasion in words fatal either to his loyalty or courage: the one
stating that "Insuper Comes de Pembrok, Henricus de Bellomonte, et multi
magnates, *cordetenus Pharisei,* a certamine recesserunt;" and the other, that "in
pedibus suis evasit ex acie, et cum Valensibus fugientibus se salvavit." In all
probability, however, the language was in both instances that of an enemy, and
deserves but little credit; though, even if it were true, "there is no great disgrace,"

f Fœdera, N. E. vol. II. p. 36.   g Esch. 3 Edw. II.
h Fœdera, N. E. vol. II. part II. p. 2.

2 q

as the learned biographer from whose memoir these extracts are taken has truly
remarked, " in seeking safety by flight when defeat was inevitable, and the whole
army pursued a similar course."[i]   In the 9th Edw. II. the Earl was a commissioner for holding a parliament in the King's absence,[j] and took an active part
in the proceedings therein.[k]   Being sent to Rome on a mission to the Pontiff, a
singular misfortune befel him, as he was taken prisoner on his return by a Bur-
gundian called John de Moiller, with his accomplices, and sent to the Emperor,
who obliged him to pay a ransom of 20,000 pounds of silver, upon the absurd
pretence that Moiller had served the King of England without being paid his
wages.   Edward used every exertion to procure the Earl's liberty, and wrote to
several sovereign princes soliciting them to interfere on the subject; but he did
not immediately succeed.   In the 11th Edw. II. Pembroke was once more in
the Scottish wars, and was appointed Governor of Rockingham Castle; and
upon the King's purposed voyage, in the 13th Edw. II. to do homage to the
King of France for the Duchy of Acquitaine, he was constituted Guardian of the
realm during his absence, being then also Custos of Scotland.   In the 15th
Edw. II. he sat in judgment on the Earl of Lancaster at Pontefract;[l] and for his
conduct on the occasion was rewarded with the grant of several manors.

With the preceding narrative, Dugdale's account of the Earl closes; nor has his
recent biographer supplied any further particulars: but the following facts are
on record, previous to citing which, the annexed notice of him in Selden's Titles
of Honor[m] merits insertion, especially as it also relates to two other knights who
were present at the siege of Carlaverock: " Anno MCCCXVI. Dominus Rich. de
Rodney factus fuit miles apud Keynsham die translationis Sancti Thomæ mar-
tyris in præsentia Domini Almarici Comitis de Pembroch, qui cinxit eum gladio,
et Dominus Mauritius de Berkley super pedem dextrum posuit unum calcar, et
Dominus Bartholomeus de Badilesmere posuit aliud super pedem sinistrum in
aula, et hoc facto recessit cum honore."

In March, 1309, the Earl of Pembroke was one of the peers appointed to
regulate the royal household;[n] in the 5th Edw. II. he was commanded not to

i Monumental Remains.   j Rot. Parl. vol. I. p. 350 b.
k Rot. Parl. vol. I. p. 352 b. 354 b. 359 a. 361 b.   l Ibid. vol. II. p. 3.
m P. 642, cited in Anstis's Collection of Authorities on the Knighthood of the Bath, p. 8.
n Rot. Parl. vol. I. p. 443.

approach the place where the parliament was held with an armed retinue, or in any other manner than was observed in the time of the late King;[o] in the 8th Edw. II. he was a commissioner to open and continue a parliament at York;[p] in the 12th Edw. II. he was sent to Northampton with others to treat with the Earl of Lancaster for the better government of the realm, and was one of the peers then appointed to be about the King's person,[q] at which time he signed the agreement between the King and that Earl;[r] he advised the reversal of the judgment against Hugh le Despenser the younger;[s] by writ tested on the 19th Jan. 14 Edw. II. 1321, he was appointed a Commissioner to treat for peace with Robert de Brus;[t] and in the 18th Edw. II. the Earl, as Justice in Eyre of the Forest of Essex, claimed the appointment of the Marshal thereof.[v]

The Earl of Pembroke accompanied Isabell the Queen of England to France in 1323; and is said to have lost his life in that year, at a tournament given by him to celebrate his nuptials with his third wife, Mary, daughter of Guy de Chastillon, Count of St. Paul's; though from the obscure manner in which his death is mentioned by some chroniclers, and the attempt which they have made to consider it as a mark of the vengeance of Heaven for his conduct relative to the death of the Earl of Lancaster, Dugdale asserts that he was murdered on the 23rd June, 1324, " by reason he had a hand" in that affair. But the former statement his recent biographer considers to be corroborated by the following lines in a long MS. poem, containing a life of the Earl, in the Cottonian collection[u], written by Jacobus Nicholaus de Dacia, who calls himself a scholar of Mary de St. Paul Countess of Pembroke; by which he probably meant that he belonged to Pembroke Hall, which she had founded:

> Mors Comitem Comitum necuit, mors ipsa cruenta
> Ipsa cruore rubrum campum facit et rubicundum.

From the annexed account of the Earl's death, however, by another contemporary writer,[w] whose statement on the subject is now for the first time cited, it would rather appear that he died of apoplexy:

---

[o] Rot. Parl. vol. I. p. 447.   [p] Ibid. p. 450.   [q] Ibid. p. 453 b.

[r] Ibid. vol. III. p. 362.   [s] Ibid. vol. I. p. 427 b.   [t] Ibid. p. 454 a.

[v] Fœdera, N. E. vol. II. p. 441.   [u] Claudius, A. xiv.

[w] Robert of Reading. Cottonian MSS. Cleopatra, A. xvi. f. 133 b. For a reference to this MS.

" Ea vero tempestate primorum consultu direxit ad partes transmarinas Rex Almaricum de Valencia Comitem de Penbrokia, virum siquidem ad queque nepharia peragenda iuxta sue propinquitatis nequiciam continue paratum, regis Francorum presencie nuncium super dictis negociis assistendum, vt eiusdem regis Francorum animum ab inceptis revocaret, ut ipsius benevolenciam affectum regis Anglorum varijs blandiciis inclinaret. Quo perveniente, ac iuxta proposita suorum verborum responsis acceptis,.per Pykardiam rediens, ad quoddam municipium mi. villa, id est, *dimidia villa*, nuncupatum, tribus leucis a Compyne distans, in vigilia sancti Johannis declinavit pransurus, ubi Christus voluit virum sanguineum et dolosum non dimidiare dies suos.   Sed finita refectionis hora thalamum ingreditur, deambulando statim in atrio corruit, ac sine confessione et viatico salutari infelicem animam subito in solo sufflavit."

The Poem alluded to is deemed, by the highly competent judge just mentioned, not to contain any thing worthy of observation; for he says that " throughout five hundred lines of exaggerated panegyric, not a single incident, anecdote, or trait of character is to be found."[x]

The Earl was thrice married; first, to Beatrix, daughter of Ralph dé Noel Constable of France; secondly, to a daughter of the Earl of Barre; and thirdly, to Mary, daughter of Guy de Chastillon Count of St. Paul: but he had no issue, and the descendants of his sisters, Isabel, the wife of John Baron Hastings; and Joan, who married John Comyn of Badenoch, are consequently his representatives.   His eldest sister, Anne, married, first, Maurice Fitz Gerald; secondly, Hugh de Baillol; and, lastly, John de Avennes; and probably died s. P. in the 3rd Edw. II.[y]

Mary Countess of Pembroke is chiefly known to the present age by an action which seldom fails to ensure immortality. She was the foundress of a College for the purposes of learning and religion, which still bears the name of Pembroke Hall; and was likewise a benefactress to several religious houses which were suppressed by the cupidity of Henry the Eighth.   She died about 1376, and on the 13th of March in that year made her will, at Braxted in·Essex, by which she

---

the Editor willingly expresses his obligation to Frederick Madden, Esq. whose profound knowledge of early English writers is only equalled by the readiness with which his information is imparted to his friends.

     x Monumental Remains.·   y·Esch. eod.' ann.   See page 149 ante.

ordered her body to be buried in the church of the sisters of Denny, where she had caused her tomb to be made; and bequeathed to the church of the Abbey of Westminster, where her husband was interred, a cross with a foot of gold and emeralds, which Sir William de Valence, Knt. brought from the Holy Land.[z]

The body of the Earl of Pembroke was conveyed to England, and buried in  the Abbey of Westminster; but upon the beautiful tomb erected to his memory it is unnecessary to say a single word, ample justice having been done to it in the work so frequently referred to, both by the artist and author.

The arms of Valence were, barry, Argent and Azure, an orle of martlets Gules.[a]

---

[z] Testamenta Vetusta, p. 100. It may not be uninteresting to observe, that there is in the possession of G. Pocock, Esq. of Lincoln's Inn Fields, a small brass coffer, which, from the arms enamelled on it, is supposed to have belonged to this illustrious woman. This curious relic was exhibited to the Society of Antiquaries a short time since, but it did not appear to excite the attention which it merited.

[a] P. 16; Cotton MSS. Caligula, A. xvii.; the seal of the Earl a⁰ 1301; and the arms on his tomb.

NICHOLAS DE CAREW.

[PAGE 16.]

That there should be such a paucity of materials extant for a memoir of this individual is surprising, for very few of his contemporaries excelled him in descent, rank, or military merit. Indeed, in the latter qualification he was so celebrated by his services in Ireland, that the Poet has particularly alluded to the circumstance; and the consideration in which he was held is sufficiently manifested by his being frequently a colleague of the Barons of the realm, though he was never summoned to parliament.

The house of Carew is supposed to have sprung from Otho de Windsor, the common ancestor of the illustrious families of Windsor and Fitz-Gerald. The grandfather and father of Nicholas de Carew had both married into distinguished Irish families; and it seems that they consequently became intimately connected with Ireland. Little notice, however, occurs of the subject of this article in records until the 29th Edw. I., when he was a party to the Barons' Letter to the Pontiff, in which he is described as " Lord of Mulesford;"[b] but from the Poem we learn that he was present in the preceding year at the siege of Carlaverock, in the squadron commanded by the Earl of Lincoln. He was, it is there said, a man of great renown, and had often displayed his valour against the rebellious people of Ireland.

He married, according to some pedigrees, Ann, daughter and heiress of the Baron Digon, Lord of Adrone in Ireland;[c] and, agreeably to others, Amicia, sister of sir John Peverell;[d] but the point is involved in great obscurity: and died in the 3rd Edw. II., leaving John his son and heir.[e] From this John de Carew has descended a most extensive family, which has ramified into almost every county in England, and was in one branch ennobled by Queen Elizabeth, and further

[b] Appendix to the Fourth Peerage Report.　　[c] Harl. MSS. 380.
[d] Kimber's Baronetage.　　[e] Esch. eod. ann.

advanced to the dignity of Earl of Totness by James the First; whilst in others it was elevated to the rank of baronets. The issue of some of the younger sons still flourish in the male line in Devonshire.

The arms of Carew are, Or, three lions passant in pale Sable.[f]

ROGER LA WARE.

[PAGE 16.]

The earliest notice of Roger la Warre, the first of his name who attained the rank of a Baron, is in the 10th Edw. I., in which year, having been in the expedition then made into Wales, he had scutage of all his tenants who held of him by military service; and in the 13th Edw. I. he obtained the King's license for a weekly market in his manor of Warrewike in Gloucestershire, with other privileges. In the 15th Edw. I. he was summoned to attend with horse and arms at Gloucester,[g] and in the 22nd Edw. I. was commanded to repair speedily to the King to deliberate on the affairs of the realm.[h] Shortly afterwards, namely on the 26th June in the same year, he was summoned to Portsmouth to accompany his Majesty into France.[i] In the 26th Edw. I. he was Governor of the Castle of Burgh in Gascony; on the 30th September, 28 Edw. I. 1299, he was ordered to be at Carlisle on the ensuing feast of St. John the Baptist, to serve against the Scots; and in the following year was present at the siege of Carlaverock, when his sagacity and valour are eulogised by the Poet of the expedition. In the 29th Edw. I. he was party to the Letter to the Pope, wherein he is called " Lord of Isefeld," but his seal is not affixed to that document.[k] From that period until

---

f Page 16; Cotton MSS. Caligula, A. xvii; and the seal of this Baron aº 1301.

g Appendix to the First Peerage Report, p. 51.   h Ibid. p. 56.   i Ibid. p. 55.

k Appendix to the Fourth Peerage Report.

the 8th Edw. II. he was frequently in the wars of Scotland; and he appears to have passed through life without being distinguished either by brilliant services, or by the commission of any crime, which would have caused his name to be more frequently recorded. He was one of the manucaptors for William de Montagu, who was a prisoner in the tower of London in the 33rd Edw. I.;[1] and in the 35th Edw. I. was attached for not having obeyed the King's writ to attend at Carlisle, or paid the usual fine.[m]

This Baron was summoned to parliament from the 6th Feb. 27 Edw. I. 1299, to the 16th June, 4 Edw. II. 1311, and died in 1320; leaving by his wife Clarice, daughter and coheir of John Baron Tregoz, John la Warr his son and heir, then forty years of age, who was summoned to parliament several years before his father's death.

The representatives of this Baron are the heirs of Mary, the daughter and eventually sole heiress of Sir Owen West, half brother of Thomas West Baron la Warr, K. G. who died s. P. in 1554, who was lineally descended from Thomas Baron West by his wife Joan, half sister and heiress of Thomas le Warr, great-great-grandson of the Baron who was present at Carlaverock. By a most extraordinary anomaly in the descent of dignities that originated in a writ of summons, the issue of Sir Owen West were passed over; and the barony was allowed to the heir male of the above-mentioned Thomas West Lord la Warr who died in 1554, namely William, the son and heir of sir George West, younger brother of sir Owen; and it has consequently been presumed to be now vested in his heir, George John, Earl de la Warr. Mary, the daughter and heiress of Sir Owen West, was twice married; first, to Sir Adrian Poynings, Knt. by whom she had three daughters, Elizabeth, Mary, and Anne; and, 2ndly,

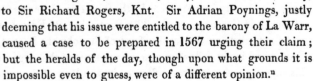

to Sir Richard Rogers, Knt. Sir Adrian Poynings, justly deeming that his issue were entitled to the barony of La Warr, caused a case to be prepared in 1567 urging their claim; but the heralds of the day, though upon what grounds it is impossible even to guess, were of a different opinion.[n]

The arms of La Warr are, Gules, semée of cross crosslets, a lion rampant Argent.[o]

---

[1] Rot. Parl. vol. I. p. 176.
MSS. 1323, f. 280.

[m] Ibid. p. 216.
[o] P. 16; and Cotton MSS. Caligula, A. xvii.

[n] MSS. in the College of Arms; also Harl.

GUY DE BEAUCHAMP, EARL OF WARWICK.

[PAGE 18.]

This nobleman, whose actions corresponded in importance with the elevated station which he held in the realm, is supposed to have derived his baptismal name from the renowned Guy of Warwick, the favourite hero of romance. He succeeded his father, William Earl of Warwick, in May or June 1296, at which time he was twenty-six years of age. Almost the earliest circumstance recorded of him is that he eminently distinguished himself in the field; for, having been summoned to serve against the Scots in the year in which his father died, he was present at the battle of Falkirk, and for his valour on that day was rewarded with the lands forfeited by Geoffrey de Mowbray. In the 27th Edw. I. he was again in the wars of Scotland, and in that year was also employed beyond the sea in the King's service. At the siege of Carlaverock, in the 28th Edw. I. he was present in the first squadron under the Earl of Lincoln, when he was about twenty-nine years old; and, though the praise bestowed upon him by the Poet is expressed in a very obscure manner, it may be interpreted to mean that none of his companions in arms were superior to him in merit. He was a party to the Letter to Pope Boniface the Eighth in 1301;[p] from which time to the end of the reign of Edward the First he was frequently in the Scottish wars, and received that monarch's dying command to protect the interests of his son, and not to allow Gaveston to return into England. The Earl partook largely of the forfeited lands of John de Baillol, and evidently derived considerable advantages from his presence in the royal army.

At the coronation of Edward the Second the Earl of Warwick carried one of the swords borne at that ceremony;[q] and in the 5th Edw. II. he joined the Earl of Lancaster against Piers de Gaveston. A similar anecdote to that related in the account of the Earl of Pembroke is preserved, explanatory of the chief cause of the Earl's hatred of that favourite; for we are informed that Gaveston, in allusion to his swarthy complexion, called him " the black dog of Arden." Though Warwick had been pardoned by the King for the part he had

---

[p] Appendix to the Fourth Peerage Report.   [q] Fœdera, N. E. vol. II. p. 36.

taken in the destruction of the Earl of Cornwall, Dugdale, upon the authority of Walsingham, considers that he had not forgiven his Majesty ; and that he therefore refused to obey his commands to attend him into Scotland.

In February, 7 Edw. II. he obtained an acquittance from the King of the jewels and plate which had belonged to Gaveston ;[r] and on the 17th May, 1309, was one of the noblemen appointed to regulate the royal household.[s] In the 5th Edw. II. he was prohibited from attending the parliament with armed followers, or in any other manner than was usual in the reign of Edward the First ;[t] and on the 4th of August, 1312, was cited with other peers to appear in the royal presence for the reformation of certain ordinances.[u]

Of the public life of this Earl nothing more is known; and his sumptuous benefactions to religious houses, and especially to the monks of Bordsley, though characteristic of the age, do not require any particular notice; excepting that it was so liberal to the latter fraternity, as to induce them to style him, in a public instrument in full chapter by which they allowed him to present two monks to their convent, " Dilecto et speciali amico."

The Earl of Warwick made his will at Warwick Castle on Monday next after the feast of St. James, July 28, 1315, by which he ordered that his body should be buried in the abbey of Bordsley, without pomp ; that Alice his Countess should have a proportion of his plate, with a crystal cup, and half his bedding, together with all the vestments and books belonging to his chapel. The other half of his beds, rings, and jewels he gave to his two daughters. To Maud, his daughter, he left a crystal cup ; and to Elizabeth, his other daughter, the profits of the marriage of Astley's heir, but whom she herself married. To Thomas, his son, he bequeathed his best coat of mail, helmet, and suit of harness, with all which belonged thereto ; and to his son John, his second best coat of mail, helmet, and harness. He further desired that the rest of his armour, bows, and other warlike implements, should remain in Warwick Castle for the benefit of his heir.

The Earl died at Warwick Castle on the 12th of August, 1316, aged about forty-four years, and was suspected to have been poisoned. He left by Alice his wife, widow of Thomas de Leybourne, and daughter of Ralph, and sister and

r Fœdera, N. E. vol. II. p. 203.   s Rot. Parl. vol. I. p. 443 b.
t Ibid. p. 447 b.   u Ibid. p. 448.

heiress of Robert de Tony, two sons, Thomas, his successor in the earldom; and Sir John Beauchamp, a celebrated knight, and one of the founders of the order of the Garter: also five daughters, Maud, who married Geoffrey Lord Say; Emma, wife of Rowland Odingsells; Isabel, wife of —— Clinton; Elizabeth, who married Thomas Lord Astley; and Lucia, wife of Robert de Napton. The

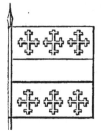

Countess of Warwick, in the year after her lord's demise, gave five hundred marks for license to marry William le Zouche of Ashby, of whom she accordingly became the wife.

The arms of Beauchamp Earls of Warwick were, Gules, crusilly, and a fess Or;[x] or, as they are now blazoned, Gules, a fess between six cross crosslets Or.

JOHN DE MOHUN.

[PAGE 18.]

The life of this individual affords no incident of the slightest interest; and all which is recorded of him is, that he performed the duties attendant upon the rank of a Baron of his times.

John de Mohun was the eldest son of John de Mohun, a Baron by tenure, by Eleanor, daughter of Sir Reginald Fitz Piers;[y] and succeeded his father, who

x P. 16; Cotton MSS. Caligula, A. xvii.; and the seal of the Earl, aᵒ 1301. Upon the reverse of his seal the Earl bore the arms of Newburgh Earls of Warwick. See Archæologia, vol. XXI. pp. 199, 200.

y This Eleanor remarried William Martin. . By the name of Eleanor de Mohun, wife of William Martin, she joined him in a conveyance of lands to their son William Martin in the 13th Edw. II. Her seal contains three shields; 1st, Martin, with a label; 2nd, Mohun, though different from the usual coat, it being a hand issuing from a maunch holding a fleur de lis; 3rd, three lions rampant, Fitz Piers. Cotton MSS. Julius, C. vii.

died in France, on the 11th June, 1279. He was born about the year 1269, and in the 22nd and 25th Edw. I. was summoned to attend with horse and arms in Gascony. In the 26th and 27th Edw. I. he was in the wars of Scotland, and in the year last mentioned exchanged his lands in Ireland with the King for the manor of Long Compton in Warwickshire. At the siege of Carlaverock he served in the first division of the English army, when he must have been above thirty years of age; but the Poet takes no other notice of him, than to describe his banner. In the 29th Edw. I. Mohun was a party to the Letter from the Barons to the Pope, in which he is described as " Lord of Dunsterre;" and was again in the Scottish wars in the 31st Edw. I. and 4th and 8th Edw. II.[z]

From the 6th February, 27 Edw. I. 1299, to the 23rd October, 4 Edw. III. 1330, a period of thirty-one years, John de Mohun was regularly summoned to parliament; and died in 1330, at the age of sixty-one. By his second wife,[a] Auda, daughter of Sir Pain de Tibetot, he had issue two sons; John, and Reginald. John, the eldest son, died in his father's life-time, leaving by Christian, daughter of John Lord Segrave, a son, John, who succeeded to his grandfather's honors, at which time he was ten years of age. Reginald, the second son, was the ancestor of the Mohuns of Cornwall, and of the Barons Mohun of Okehampton.[b] Upon the death of the last mentioned John Lord Mohun, K. G. about the year 1373, s. p. m., the barony fell into abeyance among his three daughters and

coheirs; namely, Philippa, who married, first, Walter Lord Fitz Walter, secondly Sir John Golafre, and thirdly Edward Plantagenet Duke of York, but died s. p. in the 10th Hen. VI.; Elizabeth, the wife of William de Montacute Earl of Salisbury; and Maud, who married John Lord Strange of Knockyn.

The arms of Mohun were, Or, a cross engrailed Sable.[c]

---

[z] Appendix to the Fourth Peerage Report.

[a] Glover's Collections, Harl. MSS. 807. Dugdale calls her the daughter of Sir Robert Tiptoft; from a petition on the Rolls of Parliament in the 7th Edw. III. vol. II. p. 71, it would however appear that the said Auda was his first wife, and that his second wife, who survived him, was called Sybilla.   [b] Harl. MSS. 807.

[h] P. 18; Cotton MSS. Caligula, A. xvii.; and the seal of this Baron, a⁰ 1301.

161

ROBERT DE TATESHALL.

[PAGE 18.]

This Baron was born in 1274, and succeeded his father of the same name in his dignity and possessions in 1297. In the 8th Edw. I., when he was scarcely more than six years of age, he married Eve, the daughter of Robert de Tibetot, who had for her portion six hundred marks of silver, and was then nearly thirteen years old.

In the 25th Edw. I. he was in the expedition into Gascony, and in the 26th and 28th Edw. I. attended the King in the wars of Scotland. At the siege of Carlaverock, at which time he was about twenty-seven, he served in the first squadron, but the usual attribute of valour is the only qualification assigned to him by the Poet. He was a party to the Barons' Letter to the Pontiff in 1301, and is described in it as "Lord of Bukenham."[d] In the 30th Edw. I. he petitioned the King for the office of Butler, which he claimed in right of his grandmother, Amabilla, eldest sister and coheir of Hugh d'Albini Earl of Arundel; to whom, he states, in the division of the Earl's property, that office was apportioned.[e]

Tateshall was summoned to parliament from the 6th February, 27 Edw. I. 1299, to the 13th Sept. 30 Edw. I. 1302, and died in 1303; leaving by the said Eve de Tibetot, who survived him, Robert, his son and heir, then fifteen years of

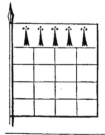

age; but he dying in his minority without issue, the *sisters*, agreeably to Dugdale, or, according to another authority to which the utmost credit is due,[f] the *aunts* of the subject of this memoir, or their children, became his representatives.

The arms of Tateshall were, Checky Or and Gules, a chief Ermine.[g]

---

[d] Appendix to the Fourth Peerage Report.   [e] Rot. Parl. vol. I. p. 154.

[f] The late Francis Townsend, Esq. MS. Collections for Dugdale's Baronage.

[g] P. 18 ; Cotton MSS. Caligula, A. xvii. ; and the seal of this Baron aº 1301. The latter, however, seems to have been engraved in the life-time of his father, as the arms are distinguished by a label.

2 T

RALPH FITZ WILLIAM.

[PAGE 18.]

The career of this Baron differs very slightly from that of his contemporaries; and the relation of it will therefore present little but a statement of barren and uninteresting facts.

He was the son of William Fitz Ralph Lord of Grimsthorp in Yorkshire, and in the 10th Edw. I. paid a fine of one hundred marks for license to marry Margery, widow of Nicholas Corbet, and daughter and coheir of Hugh de Bolebec. In the 24th Edw. I. he succeeded his brother Geoffrey Fitz William in his lands; and was summoned to serve with horse and arms in Scotland in the 25th, 26th, and 27th Edw. I. In the year last mentioned he was constituted Lieutenant of Yorkshire and Warden of the Marches, and was joined in a commission with the Bishop of Durham and others, to fortify the castles in Scotland. He was present at the siege of Carlaverock in the 28th Edw. I., in the first squadron, under the Earl of Lincoln; but the only circumstance relating to him noticed by the Poet is, that he made a fine appearance when dressed in his surcoat of arms; and in the following year he was a party to the Letter to Pope Boniface the Eighth, in which he is styled " Lord of Grimthorp."[h] In the 31st and 34th Edw. I. and 4th Edw. II. he was again in the Scottish wars, in the retinue of Aymer de Valence: in the 7th Edw. II. he was made Governor of Berwick upon Tweed, and was joined with Lord Mowbray and others in the wardenship of the Marches; and in the 8th Edw. II. he was appointed Governor of Carlisle.

The Rolls of Parliament afford the following additional particulars of this Baron. In the 34th Edw. I. his proof of having performed knight's service was respited;[i] in the 8th Edw. II. he was several times appointed with others to hold inquests;[k] in the parliament which met at Lincoln in February, 9 Edw. II. he was a Trier of Petitions from Wales, Ireland, and Scotland;[l] and on the 17th March,

h Appendix to the Fourth Peerage Report.
k Ibid. pp. 288. 304. 306. 342.
i Rot. Parl. vol. I. p. 216 b.
l Ibid. p. 350.

1310, he was one of the peers appointed to regulate the King's household.[m] In the 15th or 16th Edw. II. Alan de Hellebeck, Clerk, complained that Ralph Fitz William had been appointed by the King, guardian of the castles and lands which belonged to Sir Robert Clifford, in the county of Westmoreland, for the which trust he was fully paid by his Majesty, but that he had obliged the petitioner to take victuals from poor people and others by force, to the value of £x., without paying any thing for them, for which payment he was bound; and he consequently prayed a remedy. It was answered that Fitz William was dead, and that he must proceed against his executors.[n]

Upon the death of John Baron Greystock this Baron succeeded by settlement to that lordship, and in 1317 " Greystock" was adopted by his grandson as his surname. The relationship between Fitz William and Lord Greystock is not generally known; hence the following slight pedigree of that family, compiled from Escheats and other evidence, may prove acceptable.

Thomas de Greystock, living 1244. =

Robert de Greystock, ob. circa 1253, s. p.	William de Greystock, brother and heir, ob. 1288. =	Thomas de Greystock.=	Joan.=Ralph Fitz William.
JOHN BARON GREYSTOCK, ob. 1305, s. p. William, ob. ante 1327, s. p.	Margaret de la Val, ob. 1 Edw. III. s. p.	Elizabeth, wife of Thomas Pickering; found to be cousin and one of the heirs of Margaret de la Val, 1 Edw. III.	Alice. = 	William Fitz Ralph. =

Peter Backard; found cousin and one of the heirs of Margaret de la Val, 1 Edw. III.

RALPH FITZ WILLIAM, succeeded to the lordship of Greystock by settlement, 1305. =

Robert Fitz Ralph. =

Ralph de Greystock. =

Thus, though the descendants of this Baron assumed the name and inherited the lands of Greystock, they were not the representatives in blood of that family; unless, which does not appear to be fact, the issue of Thomas de Greystock, uncle of John Baron Greystock, had failed.

Ralph Fitz William was regularly summoned to parliament from the 24th June, 23rd Edw. I. 1295, to the 6th October, 9 Edw. II. 1315. He died " an aged man," says Dugdale, about the feast of All Saints, 1316, and was buried at

m Rot. Parl. vol. I. p. 443.   n Ibid. p. 400.

Nesham in the Palatinate of Durham.[n] By his wife Margery de Bolebec, before
mentioned, he had issue two sons; William, who died without issue in his father's
life-time; and Robert, his successor, who was forty years of age in 1316.

The barony of Fitz William, or, as it was afterwards called, of Greystock, continued vested in the male descendants of the subject of this memoir until the
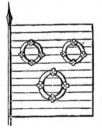 commencement of the reign of Henry the Seventh, when it
fell into abeyance among the daughters and coheirs of the
last Baron; and is now in abeyance between their representatives, the Earl of Carlisle, Lord Stourton, and Lord
Petre.

The arms of Fitz William were, Barry, Argent and Azure,
three chaplets Gules.[o]

WILLIAM DE ROOS.

[PAGE 20.]

Among the Barons of the age in which he lived, William de Roos was equally
conspicuous by his services and his fidelity to his sovereign; and although this
short memoir of him will present little or nothing which can interest our feelings,
it will at least contain ample proof of those qualities which alone commanded

---

[n] Mr. Surtees, in speaking of the relics of Nesham Abbey in his valuable History of Durham,
mentions "a very gallant monumental effigy of a Baron of Greystoke, preserved in Miss Ward's
garden at Hurworth. The effigy is, as usual, recumbent; the hands elevated and clasped on the
breast; the sword hangs from a rich baldric ornamented with quatrefoils, the shield represents a
barry coat semée of crosslets, the legs are mutilated, but rest on a lion, which seems defending
himself against several dogs." Vol. III. p. 260. At the end of that volume is a beautiful engraving of the effigy alluded to, and which was, in all probability, that of the subject of the above
notice.

[o] Page 18; Cotton MSS. Caligula, A. xvii.; and the seal of this Baron, aº 1301.

respect or excited esteem in the barbarous period in which he flourished. If then, the common error be avoided of measuring the conduct of individuals in the thirteenth or fourteenth centuries by the standard of morality which now regulates society; if we do not look for the milder virtues in the character of a soldier, and bear in mind that those pursuits which are at present deemed to dignify mankind, were then thought to be alone suitable to a cloister; and that reckless bravery, a daring and impetuous deportment, a contempt for every species of danger, together with a skilful management of his horse and arms, formed the chief if not the only objects of a nobleman's ambition, the subject of this article will possess some claim to our notice.

He was born about the year 1261, and succeeded his father Robert de Roos, in the 19th Edw. I. at which time he stood in the important situation of claimant of the crown of Scotland. His pretensions to that throne appear, however, to have been grounded on no solid foundations, for his great-grandmother, Isabel, in whose right he claimed, is generally considered to have been the bastard daughter of William the Lion; and consequently upon failure of the legitimate line of that monarch, the issue of his brother, David Earl of Huntingdon, became the next in succession. In the 22nd Edw. I. Roos was summoned to a great council upon the affairs of the realm, and he frequently received writs to attend in the field in subsequent years.

About 1295 a remarkable instance of his fidelity to Edward is recorded. Understanding that his kinsman, Robert de Roos, Lord of the Castle of Werk in Northumberland, intended to join the Scots in their invasion of England, he immediately repaired to the King at Newcastle upon Tyne; and having informed him of the meditated treason, he solicited some assistance to defend that castle, and received a thousand men for that purpose; but the Scots, being told of the circumstance, entered the village of Prestfen in the night, in which they were quartered, and killed the greater part of them. Edward lost not a moment in retrieving this loss, for he advanced from Newcastle and possessed himself of Werk Castle, and in reward of this Baron's loyalty entrusted that fortress to his custody, with power to appoint Robert de Roos, his brother, his deputy during his absence. In the 26th Edw. I. he served in Scotland in the retinue of Ralph de Monthermer; and in the 28th Edw. I. June, 1300, he was present at the siege of Carlaverock, being then thirty-nine years of age; he was on that occasion in the retinue of the Earl of Lincoln; but the Poet takes no other

2 u

notice of him than to describe his banner. In the following year he was a party to the Letter relative to the sovereignty of Scotland from the baronage of England to the Pontiff, in which he is described as " Lord of Hamelak." His services obtained a substantial reward in the 30th Edw. I. by the grant of the castle of Werk, which had been forfeited by the rebellion of its former possessor.

Roos was again in the Scottish wars in the 31st and 34th Edw. I.; and in the 1st Edw. II. was, with Robert de Umfreville Earl of Angus, and Henry Baron Beaumont, constituted the King's Lieutenant in Scotland from Berwick upon Tweed to the river Forth, as also in the Marches of Annandale, Carrick, and Galloway. This office was, however, conferred shortly afterwards upon John de Segrave; and in the 7th Edw. II. he was appointed with others Warden of the West Marches of Scotland. He was commanded to attend in the field for the last time in the 10th Edw. II., and having been summoned to parliament from the 24th June, 23rd Edw. I. 1295, to the 6th Oct. 9 Edw. II. 1315, died in 1316, at the age of little more than fifty-five, and was buried in the Priory of Kirkham. By Maud, daughter and coheiress of John de Vaux, he left issue William, his son and heir, then of full age; John, a younger son; and a daughter, Ann, wife of Pain de Tibetot.

The present representatives of this Baron, whose descendants in the male line enjoyed his honors for several centuries, are Sir Henry Hunloke, Bart.; George Earl of Essex; and Charlotte Fitz Gerald de Roos, the present Baroness de Roos, in whose favour the abeyance of the barony was terminated on the 9th May, 1806.

The arms of Roos are, Gules, three water bougets Argent.[p]

---

p Page 20; Cotton MSS. Caligula, A. xvii.; and the seal of this Baron, aº 1301.

HUGH POINTZ.

[PAGE 20.]

Less appears to be known of this Baron than of almost any other person of his rank who is noticed by Dugdale.

He was the son and heir of Nicholas Pointz of the county of Somerset, and succeeded his father in his lands in the 1st Edw. I. 1273, at which time he was of full age. In the 5th, 10th, 11th, and 15th Edw. I. he was summoned to attend with horse and arms in Wales;[q] and was present in the wars of Gascony in the 25th Edw. I.; and in those of Scotland in the 26th, 27th, and 28th Edw. I. In June in the year last mentioned, anno 1300, he was at the siege of Carlaverock, when he must have been at least forty-eight years old; and, though the Poet in speaking of him merely describes his banner, yet when noticing Brian Fitz Alan, who bore precisely the same arms, he says that that circumstance had frequently been the subject of a dispute between them. This fact will be again alluded to, both in the account of Fitz Alan and in the notes, because it is illustrative of the custom at the period that no two persons should bear the same banner. In the 28th Edw. I. Pointz was a party to the Letter from the Barons to the Pope, in which document he is described as " Lord of Cory Malet,"[r] a manor which he inherited in right of his grandmother, Helewise, sister and coheiress of William Baron Malet, and for the relief of which he paid fifty pounds in the 11th Edw. I. It appears that the seal which he affixed to that document belonged to his son, for his arms are charged with a label of five points, and is inscribed " S. Nicholai Poyntz."[s] In the 35th Edw. I. he petitioned relative to his lands in Somersetshire;[t] and, having been summoned to parliament from the 24th June, 23 Edw. I. 1295, to the 26th August, 1 Edw. II. 1307, died in the

---

[q] Appendix to the First Peerage Report, pp. 38. 43. 48. 54.

[r] Appendix to the Fourth Peerage Report.   [s] Archæologia, vol. XXI. p. 216.

[t] Rot. Parl. vol. I. p. 196.

same year. By ——, daughter of ——, this Baron had issue Nicholas, his son and heir, who was thirty years of age at his father's demise, and who was regularly summoned to parliament until his death, when his son, Hugh, inherited the barony. He died in 1333, and left one son, Nicholas Poyntz, who was never summoned to parliament, and died s. p. m., leaving two daughters and coheirs; Margaret, who married Sir John de Newburgh; and Avicia, who was the wife of John Barry, but her issue having failed, the barony created by the first writ to the subject of this memoir, is now vested in the descendants of the said Margaret Lady Newburgh.

The arms of Pointz were, Barry, Or and Gules.[u]

JOHN DE BEAUCHAMP.

[PAGE 20.]

Although the life of John de Beauchamp was not extended to a great age, he served under three sovereigns; but, so far as the barren facts which are preserved of him allow of the inference, his career was undistinguished by any action of great importance. During the turbulent scenes which he witnessed, he appears to have conducted himself with more than ordinary prudence, and to have escaped with more than ordinary good fortune the vicissitudes which attended so many of his contemporaries.

He was born in 1273, being ten years of age when he succeeded his father in the 12th Edw. I., and the first notice taken of him by Dugdale is in the 29th

---

u Pp. 20 and 36; Cotton MSS. Caligula, A. xvii.; and the seal of this Baron, aᵒ 1301.

Edw. I., when he obtained a grant from the King of a weekly market and yearly fair in his manor of Hache in Somersetshire; but it is certain that he had fulfilled some of the duties of his station some years before. In the 24th Edw. I., about which time he became of age, he was summoned to serve with horse and arms against the Scots;[x] in January following he was commanded to attend a great council at Salisbury;[y] and in the same year to be at London to accompany the expedition into Gascony.[z] In the 26th and 27th Edw. I. he was again summoned to the Scottish wars;[a] and in June, 1300, was present at the siege of Carlaverock. His deportment is described to have displayed grace and ardour, and as he was then but little more than twenty-seven years of age, we may conclude that his personal appearance attracted much attention. In the 29th Edw. I. Beauchamp was a party to the Letter from the Barons to Pope Boniface, in which he is styled " Lord of Hache;"[b] and in the 34th year of that monarch we are told that he received the honor of knighthood with Prince Edward, the King's eldest son, but it is much more probable that it was the son of this Baron who was then honored with that dignity, for it is almost incredible that he should not have been knighted many years before. Beauchamp was summoned to the field upon numerous occasions during the reign of Edward the Second; and in the 14th Edw. II. he succeeded his mother in her lands, at which time he is said to have been forty years old, but his age must have been nearer forty-seven, as he is stated to have been ten at his father's death in 1283, and which is corroborated by his having a writ of service addressed to him as early as the 24th Edw. I., when, it is evident, he was of full age. In the 2nd Edw. II. he paid a fine of xx marks to be allowed to amortize certain lands at Stoke in Somersetshire, for the support of five chaplains to sing in the chapel of St. Nicholas of that place.[c]

John de Beauchamp was summoned to parliament from the 29th December, 28 Edw. I. 1299, to the 22nd January, 9 Edw. III. 1336, in which year he died; leaving by Johanna, daughter of —— Chenduit, two sons; John, his successor in his honors, then aged thirty; and Thomas, his second son.[d]

---

[x] Appendix to the First Peerage Report, p. 72. [y] Ibid. p. 78. [z] Ibid. p. 80.
[a] Ibid. pp. 98. 100. 104. 107. 110. [b] Appendix to the Fourth Peerage Report.
[c] Rot. Parl. vol. I. p. 274 b. [d] Harl. MSS. 1559.

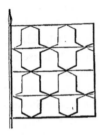

In 1360 the barony of Beauchamp fell into abeyance between the granddaughters of this Baron; namely, Cecily, who married, first, Sir Roger Seymour, ancestor of the Duke of Somerset, and, secondly, Sir Gilbert Turbeville; and Eleanor, the wife of John Merrett.

The arms of Beauchamp of Somerset are, Vaire.[e]

KING EDWARD THE FIRST.

[PAGE 22.]

Neither the limited space to which the memoirs of the individuals who were at Carlaverock must be confined, nor the immediate object with which they are introduced, will justify even a biographical sketch of this monarch. The life of a sovereign is the history of his reign; hence it would be hopeless in this place to attempt to give any satisfactory account of him whose name is so completely identified with the annals of this country. All then which will be said of Edward will relate to the information respecting him which is afforded by the Poet. At the time when he is spoken of he had just completed his sixty-first year, and we learn that he led the third squadron of the army which invested Carlaverock castle in June 1300. His conduct towards his enemies, the Poet says, resembled the lions on his banner, for to them he was fierce, haughty, and cruel; whilst his vengeance was terrible to those who excited his displeasure. Towards such, however, as submitted to his power, his kindness was soon rekindled, and he possessed every qualification which should distinguish the chieftain of noble personages. It is worthy of observation that the simile in the

---

e P. 20; Cotton MSS. Caligula, A. xvii.; and the seal of this Baron, a° 1301.

Poem respecting the royal arms, likewise occurs in some contemporary Latin verses lately published from the City archives :

Ref Anglor' nobilis vocatus Edwardus
Feror est et stabilis tanquam leopardus,
Fortis et non debilis, velox et non tardus,
Senciet id flebilis pomposus Picardus.

JOHN OF BRITTANY.

[PAGE 22.]

John de Dreux, afterwards Earl of Richmond, was the youngest son of John Duke of Brittany, by Beatrice Plantagenet, second daughter of King Henry the Third. He was born in 1266,[f] and we learn from the Poem that he was placed under the protection of his uncle, King Edward the First, at a very early age; and that he served him with great zeal and fidelity. The first information which is recorded of him by Dugdale is in 1293, when he states that he was General of the English army then sent into Gascony. In the following year, being the King's Lieutenant in Brittany, he was joined in commission with the Seneschal of Aquitaine and others to conclude a league with the King of Castile, upon which mission he accordingly proceeded. In a skirmish with the French near Bourdeaux in the 24th Edw. I. he was taken prisoner, and in the 27th Edw. I. as a reward for his eminent merits, he received a grant of one thousand pounds per annum out of the exchequer until a better provision should be made for him. At the siege of Carlaverock, in the 28th Edw. I., he is commemorated by the Poet of the event, and the particulars which he gives of him are important materials for his memoir. It has been just observed, upon that authority, that

---

[f] Anderson's Royal Genealogies.

John de Dreux was placed with the English monarch when a child, and that he had repaid his uncle's kindness by devoting himself to his service. He was, we learn, handsome and amiable, and occupied a situation in the march close to the King. The courageous behaviour of his followers also receives the Poet's commendation, for he tells us that they were fierce and daring as lions of the mountains.[g] In the 33rd Edw. I. he was constituted Lieutenant of Scotland, with a grant of three thousand marks per annum out of the issues of that kingdom ;[h] and in the same year he was summoned to parliament as a Baron, by writ addressed to " John de Brittany junior," tested at Wymingweld on the 13th July, 33 Edw. I. 1305 ; shortly after which, namely, in the parliament which met at Westminster on the Sunday next after the feast of St. Matthew following, he was appointed a Trier of Petitions.[i] On the 15th October, 1306, he was created Earl of Richmond, and was summoned to parliament by that title on the 3rd of the ensuing November. He was one of the mainpernors for Amaric de St. Amand, who was a prisoner in the Tower of London in the 33rd Edw. I.;[k] and was present in March, 1305, at the non-allowance of a papal provision.[l] On the 22nd of March, 35 Edw. I. 1307, he was commanded to attend Edward the King's son into France ;[m] in the same year he was forbidden to disturb Eleanor de Genovere in the enjoyment of her dower of the third part of the manor of Biwell ;[n] and in the 1st of Edw. II. was again constituted Lieutenant of Scotland. On the 17th March, 3 Edw. II. 1310, the Earl of Richmond was one of the peers appointed to regulate the royal household ;[o] in the 6th Edw. II. he was nominated one of the commissioners to open the parliament, when he is styled the King's dearest kinsman ;[p] and in the 12th Edw. II. was one of the noblemen engaged in the treaty between the Earl of Lancaster and the King.[q] The Earl was taken prisoner by the Scots in the 13th Edw. II. ; and Dugdale relates, upon the authority of Walsingham, that the King required for his ransom a subsidy in parliament in the 17th Edw. II., but he could not obtain it, and the money was raised by contribution from his tenants. He had, however, recovered

---

g P. 81.   h Rot. Pat. 33 Edw. I. m. 6, cited in Banks's Stemmata Anglicana.
i Rot. Parl. vol. I. p. 159.   k Ibid. p. 176 b.   l Ibid. p. 179 b.
m Fœdera, N. E. vol. I. p. 1012. n Rot. Parl. vol. I. p. 199 a. o Ibid. p. 443 b.
p Ibid. p. 448 a.   q Ibid. p. 454.

his liberty in the 18th Edw. II., when he was one of the ambassadors sent by
Edward to the King of France on the subject of the Duchy of Acquitaine.

These are the only facts which are known of one of the most eminent personages in the thirteenth and fourteenth centuries, but it is necessary to add that he
has been suspected of having designed to murder the Queen and her son Prince
Edward. No evidence of the truth or injustice of this charge can now be
adduced, and it would therefore be idle to enter into any discussion on the
subject.

The Earl of Richmond survived the accession of Edward the Third several
years, but the only circumstance related of him after that event is that, in the
1st Edw. III., he obtained a license to grant the Earldom of Richmond to his
brother Arthur Duke of Brittany; that in the 5th Edw. III. he received a similar
permission to grant to Mary St. Paul, Countess of Pembroke, some castles and
manors belonging to that earldom; that in the 7th Edw. III. leave was given him
to reside beyond the sea; and that he bestowed £300 on the building of the
church of the Grey Friars in London, and presented it with several valuable
jewels and ornaments.

This celebrated nobleman is said to have died on the 17th January, 1334,[r]
though the inquisition on his demise was not taken until the 8th Edw. III. anno
1336. He was never married; and was buried in the church of the Cordeliers
at Nantes.[s] The Earl was about sixty-eight years of age at his decease, and was
consequently thirty-four when he served under King Edward at the siege of
Carlaverock.

The arms borne by the Earl of Richmond were, Checky Or and Azure, a bordure Gules charged with lions passant gardant of the First; a quarter Ermine:[t]
or as they are blazoned in the contemporary MS. which has been so frequently
referred to, " Les armes de Garine, a un quarter de Ermine, od la bordure de
Engleterre."[u] This coat presents an example of the arrangement of different

---

[r] Anderson's Royal Genealogies; but according to the Histoire de Bretagne, tome I. p. 243,
ed. 1750, he died on the 7th January 1333-4.

[s] Histoire de Bretagne, ed. 1750, tome I. p. 243, where he is also stated to have presented to
the cathedral church of that city a cross of gold enriched with a large piece of the true cross and
many relics. Other authorities assert that the Earl was buried at Vannes in Brittany.

[t] P. 22. [u] Cotton MSS. Caligula, A. xvii.

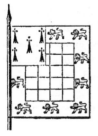

arms upon the same shield before the system of quartering was adopted, which is too curious to be allowed to pass unobserved. The arms of Dreux were checky Or and Azure: on the marriage of that house with the heiress of Brittany, they placed the coat of that family, Ermine, on a quarter; and, as a distinction, the ensigns of the subject of this memoir were surrounded by a border of England, his mother's arms.

JOHN DE BARR.

[PAGE 24.]

The trouble which has been taken to obtain some particulars of this individual has not, unfortunately, been attended with the slightest success; and it can only be conjectured from his arms that he was one of the ten children of Thibaut second Count of Bar, who died about 1296, by Jean de Toci.[x] As Henry Count de Bar, the eldest son of Thibaut, had a few years before married Eleanor, the daughter of King Edward the First, it is highly probable that the brother of his

son-in-law served in his retinue; and as his name occurs immediately after the King's nephew, John of Brittany, it would appear that he was also attached to the royal person in consequence of that alliance.

The arms of John de Barr were those of his family, Azure, semée of cross crosslets, two barbels endorsed Or, within a bordure engrailed Gules.[y]

---

x L'Art de Verifier des Dates.

y P. 24. In the church of Berwick St. John in Wiltshire, is the effigy of a knight in mail armour, whose shield is charged with the coat of Barr, and apparently within a bordure. It might possibly have been this individual, though the conjecture is unsupported by any other evidence than what the arms present.

WILLIAM DE GRANDISON.

[PAGE 24.]

The life of William de Grandison was not distinguished by any event which entitles him to consideration.   He was the younger brother of Otho de Grandison, and the first notice which occurs of him is that, for his faithful services though in a menial capacity to Edmond Earl of Lancaster, that nobleman re_ warded him with the manors of Radley and Menstreworth in Gloucestershire, by deed dated on the 11th October, 10 Edw. I. 1282.   In the following year he obtained a confirmation of that grant from the King, and also of such estovers as he was accustomed to have in the forest of Dene for repairing of his floodgates in that manor.   He petitioned to be recompensed for his loss in some premises in Dimock in the 18th Edw. I.,[z] and in the same year held an inquest at Ewelowe.[a]   In the 20th Edw. I. license was given him to make a castle of his house at Asperton in Herefordshire; and in the 22nd Edw. I. he was in the expedition into Gascony.   From the 25th to the 31st Edw. I. Grandison was frequently in the Scottish wars; and in June 1300 the Poem records that he was present at the siege of Carlaverock.   No notice of his person or character occurs, and we can only infer from other circumstances that he could not have been then less than forty years of age.   He was summoned to parliament from the 6th Feb. 27 Edw. I. 1299, to the 10th Oct. 19 Edw. II. 1325, and is mentioned as being present at the parliament which met at Carlisle in the octaves of St. Hilary, in the 35th Edw. I. 1307.[b]   It appears from the Rolls of Parliament that he petitioned for a writ *de allocate* relative to some debts due from him to the Crown,[c] and that he was on one occasion bail for his brother Otho,[d] but the precise years when these circumstances took place cannot be ascertained.   This Baron was again summoned to serve in the wars of Scotland in the 8th Edw. II., in which year he obtained an allowance of £103. 6s. 8d., to be paid out of the Exchequer, in recompense of some horses which he had lost in Gascony in the

---

z Rot. Parl. vol. I. p. 61.   a Ibid. p. 64.   h Ibid. p. 188 b.
c Ibid. p. 462 b.   d Ibid. p. 464 b.

service of King Edward the First, the value of which was certified by Henry Earl of Lincoln, who was then Lieutenant of that province.

William de Grandison married Sybilla, youngest daughter and coheiress of John Baron Tregoz. Dugdale states that they exchanged the manors of Idenne and Iham in Sussex with Edward the First for a rent of £46. 6s. 3d. out of the manors of Dertford and Cranstede in Kent, but it is manifest from their petition to the King in the 8th Edw. III. that they had exchanged the manors in question for that of Dymok; for, after stating that such was the case, they complained that the tenants of Dymok had never attorned to them, and entreated that they might be compelled to do so.[e] With that record of this Baron our information respecting him closes, excepting that he died in 1355, leaving three sons: Peter, who succeeded him in his honors, and who was then forty years of age; John, Bishop of Exeter; and Otho; also three daughters: Katherine, wife of the Earl of Salisbury; Agnes, who married John de Northwode; and Mabel, who was the wife of ——— Pateshull. Peter, the next Baron, died s. p. l. in 1358, when that dignity devolved upon John, Bishop of Exeter, his brother, upon whose demise, in July, 1369, Thomas de Grandison, his nephew, son

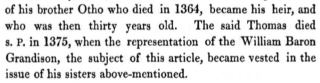

of his brother Otho who died in 1364, became his heir, and who was then thirty years old. The said Thomas died s. p. in 1375, when the representation of the William Baron Grandison, the subject of this article, became vested in the issue of his sisters above-mentioned.

The arms of Grandison are, Paly Argent and Azure, on a bend Gules three eagles displayed Or.[f]

---

e Rot. Parl. vol. II. p. 83.　　　f P. 24; and Cotton MSS. Caligula, A. xvii.

ELIAS D'AUBIGNY.

[PAGE 24.]

The information given by Sir William Dugdale of this Baron scarcely extends to six lines; nor can much be added to his statement. He succeeeded his brother Philip in the Barony in the 22nd Edw. I. 1294, at which time he was thirty years old;[g] and, from the only notice which occurs of him on the Rolls of Parliament, we learn that he was born out of the realm; for in the 23rd Edw. I. the King, in consideration of the services which he and his ancestors had rendered to him and his predecessors, granted that in all his courts he should be considered an Englishman, or, in other words, he was then naturalized.[h] He was summoned to parliament from the 2nd Nov. 23 Edw. I. 1295, to the 22nd Jan. 33 Edw. I. 1305; and it appears from the Poem that he was present at Carlaverock in June, 1300, when he was about thirty-six years of age, and upon which occasion his courteous deportment is alluded to. He died in the 33rd Edw. I. 1305;[i] and, though Dugdale says that he, " with Hawise his wife, conferred on the canons of Newhus, in the county of Lincoln, for the health of the soul of William de Albini (who gave them Saxelby and other lands in that county), all their right in the church of Saxelby, viz. the third part thereof, with certain lands in Dryholme, on the south side of Fossedike; his sons, Oliver and Ralph, confirming the grant;" it is evident, from the inquisition on his death, that his wife's name was Johanna, and that Ralph, his son and heir, was then only eleven years old.[k]

Ralph Daubeney, the son and heir of this Baron, who did not become of age until 1315, received but one writ of summons to parliament; and none of his descendants were deemed Barons of the realm until the reign of Henry the Seventh,

---

[g] Esch. eod. ann. [h] Rot. Parl. vol. I. p. 135 a. [i] Esch. eod. ann.
[k] Esch. 12 Edw. II. No. 14.

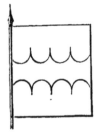

when Giles Daubeney, the great-great-grandson and heir of the Baron who was at Carlaverock, was created Baron Daubeney by patent, dated 12th March, 1486. His present representatives are the coheirs of the barony of Fitz Warine.

The arms of Daubeney are, Gules, a fess engrailed Argent.¹

EURMENIONS DE LA BRETTE.

[PAGE 26.]

Though evidently not a native of England, few persons were so constantly engaged in the diplomatic affairs of this country in the fourteenth century as this individual; and from one circumstance, which will be particularly noticed, it would appear that he enjoyed the highest reputation for sagacity and wisdom in the councils of Edward the First and Second. All which is known of him has been derived from the Fœdera, hence the few particulars which have been ascertained stand upon unquestionable authority; and they undoubtedly entitle him to much consideration.

La Brett was descended from a noble family in Gascony, and the earliest record in which he is mentioned informs us of the name of his father; for on the 4th April, 1289, by the appellation of our faithful valette, son of the late Amaneus de le Brett, Knight, the King, in reward of his services, granted him the parish

---

¹ P. 24; and Cotton MSS. Caligula, A. xvii. The arms of Daubeney are usually blazoned, Gules, four fusils in fess Argent; but see some observations in the Gentleman's Magazine, vol. XCVI. part I. p. 410, attempting to prove that such blazon is a corruption from the original bearing, both in this and in many other instances of similar charges; for example, Dinham, Marshal, Raleigh, &c.

of Pissons and other lands in Gascony and Acquitaine.[m] On the 3rd July, 1294, he was appointed one of the ambassadors from Edward to treat with those of the King of Spain;[n] and he received a similar appointment to the Pope in January, 1296, in which he is styled a Knight.[o] A few years afterwards, namely on the 22nd April, 1299, he was constituted one of the commissioners for placing certain lands and inhabitants of Gascony in the hands of the Pope;[p] and he was one of the ambassadors who executed the treaty with the Pontiff at Mostreul sur Mer on Friday before the feast of St. John the Baptist in the same year.[q]

The next occasion on which he is mentioned is in the preceding Poem, from which we learn that he was at the siege of Carlaverock; but all that is said of him relates to his banner, nor is there any evidence from which his age can be ascertained. On the 26th Sept. 1300, by the description of Amaneus Lord of la Brette, he, the Earl of Lincoln, Otho de Grandison, and Hugh le Despenser, were appointed ambassadors to the Pope;[r] and on the 25th April, and 29th October, 1307, he was selected by Edward to treat for peace between England and France.[s] The latter appointment is thus alluded to by Peter de Langtoft:

A° M.CCCII. For perille of suilk goynges the king purveied to go,
Sir Jon of Hastynges he was first of tho,
And Sir Emery the Brette, to Bascoyne forto wende,
To bide the terme sette, the treus how it suld ende.[t]

On the 6th April, 1305, he was ordered to treat with a French prelate for the exchange of certain castles;[u] and in the same year was nominated, with the Bishops of Chester and Lincoln, the Earl of Warwick, Lord le Despenser, Otho de Grandison, and others, to deliver a message from the King to parliament.[x] Upon the young Prince Edward's voyage to France in March, 1307, La Brette, with the Earls of Richmond and Warwick and other noblemen, were commanded to attend him.[y] It is evident that he survived the accession of Edward the Second, but the only notice of him in that reign deserving of atten-

[m] Fœdera, N. E. tome I. p. 708. [n] Ibid. p. 805. [o] Ibid. p. 834. [p] Ibid. p.906.
[q] Ibid. p. 907. [r] Ibid. p. 922. [s] Ibid. pp. 940. 945. [t] P. 318.
[u] Fœdera, vol. I. p. 971. [x] Rot. Parl. vol. I. p. 210 b. [y] Fœdera, vol. I. p. 1012.

tion, is one which tends to establish the high opinion that was entertained of him; for by a writ tested on the 5th April, 1312, the King, from a full reliance on his former services both to his father and himself, entreated him in the most urgent manner to attend a council on some important affairs.[z] His name again occurs in February, 1314,[a] but nothing more can with certainty be said of him, though, as it is just possible from the dates that it might have been the same person, it is necessary to observe that a Sir Amayen de la Brett, whose arms were, Gules, a lion passant gardant in chief Or, was at the siege of Calais, with a retinue of three knights, twelve esquires, and seventeen hobilers, under Edward the Third, in 1346;[b] and that the name of the "Sieur de la Brett" often occurs on the Rolls of Parliament about the same time.[c] In all probability, however, the Sir Amayen last mentioned was the son of the subject of this article, for if living he must have been nearly eighty years of age.

The merits of Eurmenions de la Brette can only be inferred from his services, and this criterion justifies the opinion that he was celebrated for his talents in council rather than for his prowess in the field. Of his marriage, issue, and

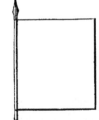

death, nothing is known; but, from the fact just mentioned, it would seem that he was succeeded in his lordship in Gascony by a son of his own name, and who also appears to have been a person of much consideration.

The arms of Eurmenions de la Brette were merely Gules.

---

[z] Fœdera, vol. II. p. 163.   [a] Ibid. p. 242.

[b] Mores' Nomina et Insignia Gentilitia, &c. p. 96.

[c] Vol. II. pp. 222 b. 236 b. 299 b. See also Calend. Rot. Pat. 34 Edw. III.

HUGH DE VERE.

[PAGE 26.]

Few of the individuals who were at Carlaverock were so distinguished by their birth and actions as Hugh de Vere. He was a younger son of Robert Earl of Oxford, by Alice, the daughter and heiress of Gilbert de Sandford. The first notice which occurs of him is in the 21st Edw. I., when, being in the wars of France, he was appointed Governor of St. Cyverine; and in the following year he was present at the ratification of the peace made between England and that country. In the 25th Edw. I. he was sent, with the Bishops of Winchester and Ely, the Earl of Pembroke, and others, to treat for peace with France, and remained in Gascony in the King's service for some time. He was ordered to Rome upon an important mission in the 26th Edw. I., and in the 29th Edw. I. was employed with the Earl of Warren to treat with the French ambassadors relative to a peace with Scotland. At the siege of Carlaverock, in June, 1300, this Baron served in the third squadron, and the Poet's description of him and his banner are equally minute. In the February following Vere was a party to the Letter from the Barons to the Pontiff, in which he is styled " Lord of Swains-chaump ;"[p] in the 33rd Edw. I. he was one of the manucaptors of Almaric de St. Amand, who was then a prisoner in the Tower of London ;[q] and in March in the same year he was present at the non-allowance of a papal provision.[r] He was again in the Scottish wars in the 34th Edw. I.; and upon the accession of Edward II. he and his wife were commanded by writ, tested on the 8th Feb. 1 Edw. II. 1308, to attend the King and Queen's coronation.[s] Hugh de Vere was summoned to parliament from the 6th Feb. 27 Edw. I. 1299, to the 3rd March, 11 Edw. II. 1318, and is presumed to have died about the 12th Edw. II. without issue.

He married, before the 25th Edw. I., Dionysia, daughter and eventually sole

---

P Appendix to the Fourth Peerage Report.   q Rot. Parl. vol I. p. 176.   r Ibid. p. 179 b.
s Fœdera, N. E. vol. II. p. 31.

3 A

heiress of Warine de Montchensy, and obtained livery of the lands of her brother, who died in that year, as a reward, Dugdale says, for his services, as she was not then of full age. This lady died without issue in the 7th Edw. II., when Aymer de Valence, afterwards Earl of Pembroke, was found to be her heir.

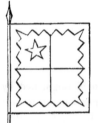

The arms of Hugh de Vere were, Quarterly Gules and Or, in the first quarter a mullet Argent; the whole within a bordure indented Sable.[t] The border was assumed as a difference from the arms of his brother the Earl of Oxford.

JOHN DE RIVERS.

[PAGE 26.]

As this family, though unquestionably Barons of the realm, escaped the attention of Sir William Dugdale, but very little is known of them. John de Rivers, who was at the siege of Carlaverock, is stated to have been the son and heir of a person of the same name, and to have succeeded him in his lands in the 22nd Edw. I.[u] Besides the circumstances already mentioned, all which is recorded of him is, that he was summoned to parliament from the 6th Feb. 27 Edw..I. 1299, to the 26th August, 1 Edw. II. 1307;[x] that he was a party to the Letter from the Barons of England, in February, 1301, to Pope Boniface the Eighth, in which he is styled " Lord of Angre,"[y] but his seal is not attached to that

---

[t] Page 26; Cotton MSS. Caligula, A. xvii.; a contemporary painting on glass in the south window of the chancel of Dorchester church in Oxfordshire; aud the seal of this Baron aⁿ 1301. From the latter it would appear that his crest was a boar passant. See some observations on the point in the Archæologia, vol. XXI.

[u] Banks's Stemmata Anglicana.   [x] Appendix to the First Peerage Report.
[y] Appendix to the Fourth Peerage Report.

document; and that in the 4th Edw. II. he paid ten marks for license to enfeoff John, his son and heir, of his said manor of Aungre.[z]

This Baron died in 1311, leaving his son John his heir, who was also summoned to parliament, and died circa 1339. Edmund, his son, died s. p. m., whose daughter, Katherine, was his heir. She was twice married; first, to William Lenthall, by whom she had a son, John, who died on the 13th Feb. 17 Hen. VI. s. p.; and, secondly, to John Hall, but it does not appear that she had any issue by him. Upon the death of John Lenthall above mentioned, in the 17th Hen. VI. William Bulkeley, of Eaton, co. Chester, son and heir of John, eldest son of ——— Bulkeley, by Christian, daughter of John second Baron Rivers, and grand-daughter of the Baron who was at Carlaverock, became his representative.

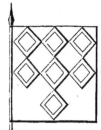

The arms of Rivers, according to the Poem, were, Mas-cally Or and Gules;[a] but the contemporary MS. so fre-quently cited states that they were, " De Goules, a vj mascles de Or;[b] and which Glover evidently deemed to be the correct blazon, as he has drawn them in a very similar manner in the MS. from which the annexed wood-cut was copied.

---

[z] Banks's Stemmata Anglicana, on the authority of Orig. 4 Edw. II. rot. 18.
[a] Page 26.   [b] Cotton MSS. Caligula, A. xvii.

MAURICE DE CREON.

[PAGE 26.]

It is extremely difficult, even if it be not impossible, to identify this knight;
for, although the family whose name and arms[c] he bore were not only one of
the most illustrious in Anjou, but were nearly related to King Edward the First,
the attempt to ascertain in what way he was connected with it has wholly failed;
nor has any thing concerning his life or character been discovered. The genealogy of the house of Craon is minutely detailed by Monsieur Augustin du Paz,
in his "Histoire Genealogique de plusieurs Maisons Illustres de Bretagne," from
which it appears that Maurice Sire de Creon, son and heir of Maurice de Creon,
by Isabel de la Marche, sister of William de Valence Earl of Pembroke, and
uterine sister of Henry the Third,[d] died in February, 1293, hence it is impossible
it could have been the individual mentioned by the Poet. No other Maurice
occurs in the pedigree until the birth of the grandson of that Baron in 1309,
consequently no light is thrown on the point by that work. In July, 1280,
Morice Sire de Craon, and Greforoi de Grenville, two of Edward the First's

---

c The arms of Craon of Anjou were, Lozengy Or and Gules, but the terms lozengè and mascallè
were often used synonymously in the fourteenth century.

d This marriage is thus proved by records, from which it will also be seen that the said Isabel
remarried the Duke of Burgundy, a fact unnoticed by Du Paz, from whom however we learn that
she died on the 14th January, 1299-1300, and was buried in the dress of the order of St. Francis
in the chapel of St. John the Baptist which her son Maurice de Creon had built in the church of
St. Francis in Angers. P. 755.

    Fœdera, vol. I. p. 278.—The grant of a pension to " our sister Isabel, who was the wife of Mau-
rice de Craon, of c marks per annum," 10th July, 35 Hen. III. 1251. See also the Calendar
to the Patent Rolls.

    Calend. Rot. Pat. 40 Hen. III.—" Marriage between Isabel de Croun, sister of the King, and
the Duke of Burgundy."

    Ibid. 54 Hen. III.—The King restored Maurice de Croun, his nephew, to the manor of Bourne,
which, the record states, had belonged to *Almaric his father*, though it is evident, from the
above extracts from that Calendar, as well as from the Fœdera, that his father's name was
Maurice. Query, if it should not have been, " Almaric his grandfather?"

Knights, addressed a letter to him, reporting their proceedings with the King of France relative to the King of Castile ;[e] and in a letter from Edward to the French monarch on the same subject, dated in 1282, he states that he had ordered " our cousin Mons[r] Morice de Croun, and our subject John de Greilly," to represent to him that, in consequence of the wars in which he was engaged in Wales, he could not assist him against the King of Spain.[f] But these notices apparently refer to the Baron who is said by Du Paz to have died in 1293 ; and it is uncertain whether the Maurice de Craon who was a guardian of Robert de Montalt in 1290,[g] was the knight who served at the siege of Carlaverock, though it is extremely probable. As the Poet merely calls him the good Maurice de Creon, and states that his

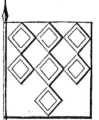

arms were the same as those borne by John de Rivers, no information is afforded on the point in question, and it would therefore be useless to say any more upon the subject.

The arms of Maurice de Craon appear to have been, Mascally Or and Gules ; or, more probably, Gules, seven mascles Or.[h]

ROBERT DE CLIFFORD.

[PAGES 27 AND 28.]

Among the Barons of Edward the First's court there was one, who, whilst equal in birth and possessions to any of his compeers, stood almost unrivalled in the splendour and extent of his services. In every military event he is recorded to have occupied a distinguished station ; nor for a long series of years did a

---

e Fœdera, tome I. p. 583.   f Ibid. p. 607.   g Rot. Parl. vol. I. p. 39 a.
. h Page 26.

circumstance of the least importance occur without that individual having shared in a pre-eminent degree in its dangers or responsibility. In this description every one who is at all acquainted with the history of the commencement of the four-teenth century cannot fail to recognize Robert de Clifford; and these remarks are not only justified by the pages of chroniclers and the national records, but they are corroborated by the Poet of the siege of Carlaverock, who has devoted a larger space to him than to any other person, and in the most emphatic and poetical manner says that he was possessed of every possible merit.

His lineage being particularly alluded to, some attention must be paid to the subject, both because it illustrates a passage in the poem, and evinces the critical knowledge of genealogy possessed by the writer. Why Scotland could testify his exalted birth is not easily explained, excepting that his possessions were in the vicinity of that kingdom; nor is the exploit which is said to have been per-formed by the Earl Marshal at Constantinople in slaying an unicorn, which probably referred to a tradition familiar at the time of some deed of one of the Marshal family in the Holy Land, elsewhere commemorated; but his descent from that house " through his mother" is thus shewn :

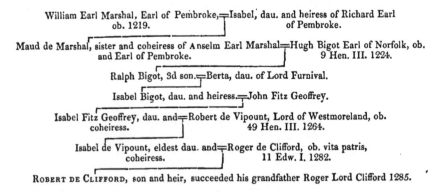

William Earl Marshal, Earl of Pembroke,═Isabel, dau. and heiress of Richard Earl
ob. 1219. of Pembroke.

Maud de Marshal, sister and coheiress of Anselm Earl Marshal═Hugh Bigot Earl of Norfolk, ob.
and Earl of Pembroke. 9 Hen. III. 1224.

Ralph Bigot, 3d son.═Berta, dau. of Lord Furnival.

Isabel Bigot, dau. and heiress.═John Fitz Geoffrey.

Isabel Fitz Geoffrey, dau. and═Robert de Vipount, Lord of Westmoreland, ob.
coheiress. 49 Hen. III. 1264.

Isabel de Vipount, eldest dau. and═Roger de Clifford, ob. vita patris,
coheiress. 11 Edw. I. 1282.

ROBERT DE CLIFFORD, son and heir, succeeded his grandfather Roger Lord Clifford 1285.

Robert de Clifford was the eldest son of Roger de Clifford, who was acci-dentally slain between Snowdon and Anglesey in 1280, and whose merits are highly eulogised by the Poet. He was born about Easter, April, 1274; and in the 14th Edw. I. 1286, he succeeded his grandfather in his baronial honours, being then twelve years of age. In the 13th Edw. I. he was found to be one of the heirs of Ralph dè Gaugy, and paid £100 for his relief; after which, the next circumstance which has been found recorded of him is, that he was summoned to attend the King with horse and arms in his expedition beyond the sea on the 4th May, 25 Edw. I. 1297;[i] and on the 26th September following he was ordered to be at Carlisle, similarly equipped to serve against the Scots, at the ensuing feast of Pentecost;[k] but Dugdale asserts that he was present at the battle of Dunbar in the 24th Edw. I.; that in the 25th Edw. I. he was sent with a hundred men at arms and twenty thousand foot from Carlisle to plunder in Scotland, and that after much slaughter he returned with considerable booty on Christmas eve. In that year he was also appointed Justice of all the King's forests beyond the Trent; in the 26th Edw. I. he was made Governor of Nottingham Castle; and in the 27th Edw. I., being constituted the King's Lieutenant and Captain General in the counties of Cumberland, Westmoreland, and Lancaster, and throughout Annandale and the Marches of Scotland, he was joined in commission with the Bishop of Durham and others to consider of the means of garrisoning the castles in that kingdom, and for guarding the Marches. Clifford was again summoned to the Scottish wars on the 7th May, 27 Edw. I. 1299;[l] and received his first writ to parliament on the 29th December in the same year.

The early age at which this nobleman was entrusted with these important duties is worthy of remark, for he did not attain his majority till 1295, and consequently could not have been above twenty-five when he was thus honoured with his sovereign's confidence, a fact which speaks forcibly in his praise. It was at this period of his life that he was noticed in the Poem, and as his conduct at Carlaverock is wholly passed over by his former biographers, it claims especial regard in this memoir. After stating that he served in the third squadron, which was led by the King in person, and extolling Clifford's valour, descent, and prudence, the writer adds, that if he were a young maiden he would bestow on him his heart and person in consideration of his renown. During the siege we are told that he particularly distinguished himself,[m] and was rewarded by being appointed Governor of the Castle when it surrendered, in consequence of which his banner was placed on its battlements.[n] Clifford was a party to the Letter from the Barons to Pope Boniface in the 29th Edw. I. February, 1301, in which

---

[i] Appendix to the First Peerage Report, p. 80.   [k] Ibid. p. 100.   [l] Ibid. p. 107.
[m] Page 77 ante.   [n] Page 87 ante.

he is described as " Castellanus de Appelby;" and in the 34th Edw. I, in recompense for his numerous services, he obtained a grant of the borough of Hartle-
pole, and of all the lands of Robert de Brus.   In the same year he was sent with
Aymer de Valence against the said Robert, who had then assumed the title of
King of Scotland, about which time the lands of Christopher de Seyton were
granted to him.   Clifford attended the death-bed of the King in 1307, and
received the dying monarch's injunctions to prevent the return of Gaveston into
the realm.   In the 1st Edw. II. he was again made Governor of Nottingham
Castle, and constituted Earl Marshal of England; and on the 31st January,
1308, he joined several other lords in an engagement to support the title and
honor of the young King with their lives and fortunes.   In the 2nd Edw. II. he
was constituted Warden of the Marches of Scotland, and soon afterwards
Governor of that kingdom; and on the 17th March, 1309-10, was one of the
peers selected to regulate the royal household.[c]   Several valuable grants of lands
were bestowed upon him in the 3rd and 4th Edw. II. in consideration of his
merits; and he was again summoned to serve in Scotland in the 4th
Edw. II.   In the 6th Edw. II. he was joined in commission with the Earl of
Hereford and others to continue a treaty begun at Margate with the Count of
Eureux and the Bishop of Poitou upon some important affairs.   On the 6th
Feb. 1313, he received an acquittance from the King for the jewels, horses, &c.
belonging to Piers de Gaveston;[p] and he firmly adhered to Thomas Earl of
Lancaster against the unfortunate favourite, for his agency in whose death he
afterwards procured the royal pardon.

Lord Clifford was regularly summoned to parliament from the 29th Dec. 28
Edw. I. 1299, to the 26th Nov. 7 Edw. II. 1313; and he terminated his career
in a manner strictly consistent with his life, for he fell in the battle of Bannockburn, on the 25th June, 1314, at the early age of forty years.   His body was
sent to King Edward at Berwick, and is supposed to have been buried at Shapp
Abbey in Westmoreland.[q]

Clifford married Maud, daughter and eventually coheir of Thomas de Clare,
Steward of Waltham Forest, son of Thomas, younger son of Richard de Clare

---

.[o] Rot. Parl. vol. I. p. 443.   [p] Fœdera, N. E. vol. II. p. 203.   See page 139 ante.
 [q] Collins's Peerage, ed. 1779, vol. VI. p. 357. .

Earl of Gloucester and Hertford, by whom, who survived him and remarried Robert Baron Welles, he had issue Roger, his successor in the barony, then aged fifteen years, but who died s. p. in 1337; Robert, brother and heir of Roger; and, according to some pedigrees, two other sons, John and Andrew; and a daughter, Idonea, the wife of Henry Lord Clifford.[r]

From Robert de Clifford, the second son of the subject of this article, descended the baronial line of Clifford, which, in the reign of Henry the Eighth, was elevated to the Earldom of Cumberland. The barony of Clifford is now possessed by Edward Southwell, the present Lord de Clifford, the abeyance having been terminated in favor of his Lordship's father in 1776.

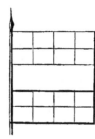 The arms of Clifford are, Checky Or and Azure, a fess Gules.[s] It is worthy of remark, as illustrative of the usage of arms in the early part of the fourteenth century, that the seal of this Baron to the Letter to the Pope in 1301, contains a shield of his arms surrounded by six annulets, and which there can be little doubt were assumed from the coat of his mother, Isabel daughter and coheiress of Robert de Vipount, Or, six annulets Gules.

---

[r] Many authorities make this Idonea the *sister* instead of the *daughter* of this Baron, but a comparison of dates renders the latter almost certain.

[s] Page 27; Cotton MSS. Caligula, A. xvii; and the seal of this Baron, a° 1301.

3 c

HUGH LE DESPENCER.

[PAGE 28.]

The vicissitudes of fortune which attended this individual, his eventful career, and, more than all, his tragical fate, have combined to render his name familiar to every historical reader. Indeed so crowded was his life with incidents, that it would be in vain to attempt to do more than present a brief outline of the most striking of them.

Hugh le Despenser was the eldest son of the celebrated Justiciary of England in the reign of Henry the Third, and succeeded his father in 1265, when he was about twenty-nine years of age. The earliest notice which occurs of him after that time is in the 15th Edw. I. when he was in the retinue of Edward Earl of Cornwall in Wales; and in the same year he paid a fine to the King of two thousand marks for having married, without license, Isabel, the widow of Patrick Chaworth, and daughter of William Earl of Warwick. In the 22nd Edw. I. he was made Governor of Odiham Castle in the county of Southampton, and was summoned to attend the King into Gascony. He was at the battle of Dunbar in the 24th Edw. I.; and on the 29th July following, during that monarch's invasion of Scotland, he dispatched " Syr Hugh Spencer and Syr John Hastynges to serche the countrey of Badenasshe."[t] In the 25th Edw. I. he attended the King into Flanders, and was one of the commissioners sent to treat of peace between England and France. Spencer was again in the Scottish wars in the 26th and 28th Edw. I.; and in June in the year last mentioned, being then nearly sixty-four years old, he served at the siege of Carlaverock, when his military prowess is particularly praised. On the 26th Sept. 1300, he was, with others, appointed ambassador to the Pope.[u] He was one of the mainpernors of Almaric de St. Amand, then a prisoner in the Tower of London, in the 33rd Edw. I.;[x] and in the same year was one of the peers nominated to treat with the Bishop of Glas-

[t] Archæologia, vol. XXI.　　　[u] Fœdera, N. E. vol. I. p. 922.
[x] Rot. Parl. vol. I. p. 176 b.

gow and the Earl of Carrick on the affairs of Scotland.[y]   In the octaves of the
feast of St. Hilary, 35 Edw. I. Spencer was present at the parliament which met
at Carlisle,[z] and was then again in the Scottish wars. On the 22nd March, 1307,
he, the Earl of Richmond, the Earl of Warwick, and Amaneus de la Brette, were
commanded to attend Prince Edward into France;[a] and at the coronation of
Edward the Second he bore a part of the regalia.[b] He was appointed Governor
of the Castles of Devizes and Marlborough in the 1st Edw. II.; and soon after
the death of Piers de Gaveston, the young monarch having fixed his affections
on Hugh le Despencer, the eldest son of this Baron, the royal favour was evinced
in a degree which proved fatal to both. During the commotion produced between
the lords and their sovereign from the presumption of the younger Despencer, his
father quitted the realm to avoid the dangers with which he was menaced. His
perpetual exile, as well as that of his son, was insisted upon by the enraged
Barons, who, after voting that measure, disbanded their forces. Edward, however, upon an insult offered to the Queen by Lord Badlesmere, to chastise that
nobleman's insolence, assembled an army with which he soon afterwards over-
threw the Earl of Lancaster at Boroughbridge in Yorkshire. His success was
instantly signalized by the advancement of the obnoxious favourites: on the
10th May, 15 Edw. II. 1322, the elder Hugh Despencer was created Earl of
Winchester, with an extensive grant of territories; and in the same year he was
appointed Warden of the King's forests to the south of the Trent. Little remains
to be said of this eminent personage, as his advanced age at the time of his elevation to that earldom, rendered him almost incapable of interfering in public
affairs, though he soon afterwards fell a victim to the mad ambition of his son.
It is needless however to relate the measures adopted by the Queen and Prince
Edward to remove the King from the influence of the younger Despencer. Upon
Prince Edward's arrival at Bristol, of which place the Earl of Winchester was
governor, the garrison rebelled against his authority, and he was brought
before the Prince, who instantly condemned him to be drawn, beheaded, and
afterwards hanged on a gibbet. This sentence was executed in the sight of the
King, as well as of the Earl's own son, on the 9th of October, 1326, he being

[y] Rot. Parl. vol. I. p. 267.   [z] Ibid. p. 188 b.   [a] Fœdera, N. E. vol. I. p. 1012.
[b] Fœdera, N. E. vol. II. p. 36.

then nearly ninety years old. Some writers assert that the Earl's body was suspended by two cords for four days, and then cut in pieces and given as food to dogs, whilst his head was sent to Winchester, in consequence of his being Earl of that city.

The Earl of Winchester married, as has been already stated, Isabel, daughter of William Earl of Warwick, and widow of Patrick Chaworth, by whom he had issue Hugh, the favourite of Edward the Second; and Joan and Eleanor, who were nuns at Sempringham in Lincolnshire. Hugh le Despencer the younger, was executed a few weeks after his father, and left issue by Eleanor, daughter and coheir of Gilbert de Clare Earl of Gloucester, the King's niece, two sons, Hugh, who died s. p., and Edward, both of whom were summoned to parliament. Thomas Lord Despenser, the son of the said Edward, obtained a reversal of the attainder of his grandfather and of the Earl of Winchester in 1397, in which year he was created Earl of Gloucester. One of the representatives of Hugh Earl of Winchester is Thomas Stapleton, the present Lord le Despenser.

The arms of Despencer are, Quarterly, Argent and Gules: the 2nd and 3rd quarters fretty Or: over all a bend Sable.[c] The 2nd and 3rd quarters are now blazoned, charged with *a fret*; but this, it is confidently contended, is a corruption from the ancient bearing.

---

[c] P. 28; Cotton MSS. Caligula, A. xvii. In that MS. the arms of the son of this Baron are said to have been distinguished by " un label de Azure ;" and it is the omission of the label in the arms in the Roll of Carlaverock which has alone identified the individual alluded to as the *elder* instead of the *younger* Despencer.

193

HUGH DE COURTENAY.

[PAGE 30.]

The history of the house of Courtenay—one of the most ancient and illustrious in Europe—having been related with unequalled eloquence by Mr. Gibbon, it would be presumptuous in this sketch of the life of the first individual of that family who attained the honours of an English earldom to allude particularly to his splendid pedigree, or to notice in detail either the exalted alliances or unmerited misfortunes of his descendants. Their alliances are, however, too intimately connected with those misfortunes, and were of too singular a nature, to be passed over in silence.

In the male line the family of Courtenay is said to have sprung from Pharamond the founder of the French monarchy, and more immediately from Reginald de Courtenay, who accompanied Henry the Second into England. By his first wife this Reginald is considered to have had a daughter, who married Peter, son of Louis le Gros King of France, and from whom the Emperors of Constantinople and the Princes of Courtenay of France descended. His second wife was Hawise, daughter and heiress of Robert de Abrincis, by whom he had issue Robert de Courtenay, Baron of Oakhampton in the reigns of John and Henry the Third. He married Mary, the daughter of William de Rivers Earl of Devon, through whom his great-grandson, Hugh de Courtenay, the subject of this memoir, derived his claim to that Earldom.

He was born in 1275, and succeeded his father Hugh in the barony of Oakhampton in February 1291, at which time he was sixteen years of age; and in 1295, though he had not then attained his majority, he performed homage and had livery of part of the lands of Isabel de Fortibus Countess of Devon, to whom he was heir. During the latter part of the reign of Edward the First he was five times summoned to serve in the wars of Scotland, and once into Wales, with horse and arms; and was present at the siege of Carlaverock in June, 1300, but no description is given of his person or merits beyond the simple title of " the good Hugh de Courtenay." He attended the parliament which met at Carlisle

3 D

in the octaves of St. Hilary, 35 Edw. I. ;[d] but no other notice of the least importance occurs of him in the reign of Edward the First, excepting that he
received the honor of knighthood at Whitsuntide in the 34th Edw. I. when that
dignity was bestowed upon the young Prince Edward and three hundred distinguished persons, among whom was Sir Philip Courtenay, the brother of the
Baron. That event is thus described by a contemporary chronicler :

> In this yere, als I told, at the Whitsonen day,
> The kyng his fest suld hold at Westmynstre fulle gay,
> His sonne Edward the Prince, and fiftene for his sake,
> Thre hundred of the Provynce, knyghtes wild he make,
> It was the kynges costage, for ilk a knyght was gest,
> Also thei mad mariage of som that were the best.
> The yong Erle of Warenne with grete nobley was thare,
> A wif thei him bikenne, the Erles douhter of Bare.
> The Erle of Arundelle his londes lauht he than,
> And toke a dampselle, William douhter of Warenne.
> Yong Sir Hugh was thare, the Spensere stout and gay,
> Gilbert douhter of Clare wedded he that day.
> It is not to wene, bot certeynly to witen,
> Joye inouh is sene, ther suilk a fest is smyten.
> In alle Bretayn was nouht, sithen Criste was born,
> A fest so noble wrought aftere no biforn.[e]

After the accession of Edward the Second, Courtenay appears to have more
particularly distinguished himself in public affairs, for in the 2nd Edw. II. he was
made a knight banneret, and was in the expedition into Scotland in the 8th
Edw. II. In the following year he claimed the territories which had belonged
to Isabel de Fortibus Countess of Devon, the proceedings relative to which are
given at great length on the Rolls of Parliament.[f] On the dispute between the
King and the Barons in the 12th Edw. II. he was appointed one of the Council
who were to be about the King's person.[g] He was a Receiver of Petitions in
the parliament which assembled at Westminster in the octaves of St. Michael in
the 14th Edw. II.[h] and was frequently engaged in the proceedings therein.[i] In

---

d Rot. Parl. vol. I. p. 188.　　e Peter of Langtoft, p. 332.　　f Rot. Parl. vol. I. pp. 334—336.
g Ibid. p. 453 b.　　h Ibid. p. 365.　　i Ibid. p. 367 b. 382 b.

the next parliament he petitioned the King and his council relative to the honor of Plympton;[k] and in the 5th Edw. III. attended the parliament which met at Westminster.[l] He was again a Trier of Petitions in the 6th Edw. III.;[m] and on the 22nd Feb. 9 Edw. III. 1335, he was created Earl of Devon; after which time nothing occurs of him on the Rolls of Parliament. Before the 8th Edw. III. he had obtained the wardship of John de Roger, for in that year he petitioned the King and his council about his lands, in which he stated that Courtenay had granted the same to Richard de Chuselden.[n]

The Earl of Devon died in his sixty-sixth year in 1340, and, considering that he was by birth, rank, and possessions one of the most powerful men of his times, and that in 1325 his eldest son had married the King's niece, his life was less chequered by vicissitudes than that of almost any of his contemporaries. This circumstance is the more remarkable, if the character given of him by the Monk of Ford be correct, who says that he was extraordinarily endowed with wisdom and knowledge, unless by "wisdom" was meant that cold and calculating prudence which enables its possessor to profit by the intemperance and calamities of others. By Agnes, sister of John Lord St. John, the Earl had issue Hugh, second Earl of Devon, who was thirty-seven years old at his father's death; John, Abbot of Tavistock; Robert; Thomas; Eleanor, wife of John Lord Grey of Codnor; and Elizabeth, who married Bartholomew de L'Isle.

The Earldom of Devon continued in the house of Courtenay, subject however to occasional forfeitures and restorations, and latterly merged in the higher dignity of Marquess of Exeter, until the reign of Elizabeth. By the next monarch the titles of Devon and Exeter were, with moral injustice at least, conferred upon far less illustrious families, notwithstanding that male descendants of the first Earl were then living in great honor at their seat of Powderham Castle. It has since been once more restored to the honors of the peerage: but their present rank forms a melancholy contrast to their ancient splendour; and when it is remembered that the misfortunes which have attended them were produced by the jealousy of the Crown, equally of their proximity to the succession and of their immense wealth and influence, there are few who reflect on the rise and fall of eminent families but would sincerely rejoice at any circumstance that might hereafter restore its representative to the most ancient of his ancestor's dignities

k Rot. Parl. vol. I. p. 405 b.   l Ibid. vol. II. p. 61 a.   m Ibid. p. 68 a.   n Ibid. p. 82 b.

—the Earldom of Devon, an event which is not improbable.[n] This memoir will be concluded by describing those alliances with the blood-royal which have been alluded to, and some of which are unparalleled in the history of any other family in this kingdom.

Hugh Courtenay, second Earl of Devon, married Margaret, daughter of Humphrey de Bohun Earl of Hereford and Essex, by Elizabeth, daughter of King Edward the First.

Edward Courtenay, eldest son of Edward Earl of Devon, married Eleano, sister and coheir of Edmund Earl of March, and sister of Ann, wife of Richard Earl of Cambridge, through whom the line of York derived its claim to the throne. He however died vitâ patris s. P.

William Earl of Devon married Katherine Plantagenet, daughter of King Edward the Fourth, and sister of Elizabeth of York, wife of King Henry the Seventh, from whom every English monarch since Richard the Third descended. By her the Earl of Devon had a son, Henry, who was created Marquess of Exeter, . but fell a victim to the jealousy of Henry the Eighth. Edward, his son, was created Earl of Devon on the 3rd Sept. 1553, and was restored to all his father's dignities in the same year. It is said that he was the object of Queen Mary's affections, whilst his own were placed on her sister the Princess Elizabeth. After passing the greater part of his life in prison, he died, not without suspicion of having been poisoned, at Padua, s. P., in 1556, when the titles of Devon and Exeter became lost to the house of Courtenay.

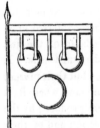

Thus in two instances did the representative of this illustrious family marry the *younger* daughter and coheir of the personage whose *eldest* daughter's issue inherited the crown.

The ancient arms of the English house of Courtenay were, Or, three Torteaux, a label Azure;[o] but the label has subsequently, with as little propriety as taste, been discontinued.

[n] Edward Courtenay, the last Marquess of Exeter, was created Earl of Devon at Richmond, on the 3rd Sept. 1553, to hold to him " *et heredibus suis masculis in perpetuum,*" and the clause in the patent giving a seat in parliament, runs, to the said Edward, " *et heredes sui masculi,*" without the usual words, " *de corpore,*" an omission which, it may be contended, was a grant of the earldom to him and his heirs male *whatsoever,* and which would vest it in the present heir male of that nobleman.

[o] Page 30; and Cotton MSS. Caligula, A. xvii. It is worthy of remark, as illustrative of the

ALMARIC DE ST. AMAND.

[PAGE 30.]

No particular merit or circumstance distinguished the life of this Baron from that of other persons of similar rank, for the duties he performed, as well as the few notices which are preserved of him, were common to nearly all of his compeers.

Almaric de St. Amand was born in March, 1285, and succeeded his brother Guy in his lands about the 15th Edw. I. In the following year £10 per annum were appropriated for his maintenance till he attained his majority, but in the 17th Edw. I. he produced proof of his being then of full age.

He was summoned to serve in Gascony with horse and arms in the 22nd Edw. I., upon which occasion his wife was assigned the manor house of Lutgareshall, with sufficient fuel, until his return. In the 25th Edw. I. he was again in Gascony; and in the 28th Edw. I. was in the Scottish wars. From the Poem we learn that he was at the siege of Carlaverock in June, 1300, when he he was about twenty-five years old, but prowess is the only merit which is attributed to him. St. Amand was a party to the Letter from the Barons to the Pope in February, 29 Edw. I. 1301, in which he is styled " Lord of Widehaye;"P and in the December preceding received his first writ of summons to parliament. He was once more in the wars of Scotland in the 31st Edw. I.; and in the 33rd Edw. I., having been Governor of Bordeaux, he was commanded to bring in the accounts of all the issues and revenues thereof during the time he held that office. Those returns seem to have produced his disgrace, as in November in that year he, with his brother, Master John de St. Amand, and William de Montacute,

---

manner in which arms were differenced, that the label was, by respective branches of the family, borne charged with mitres, crescents, lozenges, annulets, fleurs de lis, guttees, plates, and annulets with a bend over all. See Willement's Heraldic Notices in Canterbury Cathedral, and drawings of seals in the Cotton MS. Julius, C. vii.

P Appendix to the Fourth Peerage Report.

3 E

were prisoners in the Tower of London, when the Earl of Lincoln, John of Brittany, Hugh le Despenser, Hugh de Veer, Thomas de Berkeley, and Adam de Welles, became bail for his appearance whenever the King might require it.[q] From that time until the accession of Edward the Second nothing is recorded of him, excepting that he was in the Scottish wars in the 34th Edw. I. It is evident that his disgrace did not extend beyond the reign of Edward the First, for, by writ tested on the 22nd January, 1 Edw. II. 1308, he was commanded to be at Dover to receive the young King and his Queen on their landing from France;[r] and on the 8th February following both St. Amand and his wife were ordered to attend their coronation.[s] With this circumstance, however, our information about this Baron closes, and all which can be said of him besides is, that he was summoned to parliament from the 29th Dec. 28 Edw. I. 1299, to the 16th June, 4 Edw. II. 1311, and died in 1312 s. p., leaving John his brother, who from the title of " Master" being ascribed to him is conjectured to have been a priest, his heir. Almaric de St. Amand married Mary, daughter of ———, who, from an escheat in the 7th Edw. III. appears to have been the widow of John de Peyvre. She survived him, and several manors were assigned for her dowry.

Upon the death of Almaric de St. Amand, the barony created by the writ

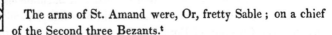

of 28 Edw. I. became extinct. John, his brother, was immediately afterwards summoned to parliament, and whose descendants are the representatives of the subject of this article; but it is extremely difficult, even if it be not impossible, to trace them.

The arms of St. Amand were, Or, fretty Sable ; on a chief of the Second three Bezants.[t]

---

q Rot. Parl. vol. I. p. 176 b.   r Fœdera, N. E. vol. II.   s Ibid. p. 31.
t Page 30; Cotton MSS. Caligula, A. xvii.; and the seal of this Baron, aº 1301.

JOHN D'ENGAINE.

[PAGE 30.]

To the few lines which contain all that Dugdale has said of this individual, not many facts can be added, for the Rolls of Parliament and other records are almost entirely silent respecting him. It may therefore be presumed that his life was wholly barren of incident, and little regret can be felt at the obscurity in which his character and conduct are equally involved.

On the 30th December, 25 Edw. I. 1296, by the appellation of " John de Engaine, junior," he was commanded to attend the marriage of the Princess Elizabeth with the Count of Holland at Ipswich on Monday in the morrow of the Epiphany;[u] and in the same year he succeeded his father, at which time he was thirty years old. He was summoned to parliament in the 27th Edw. I.; and in the 28th Edw. I. was in the wars of Scotland, and served at Carlaverock in June, 1300; but the Poet of the siege gives no other account of him than the description of his banner. He was a party to the Letter from the Barons to the Pontiff in the 29th Edw. I. in which he is styled " Lord of Colum ;" his seal, however, is not attached to that instrument.[x] Engaine was summoned to attend a parliament at Carlisle in the octaves of St. Hilary in the 35th Edw. I. though he is not marked in the record as having been present.[y] In the 8th Edw. II. he was again ordered to serve with horse and arms against the Scots; and having been

summoned to parliament from the 6th Feb. 27 Edw. I. 1299, to the 15th May, 14 Edw. II. 1321, died in 1322 without issue, when his barony became extinct. In 1342 John de Engaine, the nephew of this Baron, was summoned to parliament, whose daughters eventually became his heirs.

The arms of Engaine were, Gules, crusilly and a fess Or.[z]

---

u Fœdera, N. E. vol. I. p. 850.   x Fourth Peerage Report.   y Rot. Parl. vol. I. p. 188. ,
z Page 30; and Cotton MSS. Caligula, A. xvii.; but they are usually blazoned, Gules, a fess between six cross crosslets Or.

WALTER DE BEAUCHAMP.

[PAGE 30.]

This eminent personage enjoyed all the privileges attached to the dignity of a Baron of the realm, excepting that he is not recorded to have been summoned to parliament. He filled however many important offices, and his character is pourtrayed in a peculiarly forcible manner in the preceding Poem.

Walter de Beauchamp was a younger son of William Beauchamp of Elmley, by Isabel, sister and heiress of William Mauduit Earl of Warwick. His father, by his will dated in 1268, bequeathed to him cc marks, he being then signed with the cross for a pilgrimage to the Holy Land on the behalf of both his parents. In the 56th Hen. III. he purchased a moiety of the manor of Alcester in the county of Warwick from Peter Fitz Herbert. Nothing more seems to be known of him until the 20th Edw. I. when he was one of the manucaptors of the Earl of Hereford,[a] and in the next year he was appointed one of the Judges before whom some people of Winchester were bound to appear,[b] about which time he obtained a charter for a fair to be held yearly in his manor of Alcester. Beauchamp was made steward of the King's household in the 24th Edw. I., and in the 25th Edw. I. attended him into Flanders. In the 26th and 27th Edw. I. he served in Scotland, and was at the battle of Falkirk; and in the 28th Edw. I. he received a grant of free-warren in all his demesne lands at Alcester in Warwickshire and also at Powyck and other places in Gloucestershire. In further evidence of the rank which this individual was considered to have held, it is necessary to observe that in the writ of service tested at Stayvinagg, 26th September, 26 Edw. I. the names of those summoned are divided into two classes : against the first division the word " Comit' " occurs ; opposite to the second class is the word " Baron'," and in the latter Beauchamp's name is included.[c] In the 28th Edw. I. we learn that he was at the siege of Carlaverock, when he must have been at least fifty-two years old, which calculation supposes that he was but just of age at his father's death in 1269. The Poet says that in his opinion he was one of the best knights there present, if he had not been too rash and daring, but that

---

a Rot. Parl. vol. I. p. 76 a.   b Ibid. p. 98.   c Appendix to the First Peerage Report.

you will never hear any one speak of the Seneschal that he has not a *but*. This eulogium, however, requires some explanation. It probably means that the chief defect in his conduct as a soldier was an ungovernable impetuosity, and that his character was of so mixed a nature that the praise bestowed upon him was never unqualified: an observation, indeed, which applies to mankind in general as justly as to that individual; for few men are so entirely good as not to possess some counterbalancing errors, nor are there many so wholly vicious as to be destitute of at least one redeeming virtue. The term Seneschal evidently alluded to his office of Steward of the Royal Household, which he appears to have held until his death, for it is attributed to him as late as the 8th October, 30 Edw. I.[d] In the 29th Edw. I. Walter de Beauchamp was a party to the Letter from the Barons to Pope Boniface, in which he is called " Lord of Alcester," and was again in the wars of Scotland in the 31st Edw. I., in which year his public services apparently terminated, as nothing further is known of him excepting that he died on the 16th February, 1303, and was buried in the Grey Friars near Smithfield in London. He married Alice, daughter of ——— Tony, and in consequence of their being within the fourth degree of consanguinity, the ceremony was afterwards confirmed by Godfrey Bishop of Worcester, and their children legitimated. That Prelate is said to have been ordered to do so by the Pope, because they were ignorant of the fact at the time of their union. The said Alice survived her husband, for in the 35th Edw. I. by the description of Alice who was the wife of Walter de Beauchamp, and executrix of his will, she petitioned the King to be allowed to repay the sum of £cxx. xd., which her husband was indebted to the Crown, by annual instalments of £x.[f] By her he had three sons: Walter; William; who both appear to have died s. P.; and Giles.[g]

Walter, their son and heir, was repeatedly summoned to the field, but the first person of the family who sat in parliament after the death of the Seneschal, was Sir John Beauchamp, the great grandson of his son Giles, who was created Lord Beauchamp of Powyck by Henry the Sixth.

The arms of Beauchamp of Alcester were, Gules, a fess between six martlets Or.[h]

---

d Fœdera, N. E. vol. I. p. 944.　　e Fourth Peerage Report.　　f Rot. Parl. vol. I. p. 199 b.

g Dugdale's Warwicksh. ed. 1765, p. 536.　h P. 30; Cotton MSS. Caligula, A. xvii.; and seal, 1301.

JOHN DE BOTETOURT.

[Page 32.]

John de Botetourt appears to have had the merit of being the founder of his family, for we are even ignorant of the name of his father and of the time of his birth. The first which Dugdale says he has seen of the name after the reign of Henry the Second was in the 19th Edw. I., when this individual was made Governor of St. Briavel's Castle in the county of Gloucester, and Warden of the Forest of Dene. In the 21st Edw. I. he was appointed a Justice of gaol delivery;[i] and in the next year was summoned to serve in Gascony, at which time he was Admiral of the King's fleet; and in the 24th Edw. I. he again served in the expedition into Gascony, and was in the wars of Scotland in the 25th, 26th, and 28th Edw. I. By writ tested on the 30th Dec. 1296, he was commanded to attend the marriage between the Princess Elizabeth and the Count of Holland, at Ipswich, on Monday in the morrow of the Epiphany following.[k] He was present at Carlaverock in June, 1300, and his character as given by the Poet is of the most amiable description. In the 29th Edw. I. he was a party to the Letter to the Pontiff from the Barons at Lincoln, in which he is styled " Lord of Mendlesham,"[l] though he had never then been summoned to parliament. Covenants were entered into in the 33rd Edw. I., at which time he was still Warden of the Forest of Dene,[m] that Joane his daughter should marry Robert, the son and heir of Richard Fitz Walter. In that year he was also appointed, with William Haulward and Nicholas Fermband, to hear and determine certain transgressions committed at Bristol;[n] and to treat with some Scots on the affairs of Scotland.[o] Shortly afterwards he received £c. for the King's service,[p] and was present at the non-allowance of a papal provision in April, 1305,[q] when he was appointed one of the Justices of Trailbaston.[r] Botetourt was in the Scottish wars

---

i Rot. Parl. vol. I. p. 95 b.   k Fœdera, N. E. vol. I. p. 850.
l Appendix to the Fourth Peerage Report.   m Rot. Parl. vol. I. p. 163 b.
n Ibid. p. 168 b.   o Ibid. p. 267 a.   p Ibid. pp. 169 b. 194 a.
q Ibid. p. 179 b.   r Fœdera, N. E. vol. I. p. 970; and Rot. Parl. vol. I. p. 330 b.

in the 34th Edw. I., and in the next year Joan de Wake obtained a re-seisin of certain lands in Lydell against him.ˢ

Immediately after the accession of Edward the Second he was again constituted Governor of the Castle of St. Briavel; and in the 1st Edw. II. joined several other Barons in executing the instrument by which they pledged themselves to support the young monarch, his crown, and dignity. In the 3rd Edw. II. he was one of the peers appointed to regulate the royal household;ᵗ in the 4th Edw. II. he was in the wars of Scotland; and in the year following was Governor of Framlingham Castle in Suffolk. About the same time he bound himself to support the Earl of Warwick against Piers de Gaveston; and in the 6th Edw. II. was joined in a commission with the Earl of Hereford and others to treat with the embassy from the Pontiff at Margate. He was once more Admiral of the King's fleet in the 8th Edw. II.; and in the 12th Edw. II. served against the Scots. A petition having been presented to the King in the 8th or 9th Edw. II. from Herman Clipping, a German merchant, complaining that, as he was lately going to Ipswich with a ship full of hard fish, John de Holebrok forcibly entered his ship by night, and carried away seven hundred fish, of the value of LXX s., and severely beat John Lange his servant because he opposed him, John Botetourt and others were appointed to hear and determine the cause.ᵘ He was one of the Barons at Northampton who treated with the Earl of Lancaster in the 12th Edw. II.;ᵛ and having been summoned to parliament from the 13th July, 33 Edw. I. 1305, to the 13th September, 18 Edw. II. 1324, closed a long and honorable life in the same year, and apparently at an advanced age, for he could scarcely have been less than thirty in the 19th Edw. I. when he was appointed Governor of St. Briavel's Castle, and which calculation would render him about forty when he was at Carlaverock, and above sixty-four at his demise. He married, in the 30th Edw. I. Maud, sister and heiress of Otho de Beauchamp, and widow of William de Munchensi of Edwardstone, by whom he had issue Thomas, his eldest son, who died v. P., leaving a son, John, who succeeded his grandfather in his honors; John; Otho; and two daughters; Elizabeth, who married first William Lord Latimer, and secondly Robert de Ufford; and Joan, who was contracted to marry Robert Fitz Walter. Upon the death of John, the

ˢ Rot. Parl. vol. I. pp. 201 a. 214 b.   ᵗ Ibid. p. 443 b.   ᵘ Ibid. p. 340 a.
ᵛ Ibid. p. 453.

second Baron Botetourt, in 1385, the barony fell into abeyance, and continued in that state until 1764, a period of nearly three hundred and eighty years, when

it was terminated in favour of Norborne Berkeley, Esq. one of the coheirs. His Lordship died in 1776, s. p., when it again fell into abeyance, and remained so until 1803, in which year it was allowed to Henry fifth Duke of Beaufort, son and heir of the last Baron's sister, and is now possessed by Henry Charles, the present Duke of Beaufort, K. G.

The arms of Botetourt are, Or, a saltire engrailed Sable.[x]

EUSTACE DE HACCHE.

[PAGE 32.]

This Baron is said to have commenced his career as a menial servant to the King, being in that capacity in the 7th Edw. I., about which time he obtained a charter for free warren in all his demesne lands at Hacche in Wiltshire, and at Morton-Merhull and Cestreton in the county of Warwick; and in the 18th Edw. I. his essoin of King's service was disallowed.[y] By his merits or his good fortune he soon emerged from the comparative humble station in which he is first presented to our notice, for in the 21st Edw. I. he was joined with John de Botetourt and William Hamelyn in a commission of gaol delivery;[z] and in the 22nd Edw. I. he was made Governor of Portsmouth. In the same year he accompanied the Earl of Lancaster in the expedition into Gascony, and in the 24th and 25th Edw. I. was in the wars of Scotland, and in the 26th Edw. I. at the battle of Falkirk. Rising still higher in the opinion of his sovereign, he was in

---

[x] Page 32; Cotton MSS. Caligula, A. xvii.; and the seal of this Baron aᵒ 1301.

[y] Rot. Parl. vol. I. p. 50 a.　　　　　　　　[z] Ibid. p. 95 b.

in the 27th Edw. I. summoned to parliament as a Baron of the realm; and in the 28th and 29th Edw. I. was again in the Scottish wars. In June 1300 we are told by the Poet of the siege of Carlaverock that he was present, though no account is given of his character; and in the February following he was a party to the Letter to Boniface VIII., in which he is styled "Eustace Lord of Hacche." In the 31st Edw. I. he once more served in Scotland; and having been summoned to parliament from the 6th Feb. 27 Edw. I. 1299, to the 22nd Jan. 33 Edw. I. 1305, died in the next year without male issue. Of the age of this Baron we have no information, nor does the name of his wife occur, but he left his daughter Julian his heiress, who married John Hansard.

In the year after the death of Eustace de Hacche, his executors petitioned the King to be paid what was owing to him by the Crown for his robes, wages, and

 horses lost in the wars of Scotland. They stated that he had by his will left many legacies to the Holy Land and to his servants, which could not be paid unless their request was granted, and succeeded in obtaining a special precept to John de Drokensford the keeper of the great wardrobe, commanding him to settle with them accordingly.[a]

The arms of Hacche were, Or, a cross engrailed Gules.[b]

---

[a] Rot. Parl. vol. I. p. 199 a.

[b] Page 32; Cotton MSS. Caligula, A. xvii.; and the seal of this Baron aᵒ 1301.

ADAM DE WELLES.

[PAGE 32.]

The family of Welles, though of much consideration from the reign of Richard the First, never attained the baronial rank until this individual was summoned to parliament in the year 1299. He was the son of William de Welles by Isabel de Vesci, but Dugdale does not state in what year he succeeded his father, who was living in the 11th Edw. I., and the earliest notice which that writer takes of him is in the 22nd Edw. I., at which time he states that he was in the retinue of William de Vesci in the King's service in Gascony. In the 25th Edw. I. he was similarly engaged, in consideration of which he obtained a writ from the King to the Treasurer and Barons of the Exchequer, forbidding them to take any of his wools of that year's growth; and in the 27th Edw. I. he was made Constable of the castle of Rockingham and Warden of that forest, and received his first writ of summons to parliament. Welles was in the wars of Scotland in the 28th Edw. I., and served at the siege of Carlaverock; and in February, 1301, by the style of " Adam Lord Welle," was a party to the celebrated Letter from the Barons at Lincoln to the Pontiff, relative to his Holiness's claim to the sovereignty of Scotland.c In the 30th Edw. I. he had a charter for free warren in certain of his demesne lands in the county of Lincoln.d He was in the Scottish wars in the 31st and 32nd Edw. I.; in the 33rd Edw. I. he was one of the manucaptors of Almaric de St. Amand, who was then a prisoner in the Tower of London;e and in March in the same year he was present at the non-allowance of a papal provision.f In the 35th Edw. I. some proceedings occurred about the debts due from John de Hoyland to the King, whose lands were then held by this Baron.g His services in Scotland were rewarded by Edward the Second; for in the fourth year of his reign he granted him in tail general forty-two pounds out of lands in Besely, Hawordly, Gunnerby, &c. which had belonged to Thomas

c Appendix to the Fourth Peerage Report. d Calend. Rot. Chart. p. 133.
e Rot. Parl. vol. I. p. 176 b. f Ibid. 179 b. g Ibid. pp. 205 b. 206.

de Woodhay and William Garlond;[h] and he obtained a precept from the Crown to the Treasurer and Barons of the Exchequer to respite the payment of such debts as were then due from him until the ensuing Easter.

Lord Welles was summoned to parliament from the 6th February, 27 Edw. I. 1299, to the 16th June, 4 Edw. II. 1311, in which year he died, leaving by Joane his wife, who according to some pedigrees was the daughter and heiress of John Baron Engaine,[i] two sons; Robert, his successor in the dignity, but who died s. P. in 1320; and Adam, who was the third baron.

The barony of Welles continued vested in the male descendants of Adam the first peer until the reign of Edward the Fourth, when it was enjoyed by Richard Hastings, who had married the heiress of Richard the seventh baron. They, however, both died s. P., and the barony fell into abeyance between the representatives of the four daughters of Leo the sixth baron. Sir John Welles, K. G. son of the said Leo Lord Welles, by his second wife, was created a Viscount in 1487, and not only thus attained to a higher dignity than any of his ancestors, but formed a most splendid alliance, having married Cecily Plan-

tagenet, daughter of King Edward the Fourth, and sister of Elizabeth of York, the progenitrix of the royal family of this country; by her he had a daughter, Ann, who survived her father but a very short time, and with her the Viscount's issue became extinct.

The arms of Welles are, Or, a lion rampant, double queued, Sable.[k]

---

h Calend. Rot. Pat. part 2. p. 72.   i Harl. MSS. 3288. f. 143.

k Page 32; Cotton MSS. Caligula, A. xvii.; and the seal of this Baron, aᵒ 1301.

ROBERT DE SCALES.

[PAGE 32.]

Of " the handsome and amiable Robert de Scales," very little is recorded. He was the eldest son of a person of the same names, whom he succeeded about the 50th Hen. III.; and in the 14th Edw. I., being in the expedition then made into Wales, had scutage of all his tenants who held their lands of him by military service.   In the 18th Edw. I. he petitioned the King on the same subject;[1] and in the 22nd Edw. I. was commanded to be at Portsmouth on the first of the following September, to attend the King into France. He was in the expedition into Flanders in the 25th Edw. I.; and served in the wars of Scotland in the 28th Edw. I., in which year he was present at the siege of Carlaverock; and in the 29th Edw. I., by the title of " Lord of Neuseles," was a party to the Letter to Pope Boniface the Eighth from the Barons of this country.[m]   Scales was summoned to parliament from the 6th February, 27 Edw. I. 1299, to the 22nd Jan. 33 Edw. I. 1305, and died in the year last mentioned, leaving by Isabel, daughter of Sir — Burnell, Knight, or, according to other pedigrees, by Margery, daughter and coheiress of Fulke Beaufyne,[n] Robert, his son and heir, who succeeded to his honors, and a daughter, Eleanor, who married John Lord Sudley.[n] The barony of Scales was inherited by the male descendants of this Baron until the reign of Edward the Fourth, when Anthony Woodville, the eldest son of Richard Earl Rivers, having married the daughter and heiress of Thomas, seventh

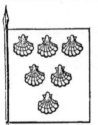

Baron, was summoned to parliament as Lord Scales. They both died without issue, when the barony fell into abeyance between the descendants of Margaret, wife of Sir Robert Howard, and Elizabeth, who married Sir Roger de Felbrigge, the daughters of Roger fourth Lord Scales; in which state it still continues.

The arms of Scales are, Gules, six escallops Argent.[o]

---

1 Rot. Parl. vol. I. p. 47 a.   m Appendix to the Fourth Peerage Report.
n Harl. MSS 245. f. 25. Glover's Collections.
o P. 32; Cotton MSS. Caligula, A. xvii.; and the seal of this Baron, a° 1301.

EMLAM TOUCHES.

[PAGE 34.]

The name of Emlam Touches is not once to be found in any of the records from which the greater part of the particulars of his contemporaries have been derived; hence we are in total ignorance of his birth, services, or character. In the Roll of Arms in the Cottonian MS. Caligula, A. xvii., a Sir William Thochet occurs, whose arms are described to be precisely those of this individual, and hence it may be inferred that he was of the same family. It will be seen by a reference to the Poem that the baptismal name of Emlam has been subsequently added in one copy, whilst it is wholly omitted in the other. A William Touchét was summoned to parliament from the 28th to the 34th Edw. I., but his arms, as

 they appear on his seal affixed to the Barons' Letter, were totally different, being semée of cross crosslets a lion rampant; nor, for the same reason, does it seem likely that this Knight was connected with the family of Touchet afterwards Barons Audley, who bore, Ermine, a chevron Gules.

The arms of Emlam Touches were, Gules, martlets Or.[p]

P Page 34.

THE EARL OF LENNOX.

[PAGE 34.]

The nobleman to whom this title is attributed in the Poem, was Patrick eighth Earl of Dunbar, who succeeded his father in that dignity in 1289, being then forty-seven years of age.[q] In the same year he was a party to the instrument from the nobility of Scotland, by which they signified their approval of the marriage then meditated between Prince Edward of England and Margaret the young Queen of Scotland, in which he is styled " Comes de Marchia;"[r] and on the 3rd August 1291 was himself one of the claimants to the crown of that kingdom, in right of his great grandmother, Ada, daughter of William the Lion; having, with the other claimants, in the June preceding, agreed to refer their pretensions to King Edward the First as sovereign lord of that realm.[s] Dunbar, however, soon withdrew his claim, and became one of the nominees of his grandfather Bruce in the competition; but before the close of the year 1291 he swore fealty to the English monarch, to which pledge he adhered with the utmost zeal and fidelity. He was summoned to attend him with horse and arms into Gascony in 1294; and in 1296, notwithstanding Dunbar's attachment to the English interest, his wife, with far greater patriotism, supported the cause of her country, and held his castle against the invaders for some time. Dunbar was the King's Lieutenant beyond the Scottish sea in November, 26 Edw. I.;[t] and on the 26th September, 1298, he was commanded to serve against Edward's enemies in Scotland.[u] In June, 1300, he was in the English army at the siege of Carlaverock, when he must have been about fifty-eight years old; after which year all which appears to be known of him is, that in the 33rd Edw. I. he was one of the ten persons elected by the commons of Scotland to attend the English parliament on

q All the particulars of the Earl given in the text, for which no other authority is cited, are taken from Wood's Douglas's Peerage. The editor of that edition has added " query" whenever the age of that nobleman is alluded to.

r Fœdera, N. E. vol. I. p. 730.   s Ibid. p. 755.   t Calend. Rot. Pat. p. 59.

u Fœdera, N. E. vol. I, p. 899.

the affairs of that kingdom, but he did not do so;[x] that on the 30th September, 1 Edw. II. 1308, he was ordered to assist in repressing an attempt to subvert the English power in Scotland;[y] that on the 18th November following he was a main-pernor for the Earl of Strathearn;[z] and that he died in 1309, leaving by Margery, daughter of Alexander Comyn Earl of Buchan, a son, Patrick, who became ninth Earl of Dunbar, and who will form the subject of the next article.

It is difficult to explain upon what grounds the Poet styled the Earl of Dunbar " Earl of Lennox;" but it would appear that there was great uncertainty about his proper title, for Douglas informs us that he was for the first time called " Earl of March" in 1291, in the record of that year which has just been cited.

The arms of the Earls of Dunbar were, Gules, a lion rampant Argent, within a bordure of the Second, charged with roses of the First.[a]

PATRICK DE DUNBAR.

[PAGE 34.]

Either because this individual lived one generation nearer to the present age, or from his services being more numerous and important than those of his father, the account given of him by Sir Robert Douglas fills above twice the space appropriated to that nobleman. The first notice which occurs of him is that he served under Edward the First at Carlaverock in 1300, at which time he could not have been much more than fifteen years old, for, on succeeding to the honors of his family in 1309, he was only twenty-four years of age. He commenced his political career by following his father's example of supporting the King of

[x] Rot. Parl. vol. I. p. 267 a.   [y] Fœdera, N. E. vol. II. p. 8.   [z] Rot. Scotiæ, vol. I. p. 59.
[a] P. 34; and the seal of this Earl described in Nisbett's Heraldry, p. 273.

England; and after the battle of Bonnockbourn he received Edward the Second
into his castle of Dunbar. Suggestions of interest or patriotism soon afterwards
induced him to make his peace with King Robert, and he attended the parliament at Ayr in April, 1315, when the succession to the crown of Scotland was
settled. Nor was his adherence to his own sovereign of a negative description;
for being Sheriff of Lothian in March, 1318, he powerfully contributed to the
capture of Berwick from the English. In 1320 he signed the Letter to the Pope
asserting the independence of Scotland; and in 1322 commanded part of David
the Second's forces.   He was appointed Governor of Berwick Castle, and
was besieged by Edward the Third in 1333, but that fortress having surrendered
on the 19th July in that year in consequence of the battle of Halidon-hill, he was
received into the conqueror's protection, and engaged to garrison it with English.
This agreement admits of inferences which are irreconcileable with the Earl's
faith and honor, and at least cast a doubt upon the motives of his former conduct.   After attending Edward Baliol at the parliament of Edinburgh in February 1334, he once more renounced his allegiance to the King of England,
and served against his forces with much success in July 1335, when his lands in
England were seized by the Crown; for in the same year Henry de Percy obtained a grant of the lands in the county of Northumberland which had belonged
to Patrick Earl of March.[a] Whilst actively and honorably employed in repelling
the invasion of his country, his Countess, Agnes, daughter of Randolf Earl of
Moray, who was familiarly termed " Black Agnes," heroically defended his
castle of Dunbar against the Earl of Salisbury in January 1338; and after sus-
taining a siege of nineteen weeks obliged him to retire.

   At the battle of Durham on the 17th October, 1346, the Earl of Dunbar, with
the Steward of Scotland, commanded the left wing of the royal army, and, though
defeated, managed to secure their retreat. The Earl of Moray having lost his
life on that occasion, the Countess of Dunbar became his sole heiress, and her
husband consequently assumed the title of that earldom. In 1357, when he is
next mentioned by Douglas, he exerted himself for the liberation of his captive
sovereign, and became one of the sureties for the fulfilment of the terms upon
which he was released; in reward of which services that monarch bestowed a
pension and other favors upon him.

---

b Calend. Rot. Pat. p. 122.

Dunbar was a Commissioner for settling the affairs of the Marches in 1367; and in March 1369 was one of the peers appointed by the parliament of Perth to watch over the general affairs of the kingdom. Having made a pilgrimage to the shrine of Thomas â Becket, and being eighty-four years of age, he resigned his Earldom of March and his estates to his eldest son George, to whom they were confirmed by David II. by a charter dated on the 25th July, 1368, wherein this nobleman is described as " Patricius Dunbar, Miles, ultimus Comes ejusdem." His natural and political life closed within a very short time of each other, for he did not long survive the surrender of his honors; and left by his celebrated wife, Agnes Randolph, sister and heiress of the Earl of Moray, George tenth Earl of Dunbar; John Earl of Moray; Margaret, who married William first Earl of Douglas; Agnes, wife of James Douglas Lord of Dalkeith; and Elizabeth, wife of John Maitland of Lethington, ancestor of the Earls of Lauderdale.

The early part of the career of the Earl of Dunbar was marked by tergiversation for which it would be impossible to find a justifiable cause; but these breaches of faith were in a great measure redeemed by the firmness with which in the last thirty-five years of his life he adhered to the interests of his country, and during that long period he stands conspicuous as one of the most

constant and intrepid of its defenders. His male descendants enjoyed his honors until 1435, when they were declared to have been forfeited.

The arms borne by this nobleman at Carlaverock were differenced from those of his father by a label Azure,[c] a mark of filiation which he probably abandoned on succeeding to his honors.

---

c Page 34.

RICHARD SIWARD.

[PAGE 34.]

If the numerous occasions on which this individual is mentioned in the public records of the reigns of Edward the First and Second, and the importance which was evidently attached to him, be considered, it is extraordinary that we should be entirely destitute of genealogical particulars respecting him.

He seems almost to be the first and last of his family, unless we entertain the conjecture of a recent writer,[d] that he was descended from Syward the great Saxon Earl of Northumberland; but the want of those facts is more than compensated by the many proofs that exist of his services, from which it is manifest that he was one of the most celebrated men of his times.

It is almost certain that he was a native of Scotland, though, like the Earl of Dunbar and others of his countrymen, he occasionally wavered between his fidelity to his own sovereign and the King of England.

When he is first presented to our notice he was undoubtedly an adherent of King Edward, for on the 18th November, 21 Edw. I. 1292, he was appointed by him Governor of the castles of Dumfries, Wigtown, and Kirkcudbright.[e] On the 22nd of April, 1294, he obtained a grant of the marriage of the widow of Simon Fresel;[f] and on the 15th October in the same year he was commanded to attend that monarch with horse and arms in the expedition into Wales.[g] Before the end of 1295, however, Syward returned to his allegiance to the crown of Scotland, and was taken prisoner in the castle of Dunbar on the 29th of April, 1296,[h] a fact which not only stands upon the authority of chroniclers, but is corroborated by the circumstance of a precept having been addressed to the Earl of Warren and Surrey by King Edward, tested the 4th Sept. 1296, commanding him to assign £40 out of the lands of Richard Syward, who was then a prisoner, for the support of Mary his wife, and of Eliza-

---

d Banks's Stemmata Anglicana.   e Rotuli Scotiæ, vol. I. p. 12 a.
f Rot. Scot. vol. I. p. 20 a.   g Appendix to the First Peerage Report, p. 61.
h Archæologia, vol. XXI. and Hemyngford.

beth the wife of Richard his son.[i] His fidelity did not, it seems, withstand the temptation to which his imprisonment exposed him; and in the very next year he again attached himself to Edward's interest, for we find that on the 30th of July, 1297, at which time he was a prisoner in the Tower of London, having, the instrument states, been taken at Dunbar, several English noblemen became bail that he would accompany the King in his expedition beyond the sea, and faithfully serve him against the King of France; and John his son was given as a hostage for the fulfilment of his engagement.[k] In the ensuing September all his lands were restored to him.[l] If Peter de Langtoft is to be credited, Syward was a partizan of Edward's when the castle of Dunbar was besieged, for, in speaking of that event, he says—

> A knight was tham among, Sir Richard Seward,
> Tille our faith was he long, and with Kyng Edward,[m]

and proceeds to describe the artful manner in which he managed to place that fortress into his hands; but this account is totally irreconcileable with the positive fact that he was a prisoner from the time of the surrender of the castle until July in the next year. Certain it is, however, that from the moment in which he was released from the Tower he served England with zeal and good faith, and speedily obtained the confidence of its monarch. On the 26th September, 1298, 7th May and 16th July, 1299, Syward was summoned by the title of "Baron," to serve in the Scottish wars;[n] and in the following year he was present at the siege of Carlaverock, "in company," the Poem informs us, with his countrymen, the Earl of Dunbar and his son, and Simon de Fresel. In the Wardrobe Book of the 28th Edw. I. his name frequently occurs: on one occasion he received £2. 13s. 4d. for a horse which died in July at Kirkcudbright;[o] and on another, when he is styled a Banneret, he was allowed wages for his retinue, which consisted of two knights and seven esquires.[p] Syward was again summoned to serve in Scotland on the 1st March, 1301;[q] was Sheriff of Dumfriesshire in the 33rd Edw. I.;[r] and was commanded to assist in repressing the rebellion of Robert

---

i Rot. Scot. vol. I. pp. 27, 28. k Ibid. p. 43 c. l Ibid. p. 49. m P. 275.
n Appendix to the First Peerage Report, pp. 100, 107, 110. o Page 175. p Page 198.
q Appendix to the First Peerage Report, p. 129. r Rot. Parl. vol. I. p. 267 b.

Brus, by writ tested on the 21st June, 1308.[s]   On the 16th August . following
he was appointed to command a district in Galloway for King Edward the
Second;[t] and was Governor of. Dumfries in 1309, when a certain quantity of
wine was ordered to be delivered to him for that castle.[u]

With that record all account of Richard Syward terminates, and it is therefore
most probable that he died about the year 1310.   From some of the preceding

extracts it is evident that his wife's name was Mary, and that
he had two sons ; Richard, who had attained manhood, and was
married to Elizabeth ——, as early as the year 1296;
and John; but nothing further has been discovered about
them.

The arms of Richard Syward were, Sable, a cross fleury
Argent.x

SIMON DE FRESEL.

[PAGE 36.]

Simon de Fresel, or more properly Simon Fraser, eminently distinguished
himself in the political transactions of his country; and the pages of contemporary chroniclers, as well as the records of the kingdom, bear ample testimony
to his bravery and activity in the field.

He was the eldest son of Simon Fraser, the ancestor of the baronial houses of
Saltoun and Lovat; and the earliest account given of him by Sir Robert Douglas
is in the 25th Edw. I., when we are informed he was Edward's prisoner, but having
undertaken to support him in his foreign wars, pledged his wife and children for
the faithful performance of his engagement.   It would appear that, like Syward,

---

s Fœdera, N. E. vol. II. p. 52.   t Rotuli Scotiæ, vol. I. pp. 56 and 57.   u Ibid. p. 64.

x Page 34; and Cotton MSS. Caligula, A. xvii.

he was captured in the castle of Dunbar, and that he purchased his release at the expense of his honor, by swearing fealty to the conqueror. On the 26th September, 1298, and 7th May, 1299,[y] by the appellation of a Baron, he was summoned to serve with horse and arms against his countrymen under Edward's banner; and was at the siege of Carlaverock in June, 1300, in which year he appears to have been Warden of the Forest of Selkirk, for by that designation the truce between the two kingdoms was notified to him on the 30th of October. In the same year, by the description of " Dom. Simon Fraser, Baneret," he was allowed £64. 18s. as wages for his retinue, which consisted of three knights and twelve esquires;[z] but with the flexibility of conscience which characterized the greater part of the Scottish nobility at the period, he seceded from Edward in 1302, and having joined Comyn, one of the Regents of Scotland, defeated part of the English army at Roslin on the 24th February, 1303. His rigour towards " Sir Ralph the Coffrers," who fell into his hands on that occasion, is curiously described by Peter of Langtoft,[a] but the passage is too long for insertion. Edward having succeeded in once more subduing Scotland, Fraser was excepted from the general conditions of the capitulation at Strathorde in February, 1304, as it was specially provided that he should be banished for three years from Edward's dominions, and should not be permitted during that time to enter the territories of France; and in 1305 a fine of three years rent was imposed upon his estate. He was present at the defeat of Robert King of Scotland in 1306, which event was immediately followed by the execution of this distinguished soldier and of the still more distinguished Wallace.

Those events are thus described by Langtoft:

> The Freselle ther he fled, gone after was he fonden,
> Now taken he is and led unto the toure of Lundon,
> Ther his dome he feyng als traytoure salle pe witen,
> First drawen and sithen heyng, and his hede of smyten.
> Allas, it was to mene, his bertuz and his pruesse,
> So fele in him were gene, that perist for falsnesse,
> His hede unto the brigge to sette was it sent,
> The body lete thei ligge, and som therof thei brent.[b]

---

[y] Appendix to the First Peerage Report, pp. 100, 106.

[z] Liber Quotidianus Contrarotulatoris Garderobæ anno Regis Edwardi Primi 28o. p. 198.

[a] Page 319.   [b] Page 335.

But a much more minute and curious account is given of the tragical termination of Fraser's life in a fragment of an inedited chronicle in the British Museum
of the fifteenth century,[c] from which Mr. Ritson printed the subjoined extract
in illustration of a poem which will be more fully noticed.

" The fryday next before assumpcioun of oure lady, King Edeward mette
Robert the Brus bisides seynt Johns toune in Scotland and with his companye, of
whiche companye King Edewarde quelde sevene thowsand. When Robert the
Brus saw this myschif and gan to flee, and hovd hym that men mygte nougt hym
fynde, but S[r] Simond Frisell pursuede hym socore, so that he turnede ayen and
abode bataille, for he was a worthy knyght and a bolde of body, and the
Englisshe men pursuede hym sore yn every syde, and quelde the stede that S[r]
Symond Frisell rood uppon, and ther toke hym and lad hym to the host. And
S[r] Symond began for to flater and speke faire, and saide, Lordys, I shall yeve you
iiij thousand marke of sylver and myne hors and harneys and all my armure and
vicome. Tho answerd Theobaude of Pevenes, that was the Kinges archer, Now
God me so helpe hit is for nougt that thou spexte, for alle the gold of Engelonde
I wold the noght lete gone withoute commaundement of King Edeward. And
tho was he lad to the King. And the King wolde not see hym, but commaunded
to lede hym awey to his dome to London on our Ladyes even nativite, and he
was honge and drawe, and his heede smyten of, and honged ayene with chynes
of jren oppon the galwes, and his hede was sette oppon London brug on a sper.
And ayens Cristesmasse the body was brent, for enchesoun that the men that
kepte the body by nyghte sawe menye devellis rampande with jren crokes, ren-
nynge uppon the gallews and horribliche tormented the body, and meny that ham
sawe, anoon after thei deied for dred, or woxen mad, or sore sykenesse thei
had."

In one of the Harleian Manuscripts[d] there is a ballad written on the subject,
a few years after the circumstance took place, and which was published by
Ritson.[e] The following stanzas are so extremely interesting, from the manner in
which Fraser is alluded to, that, notwithstanding the length to which they
extend, it is impossible to avoid inserting them. After noticing the capture and
the fate of his unfortunate companions, the poet says:

---

c Harl. MSS. 266.   d No. 2253.   e Ancient Songs.

Thenne saide the iustice that gentil is ant fre,
Sire Simond Frysel, the kynges traytour hast thou be,
In water ant in londe that monie myhten se,
What sayst thou thareto, hou wolt thou quite the?
    Do say.
      So foul he him wiste
      Nede waron truste
        Forto segge nay.

Ther he was ydemed, so hit wes londes lawe,
For that he wes lordswyk furst he wes to drawe,
Upon a retheres hude forth he wes ytuht,
Sum while in ys time he wes a modi knyht,
    In huerte.
      Wickednesse and sunne
      Hit is lutel wunne,
        That maketh the body smerte.

For al is grete poer yet he wes plaht,
Falsnesse and swykedom al hit g'eth to naht,
Tho he wes in Scotlond lutel wes ys thoht,
Of the harde iugement that him wes bysoht
    In stounde.
      He wes foursithe forswore
      To the king ther bifore,
        And that him brohte to grounde.

With feteres and with gyves ichot he wes to drowe,
From the tour of Londone, that monie myhte knowe,
In a curtel of burel aselkethe wyse,
Ant a gerland on ys heued of the newe gupse,
    Thurh Cheepe;
      Moni mon of Engelond,
      For to se Symond,
        Thideward con lepe.

Tho he come to galewes furst he wes an honge,
Al quick byheueded, thah him thohte longe,
Seththe he wes ypened, is boweles ybrend,
The heued to Londone brugge wes send,
To shonde :
So ich ever mote the
Sum while wende he
Thes lutel to stonde.

He rideth thourh the site as y telle may,
With gomen and wyth solas, that wes here play,
To Londone brugge hee nome the way,
Moni wes the wyves chil that ther on laketh a day,
Ant seide alas
That he wes ibore,
And so villiche forlore,
So feir mon ase he was.

Now stont the heued aboue the tubrugge,
Faste bi Waleis, soth forte sugge,
After socour of Scotlond longe he mowe prye,
Ant after help of Fraunce, wet halt hit to lye,
Ich wene.
Betere him were in Scotlond,
With is ax in ys hond,
To pleyen othe grene.

Ant the body hongeth at the galewes faste,
With yrnene claspes longe to laste,
Forte wyte wel the body, and Scottysh to garste,
Foure and tuenti the beoth to sothe ate laste,
By nyhte,
Yef eny were so hardi
The body to remny,
Also to dyhte.

Fraser left two daughters his coheirs, one of whom married Sir Patrick Fleming, ancestor of the Earls of·Wigton; and the other, named Mary, was the wife of Sir Gilbert Hay, ancestor of the Marquess of Tweedale. From Alexander Fraser his brother the Barons Saltoun and Lovat descended.

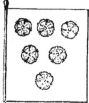

The arms of Simon Fraser were, Sable, semée of roses Argent;[f] but the descendants of his brother bear, Azure, three cinquefoils Argent.[g]

BRIAN FITZ ALAN.

[PAGE 36.]

The description given by the Poet of this Baron tends to impress us with a favorable idea of his person and character. Courtesy and honor are among the best attributes even in a refined state of society; and it would seem that they were as highly estimated in the rude age in which Fitz Alan lived. Had we not possessed that testimony to his merits, this notice of him would have been even more barren than it is, for nearly all the usual sources present no information respecting him; hence the little which is known has been almost wholly derived from the invaluable labours of Sir William Dugdale.

He succeeded his father, Brian Fitz Alan, before the 5th Edw. I.; and on the 6th April, 10 Edw. I. 1282, and 14th June, 1287, was summoned to serve with horse and arms in Wales.[h] In the 19th Edw. I. he obtained permission to make a castle of his house at Kilwardeby in Yorkshire; and in the following year,

---

f Page 36.

g Wood's Douglas's Peerage of Scotland, from which such facts in the above memoir of Simon Fraser have been taken as are not stated to have been derived from other authorities.

h Appendix to the First Peerage Report, pp. 39, 51.

being one of King Edward's vicegerents. in Scotland, he, with others, received
that monarch's precept to give John de Baillol possession of the kingdom.   He
was a witness to that personage's surrender of his crown on the 10th July, 1296,
about which time he was constituted the King's Lieutenant in Scotland.   Fitz
Alan was present at the siege of Carlaverock in June 1300 ;[i] and in the ensuing
February was a party to the Letter from the Barons to Pope Boniface, in which
he is styled " Lord of Bedale."[k]   His seal affixed to that document has been the
subject of remark,[l] for, instead of containing his arms, it presents a whimsical
assemblage of animals, apparently consisting of two birds, a. rabbit, a stag, and a
pig or boar, all of which are looking to the dexter excepting the latter, which is
regarding the chief; and is inscribed with this curious legend :

TOT. CAPITA. TOT. SENTENCIE.

The inference to be drawn from this singular seal tends to establish that its
owner was eccentric or satirical; for it must either have been used from un-
meaning caprice, or with the intention of ridiculing the devices on the signets of
his contemporaries.   The allusion in the Poem to the arms of Fitz Alan is too
important to be allowed to pass unnoticed.   It not only informs us of an event
in his life, by proving that he had been involved in a dispute with Hugh Pointz,
but shows that it was always one of the fundamental laws of arms that no two
persons should bear the same ensigns, and that there was then sufficient pride
felt on the point to resent its infringement.

All which is further known of Fitz Alan is that he was summoned to parliament from the 23rd June, 23 Edw. I. 1295, to the 22nd January, 33 Edw. I.
1305, though he died in 1302.   The name of his wife is not stated, but it is
almost certain that he married late in life; for, according to a note[m] of the inquisition held on his death, Maud his daughter was his heir, though on the death
of his brother Theobald Fitz Alan in the 1st Edw. II. 1307-8, his heirs are
said to have been Maud and Katherine, the daughters of his brother Brian Fitz
Alan, the former of whom was then aged seven years and the latter five, so that
Katherine, who made proof of her age in the 12th Edw. II. was probably a post-
humous child.   A discrepancy, however, exists on the subject ; for, agreeable to

---

i Page 36 ante.   k Appendix to the Fourth Peerage Report.
l Archæologia, vol. XXI p. 213.   m Penès auctoris.

a note of the inquisition on the death of this Baron his daughter Maud was then eight years old, and Dugdale says that Katherine was at the same time aged six, which, if the other statement be correct, was impossible. Of these daughters, Maud married Sir Gilbert Stapleton, and, according to a pedigree in Dodsworth's MSS., secondly, Thomas Sheffield;[n] and Katherine became the wife of John Lord Grey of Rotherfield.

Brian Fitz Alan was buried in the south aisle of Bedale church in Yorkshire, and a sumptuous monument was there erected to his memory, a beautiful engraving and accurate description of which are given in Blore's " Monumental Remains."

The arms of Fitz Alan were, Barry Or and Gules;[o] but they are described in the contemporary roll in the Cottonian collection,[p] as, Gules, three bars Or. The latter agrees with the shield on the monument just mentioned, which is charged with barry of six, and the same coat occurs in several places in the windows of Bedale church. Dugdale informs us that the seal of this Baron's grandfather attached to a deed in the Cottonian library, contained the same bearings.

---

n Blore's Monumental Remains.   o Page 36.   P Caligula, A. xvii.

ROGER DE MORTAIGNE.

[PAGE 36.]

A few facts are recorded of a Roger de Mortaine about the period in which this knight lived, but it is impossible to identify him as the person to whom they relate, though there can be little doubt on the subject.

His name is of great antiquity; but the pedigree of his family has never, it is believed, been compiled in an authentic manner, nor are there, perhaps, sufficient materials for the purpose.

It would appear that he was the son and heir of Roger de Morteyne who died in vitâ patris, and that he succeeded as heir to his grandfather William de Morteyne's lands in the counties of Leicester, Notts, Lincoln, and Derby, in the 12th Edw. I., at which time he was twenty-one years of age.[q] In the 26th Edw. I. 1298, on the death of William de Luda Bishop of Ely, Isabella, the wife of Roger de Morteyn, and William Tuchet, were found to be the heirs to that prelate's lands in Buckinghamshire;[r] and in the 33rd Edw. I. the said Roger and Isabella petitioned the King relative to the division of the Bishop's possessions, in which it is also said that William Tuchet was his other coheir, and that Luda was indebted to the crown at the time of his decease the sum of £128. 4s. 5½d.[s]

From the preceding Poem we learn that a Roger de Morteyne was at the siege of Carlaverock in June 1300, when, if he was the individual who succeeded his grandfather in the 12th Edw. I. he must have been about thirty-seven years old. That he was ambitious to distinguish himself is the only description given of him by the Poet. After that time there is no other record of the name than that in the 1st Edw. II. a Roger de Morteyne held the manor of Eyam and the castle of Peak in Derbyshire;[t] and in the next year

q Esch. 12 Edw. I.   r Esch. eod. ann.   s Rot. Parl. vol. I. p. 182 b.
t Calend. Inquis. ad quod damnum, p. 220.

was enfeoffed of several manors in Lincolnshire and Cumberland.[u]

The arms of Roger de Mortaigne, according to the Poem, were, Or, six lions rampant double-queued Azure; but in the Roll in the Cottonian MS.[x] they are thus blazoned, " De Or, a vj lioncels de Sable, od les cuowes forchees."

WALTER DE HUNTERCOMBE.

[PAGE 36.]

Notwithstanding the slight notice taken of this individual by the Poet, few of those whom he commemorates had more legitimate claims upon his attention; for his services were long, zealous, and important.

Walter de Huntercombe succeeded his father in his lands in the 55th Hen. III. at which time he was of full age; and shortly afterwards married Alice, third daughter and coheiress of Hugh de Bolebec, and who, in the 2nd Edw. I., was found to be one of the coheirs of Richard de Muntfichet, in right of her grandmother Margery, his sister.[y] In the 5th Edw. I. he paid £50 for his relief of the barony of Muschamp; and on the 12th December in that year was summoned to serve with horse and arms against the Welsh:[z] he received similar writs tested 6th April and 24th May, 10 Edw. I.,[a] and 14th June, 15 Edw. I.[b] He was one of the peers who were present in parliament in the 18th Edw. I. when a grant was made to the King, for the marriage of his eldest daughter, of the same aid as had been given to Henry the Third for the marriage of his daughter

---

[u] Calend. Inquis. ad quod damnum, p. 223. [x] Caligula, A. xvii.
[y] Esch. 2 Edw. I. [z] Appendix to the First Peerage Report, p. 37. [a] Ibid. pp. 40, 44.
[b] Ibid. p. 51.

3 M

the Queen of Scotland;[c] and shortly afterwards the isle of Man was entrusted
to his charge, but which he only held three years, as; in obedience to the King's
commands, he surrendered the trust to John de Baillol in the 21st Edw. I.   In
the 19th Edw. I., by writ tested on the 16th April at Darlington, he was ordered
to be at Norham equipped for the field by the ensuing Easter;[d] and obtained a
charter of free-warren in all his demesne lands in the county of Northumberland
before the end of that year.   On the 26th June, 1294, Huntercombe was ordered
to join the expedition then made into Gascony.[e]   His military services during
the remainder of the reign of Edward the First were incessant, for he was in the
Scottish wars in the 25th, 26th, 28th, 31st, and 34th years of that monarch; was
Governor of Edinburgh Castle in the 26th; Lieutenant of Northumberland in
the 27th Edw. I.; and afterwards Warden of the Marches there.   In the 28th
Edw. I. we find from the Poem that he was at the siege of Carlaverock; and in
the next year he was a party to the Letter to Pope Boniface, in which he is
called "Walter Lord of Huntercombe."   It appears from the Wardrobe accounts
of the 28th Edw. I. that he was allowed £10 as a compensation for a black nag
which was killed by the Scots at Flete, on the 6th August, 1299.[f]   But the
nature and extent of Huntercombe's services are best shewn by his own statement of them in his petition to the King in the 35th Edw. I., praying a remission
of his scutage for the expeditions in which he had been engaged, with which
prayer the Crown complied.   He says that he had been in all the wars of Scotland up to that time; namely, in the first war at Berwick with twenty horse;
then at Stirling with thirty-two horse in the retinue of the Earl Warren; then at
Le Vaire Chapelle with thirty horse in the retinue of the Bishop of Durham;
afterwards at Gaway with sixteen horse; and that he sent eighteen horse to
the last battle, though he was not present himself, being then Warden of the
Marches of Scotland and Northumberland.[g]   From that year nothing more is
known of this Baron, excepting that he was summoned to parliament from the
23rd June, 23 Edw. I. 1295, to the 16th June, 14 Edw. II. 1311, and died in
1312; but after the 35th Edw. I. he was probably prevented by age from taking
an active part in public affairs, for even allowing him to have been but
twenty-one in the 55th Hen. III. he must have been above sixty in 1307; which

---

c Rot. Parl. vol. I. p. 24.   d Appendix to the First Peerage Report, p. 54.
e Ibid. p. 55.   f Page 175.   g Rot. Parl. vol. I. p. 194 b.

calculation makes him to have been about fifty when he was at Carlaverock, and sixty-four at his decease.   Though he was twice married he died without issue.

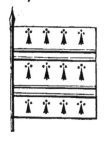

His first wife was Alice de Bolebec, before mentioned; but we only know that the Christian name of his second was Ellen, and that she survived him.   Nicholas Newbaud, his nephew, son of his sister Gunnora, was found to be his heir.[h]

. The arms of Huntercombe were, Ermine, two bars gemells Gules.[i]

WILLIAM DE RIDRE.

[PAGE 38.]

William de Ridre appears to have been the individual who in most other places is called William de Rithre or Rythre.   The first occasion on which the name has been found is in the 18th Edw. I. on the Rolls of Parliament, when he was one of the manucaptors of William de Duclas.[k]   In the 25th Edw. I. he was in the expedition into Gascony, and was in the wars of Scotland in the 26th, 29th, 31st, and 32nd Edw. I.   From the Poem we learn that he was at the siege of Carlaverock in June 1300; and he received his first writ of summons to parliament in the, preceding December.   The accounts of the Wardrobe of Edward the First in the 28th year of his reign, inform us that " Dom. Will. de Rithre, Banerett," received £67. 13s. for the wages of himself and his retinue, that is to say:—for himself, two knights, and five esquires, from the 14th July, on which day his horses were valued, to the 29th September, when one of his knights,

---

h Esch. 6 Edw. II.
i Page 36; Cotton MSS. Caligula, A. xvii.; and the seal of this Baron, a⁰ 1301.
k Vol. I. p. 34.

namely, "Dom. William de Beeston," returned, being seventy-seven days, £50. 15s.;—for himself, one knight, and five esquires, from the 29th September to the 13th October, on which day another of his knights returned, being fourteen days, £7. 14s. 5d.;—and for himself and his five esquires, from the 13th October to the 3rd November, being twenty-two days, £9. 18s.[1] He is mentioned as having been present in the parliament which met at Carlisle in the octaves of St. Hilary in the 35th Edw. I. aº 1307,[m] but nothing more is known of him.

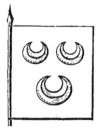

Rythre was summoned to parliament from the 29th December, 28 Edw. I. 1299, to the 26th August, 1 Edw. II. 1307, about which year he died, and was succeeded by his son, John de Rythre, who was Governor of Skipton Castle in the 11th Edw. but was never summoned to parliament.

The arms of Rythre were, Azure, three crescents Or.[n]

THOMAS DE FURNIVAL.

[PAGE 38.]

The praise which has been bestowed upon the knights who were at Carlaverock in the preceding pages, has been almost unvaried in its nature; since scarcely any other merits have been ascribed to them than what characterize soldiers in the rudest state of society. If they performed actions of a more praiseworthy description no record of them has been preserved; and they are consequently only known to us by their military services. It is therefore a pleasing relief to the monotony of these sketches to find one individual among them still remembered in the place where he resided, as a Benefactor; and it will be seen that, considering the age in which Thomas de Furnival lived, few have higher claims to the appellation.

---

[1] Rot. Parl. vol. I. p. 188.   m Page 198.   n Page 38; and Cotton MSS. Caligula, A. xvii.

The exact period of his birth is no where stated, but he succeeded his father, Thomas de Furnival, in his lands, before the 7th Edw. I. anno 1279; and having performed homage, he obtained livery of them in the 9th Edw. I., at which time he was of full age. In the 10th and 11th Edw. I. he was commanded to serve with horse and arms against the Welsh;[o] on the 8th of June, 1294, he was summoned to attend a great council or parliament;[p] and on the 14th of that month he was ordered to be at Portsmouth in September following, thence to join the expedition into Gascony.[q]

In the next year Furnival was summoned to parliament, and in the 26th Edw. I. was in the wars of Scotland; in the 27th Edw. I. he was constituted Captain-general and Lieutenant to the King in the counties of Nottingham and Derby; and was again in the Scottish wars in the 28th, 32nd, 34th, and 35th Edw. I. The Poem informs us that he was at the siege of Carlaverock in June, 1300, at which time he was about forty years of age, and the account given of him is amusing. After a compliment to his personal appearance, we are told that "when seated on horseback he did not resemble a man asleep," by which was probably meant that he always acquitted himself with honour in the field. Furnival was a party to the Letter from the Barons to Pope Boniface in February, 1301, in which he is styled "Lord of Sheffield;"[r] and in the 4th and 8th Edw. II. he was again commanded to serve in the wars of Scotland. He was summoned to parliament from the 24th June, 23 Edw. I. 1295, to the 27th January, 6th Edw. III. 1332; and died on the 3rd February, 1332; when, allowing that he was only twenty-one in the 9th Edw. I., he must have been seventy years of age.

The conduct which entitles the memory of Thomas de Furnival to respect, and which has caused him to be still familiarly termed at Sheffield "the great grantor," was the emancipation of his tenants from their vassalage; the regular establishment of a municipal court, with trial by jury; and the institution of a market and fair, in his demesnes.[s] In estimating his character, all his military services sink into nothing when contrasted with the important benefits which he thus conferred upon those under his protection: the praise which belongs to the

---

[o] Appendix to the First Peerage Report, pp. 40. 47. [p] Ibid. p. 56. [q] Ibid. p. 57.
[r] Appendix to the Fourth Peerage Report. [s] Hunter's History of Hallamshire.

former he shares in common with most of his contemporaries, but the everlasting honour which must be ascribed to the latter, is peculiarly his own.

It would seem from Dugdale's statement that this Baron had Thomas, his son and heir, and other children, by his wife Elizabeth, daughter of Sir Peter de Montfort, of Beldesert Castle in Warwickshire, Knight, and widow of William de Montacute; and which is corroborated by the inquisition on the death of the said Elizabeth in the 28th Edw. III., where the following statement occurs: " Elizabetha de Montacute, uxor Willielmi de Montacute, et quondam nupta Thomæ de Furnival, per quem exitum habuit Thomas de Furnival, qui filium habuit Thomas de Furnival;"ᵗ but it is opposed by the fact that William de Montacute, her first husband, died in the 13th Edw. II. 1328-9, and that Thomas Furnival, the son of her second husband, was born in 1302, twenty-six years before the death of his mother-in-law's first husband; and also by the circumstance that among the persons whose souls this Elizabeth orders to be prayed for in the chauntry which she founded in the monastery of St. Frideswide at Oxford, she takes no notice of any children by Furnival, though he was to be remembered in the religious services, whilst all those by Montacute are particularly mentioned. In the pedigree of Furnival in the " History of Hallamshire," this Baron is said to have had two wives; first, Joan, daughter of Hugh le Despenser, by whom he is stated to have had his son and heir, Thomas 2nd Baron Furnival; and, secondly, the above-mentioned Elizabeth Montfort. Besides the sons before noticed, he is considered to have had three daughters; Maud, the wife of John Baron Marmion; Katherine, who married William de Thweng; and Eleanor, the wife of Peter, Baron de Mauley.

Thomas the next Lord Furnival was summoned to parliament in his father's life-time and dying in 1339, was succeeded by his son of the same name, upon whose decease in 1364 s. p., the dignity devolved upon his brother William, the fourth Baron. He died s. p. m. in 1383, and in the same year Thomas Neville, brother of Ralph first Earl of Westmoreland, the husband of Joan, daughter and sole heiress of the last Baron, was summoned to parliament as Baron Neville of Hallamshire, and died s. p. m. in 1406, leaving by his first wife, Joan Furnival, a daughter Maud; and by his second wife, Ankaret, daughter of John Lord

---

ᵗ From a MS. note in the possession of the Editor.

Strange of Black'mere, a daughter, Joan, who married Sir Hugh Cooksey, Knt.[v] Maud married John Talbot, afterwards the celebrated Earl of Shrewsbury, who in her right was summoned to parliament as Lord Furnival in 1409. The barony

of Furnival continued vested in the Earls of Shrewsbury until the death of George Talbot, the 7th Earl, s. p. m. in 1616, when it fell into abeyance among his daughters and coheirs; and is now in abeyance between their representatives, namely, the present Lords Stourton and Petre.

The arms of Furnival are, Argent, a bend between six martlets Gules.[u]

JOHN DE LA MARE.

[PAGE 38.]

The particulars which are preserved of this Baron are remarkable only for their brevity. He was descended, Sir William Dugdale informs us, from a family which possessed lands in Oxfordshire from the time of Stephen; but he does not state the name of his father, the time of his birth, or the period when he succeeded to his inheritance. The first occasion on which he is mentioned appears to have been in the 22nd Edw. I., having on the 14th of June in that year been commanded to serve with horse and arms in the expedition into Gascony.[x] In the 26th Edw. I. he was in the wars of Scotland; and in the year following was summoned to parliament among the Barons of the realm. It is evident that he was again in the Scottish wars in the 29th Edw. I., as we learn

---

[v] Dugdale says both daughters were by Joan de Furnival, but the statement in the text stands on the authority of a pedigree in the College of Arms, B. 2. f. 17.

[u] Page 38; Cotton MSS. Caligula A. xviii.; and the seal of this Baron in 1301.

[x] Appendix to the First Peerage Report, p. 57.

from the Poem that he served in the third division of the English army at Carlaverock in June 1300, though nothing more is there said of him than the description of his arms. The subjoined account of his retinue is extracted from the
" Liber Quotidianus Contrarotulatoris Garderobæ," of that year:—

" Domino Johanni de la Mare, Báneretto, pro vadiis suis, duorum militum et
viij scutiferorum suorum a xiij die Julij, quo die equi sui fuerunt appreciati, usque
v diem Septembris, quo die unus de militibus suis, videlicet, Dominus Johannes de
la Mare, et Rogerus de Levyngton, vallettus ejusdem, recesserunt de exercitu Regis,
primo die computato et non ultimo per liiij dies, exceptis vadiis trium scutiferorum suorum, videlicet, Johannis de Glaston, Hug' de Ingelton, et Willielmi de
Styvinton, per xl dies, xxj die Augusti pro ultimo computato, per quos fecerunt
servicium pro eodem Domino Johanne post appreciationem equorum suorum,
xxxvij *li.* iiij *s.* Eidem, pro vadiis suis, unius militis et vij scutiferorum suorum,
a v die Septembr' usque xxvj diem ejusdem mensis, utroque computato per xxij
dies, xiiij *li.* vj *s.* per compotum factum cum eodem, per duas vices apud la Rose
et Holm', mense Septembris. Summa lj *li.* x *s.*" [y]

In the 33rd Edw. I. he petitioned the King to be forgiven the payment of one
hundred marks, with which request his Majesty complied.[z]

De la Mare was regularly summoned to parliament from the 6th February,
27 Edw. I. 1299, to the 26th July, 7 Edw. II. 1313; and died in the 9th

Edw. II. 1315-16, apparently without issue, for his sister
Isabella, wife of Thomas de Maydenhache, is stated to have
been his heir, and who was then fifty years of age:[a] in that
case his barony then became extinct. Joan, his widow, survived him.[b]

The arms of John de la Mare were, Gules, a maunch
Argent.[c]

. y P. 197.   z Rot. Parl. vol. I. p. 159 b.   a Esch. 9 Edw. II. No. 274.   b Ibid.
c Page 38; and the Cotton MSS. Caligula, A. xviii.

JOHN LE STRANGE.

[PAGE 38.]

John le Strange succeeded his father in the 4th Edw. I., at which time he was twenty-two years of age;d and obtained livery of his lands in the 6th Edw. I. On the 28th June, 11 Edw. I. 1283, he was summoned to be at Shrewsbury on the morrow of the feast of St. Michael next following, to attend a council relative to the proceedings of Llewellyn late Prince of Wales;e and in the next year answered for three hundred marks to the King which his grandfather John le Strange had borrowed of the inhabitants of Cheshire to support the Welsh wars. In the 22nd Edw. I. he was summoned to serve with horse and arms in the expedition into Gascony;f and on the 26th September, 26 Edw. I. 1298, was commanded to attend at Carlisle at the ensuing Easter with his followers against the Scots.g Le Strange was first summoned to parliament in December, 28th Edw. I. 1299, and in June in the next year he was at the siege of Carlaverock, when he must have been above forty-five years old. Of his retinue about that time the following record is preserved:

" Domino Johanni Extraneo, banerctto, pro vadiis suis duorum militum et vij scutiferorum; a vj die Julii, quo die equi sui fuerunt appreciati in guerra predicta, usque xxiij diem Augusti, quo die recepit de exercitu Regis apud Douceur, primo die computato et non ultimo, per xlviij dies, per compotum secum factum apud Westm', mense Novembr', anno xxx. xxxvj *li.*"h

In February, 1301, Le Strange was a party to the Letter from the Barons to the Pope, in which, and on his seal affixed to that document, he is styled " Lord of Knokyn."i He was again in the wars of Scotland in the 31st Edw. I.; and in the 33rd Edw. I. according to Dugdale, " was made a knight by bathing and other sacred ceremonies;" but it is almost certain that it was his son and heir apparent who then received that honour, as he attained his majority in that year.k

---

d Esch. 4 Edw. I.   e Appendix to the First Peerage Report, p. 50.   f Ibid. p. 58.
g Ibid. p. 100.   h Liber Quotidianus Garderobæ, 28 Edw. I. p. 202.
i Appendix to the Fourth Peerage Report.
k In Anstis's " Authorities relative to the Order of the Bath," p. 5, there is an account of the robes granted to him on the occasion.

In the 1st Edw. II. he was permitted to make a castle of his house at Medle
in Shropshire; and having been summoned to parliament from the 29th Dec. 28
Edw. I. 1299, to 12th Dec. 3 Edw. II. 1309, died in 1310, aged fifty-six; leaving
issue by Maud, daughter and heiress of Roger de Eiville, John, his son and heir,
then twenty-seven years old; a younger son, Eubolo; and a daughter, Elizabeth.[1]   Maud his widow remarried, before the 8th Edw. II., Thomas Hastang;[1]
for Hastang and the said Maud petitioned the King, stating that Lord Strange
and herself had bought the marriage of the son and heir of Madok ap Griffith
Maillor for their daughter Elizabeth for £50; that the lands of the said Griffith
having been seized into the King's hands, he had given the custody of them to
Lord Strange until the heir became of age; that after Strange's death it had
pleased his Majesty to give the said lands to the custody of Sir Edward Hake-
bute or Hakebutel; and they prayed to have the said lands entrusted to their
keeping, and also that regard should be paid to the circumstance that the children were contracted in the life-time of their fathers, and to the £50 which
had been given for the said marriage.[1]   A petition on the same subject follows
from Roger Mortimer of Chirk.[1]

The Barony of Strange of Knockyn was vested in the male descendants of this
Baron until 1477, when John le Strange, 8th Baron, died s. p. m.   Joan, his
daughter and heiress, having married George Stanley, son and heir apparent of
Thomas 1st Earl of Derby, he was summoned to parliament in 1482 as Lord

Strange, and the dignity continued in the Earls of Derby.
until the death of Ferdinand the fifth Earl in 1594, when it
fell into abeyance between his three daughters and coheirs;
and is now in abeyance among their descendants and repre
sentatives.

The arms of Strange of Knockyn are, Gules, two lions
passant Argent.[m]

---

1 Rot. Parl. vol. I. p. 306.

m Page 38; Cotton MSS. Caligula, A. xviii; and the seal of John Baron Strange in 1301.

JOHN DE GREY.

[PAGE 40.]

There is scarcely an important event in English history, but in which some member of the illustrious house of Grey bore a conspicuous part; and, as in this instance, it frequently happened that the representatives of two or more of its numerous branches are recorded to have participated therein. Of Henry Lord Grey of Codnor, the head of the family, who served in the first squadron, some particulars have already been given; and of John de Grey, who was descended from Robert, a younger son of Henry de Grey, the great grandfather of the said Henry, it is now necessary to state all which is known.

He succeeded his father, Robert, in his lands of Rotherfield in Oxfordshire in 1295, at which time he was about twenty-four years of age; and on the 26th Jan. 25 Edw. I. 1297, was summoned to attend a great council or parliament at Salisbury on the feast of St. Matthias next following.[n] In the same year he was returned from the county of Oxford as holding lands or rents *in capite* or otherwise, to the amount of £20 yearly and upwards, and as such was summoned to serve in person with horse and arms;[o] and was a commissioner of array in "Maylor Sexneth," and in other demesnes and lordships in the Marches.[p] In the 27th Edw. I. he was in the wars of Scotland; and in June in the following year, 1300, we learn from the Poem that he was at the siege of Carlaverock, when he must have been nearly thirty years of age; but no description of his personal appearance or character occurs, though it seems

---

n Appendix to the First Peerage Report, p. 78. Although he succeeded to lands which seem to have been held *in capite*, and hence may be supposed to have been a Baron by tenure, it is very doubtful whether he was considered by his contemporaries as a Baron of the realm, since it is by no means certain that the meeting alluded to was a regular parliament, and he was never again summoned to any legislative assembly. This doubt is not a little increased by the fact that, in the Roll of Arms in the Cottonian MS. Caligula, A. xviii, which was undoubtedly compiled in the early part of the reign of Edward the Second, his name is introduced among the knights in the county of Essex towards the end, instead of among the peers at the commencement of the manuscript.　　o Palgrave's " Parliamentary Writs," p. 290.　　p Ibid. p. 306-7.

that he was actively engaged in the siege.[q] These few sentences contain all which can be said of this individual, excepting that he died in 1312, aged about forty-two; and by his wife Margaret, daughter and coheiress of William de Odyngsells of Maxton in Warwickshire, left issue John, his son and heir, then ten years old, who was summoned to parliament soon after he became of age. The barony continued vested in the male descendants of the subject of this notice until 1387, when Robert fourth Lord Grey of Rotherfield died s. p. m., on which event it devolved on Joan, his daughter and sole heiress, who married John Lord Deincourt, and by him left issue two daughters and coheirs; of whom, Alice married William Lord Lovell; and Margaret, the other, became the wife of Ralph Lord Cromwell: she died s. p., when the barony became vested in John Lord Lovell, the son of the said Alice; but was forfeited on the attainder of his son and heir, Francis Viscount Lovell, K..G:, in 1487.[r]

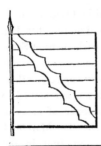

The arms of Grey of Rotherfield are always considered to have been, Barry of six Argent and Azure, a bend Gules; and which is corroborated by the description of them in the contemporary roll so frequently referred to,[s] and by the seal of John Lord Grey of Rotherfield in the 35th Edw. III.;[t] but the Poem states that the bend in the arms of the John de Grey who was at Carlaverock was *engrailed.*

---

[q] Page 79 ante.

[r] That such was the fact appears from evidence. It is necessary to observe that the erroneous account of the family of Grey of Rotherfield in the " Synopsis of the Peerage," was taken from a pedigree by Vincent in the College of Arms.

[s] Cotton MSS. Caligula, A. xviii.

[t] Appended to a charter in the British Museum.

WILLIAM DE CANTILUPE.

[PAGE 40.]

In common with many of his contemporaries, the merits and services of this individual are alike forgotten; and a very brief notice will contain all which can be gleaned respecting him from the records of his time.

He was the eldest son of Nicholas de Cantilupe, by Eustachia, the sister and at length sole heiress of Hugh Fitz Ralph, Lord of Gresley in Nottinghamshire. In the 22nd Edw. I. he was summoned to serve in the expedition into Gascony; and in the 26th, 27th, and 34th Edw. I. was in the Scottish wars. The Poem informs us that he was also there in the 28th Edw. I., as he was present at the siege of Carlaverock in June 1300; and the writer praises him because he had "at all times lived in honour." The Wardrobe accounts of that year present the subjoined notice of him and his retinue:

" Domino Willielmo de Cantilupo, baneretto, qui solebat com̃edere in aula Regis ante statutum factum apud Sanctum Albanum de aula non tenenda, et non com̃edenti amplius sed percipienti certa vad', videlicet, per diem vj *s.* pro se et milite suo per statutum predictum, pro hujusmodi vadiis, a xxvij die Junii, quo die venit primo ad curiam post statutum predictum, usque secundum diem Julii, utroque computato, per vj dies, per quos fuit in cur' et extra rotulum hospicii, per compotum factum cum Domino Ricardo de Nevill, militi suo, apud Drumbou, j *li.* xvj*s.*" [u]

On the 29th December, 1299, Cantilupe was summoned to parliament; and in February, 1301, was a party to the Letter from the Barons to Pope Boniface the Eighth, in which he is styled " Lord of Ravensthorp:"[v] in January, 1303, he was ordered to place himself with all his forces under the command of John de Segrave, the King's Lieutenant in Scotland;[w] and on the 9th of April following the knights and men at arms in the county of York were enjoined to obey his instructions concerning the expedition against the Scots.[x] Having been summoned to parliament from 1299 until the 5th August, 2 Edw. II., 1308, he died in

[u] Pp. 200-1. [v] Appendix to the Fourth Peerage Report.
[w] Palgrave's " Parliamentary Writs," p. 369. [x] Ibid. p. 371.

1309, leaving William his son and heir, fifteen years old; but who was never summoned to parliament, and died s. p., when the dignity devolved upon his brother, Nicholas de Cantilupe, who was regularly summoned to and sat in parliament from 1337 until his decease in 1355. Upon the death of his grandson William in the 49th Edw. III., the issue of the Baron who was at Carlaverock failed; and the dignity became extinct.[y]

The arms of Cantilupe are said in the Poem to have been, Gules, a fess Vaire between three fleurs de lis issuing from leopards' heads Or;[z] or, as they would now be blazoned, three leopard's faces jessant fleurs de lis. In the contemporary roll in the Cottonian manuscript,[a] they are, however, thus described, " De Goules, a une fesse de Veer, a iij testes de lupars de Or;" whilst on the seal of this Baron, affixed to the Letter to the Pope in 1301, his arms are represented without the leopards' heads, and simply as a fess Vaire between three fleurs de lis.[b]

HUGH DE MORTIMER.

[Page 40.]

Though a descendant from the common ancestor of the house of Mortimer, afterwards Earls of March, this branch assumed very different arms; and after having existed for a few generations, the male line failed with the Hugh de Mortimer whose career is the subject of this article.

In the reign of Henry the Second, Robert de Mortimer, a younger son of Hugh, second Baron Mortimer by the tenure of Wigmore Castle, acquired Richard's Castle in Shropshire by marrying Margery, the daughter and heiress of Hugh de Say. His grandson, Robert de Mortimer, by Joyce, the daughter and heiress of William le Zouche, had issue Hugh, his son and heir, who succeeded his father in his lands in 1287; and obtained livery of them in 1295, about which.

---

y MS. Collections for Dugdale's Baronage by the late Francis Townsend, esq. Windsor Herald.
z Page 40.   a Caligula, A. xviii.   b Archæologia, vol. XXI. p. 212.

time he probably became of age. In the same year he was attorney for the commonalty of the baronies of Haverford and Roche, in some proceedings connected with the claim of the Earl of Pembroke in Wales:[c] in the 25th Edw. I., he was returned from the counties of Hereford, Northampton, Salop, and Stafford as holding lands or rents to the amount of £20 yearly and upwards, either *in capite* or otherwise, and as such was summoned to perform military service beyond the seas;[d] and in the 27th Edw. I. he was in the wars of Scotland. The Poem informs us that he was also at the siege of Carlaverock in June 1300; and of his retinue in the Scottish wars the following account occurs in the Wardrobe Book of that period:

"Domino Hugoni de Mortui Mari, baneretto, pro vadiis suis, duorum militum et iiij scutiferorum suorum, a xxvj die Julii, quo die equi sui fuerunt appreciati, usque iiij diem Augusti, quo die equi unius militis et unius scutiferis sui fuerunt appreciati, primo die comp' et non ultimo, per ix dies v *li.* viij *s.* Eidem, pro vadiis suis iij militum et v scutiferorum suorum, a iiij die Augusti usque j diem Septembr', utroque comp', per xxix dies, xxj *li.* xv *s.* per compotum factum cum eodem apud Drumbou j die Septembr'. Summa xxvij *li.* iij *s.*"[e]

Hugh de Mortimer was summoned to parliament on the 6th February and 10th April, 27 Edw. I. 1299; and also received writs to attend a great council two years before, namely, on the 26th January and 9th September, 25 Edw. I. 1297. He died in 1304, leaving by Maud his wife, who died in 1316, two daughters, Joan and Margaret, who were his coheirs. The former, who was then twelve years old, married, first, Sir Thomas Bikenore, who was her husband in 1316; and, secondly, Sir Richard Talbot, whose posterity enjoyed the lordship of Richard's Castle. Margaret, the second daughter, was eight years old at the death of her father, and in 1316 was the wife of Sir Geoffrey Cornwall, ancestor by her of the Barons of Burford.[f]

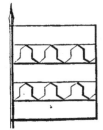

The arms of Mortimer of Richard's Castle were, Gules, two bars Vaire.[g]

.,[c] Rot. Parl. vol. I. p. 140 a.   [d] Palgrave's "Parliamentary Writs," pp. 286, 288, 291.

[e] Pp. 199-200. .   [f] See an elaborate pedigree in Baker's Northamptonshire, p. 415.

[g] Page 40; and several seals of this Baron preserved in divers collections.

SIMON DE MONTACUTE.

[PAGE 40.]

The family of Montacute or Montagu, one of the most illustrious in the Peerage of England, have not only been ennobled in various branches, but have attained the highest honours to which a subject can aspire.

Simon de Montacute, of whose life it is the object of this notice to give a brief account, was the common ancestor of every peer of his name; and succeeded his father, William de Montacute, in the early part of the reign of Edward the First. In the 10th of that monarch he was commanded to serve with horse and arms against the Welsh;[e] and in the 11th Edw. I. was summoned to a parliament at Shrewsbury:[f] in the 18th Edw. I. he obtained a grant of numerous manors from the King; and in the same year the ratification of an agreement between him and Matthew de Forneas, relative to a claim to some lands, was deferred.[g] He was summoned to attend a great council on the 8th June, 1294;[h] and on the 14th of the same month to attend at Portsmouth, properly equipped, thence to join the expedition into Gascony.[i] In the 26th Edw. I. he was in the wars of Scotland: in the next year he was appointed Governor of Corfe Castle in Dorsetshire; and in 1300 was returned from the counties of Somerset and Dorset as holding lands or rents, either *in capite* or otherwise, to the amount of £40 yearly and upwards, and as such was summoned to perform military service against the Scots.[j] At the siege of Carlaverock in that year he is stated to have brought up the third squadron of the English army,[k] a situation which, it would appear from another part of the Poem, was only conferred upon an experienced soldier.[l] From one of the notices of Montacute in the Wardrobe accounts of the 28th Edw. I. it seems that, on the 29th July, 1300, he was sent from Kirkcudbright to Ireland, and returned in the September following:

---

[e] Appendix to the First Peerage Report, p. 48.   [f] Palgrave's "Parliamentary Writs," p. 16.
[g] Rot. Parl. vol. I. p. 55.   [h] Appendix to the First Peerage Report, p. 56.   [i] Ibid. p. 57.
[j] Palgrave's "Parliamentary Writs," p. 336.   [k] Page 41.   [l] Page 47.

" Domino Simoni de Monte Acuto, baneretto, pro vadiis suis, duorum militum et quinque scutiferorum suorum, a xiv die Julii, quo die equi sui fuerunt appreciati, usque xxix diem ejusdem mensis, quo die idem Dominus Simon, simul cum Domino Petro de Donewico, missus fuit per Regem de Kirkcudbright in Hibern' pro victualibus ibidem querend', primo die computato et non ultimo per xv dies, ix *li.* xv *s.* Eidem, pro vad' duorum militum et dictorum quinque scutiferorum morancium in exercitu Reg', cum ejus suis appreciatis, a xix die Julii usque xviij diem Septembr', quo die unus eorundem militum, videlicet, Dominus Humphridus de Bello Campo, simul cum uno scutifero suo, recessit de exercitu Reg' versus partes proprias, primo die computato et non ultimo per lj dies, xxij *li.* xix *s.* Eidem, pro vadiis unius militis et quatuor scutiferorum suorum, a xviij die Septembris usque xx diem ejusdem mensis, utroque computato per iij dies, xviij *s.* Eidem, pro vadiis suis, unius militis, et quatuor scutiferorum suorum, a xxj die Septembris, quo die idem Dominus Simon rediit ad Regem apud Holm' de partibus Hibern', usque tercium diem Novemb', utroque computato per xl dies, xxij *li.* per compotum factum cum eodem apud Karliol' x die Novembr'. Summa lv*li.* xij *s.*"[m]

Another entry is :

" Domino Simoni de Monte-Acuto, pro fretto unius navis cariantis equos ejusdem et Domini Petri de Donewyco redeundo de Hibern' usque Skymburnesse in nuncium Regis, per manus proprias apud Holm' xxviij die Septembr'. j *li.*"[n]

In February, 29 Edw. I., 1301, he was a party to the Letter from the Barons to Pope Boniface, in which he is styled " Simon Lord of Montacute."[o] Dugdale says in the 34th Edw. I. in consideration of his services in the king's wars' he obtained pardon for a debt of cxx *li.* viij *s.* iiij *d.* due from his father to his Majesty's exchequer; and in the same year, on his petition, search was ordered to be made in the exchequer for an account of his debts due to the King, of the payment of which he was granted a respite till it could be made, but he was not allowed to attermine without the King's permission.[p] In the 33rd Edw. I. he was one of the bail for William de Montacute, who was then prisoner in the Tower of London.[q]

---

[m] Page 199. [n] Page 83. [o] Appendix to the Fourth Peerage Report.
[p] Rot. Parl. vol. I. p. 166. [q] Ibid. p. 176.

Having been summoned to the parliament held at Carlisle in the octaves'of
St. Hilary in the 35th Edw. I. 1307, he was excused from attending because he
was in Scotland;[r] in the 2nd Edw. II. he was appointed Constable of Beaumaris
Castle in the island of Anglesea; in the 4th Edw. II. he was constituted Admiral
of the King's fleet then employed against the Scots; and in the 7th Edw. II.
he obtained a license to make a castle of his house at Yerdlington in Somersetshire.

Among the petitions on the Rolls of Parliament of the reigns of Edward the
First and Second, is one from this Baron, praying that, in consideration of his
long services, the King would pardon him the payment of c marks, which "Mons[r]
William Martin," who is described as " late one of the King's justices," in 1306,[s]
adjudged him to have forfeited for not having appeared before him in the King's
court, as he was ignorant that he was in his part of the country; with which
prayer his Majesty complied.[t] In the 8th Edw. II. he was for the last time
commanded to serve in Scotland; and having been regularly summoned to parliament from the 26th September, 28 Edw. I. 1300, to the 6th October, 9 Edw.
II. 1315, closed a long life, distinguished by arduous and faithful services in the
field, in 1316. He married Aufricia, sister and heiress of Orry King of the isle
of Man,[u] and by her had issue William, his successor in the barony, and Simon,
a younger son.

William de Montacute, the son of this Baron, died in 1319, and was succeeded
by his son of the same name, who in 1337 was created Earl of Salisbury; of
which dignity his descendants continued possessed until 1428, when that title
was conferred on Richard Neville, who had married Alice de Montacute, the
daughter and heiress of the last Earl. The barony of Montacute and that Earldom became forfeited in 1471 by the attainder of their son, Richard Earl of
Warwick and Salisbury.

---

[r] Ibid. p. 188.   [s] Rot. Parl. vol. I. p. 196 b.   [t] Ibid. p. 477 a.

[u] Among the " Ancient Charters" in the British Museum is one marked V. 73, by which " Au-
frica de Counnoght, heir of the lands of Man," granted all her right in the same to " nobili et
potenti viro D'no Simon' de Monte Acuto." It is dated at Bridgewater in the county of Somerset,
on Thursday the vigil of the feast of the Annunciation, 1305, i. e. 24 March, 1306. In a deed
in the same collection of the early part of the reign of Edward the Third, William de Montacute,
his grandson, calls himself " Lord of Man."

. ʳ. The arms of Montacute are usually considered to have been, Argent, three fusils conjoined in fess Gules; and which occur on the ʾseal of Lord Monta-cute in 1301;ˣ but in the Roll in the Cottonian MS. they are thus blazoned: " Quartile de Argent e de Azure; en les quarters de Azure les griffons de Or, en les quarters de Argent daunces de Goules;"ʸ whilst in the Poem, this Baron is

 said to have borne a blue banner and shield, charged with " a griffin rampant of fine gold."ᶻ The fact appears to have been that Simon de Montacute bore two coats; the one, Argent, three fusils, which it is most probable was a corrup-tion of a fess dancette, or a dance, Gules; and the other, Azure, a griffin segreant Or; for on the secretum to his seal just noticed, is a griffin in that position.ᵃ

EDWARD PRINCE OF WALES,

AFTERWARDS KING EDWARD THE SECOND.

[PAGE 42.]

The same reasons which prevented a memoir being given of King Edward the First, oblige this notice of his son, the Prince of Wales, afterwards Edward the Second, to be ʾconfined to remarks illustrative of what is said of him in the Poem.

Edward was born on the 25th April, 1284, and was consequently, as is there stated, in his seventeenth year in June 1300. The Poet informs us that he led the fourth squadron of the English army at the siege of Carlaverock, and which, he adds, was his first appearance in the field. Besides this fact in the biography of that Prince, the description given of his personal and mental endowments is ʾinteresting; though the portrait may perhaps be deemed a flattering likeness.

x Archæologia, vol. XXI.pp. 216-17.   y Cotton MSS. Caligula, A. xviii.   z Page 40.
a See some remarks on the subject in the Gentleman's Magazine, vol. XCVI. Part i. p. 412.

He says, Edward was well proportioned and handsome, courteous and intelligent, a good horseman, and was animated with a strong desire to display his courage. The young prince seems to have been entrusted to the especial care of John de St. John, " who went every where with him ;"[b] and from a subsequent passage it may be inferred that, besides St. John, the Barons Tony, Tyes, Latimer, Leyburne, and Roger de Mortimer, were appointed as his body-guard, if such an expression may be allowed in reference to that period..[c]

Such is the contemporary sketch presented of a prince in his minority, who subsequently became celebrated only for his misfortunes; and the history of whose reign is a mere record of weakness, tergiversation, and crime.

The arms borne by Edward in his father's life-time were those of England, Gules, three lions passant gardant Or, differenced by a label Azure.[d]

JOHN DE SAINT JOHN.

[PAGE 42.]

Notwithstanding that the Poet in speaking of this distinguished knight has not indulged in any eulogy upon his merits, beyond attributing to him the simple epithet of brave, he was the oldest and most experienced commander in Edward's army. The confidence reposed in him by his sovereign is manifest from his being entrusted with the care of the Prince of Wales, whom, there can be no doubt, he was appointed to instruct in the duties of a soldier, a knight, and a chieftain. Nor could the King's choice have fallen upon a more worthy object, if the splendid catalogue of his services, which will be more fully alluded to, may be received as evidence of his eminent merits.

---

[b] Pp. 42-43.   [c] Pp. 46-47.   [d] Page 40.

He succeeded his father, Robert de St. John, in his lands in the 51st Hen. III. 1267, and was immediately appointed to his situation of Governor of Porchester Castle; on the 12th Nov. 4 Edw. I. 1276, he was one of the "magnates" present at the council of Westminster on judgment being given against Lewellyn Prince of Wales;[e] in the 5th Edw. I. he was summoned to serve with horse and arms against the Welsh;[f] and again in the 11th Edw. I.[g] St. John was one of the peers present in parliament on the morrow of the feast of the Trinity, 18 Edw. I. 1290, when a grant was made to the King for the marriage of his eldest daughter;[h] and in the same year he was involved in a dispute with William de Valence relative to the manor of Cumpton, which had belonged to Robert de Pundelande.[i] He was constituted the King's Lieutenant in the Duchy of Acquitaine, with an assignment of two thousand pounds tournois yearly for his expenses, in the 21st Edw. I., to be paid by the Constable of Bordeaux. His services about that period are thus described by Dugdale : " Whereupon being sent into Gascoigne with five hundred men at arms and twenty thousand foot, he manned and fortified all the cities and castles in those parts ; but before the end of that year, upon a truce made with the French, he sold the provisions which were laid up in these garrisons, and came for England by the way of Paris. Shortly after which he was sent over to John de Britannia, Earl of Richmond, the King's nephew, and general of his army in Gascoigne ; and in 1295, 23rd Edw. I., continuing in those wars, assaulted the city of Bayon by sea, with such success, that it was soon rendred to him ; whereupon he laid siege to the castle there, and took it within eight days : thence he advanced towards Bellagard, at that time besieged by the Earl of Arras ; but meeting with the enemy, whose strength was too big for him, was taken prisoner and sent to Paris. It is said that being thus prisoner, Alfonsus King of Leon redeemed him ; and that being so enlarged and trusted by Alfonsus, he delivered up his country to the enemy." Upon the act of treachery thus imputed to St. John it would be a waste of words to offer any comment, for it stands upon the authority of a writer who did not live until about a century afterwards: and from the way in which Dugdale speaks of it, it would appear that he considered the charge to be at least doubtful. The defeat and capture of St. John at Belgarde is thus quaintly related by a rhyming Chronicler of the period :

---

[e] Palgrave's " Parliamentary Writs," p. 5.   [f] Appendix to the First Peerage Report, p. 38.
[g] Ibid. p. 47.   [h] Rot. Parl. vol. I. p. 25.   [i] Ibid. p. 39—68.

The Wednesday next at even befor Kandilmesse
A spie did Sir John leve that Frankis oste non was,
Namely, in that pas, that he suld lede him bi,
He lied, that Judas, ten thousand wer redi.
Sir Jon mad him prest, he trost that losengere,
His bataile was formest, displaied his banere,
And passed alle the pas, that thei alle so dred,
Biside enbussed was fiften hundred sped,
In foure grete escheles alle to batail sette,
The first he disconfet wele, the tother with him so mette,
Sir Jon fulle hardely to fight did his peyn,
And bad Sir Henry Lacy, that he sulde turne agayn,
This oste is gret biforn, I rede that ye fle,
Ther vitaile was alle lorn, herneis, and ther mone,
Sir James of Beauchamp wonded, and may not stand,
In a water stampe he was dronkled fleand,
Sir Jon thorgh tham brast, bifore ye herd me neven,
Was taken at the last, and his knyghtes elleven,
And of his squierie gentille men auhtene,
Ther pride and ther folie, I trowe, on tham was sene.[j]

In the 25th Edw. I. he was again in the wars in Gascony; in 1299 he was
sent with a great force into Scotland; and in June in the next year he, in fact,
commanded the fourth squadron of the army at the siege of Carlaverock, though
it was nominally led by the Prince of Wales.

The entries respecting this eminent soldier in the Wardrobe Accounts of the
28th Edw. I., are not only interesting from the manner in which they elucidate
many of the arrangements for the payments of an army at the commencement of
the fourteenth century, but, from their proving the important situations filled by
St. John, and giving the names of many of his retinue.

The first is an allowance of money for such of his horses as had died in the
King's service; and as it shows the value of almost every description of those
animals above five hundred years since, it is not a little curious:

---

[j] Peter of Langtoft, ed. 1810, pp. 288-289.

" Domino Johanni de Sancto Johanne, pro restauro diversorum equorum appreciatorum pro quibusdam militibus et scutiferis suis, mortuorum in servicio Regis, et redditorum ad karvannum per vices anno presenti, tam moranti in partibus Cumbr', pro custodia dicte Marchie inter vj diem Januar' et festum nativitat' Sancti Johannis Baptiste, quam in exercitu Regis in partibus Scotie, videlicet, unius dextrarii nigri appreciati pro Domino J. de Sancto Johanne, filio suo, lx marc'—unius dextrar' nigri cum stella in fronte appreciati pro Domino Ricardo de Borhunte, lxxx marc'—unius equi badii bauzeyn appreciati pro Domino Hugone de Sancto Johanne, xl marc'—unius runcini powis appreciati pro Hugone de Cheyny, xij li'—unius runcini grisei ferrandi appreciati pro Ricardo de Clifford, x marc'—unius runcini nigri appreciati pro Ranulpho le Chaumberleng, viij marc'—unius runcini ferrandi pomele appreciati pro Roberto de la Poynte, xx marc'—unius runcini badii cum stella in fronte appreciati pro Waltero Crespyn, xxv marc'—unius equi albi appreciati pro Simone du Park, xx marc'—unius runcini ferrandi pomele appreciati pro Nicholao de Romesey, x marc'—unius runcini sori appreciati pro Alexandro le Mareschal, xx marc'—unius runcini nigri cum duobus pedibus posterioribus albis appreciati pro Nicholao Gentil', xxx marc'—et unius runcini badii cum stella in fronte appreciati pro Johanne le Chaumberleng, xxv marc'—per compotum factum cum Domino Thoma Paignel, milite suo, apud la Rose mense Septembris. Summa ccxliiij *li*." [k]

From the next payment to him we learn that certain marches were entrusted to his custody :

" Domino Johanni de Sancto Johanne, Capitaneo et Custodi Marchie Cumbr' et Wall' Anand', de dono Regis pro quibusdam expens' secretis factis per ipsum per ordinationem Regis et consilii sui factum apud Novum Monasterium in vigilia Epiphanie anno presenti, morando in partibus predictis, in den' allocat' eidem ad comp' factum cum Domino Thoma Paynel, milite suo, apud la Rose, xxv die Septembr'. ccccxiij *li*. xij *s*." [l]

The account of the wages of his retinue proves the rank which he held in the English army, for it seems that they consisted on one occasion of two or three bannerets, twelve esquires, and fifty-four knights :

" Domino Johanni de Sancto Johanne, baneretto, pro vadiis suis, quinque militum et xxviij scutiferor' suor', cum equis appreciatis, a xxv die Junij usque xij

k Page 176.   l Ibid. p. 183.

diem Julij, utroque computato per xviij dies, xxxvij *li.* xvj *s.* Eidem, pro vadiis suis et Dominor' Roberti de Tonny et Henr' de Tyeys, banerettorum, xj militum, et lj scutiferorum suorum, a xiij die Julij, quo die equi Dominorum dictorum Roberti et Henrici et Domini Radulphi de Gorges, quinque militum et xxiij scutiferorum eorundem fuerunt appreciati, usque xix diem ejusdem mensis, utroque computato per vij dies, xxix *li.* xv *s.* Eidem, pro vadiis suis, eorundem banerettorum, xij militum, et lxiiij scutiferorum suorum, a xx die Julij, quo die equi unius militis, videlicet, Domini Willielmi de Karło et xiij scutiferorum suorum, et Domini Roberti de Tonny, fuerunt appreciati, usque xxx diem Augusti, quo die conventum fuit cum eo ad morandum apud Loghmaban tanquam Capitaneus et Custos Marchie Cumbr' Vall' Anand et parcium circumjacentium, primo die computato et non ultimo per xlj dies, ccv *li.*—per compotum factum cum Domino Thoma Paignel, milite suo, apud la Rose xxvj die Septembr'. Summa cclxxij *li.* xj *s.*"[m]

A John de St. John was a party to the Letter from the Barons to the Pope in February, 1301, but it was most probably the son of the subject of this notice, as the father is not recorded to have been ever summoned to parliament.[n] That fact is not a little singular, for he was undoubtedly present in parliament in the 18th Edw. I., and possessed a large share of his sovereign's confidence and esteem: it may perhaps be explained by his being constantly occupied in the wars of his times, and that in consideration of his long services he was exempted from what was then considered an onerous duty, though it subsequently, became and continues to be, an object of political ambition.

St. John died towards the end of 1302; and though the time of his birth is not stated, he was, it may be safely conjectured, an old man at his decease. By Alice his wife, daughter of Reginald Fitz Piers, who survived him, he left issue John his son and heir, who was likewise at Carlaverock, and who will consequently be again noticed.

The arms of St. John were, Argent, on a chief Gules two mullets Or;[o] and his crest, a lion passant between, what seems to be meant for, two palm branches.[p]

---

m Page 200.   n Archæologia, vol. XXI. p. 225.

o Page 42; Cotton MSS. Caligula A. xviii.; and the seal of John de St. John, 1301.

p The seal of John de St. John in 1301, which, though supposed to have been used by the son of this Baron, undoubtedly belonged to his father. See Archæologia, vol. XXI. pp. 224-226.

ROBERT DE TONY:

[PAGE 42.]

The place assigned to this Baron and to Henry le Tyes who immediately follows, proves the extreme accuracy of the Poet; for in one of the extracts given
in the preceding memoir from the Wardrobe Accounts, it is stated that these
knights were in the retinue of John de St. John; and they, with a few others, are
said in another part of the Poem to have formed the guard of the young Prince
Edward.q In the description of the siege, when Tony is again spoken of, his name
occurs next to that of Ralph de Gorges, who is also included in the retinue of
St. John in the entry referred to.

Of this individual very little is known; nor is that little particularly deserving of attention. He succeeded his father, Ralph de Tony, a baron by
tenure, in 1294, when he was of full age; and shortly afterwards was ordered to
serve in the wars of Gascony, and the next year in those of Scotland. On the
13th July, 25 Edw. I. 1297, he was commanded to raise a hundred men from the
townships of Elvet, Ughmenith, and Estmenith;r in the 27th Edw. I. he obtained a grant of fairs and markets in divers of his manors; and in the same
year was summoned to parliament. We learn from the Poem that he was at
the siege of Carlaverock in June 1300; and the Wardrobe Accounts show, as
has been already observed, that he and his followers formed part of the retinue
of John de St. John, and were attached to the person of the Prince of Wales.
The notice of Tony by the Poet is curious; he says he fully proved that he was
a " Knight of the Swan," or perhaps " that he is from" or " with a Knight
of the Swan." The line,

Ke il est du chevalier a cigne,

is obscure, but some remarks, attempting to explain it, will be found in the
notes. He appears to have particularly signalized himself during the siege, as

q Page 46. r Palgrave's " Parliamentary Writs," p. 294.

3 s

he is said to have severely harassed those who were on the battlements of the castle.[r] He was a party to the Letter from the Barons to Pope Boniface in February 1301, and is styled in that document, " Robertus de Touny, Dominus de Castro Matil."[s]

In the 34th Edw. I. Tony fell into disgrace, in consequence of his having left the wars of Scotland, in which he served in the retinue of the Earl of Hereford, without the King's license; and precepts were sent to the sheriffs of Worcester, Essex, Hertford, Middlesex, Cambridge, Huntingdon, Norfolk, Suffolk, Hereford, and Gloucester, to seize his lands, goods, and chattels, in those counties, and to arrest his body.[t] Writs of summons to parliament were addressed to him from the 10th April, 27 Edw. I. 1299, to the 16th June, 4 Edw. II. 1311, though he died in the year preceding. He married Maud, daughter of ———, but by her, who remarried in the 10th Edw. II. William le Zouch of Ashby, he had no issue; and

his sister Alice, the widow of Thomas de Leybourne was found to be his heiress, and at that time twenty-six years old. She married soon afterwards Guy de Beauchamp, Earl of Warwick; and after his demise William Zouch, of Mortimer.

The arms of Tony were, Argent, a maunch Gules.[u]

---

[r] Page 75.   [s] Appendix to the Fourth Peerage Report.

[t] Palgrave's " Parliamentary Writs," p. 378.

[u] Page 42; Cottonian MSS. Caligula, A. xviii; and the seal of this Baron in 1301. It is remarkable, as tending to elucidate the expression of the Poet relative to " the Knight of the Swan," that the shield on that seal is surrounded by lions and *swans* alternately.

HENRY LE TYES.

[PAGE 44.]

The particulars which Sir William Dugdale has given of this individual render us but very imperfectly acquainted with his career. Every one who has referred to the " Baronage of England," must have been struck with the different manner in which the first and second volumes of that work are executed. The former is distinguished by the most laborious research and extraordinary accuracy, and confers honour upon its author; but the latter is unfortunately of a very different character, and is much more remarkable for the paucity of its statements and its errors. This is not the place, however, in which an explanation of the cause of that fact can be attempted, but it is to the existence of it that so little can be said of many of the Barons who were at Carlaverock.

Besides the remark that " in the time of Henry the Third Henry le Tyes held Shoresbury in the county of Oxford, by the grant of Richard Earl of Cornwall, which was part of the barony of Robert de Drucis," Dugdale takes no other notice of him than to state that in the 28th Edw. I. he obtained a charter from the King for a market every week, on Tuesday, in his manor of Mousehole in Cornwall, and a fair on the eve, day, and morrow after the feast of St. Barnabas the Apostle; that he also received a grant of free warren in all his demesne lands at Allerton in that county, Shereburne in Oxfordshire, and Hardwell in Berkshire; and that he died in the first of the reign of Edward the Second.

To this slight account of Henry le Tyes very little can be added; but that little is of considerable importance as evidence of his military services, and of the rank he held in life.

In the 10th Edw. I. 1283, he was summoned to perform military service due from the Bishop of Bath and Wells;[v] on the 8th of June, 22 Edw. I. 1294, he was commanded to attend a great council or parliament;[w] and on the 14th of that month to serve with horse and arms in the expedition then sent into Gascony.[x] On the 1st March, 25 Edw. I. 1297, he was appointed a Commissioner in the county of Southampton to receive the recognizances of such of the clergy as

---

[v] Palgrave's " Parliamentary Writs," pp. 228, 235.

[w] Appendix to the First PeerageReport, p. 56.   [x] Ibid. p. 57.

were willing to obtain the King's protection;[v] and on the 4th of May following was commanded to be at London similarly equipped on the feast of St. John the Baptist next following, to serve against the King's enemies beyond the sea.[u] In July in the same year he was returned from the counties of Cornwall and Oxford, as holding lands or rents to the amount of £20 yearly and upwards, either *in capite* or otherwise, and as such was summoned to perform military service in person with horse and arms in parts beyond the sea;[x] and again in October in that year.[y] On the 26th September, 26 Edw. I. 1298, he received the King's writ to attend at Carlisle to serve in the wars of Scotland, in the record of which he is called a Baron;[z] and he was also ordered to the same place on the 16th July in the next year,[a] having in the February preceding been for the first time summoned to parliament.[b] That Tyes was in the Scottish wars in June 1300 is manifest both from the Poem and the Wardrobe Accounts of that year; from the former we learn that he was then at the siege of Carlaverock, and from both, that he served in the retinue of John de St. John.[c]

He was a party to the Barons' Letter to the Pope in February 1301, in which he is called " Lord of Chilton ;"[d] and was repeatedly commanded to serve in the King's wars againt the Scots from the 30th to the 35th Edw. I.[e] Having been regularly summoned to parliament from the 6th February, 27 Edw. I. 1299, to the

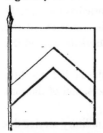

26th August, 1 Edw. II. 1307, he died in 1308, leaving Henry his son of full age, who was also summoned[f] from the 6th Edw. II. 1313, until the 14th Edw. II. 1321, when he was beheaded and attainted. He died without issue, leaving his sister, Alice, the wife of Warine L'Isle, his heiress; and whose descendants are the representatives of this Baron.

The arms of Henry le Tyes were, Argent, a chevron Gules.[g]

---

v Palgrave's " Parliamentary Writs," p. 394.   u Appendix to the First Peerage Report, p. 78.
x Ibid. pp. 282. 290.   y Ibid. p. 90.   z Ibid. p. 101.
a Ibid. p. 109.   b Ibid. p. 104.   c Page 248 ante, and p. 200 of those Accounts.
d Appendix to the Fourth Peerage Report.   e Ibid. See Digest, p. 865.
f Dugdale has erroneously said that Henry le Tyes, the subject of this article, was summoned until the 14th Edw. II.; but it was evidently his son to whom all the writs from the 6th to the 14th Edw. II. were addressed.
g Page 44; the Cottonian MS. Caligula, A. xviii.; and the seal of this Baron in 1301. His shield on that seal is surmounted by a Saracen's or blackamoor's head looking to the sinister, and which was probably his crest. Archæologia, vol. XXI. p. 218.

WILLIAM LE LATIMER.

[PAGE 44.]

This veteran knight is first presented to our notice by Sir William Dugdale, as being appointed to a military and civil situation of equal importance, forty-seven years before he is commemorated by the Poet. In the 38th Hen. III. 1253, he says he was constituted Sheriff of Yorkshire and Governor of York Castle; and in the 39th Hen. III. Governor of the castle of Pikeryng in that county. In the 42nd Hen. III. he was ordered to attend with horse and arms to rescue the King's son-in-law, the King of Scotland, then a minor, from the hands of his rebellious subjects;[h] in the 43rd Hen. III. he was made Escheator-general in all the counties of England north of the Trent; and in the following year succeeded the Earl of Albemarle as Governor of the castle of Cockermouth. He bought the wardship of the heirs of Hugh de Morewyk and the benefit of their marriages of the King for MCC marks in the 45th Hen. III.; and in the 47th Henry III. obtained the royal precept for the restitution of his lands, which had been seized during the baronial wars, when he seems to have been also deprived of all his official situations. During those wars he was a firm adherent to the Royal party; and on the Tuesday after the feast of St. Lucie, 17 December, 1262, he was one of the peers who undertook that the King should submit to the arbitration of the French monarch relative to the ordinances of Oxford. Immediately after Henry recovered the free exercise of his prerogative, he rewarded Latimer's fidelity by re-appointing him to the shrievalty of Yorkshire, and to the government of York and Scardeburgh castles; and moreover, in the 50th year of his reign, granted him C marks for the expences which he had incurred.

Upon the Prince, afterwards Edward the First, assuming the Cross in the

54th Hen. III., this Baron also adopted that sacred badge, and it may be presumed attended him to the Holy Land. In December, 5 Edw. I. 1276, and in May, 10 Edw. I. 1282, he was summoned to serve against the Welsh;[i] and was one of the peers present in parliament on the morrow of the feast of the Trinity, 29th May, 1290, when a grant was made for the marriage of the King's eldest daughter.[k] Latimer in the same year gave xx *s.* to John de Yarmouth on his quit-claim of a messuage in Yarmouth;[l] and complained that Richard de Holebrook, the King's steward of the forest of Rockingham, had committed waste in his manor of Corby, a long account of the proceedings on which are on the Rolls of Parliament.[m] In April, 19 Edw. I. he was ordered to be at Norham at Easter following, equipped for the field;[n] and in the 21st Edw. I., Dugdale says, " he accompanied John de St. John, that famous soldier, into Gascony." Whilst abroad, that writer adds, he obtained permission for his wife and family to reside in Skypton Castle, with an allowance of fuel from the woods there. Latimer was in the same year one of the manucaptors for William de Luda, Bishop of Ely, who was then involved in a dispute with the Archbishop of Dublin, in consequence of a quarrel between the servants of their respective households;[o] and he incurred the same responsibility for William de Montacute, who was prisoner in the Tower of London, in the 33rd Edw. I.[p]

Although Latimer is said to have gone into Gascony under St. John in the 21st Edw. I., he was summoned on the 14th June in the next year to be at Portsmouth on the 1st of the ensuing September, to join the expedition into that province;[q] where he was again in the 25th Edw. I., about which year he obtained a grant of the marriage of Isabel, daughter and heiress of Simon de Sherstede, for his son and heir apparent, John le Latimer. In the 26th Edw. I. he attended Edward into Scotland; and in the following year was appointed one of the commissioners for fortifying the castles in that country. He was at the siege of Carlaverock in June, 28th Edw. I. 1300; and when, even allowing that he was but twenty-three on being appointed Governor of York Castle and Sheriff of York-

---

[i] Appendix to the First Peerage Report, pp. 37 and 44.

[k] Rot. Parl. vol. I. p. 25 a.   [l] Ibid. p. 33 b.   [m] Ibid. pp. 35 b, 36 b.

[n] Appendix to the First Peerage Report, p. 55.   [o] Rot. Parl. vol. I. p. 112.

[p] Ibid. p. 176.   [q] Appendix to the First Peerage Report, p. 58.

shire in 1253, he must have been seventy years of age; and the probability is that he was much older. The Wardrobe Accounts of that time contain the subjoined notices respecting him, from which it appears that his son William le Latimer was also in those wars:

"D'no Willielmo Latimer, seniori, pro feodo suo hiemali anni presentis xxviij, per compotum factum apud Westmonast', xij die Marcij, vj *li.* xiij*s.* iiij*d.*

"D'no Willielmo Latimer, juniori, pro eodem, per compotum secum factum ibidem eodem die, qui denar' allocatur eidem patri suo,vj *li.* xiij *s.* iiij*d.*" *

Of his retinue in the 29th Edw. I., in which year he was in the garrison of Berwick, and received a grant of the manor of Danby in Yorkshire for his life, with remainder to his son William and Lucia his wife, and to her right heirs, the same Accounts contain the following particulars:

"Domino Willielmo le Latimer, seniori, baneretto, pro vadiis suis, vj militum et xiij scutiferorum suorum, cum equis coopertis, morancium in comitiva Domini Edwardi filii Regis, in guerra predicta, a primo die Julij usque xxviij diem Septembr', utroque computato 'per xc dies, per comp' factum cum eodem apud Nettelham, ix die Februar', anno xxix. cxxx *li.* x *s.*" *

In February, 29 Edw. I. 1301, he was a party to the Letter from the Barons assembled at Lincoln to Pope Boniface; and it must here be remarked that the entry extracted above, affords additional evidence that all the peers whose names are mentioned in the Letter to the Pontiff were actually present in parliament when it was written; for on the 9th of February, 1300, we find Latimer was within four miles of the city where he is presumed to have been on the 29th of that month; and to which he was doubtless then on his journey. In the 30th Edw. I. he received a grant of fairs and markets in his manors in Surrey, Kent,

r Page 189.　　　　　　　　s Page 201.

t Appendix to the Fourth Peerage Report. The fact of his being within four miles of Lincoln on the 9th of February, and the description given of the Lord Latimer whose seal is affixed to that instrument, "Willielmus le Latimer, Dominus de Corby," without the addition of the word "junior," renders it almost positive that it was this Baron rather than his son who was a party to it; but it must not be forgotten that the father was not expressly summoned to the parliament then held at Lincoln, though he was so to the previous one, but which, being an adjourned parliament, he had a right to attend by virtue of the writ to the previous assembly, whilst the son is expressly recorded to have received a writ to be at Lincoln on that occasion.

and York; and in the 31st Edw. I. was for the last time in the wars of
Scotland.

The earliest writ of summons on record to this Baron was tested on the 29th
December, 28th Edw. I. 1299, though he manifestly sat as a peer of parliament
ten years before; and he was regularly summoned from the 28th Edw. I. to the
22nd January, 33rd Edw. I. 1305, and died in the same year.

The constant services of this distinguished soldier for nearly half a century,
and his unvaried loyalty to his sovereign when menaced by his rebellious barons,
render any eulogy unnecessary; and his conduct seems fully to justify the compliment paid him by the Poet, who personifies Prowess, and supposes that she
had chosen Latimer for her friend.

His wife was Alice, the eldest daughter and coheiress of Walter Ledet alias
Braybrooke, who died in 1316, by whom he had two sons; John, who has been
before spoken of; and William.   John died in his father's lifetime without
issue; and William was summoned to parliament one year before his father is
recorded to have received a writ of summons. According to the inquisition on the
death of his mother in 1316, William le Latimer was born about the year 1276,
which proves the error into which Dugdale has fallen in saying that in the 50th
Hen. III. he accounted for divers sums due to the King; that in the 54th Hen.
III. he was personally in the court of Exchequer; and that in the same year he
performed the duties of sheriff of Yorkshire for his father.   In all probability
both these circumstances occurred to the subject of this article; that it was the
father of this Baron to whom all which has been attributed to him until the
early part of the reign of Edward the First, related; and consequently that the
William le Latimer who was at Carlaverock was by no means so old a man, or
his services so extensive in point of time, as has been supposed. As, however,
there is only one part of Dugdale's statement which can be demonstrated to be
positively wrong, and as it is possible that the Baron who served at Carlaverock
was born sufficiently early to have held the offices attributed to him in 1253, it
was not thought decorous towards so respectable an authority to differ so entirely
from his statement without more satisfactory evidence of his error.

The barony of Latimer, on the death of William, fourth Lord Latimer, K. G.,
the great grandson of the first Baron, in 1380, devolved on his daughter and
heiress Elizabeth, who married, first, John Lord Neville of Raby, to whom she
was second wife; and secondly, according to some authorities, Robert Lord Wil-

loughby of Eresby. Her son and heir, John Neville, **was** summoned to parliament as Lord Latimer in 1404 ; and died s. P. in 1430. Lord Willoughby de Broke, the descendant of his sister and heiress Elizabeth, is the present representative of the house of Latimer; and is entitled to the barony.

The arms of Latimer are, Gules, a cross patée Or.[u]

WILLIAM DE LEYBOURNE.

[PAGE 44.]

It would be difficult, even in the present state of literature, to find a more emphatic phrase to describe the uncompromising spirit which was the characteristic of a rude soldier of the fourteenth century, than that which the Poet has used with respect to William de Leybourne. He was, he says, a man " without *but* and without *if;*" or, in other words, one who was not to be diverted from his purpose by any trifling impediment, but, having once resolved on a particular object, pursued it with a zeal and perseverance which generally ensure success.

He was the eldest son of Roger de Leybourne, of whom Dugdale has given many particulars, by his first wife, Eleanor, daughter of Stephen de Turnham, and succeeded his father in his lands in the 56th Hen. III. 1272. In the 5th Edw. I. 1277, he was summoned to serve with horse and arms against the Welsh;[v] again in the 11th Edw. I.;[w] and in the 22nd Edw. I. was made Constable of Pevensey Castle. On the 24th of June in the same year, 1294, he was commanded to be at Portsmouth on the 1st of the following September to join the expedition

---

[u] Page 44 ; Cottonian MS. Caligula, A. xviii.; and the seal of this Baron in 1301. Though thus blazoned in both the MSS. cited, it must be observed that the word " patée" evidently means what is now termed " flory," for it is so represented on the seal alluded to ; and which was also the opinion entertained of it by Glover, from whose drawing the banner in p. 44 has been exactly copied.

[v] Appendix to the First Peerage Report, p. 37.　　　　[w] Ibid. p. 43.

3 u

into Gascony, when he was appointed Admiral of that part of the King's fleet
which was at Portsmouth. In March, 25 Edw. I. 1297, he was constituted a
commissioner in the county of Kent for the purpose of receiving the recognizances of such of the clergy as were willing to obtain the King's protection;[x]
and in May following he was ordered to be at London in readiness to serve
beyond the seas on the Sunday next after the feast of St. John the Baptist following; in January, 28 Edw. I. 1300, he was one of the commissioners appointed
to summon the knights of the county of Kent to meet the King for the purpose
of performing military service against the Scots; and by writ tested on the 11th
of the ensuing April, at St. Alban's, he was enjoined to enforce the muster of the
levies of the men at arms in that county, and to return the names of the defaulters
into the Wardrobe.[y] Leybourne was first summoned to parliament in February,
27 Edw. I. 1299; he was in the wars of Scotland in the 28th Edw. I. 1300; and
the Poem informs us that he was present at the siege of Carlaverock in June
in that year.

The Wardrobe Accounts of the time contain two entries respecting him:

" D'no Willielmo de Leybourne pro feodo suo hiemali anni presentis xxviij;
per manus D'ni Willielmi de Lecton, capellani sui, apud Berewicum super Twedam, xxvij die Decembr'. vj *li.* xiij *s.* iiij *d.*"[z]

The other relates to the wages of his retinue:

" Domino Willielmo de Leyburn, baneretto, pro vadiis suis, quinque militum et
tresdecim scutiferorum suorum ab viij die Julij, quo die equi sui fuerunt appreciati, usque vj diem Augusti, utroque computato per xxx dies, predicto D'no
Willielmo per diem iij *s.*—cuilibet militi suo per diem ij *s.*—et cuilibet scutifero
suo per diem xij *d.*—xl *li.* x*s.* Eidem, pro vadiis suis, vj militum et xv scutiferorum suorum, a vij die Augusti, quo die equi unius militis et ij scutiferorum suorum fuerint appreciati, usque ultimum diem ejusdem mensis, utroque computato
per xxv dies, xxxviij *li.* xv *s.*—per comp' factum cum Domino Willielmo de Cray,
milite suo, apud Drumbogh, primo die Septembr'—lxxix *li.* v *s.*"[a]

In February, 1301, Leybourne was one of the Barons who sealed the Letter to
Pope Boniface relative to his claim to the throne of Scotland, in which he is
styled " Willielmus Dominus de Leyborn."[b] He was again in the Scottish wars

[x] Palgrave's "Parliamentary Writs," p. 394.   [y] Ibid. pp. 330 and 342.   [z] Page 188.
[a] Page 195.   [b] Or " Leyburne." Appendix to the Fourth Peerage Report.

in the 29th and 32nd Edw. I. 1301, 1304; and in the 35th Edw. I. 1307; obtained a charter for a market and fair in his manor of Preston in Kent.

Writs of summons to parliament are recorded to have been addressed to him from the 6th February, 27 Edw. I. 1299, to the 16th of June, 4 Edw. II. 1311, though it is certain that he died in 1309. By his wife Julian, but whose other name is not stated, he had issue a daughter, Idonea, for whose husband he obtained Geoffrey, the son and heir of William de Say, in the 24th Edw. I.; and a son, Thomas, who died in 1307 in his father's lifetime, leaving Julian, his daughter, his heiress, and who was found heiress to her grandfather, the subject of this article, on his demise, and was then six years old. She married, first, John Baron

Hastings; and, secondly, William de Clinton Earl of Huntingdon; but her issue failed in 1389, on the death of the last Hastings Earl of Pembroke, s. p., when the representation of this Baron apparently became vested in the heirs of his daughter Idonea de Say above mentioned.

The arms of Leybourne were, Azure, six lions rampant Argent.[c]

ROGER DE MORTIMER.

[PAGE 44.]

As this celebrated Baron was engaged in almost every expedition, and in many of the political events, which occurred from the year 1283 to 1330, a period of above fifty-three years, his life presents ample materials for that monotonous species of biography which consists of mere notices—of services in the field; of summonses to the legislative assembly; of occasional acts of rebellion and outrage; and of their consequent punishments or pardons. In these incidents

---

c Page 44; Cotton MSS. Caligula, A. xviii.; and the seal of this Baron in 1301.

the long career of Roger de Mortimer abounded; and, however dull the following facts relating to him may be in perusal, the labour of collecting them could only have been adequately rewarded, if the result had produced a memoir of general interest.

He was the second son of Roger Baron Mortimer of Wigmore, by Maud de Braose; and as his eldest brother Edmund was, according to Dugdale, twenty-seven years old in 1282, he was probably born about the year 1260. The first circumstance recorded of him is that, in March, 11 Edw. I. 1283, the year following that in which his father died, when he probably succeeded to lands that imposed on their tenant the duty of serving in the field, he was summoned to attend with horse and arms against the Welsh.[d] In the 14th Edw. I. he obtained a charter of free warren in his lordships of Sawarden, Winterton, Hampton, and others, in Herefordshire and Shropshire: he was also possessed of the lordship of Chirke, of which from its importance he was generally described. That territory is said to have fallen into his hands in no very creditable manner; for the wardship of Lewelin, younger son of Griffith ap Madoc Prince of Wales, to whom the lordships of Chirke and Nanheydwy belonged, having been entrusted to this Baron, he " so guarded his ward that he never returned to his possessions, and shortly after obtained these lands to himself by charter,"[e] a statement which is at least doubtful. On the 16th July, 15 Edw. I. 1287, he was directed to raise four hundred foot soldiers from his lordships to march against Resus filius Mereduci; and on the 14th of November was enjoined to reside on his demesnes until the rebellion of that individual was quelled.[f] Mortimer was commanded to answer relative to jurisdiction in the barony of Haverford West in the 18th Edw. I., and he appeared accordingly in the 20th Edw. I.: the whole proceedings on the subject are detailed at length on the Rolls of Parliament, whence we learn that he held certain lands of the Earl of Hereford.[g] In the 21st Edw. I. he was in the expedition into France, in which year he was appointed Governor of Burgh upon the Sea, anciently called Mount Alban, in that kingdom. He was summoned on the 14th June, 1294, to be at Portsmouth on the 1st of the ensuing September,

d Appendix to the First Peerage Report, p. 48.
e Powel's History of Wales, p. 212, quoted by Dugdale.·
f Palgrave's " Parliamentary Writs," pp. 251, 253.
g Rot. Parl. vol. I. pp. 34 a, 70 a, 71 b, 139 b, and 140 b.

there to join the expedition into France,[h] and undoubtedly obeyed the writ, for he is expressly stated to have received letters of protection in that year in consequence of his being in the King's service in Gascony;[i] and for the same cause he and his tenants were exempted from the payment of any part of the tenth then granted to the crown. He was again in Gascony in the 25th Edw. I.: on the 26th September, 26 Edw. I., 1298, he was commanded to be at Carlisle in the Easter following with horse and arms, in the record of which he is styled a Baron;[k] in the same year he was a commissioner of array in Landuho, Moghelan, and La Pole:[l] in the 27th Edw. I. he was summoned to parliament;[m] and on the 7th May, 16th July, and 17th September, 1299, was again ordered to be at Carlisle to serve against the Scots.[n] He was, the Poem informs us, at the siege of Carlaverock in June 1300, at which time he must have been about forty years of age; and it confirms Dugdale's statement that he was then in the retinue of the Prince of Wales. It is recorded in the Wardrobe Accounts that he received his winter's fee of £6. 13s. 4d.[o] in the same year; and they give the following particulars of his retinue:

" Domino Rogero de Mortuo Mari, baneretto, pro vadiis suis, duorum militum, et xiiij scutiferorum suorum, a xxviij die Julij, quo die equi sui fuerunt appreciati, usque xxix diem Augusti, utroque computato per xxxiij dies, xxxvj *li.* vj*s.* Eidem, pro expensis oris sui et unius militis sui, a ix die Julij, quo die venit ad curiam apud Karlaverok, usque xxviij diem ejusdem mensis, quo die equi sui fuerunt appreciati, primo die computato et non ultimo per xix dies, per quos fuit in cur' et extra rotulum hospicii, percipienti per diem vj*s.* per statutum factum apud Sanctum Albanum de hospicio, v*li.* xiv*s.* per compotum factum cum eodem apud Lincoln', xx die Feb' anno xxix. Summa xlij *li.*"[p]

The places mentioned in that entry are singularly corroborative of two statements respecting Mortimer; the one, in the Poem, that he was at the siege and capture of Carlaverock in June 1300; and the other, that he was a party to the Letter from the Barons of England assembled in the parliament at Lincoln on the 29th February 1301; for it appears that on the 9th of July 1300 he attended the court at Carlaverock, and on the 20th of February his accounts were settled

---

[h] Appendix to the First Peerage Report.   [i] Rot. Parl. vol. I. p. 140.
[k] Ibid. p. 100.   [l] Palgrave's " Parliamentary Writs," pp. 313, 315.
[m] Rot. Parl. vol. I. p. 104.   [n] Ibid. pp. 107, 110, 112.   [o] Page 189.   [p] Page 202.

at Lincoln. In the Letter to the Pope, Mortimer is styled " Lord of Penketlyn,"^q one of the manors which he held of Humphrey de Bohun, Earl of Hereford. He was summoned to the Scottish wars by two writs ; the first tested at Lincoln on the 1st of March, 29 Edw. I. 1301;^r the other on the 7th of November, 30 Edw. I. 1302;^s and was present in the parliament held at Carlisle in January 1304;^t on the 5th of April in which year he was ordered to attend at Westminster to determine upon the aid to be granted to Edward on knighting his eldest son. Soon after this time Mortimer swerved from the fidelity which had hitherto marked his conduct, as in the 35th Edw. I. he and some other peers were accused of having quitted the King's service in Scotland and gone beyond the sea ; in consequence of which, orders were issued to the Escheator of the crown on each side of the Trent, dated on the 15th November, 1306, directing them to seize their lands and chattels.^u

Upon the accession of Edward the Second he was restored to favour ; and was constituted the King's Lieutenant and Justice of Wales, having all the castles of the principality committed to his charge. In the 2nd Edw. II. he was made Governor of Beaumaris Castle ; and in the 4th Edw. II., of those of Blaynleveng and Dinas : in that year and in the 7th Edw. II. he was again in the wars of Scotland :^x in the 8th Edw. II. he petitioned that he might be allowed the expenses he incurred, when Justice of Wales, in raising a force to repel the attack which Sir Griffith de la Pole made on the castle of Pole, on which occasion he spent altogether £332. 19s. 2d. ;^y and in the same year stated that he held the land of Griffith, son of Madoc ap Griffiths, and prayed to be allowed to retain the same during his minority.^z Early in the 9th Edw. II. he was one of the manucaptors for Hugh le Despenser, who was accused of having assaulted and drawn blood from Sir John de Roos in the cathedral court of York, in the presence of the King and the parliament.^a In the 10th Edw. II. Mortimer was constituted Justice of North Wales ; and in the 11th Edw. II. was ordered to provide an hundred men out of his lordships of Blaynleveng o Talgarth, and two hundred out of

---

^q Appendix to the Fourth Peerage Report.
^r Appendix to the First Peerage Report, p. 129.   ^s Ibid. p. 152.
^t Rot. Parl. vol. I. p. 188.   ^u Ibid. p. 216.
^x Appendix to the First Peerage Report, pp. 203, 235.
^y Rot. Parl. vol. I. p. 305 b.   ^z Ibid. p. 306 b.   ^a Ibid. p. 352 b.

his territory of Lanledu, for the wars of Scotland   He was again in the Scottish wars in the 12th and 13th Edw. II. and was assigned c *li.* for his services therein; and in the 12th Edw. II. he was appointed Governor of Buelt Castle in Wales. On the 28th March, 1321, he was commanded to attend at Gloucester on the 5th of April following, to devise how the insurrection in Wales might be suppressed;[b] and in the 15th Edw. II. was again made Justice of Wales, on the 28th November, in which year, anno 1321, he was summoned to appear personally before the King.[c] Having taken an active part against the Despensers, the favourites of the young monarch, he exposed himself to Edward's enmity; and two records are extant, which, though from immediately opposite parties, tend equally to prove the unenviable situation in which he was placed. In the 15th Edw. II. he joined the Earl of Hereford in his quarrel against the Spencers,[d] and having entered and burnt Bridgenorth, his Majesty declared him and the other Barons to have forfeited their lands :[e] about the same time the commonalty of North and South Wales petitioned the crown, praying that as Mons[r] Roger de Mortimer the nephew, and Mons[r] Roger de Mortimer the uncle, who had the custody of Wales, had risen against him and seized his castles, they might not be pardoned for their offences.[f] From this time the only thing certain which can be said of the subject of this article, is that in the 1st Edw. III. 1327, he and his nephew were restored to all their lands which had been forfeited in the 16th Edw. II., and the whole of the proceedings on the occasion were reversed;[g] that in the 4th Edw. III. he is styled in a writ from the King, "Justic' suo Wall' vel ejus locum tenenti in partibus North Wall' et Camerario suo North Walliæ;"[h] and he was also described by the former of these titles in the 2nd Edw. III.;[i] hence the assertion of Leland that he died in the Tower of London, to which his

---

b Fœdera, N. E. vol. II. p. 445, and Rot. Parl. vol. I. p. 455 b.   c Ibid. p. 461.

d In the petitions from Hugh le Despenser the son, to Richard the Second, the injuries inflicted upon his lands and property in this insurrection àre very minutely detailed, together with the names of the leaders, among which are those of this Baron and his nephew; Rot. Parl. 21 Ric. II. vol. III. pp 361-2. It is also necessary to state that a Roger de Mortimer was appointed to treat with the Earl of Lancaster relative to the political dissentions which then agitated the realm; but as the usual addition of " de Chirk" does not occur, it is presumed to have been Lord Mortimer of Wigmore, the nephew of this Baron.

e Fœdera, N. E. vol. II. p. 471.   f Rot. Parl. vol. I. p. 400 a.

g Calend. Rot. Pat. p. 100.   h Rot. Parl. vol. II. p. 35 c.   i Ibid. p. 17 b.

nephew and himself were committed by Edward the Second for the conduct just noticed, is proved to be erroneous: nor is the statement of other writers, that he died there on the 3rd of August, 1336, much more probable, as it is evident that he was restored to his office of Justice of Wales soon after the accession of Edward the Third, and continued to hold it with others of equal importance in that province until 1330.   It is possible, however, that he fell into disgrace after that time, when all authentic accounts of him cease; and perhaps died in the Tower a few years afterwards: it is positive that he lived until 1336, and must have been nearly eighty at his demise.   By his wife Lucia, daughter and heiress of Sir Robert de Wasse, knt., he is said to have had issue Roger, who left a son, John de Mortimer; but neither of them ranked as barons of the realm.

Roger de Mortimer was summoned to parliament from the 6th February, 27 Edw. I. 1299, to the 15th of May, 14 Edw. II. 1321, about which year he in-

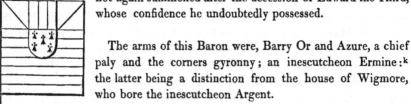

curred the King's enmity; and it is remarkable that he was not again summoned after the accession of Edward the Third, whose confidence he undoubtedly possessed.

The arms of this Baron were, Barry Or and Azure, a chief paly and the corners gyronny; an inescutcheon Ermine:[k] the latter being a distinction from the house of Wigmore, who bore the inescutcheon Argent.

---

[k] Page 44; the Cottonian MS. Caligula, A. xviii., in which he is called " Sire Roger de Mortimer le oncle;" and the seal of this Baron anno 1301.

THOMAS EARL OF LANCASTER.

[PAGE 46.]

It would require no common talents to do justice to the life and character of Thomas Plantagenet Earl of Lancaster; for whilst by one party he was venerated as a martyr and canonized as a saint, he was considered by the other as a hypocrite and a rebel. The difficulty of deciding between these conflicting opinions is by no means lessened upon viewing the materials for his history; for the contemporary accounts which have been handed down to us are so deeply imbued with the prejudices of their authors, that but little reliance can be placed on the fidelity of their statements. In the following sketch it will be impossible to do more than detail the principal events of his life; and as an inquiry into the motives of his conduct would extend the article to a length totally inconsistent with its object, it will not be attempted.

Thomas Plantagenet was the eldest son of Edmond, Earl of Lancaster, Chester, and Leicester, Steward of England, second son of King Henry the Third; and succeeded his father in all those dignities in 1295, at which time he was of full age. His mother was Blanch, daughter of Robert Count of Artois, third son of Louis VIII. King of France.

On the 26th Sept. 26 Edw. I. 1298, he was commanded to serve in the wars of Scotland,[1] which appears to have been the first writ of service addressed to him; and on the 6th February in the next year he was summoned to parliament.[m] In May following he was ordered to be at Carlisle " on the morrow of the gule of August," the 2nd of August ensuing, with horse and arms, to serve against the Scots,[n] a command which was repeated in several subsequent writs postponing the day of meeting there, from time to time, until the feast of St. John the Baptist, 1300.[o] The English army then assembled, and immediately afterwards besieged Carlaverock; on which occasion the Earl served in the squadron led by his cousin

---

[1] Appendix to the First Peerage Report, p. 100. [m] Ibid. p. 103. [n] Ibid. p. 107.
[o] Ibid. pp. 112, 118.

the Prince of Wales, and was about twenty-five years old. He is rarely, even if he
is once, mentioned in the Wardrobe Accounts of the period, an omission which
is not a little remarkable.   Lancaster was a party to the Letter from the Barons
to the Pope in February, 1301 :[p] his seal affixed to that document has given rise
to some observations, from his being described on it as " Earl of Lancaster, Leicester, and Ferrers ;"[q] and he was again in the wars of Scotland in the 31st, 32nd,
and 34th Edw. I. At the coronation of Edward the Second the Earl of Lancaster
bore the Sword of Mercy, or Curtana :[r] on the 17th March, 3 Edw. II. 1310, he
was appointed one of the Peers to regulate the kingdom and the royal household:[s]
in the 4th Edw. II. he married Alice, daughter and heiress of Henry de Lacy, Earl
of Lincoln, a memoir of whom has been given in a preceding page,[t] when to his
own immense possessions he added those of that powerful house ; and on the 28th
Nov. 1311, he was commanded not to attend the ensuing parliament with an
armed retinue, or otherwise than in the usual manner.[v] About the 5th Edw.
II. he first distinguished himself in political affairs by heading the party of
Barons against Piers de Gaveston, the favourite of the young King; and it is
said that his father-in-law, the Earl of Lincoln, enjoined him on his death-bed to
maintain that quarrel to the utmost of his power. The confederated nobles
having bound themselves to expel Gaveston, appointed Lancaster their general ; and whether his zeal against the favourite arose from patriotism or personal
hatred,' he prosecuted their views with zeal and success; but the details of
these transactions, and the important part taken in them by the Earl, are too
well known to justify repetition. After Gaveston's death his goods were placed
in the hands of the Earls of Lancaster and Warwick, Lord Percy, and others,
who obtained an acquittance for them from the King on the 7th February, 6
Edw. II. 1313.[u]

Being absent on the King's service, probably in the Scottish wars, in January,
8 Edw. II. 1315, commissioners were appointed to hold the parliament which
then assembled at Lincoln until his arrival ;[x] in which parliament Edward caused
it to be signified to him and his adherents that he entertained sincere good will

p Appendix to the Fourth Peerage Report.   q Archæologia, vol. XXI. p. pp. 201-203.
r Fœdera, N. E. vol. II. p. 36.   s Rot. Parl. vol. I. p. 443.
t Pp. 89-98.   v Rot. Parl. vol. I. p. 447 b.
u Fœdera, N. E. vol. II. p. 203. For a list of part of these articles see pp. 139-40 ante.
x Rot. Parl. vol. I. p. 350 a.

towards them, and that he particularly wished the Earl to be at the head of his council; who, having consented, was sworn accordingly.[y] In the 12th Edw. II. a new treaty was entered into between Lancaster and King Edward, certain lords having been sent from Northampton to confer with him relative to the welfare and honor of the King and his realm. An agreement was accordingly drawn up with the view of terminating the dissentions between the two parties, a copy of which is preserved, but it is too long to be more fully alluded to in this place.[z] Thus his quarrel with Edward was amicably terminated; but their friendship was of short duration, even if it was for a moment sincere. Another favourite, Hugh le Despencer, occupied the place of Gaveston, and became the source of new suspicions and jealousy; and in the 14th Edw. II. the discontented Barons openly evinced their disgust by proclaiming both the Despencers traitors to their country. In this crisis Hugh le Despencer seized upon some lands which were the subject of a dispute between the Earl of Hereford and Lord Braóse. Hereford represented the insult offered to the laws and himself to the Earl of Lancaster, who appears to have gladly seized the excuse for appealing to arms against his sovereign. Having collected his forces, he proceeded to St. Alban's, openly avowing his resolution to reform the abuses in the government of the kingdom ; and sent the Bishops of Ely, Hereford, and Chichester to the King, to require the banishment of both the Spencers, and letters of amnesty to himself and his adherents. These demands being refused, the Earl marched to London; and soon after his arrival Edward finding he had no alternative gave way, and the obnoxious favourites were formally banished. But this apparent compliance with the wishes of his rebellious subjects was of no longer duration than was sufficient to enable the King to raise an army capable of opposing them; and in the next year he took the field. At that moment some of the Earl's adherents quitted his banner, and were received under that of Edward. The King, finding himself thus strengthened, immediately pursued Lancaster, who posted himself at Burton upon Trent; but being deserted by many of his followers he took to flight, and the Earls of Kent and Surrey were despatched in pursuit. It would be useless to repeat the details of all the events which preceded the termination of his career, for they are familiar to every historical reader; hence it is sufficient to observe that having reached Boroughbridge on his way to Pomfret, he found Sir Andrew

---

[y] Rot. Parl. vol. 1. p. 351 b.   [z] Ibid. pp. 453-454.

Harcla, drawn up to oppose him; that in the attempt to force the passage
he was repulsed, his most powerful ally, the Earl of Hereford, being slain;
and his whole army was routed.   Incapable either of defence or flight, Lancaster was seized without resistance, and conducted to the King at Pomfret.   His
treason was deemed too notorious to require, and the eagerness to dispatch him
was too great to allow, of the delay necessary for the observance of the usual
forms of law.   He was merely brought before the King, and the Earls of Kent,
Richmond, Pembroke, Warren, Arundel, Athol, and Angus, some Barons, and
other great men of the kingdom,[a] who sentenced him to be drawn, hanged, and
beheaded.   In consequence of his royal descent, the more disgraceful parts of
his sentence were omitted; and he was merely beheaded,[b] on the morrow after
the feast of St. Benedict, 22 March 1322, at Pomfret, and was buried in the
priory of St. John at that place.[c]

   Such was the veneration of the multitude for the Earl of Lancaster, that they
worshipped his effigy, which, with those of others, was sculptured on a tablet in
St. Paul's cathedral in London, until the King expressly forbad them to do so by
a mandate to the Bishop of London, dated 28th June, 1323.[d]   The commons
prayed the King in 1327, for the honour of God and of Holy Church, and for the
benefit of the kingdom, to supplicate the Pope to canonize the noble Earl of Lancaster and Robert Winchelsea, Archbishop of Canterbury,[e] who replied that it
appeared to his council that the advice of the prelates should be taken.[f]   His
memory continued to be held in the highest veneration for several centuries,
miracles being said to have been wrought at his tomb, attended by the usual
sign of sanctity, blood issuing from it; and many instances are mentioned

---

   a Rot. Parl. vol. II. p. 3.

   b Rot. Parl. vol. II. pp. 3, 4, 5, where the whole proceedings against the Earl are recorded.

   c In the Act of Resumption, 34th Hen. VI. alluding to that priory, it is said, " And how that
the blissyd and holy Erle, Thomas late Erle of Lancastre, owre dere and nygh cosyn, is honorably
tumylat and restyng within the priory of Seint John Th'appostill aforseid, to the honour and wor-
shuppe of God, plaisir and comfort of us." Rot. Parl. vol. V. p. 308.

   d Vincent, in his " Discoverie of Errors," p. 295, has given a copy of the record alluded to. The
words are, " in qua statuæ sculpturæ seu imagines diversorum, et inter cætera effigies Thomæ
quondam Comitis Lancastriæ."

   e Rot. Parl, vol. I. p. 7 a.   f Ibid. p. 11 a.

of offerings being made at his shrine.[g]   It would be dangerous to draw
any positive conclusion as to the real character of this once powerful
nobleman. That he was the popular idol is but *primâ facie* evidence of his
worth ; nor are the epithets bestowed on him by those of the royal party more
conclusive proofs of his crimes. In both instances in which he appeared in arms
against his sovereign, there were undoubtedly wrongs which cried loudly for
redress ; but whether he was animated alone by a desire to remove the grievances
under which the country suffered, to rescue the King from the thraldom in which
he was held, and to enforce the execution of strict and impartial justice throughout the realm ; or, made these the mask, either of his own personal ambition, or
of individual hatred towards Edward and his minions, is a question upon which
it is scarcely possible to throw any light, and hence extremely difficult to form an
accurate judgment.

The Earl of Lancaster died without issue, and his lands and dignities were declared to be forfeited ; but all the proceedings against him were reversed immediately after the accession of Edward the Third, in favour of his brother and heir,
Henry, the subject of the next memoir. Alice his Countess survived him ; but
he repudiated her some years before his death, and, as is stated in a former

page, she married, secondly, Eubolo le Strange, who was her
husband in 1330,[h] and, thirdly, Hugh le Frenes, but died
issueless in October, 1348.[h]

The arms of the Earl of Lancaster were those of England, Gules, three lions passant gardant Or ; with a label
of France, his mother's arms, Azure, semée of fleurs de
lis, Or.[i]

---

g Humphrey Earl of Hereford ordered by his will in 1361, that " a man should be sent to Pomfret to offer xl s. at the tomb of Thomas late Earl of Lancaster." Testamenta Vetusta, p. 68.
h Page 98.
i Page 46; Cotton MSS. Caligula A. xviii.; and the seal of the Earl, 1301.

3 z

HENRY DE LANCASTER.

[Page 48.]

As has been observed in the preceding memoir, Henry de Lancaster was the second son of Earl Edmond by Blanch of Artois; and we may presume was born about the year 1276.[k]
Upon the death of his father he had livery of the town, castle, and honour of Monmouth: in September, 26th Edw. I. 1298, he was commanded to serve against the Scots, in the record of which writ he is styled a Baron, and is placed at the head of the list of those of that rank.[l] In the next year he was summoned to parliament; and on the 7th May, 16th July, and 30th December, 1299, he received writs of service for the wars of Scotland;[m] and was, it appears from the Poem, present at Carlaverock in June, 1300. Lancaster was a party to the Letter from the Barons at Lincoln to Pope Boniface, in February, 1301, in which he is styled " Henry of Lancaster, Lord of Munemue," but on his seal attached to that document he is called " Lord of Monemutæ," both being intended for Monmouth.[n] He was again in the expeditions into Scotland in the 32nd and 34th Edw. I.: on the 22nd January, 1 Edw. II. 1308, he was commanded to attend at Dover to receive the King and Queen on their return from France;[o] and at the coronation of Edward the Second he bore the rod or sceptre with a dove on the top.[p] In March, 1310, he was one of the peers appointed to regulate the state of the royal household and of the kingdom.[q] He was enjoined to serve

---

[k] A MS. note of the inquisition held in the 1st Edw. III. of the lands of which Thomas Earl of Lancaster was possessed, states that Henry was then forty years old, in which case he was born about the year 1287; but this must be erroneous, for he was most probably of full age when summoned to serve in the Scottish wars in 1298, and in 1301 he sat in parliament as a peer of the realm.
[l] Appendix to the First Peerage Report, p. 100.   [m] Ibid. pp. 107, 109, and 118.
[n] Appendix to the Fourth Peerage Report.
[o] Fœdera, N. E. vol. II. p. 31.   [p] Ibid. p. 36.
[q] Rot. Parl. vol. I. p. 443 b.

in Scotland in the 7th and 8th Edw. II.; and in the 11th Edw. II. was ordered to provide one hundred foot soldiers out of his lands in Wales for the wars there.

It appears that Henry de Lancaster did not in any degree participate in the rebellion of his brother, for he not only continued to be summoned to parliament after the Earl's execution, but, probably as a compensation for the honours he had lost in consequence of his brother's attainder, Edward created or rather restored him to the dignity of Earl of Leicester on the 29th March, 17 Edw. II. 1324; and on the 4th of August in that year he was summoned to parliament by that title.

Notwithstanding this mark of the King's favour, his patriotism was superior to his gratitude: he confederated with his cousin, the Earl Marshal, against the royal authority, or rather against the mere shadow of it, the real power of the crown being then usurped by the Queen and her paramour, Mortimer. The deposed monarch was for a short time in his custody; and when Edward the Third was proclaimed, the Earl of Lancaster girded him with the sword of knighthood, and was entrusted with his tuition as soon as he was crowned.

The earliest act of the first parliament of Edward the Third was to reverse all the proceedings against Thomas Earl of Lancaster; and his brother being his heir, he consequently succeeded to the earldoms of Lancaster and Chester, and to his immense possessions. In the 1st Edw. III. he was appointed Captain-general of all the King's forces in the Marches of Scotland. About this period, from some cause now unknown, it is said that the Earl refused to attend the parliament that was to meet at Salisbury in the quindesme of St. Michael, 2 Edw. II. anno 1328, which offended the young monarch, who, being impressed with the belief that he meant to destroy him, raised a great force, and marched against him to Bedford; but through the influence of the Earl Marshal and the Earl of Kent the quarrel was speedily reconciled. In the 14th Edw. III. 1340, he was appointed one of the council to assist the Duke of Cornwall, who was constituted guardian of the realm in the King's absence,[r] after which he does not appear to have been ever connected with public affairs. The Earl of Lancaster died in 1345; and allowing him to have been only twenty-one in 1298, when first summoned to the field, he must have been very nearly seventy at his decease. He

---

r Rot. Parl. vol. II. p. 114 b.

married Maud, the daughter and heiress of Sir Patrick Chaworth,[s] in the 27th Edw. I. 1299, and by her had Henry, his son and heir, who was of full age at his father's death; and six daughters; Blanch, wife of Thomas Lord Wake; Maud, who married William de Burgh, Earl of Ulster, and afterwards Ralph de Ufford, son of the Earl of Suffolk; Joan, the wife of John Lord Mowbray; Isabel, Prioress of Ambresbury; Eleanor, who married, first, John Lord Beaumont, and, secondly, Richard Earl of Arundel; and Mary, who became the wife of Henry Lord Percy.

The Earl of Lancaster was buried at Leicester, where a handsome tomb was erected to his memory. His son and successor was of full age in 1345; he was created Duke of Lancaster in the 25th Edw. III. was one of the founders of the order of the Garter, and died s. p. m. in 1360. Maud, his eldest daughter and coheiress, married William Duke of Bavaria, but died issueless; Blanch, his second daughter, was the first wife of John of Gaunt, who, in consequence of his marriage, was created Duke of Lancaster.

The arms of the Earl of Lancaster, in the lifetime of his elder brother, were, Gules, three lions passant gardant Or, England, with a baton Azure;[t] but whether he changed them on becoming the heir male of his house in 1321 has not been ascertained; Henry Duke of Lancaster, his son, bore the arms of his uncle and grandfather, England, with a label of France.

---

[s] Rot. Parl. vol. I. p. 315. A drawing of a seal of the Earl in 1318, in the Cottonian MS. Julius, C. vii. represents the secretum as being impaled with Chaworth.

[t] Page 48; Cotton MSS. Caligula, A. xviii.; and the seal of this Baron in 1301.

WILLIAM DE FERRERS.

[PAGE 48.]

This nobleman was the eldest son of William de Ferrers, second son of William eighth Earl of Derby, who, having obtained the lordship of Groby in Leicestershire, part of the inheritance of his mother, Margaret, daughter and co-heiress of Roger de Quincy, Earl of Winchester, adopted her arms as his paternal coat.

William de Ferrers, the subject of this notice, succeeded his father at Groby in 1288, when he was eighteen years of age. In the 22nd Edw. I. 1294, he was commanded to serve in person against the King of France in parts beyond the sea;[u] and about that time was a witness to the proceedings relative to John Baliol, King of Scotland:[x] in the 25th Edw. I. 1297, he was summoned to attend a council or parliament at Salisbury;[y] and in the same year letters of credence were addressed to him as a Scottish Baron, " dwelling on this side the Forth," concerning military service to be performed by him.[z] He was repeatedly enjoined to serve with horse and arms from the 26th Edw. I. 1297, to the 29th Edw. I. 1300;[a] and in June in that year he was present at the siege of Carlaverock in the fourth squadron, at which time he was above thirty years old. In February, 1301, Ferrers was a party to the Letter from the Barons at Lincoln to the Pope, in which he is styled " Lord of Groby ;"[b] and he was again frequently summoned to serve against the Scots from the 29th to the 35th Edw. I.[a] On the accession of Edward the Second he was ordered to attend the coronation ;[c] and was several times commanded to perform military service against the Scots during that reign.[d] In the 9th Edw. II. he was one of the manucaptors of Hugh le Despencer, who was accused of having wounded Sir John de Roos, Knt. in the

u Palgrave's " Parliamentary Writs," p. 262.
y Palgrave's " Parliamentary Writs," p. 52.
a Ibid. Digest, p. 596.
c Appendix to the First Peerage Report, p. 176.
x Rot. Parl. vol. I. p. 115 b.
z Ibid. p. 285.
b Ibid. pp. 102-3.
d Ibid. p. 181 et seq.

presence of the King and Parliament, in the cathedral church of York.[e] Excepting that Ferrers was summoned to parliament from the 26th September, 28 Edw. I. 1300, to the 20th February, 18 Edw. II. 1325,[f] the preceding are all the facts which appear to be recorded of his life; and it is not necessary to point out the impossibility of drawing from them any deductions illustrative of his character. He died in 1325, aged about fifty-five, leaving by his wife, who, according to some authorities, was Margaret the daughter of John Lord Segrave, Henry his son and heir, then twenty-two years old.

The barony of Ferrers of Groby was enjoyed by the male descendants of this Baron until the death of William, fifth Baron by writ, in 1445; and in the next year Sir Edward Grey, husband of Elizabeth, his granddaughter and heiress, was summoned to parliament in her right as Lord Ferrers of Groby: their grandson, Thomas Grey, was created Marquess of Dorset, and his son, Henry, Duke

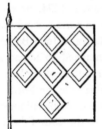

of Suffolk; but this barony, with all his other dignities, became forfeited, on the Duke's attainder in 1554. The present representative of William Lord Ferrers who is commemorated in the preceding Poem, is her Grace, Ann Eliza, Duchess of Buckingham and Chandos.

The arms of Ferrers of Groby were, Gules, seven mascles voided of the Field.[g]

---

e Rot. Parl. vol. I. p. 352 b.

f Palgrave's " Parliamentary Writs," Digest, p. 596, and the Appendix to the First Peerage Report.

g Page 48; Cotton MSS. Caligula, A. xviii., where the charges are, however, described as " losenges ;" and the seal of this Baron in 1301, on which his arms are represented on the breast of a double-headed eagle. · See Archæologia, vol. XXI. p. 210.

RALPH DE MONTHERMER.

[PAGE 48.]

It is singular that nothing should be known of the origin of an individual who became the son-in-law of the King of England, and possessed in right of his wife the powerful earldoms of Gloucester and Hertford. Until his marriage with Joan d'Acres, widow of Gilbert de Clare, Earl of Gloucester and Hertford, and daughter of King Edward the First, early in 1297, his name does not once occur in the records of the period; and it may therefore be conjectured that both his birth and station were obscure, and that he was solely indebted to his splendid alliance for the wealth and honours he obtained. We are told indeed that he had long nourished a passion for the Countess, and that he had suffered deeply for her;[h] but this must be the language of poetry instead of truth, unless his attachment commenced during the lifetime of her first husband, who did not die until 1295. The fact probably was, and many similar instances could be cited, that Joan Plantagenet's first marriage was one of policy rather than affection; and that in her second she gratified her heart rather than her pride. At the time of her union with Monthermer she was scarcely more than twenty-four years old, and perhaps his age was about the same. The account which is given by Dugdale of her second marriage supports these suggestions, as he says, " she matched herself to a plain esquire, called Ralph de Monthermer, clandestinely, without the King her father's knowledge, whom afterwards she sent to her father to receive the honour of knighthood. But when the King understood that she had much debased herself by marrying so meanly, being highly incensed, he caused all her castles and lands to be seized on, and sent her husband, Monthermer, to strait imprisonment in the castle of Bristol. Nevertheless at length, through the mediation of that great prelate Anthony Beck, then Bishop of Durham, a reconciliation was made."[i] Besides the disparity between the rank of the parties, another cause for Edward's displeasure may be found in the fact that he intended she should have married, to her second husband, Amadeus Count of Savoy; for

---

,h Page 48 ante.   i Baronage, tome I. p. 215.

it appears that Otho de Grandison was specially instructed to treat for that alliance on the 16th March, 25 Edw. I. 1297.[k]

The first occasion on which Monthermer is mentioned, is in the 25th Edw. I., when, by the appellation of a Knight, he is stated to have married Joan Countess of Gloucester and Hertford, and to have done homage to the King on Friday the morrow of St. Peter ad Vincula, 2nd August, 1297, at Eltham; immediately after which she performed the same ceremony:

"Memòrandum quod Radulphus de Mahermer, Miles, qui Johannem Comitissam Glouc' et Hertford' duxit in uxorem, fecit fidelitatem Domino Regi die Veneris in crastino Sancti Petri ad Vincula apud Eltham, et postmodum filio Regis, et incontinenter ibidem fecit Comitissa fidelitatem eisdem."[l]

By a writ tested on the 31st July, 1297, the Countess's lands, with some exceptions, were restored to her, upon condition that she should provide one hundred men at arms to serve in the King's wars in France, of whom she was to appoint any captain excepting her husband, Ralph de Monthermer, he having the King's license to remain in England.[m] On the 8th of September following he was summoned to appear with horse and arms at Rochester:[n] on the 10th of April, by the title of " Ralph de Monthermer, Earl of Gloucester and Hertford," he was commanded to attend a parliament at Salisbury, accompanied by as small a retinue as possible;[o] and in June, 26th Edw. I. 1297, his bailiffs were enjoined to assist the commissioners of array in raising foot soldiers against the Scots.[p] By these appellations he continued to be summoned both to parliament and to perform military service until 1307:[q] he was present at the siege of Carlaverock in June 1300; and in the parliament held at Lincoln in February 1301,[r] when the peers of England addressed the memorable Letter to the Pope which has been so frequently noticed in these memoirs, he was a party to that instrument by the same titles.   Upon the occasion of Monthermer attending at York, some years before, Peter of Langtoft says,

> The Erle Jon of Surray com with grete powere,
> Of Gloucestre stoute and gay, Sir Rauf the Mohermere,
> And his wif, Dame Jone, whilom Gilberde's of Clare.[s]

---

k Fœdera, N. E. vol. I. p. 861.

l Rot. Fin. 25 Edw. I. m. I. cited in a note to Palgrave's " Parliamentary Writs," p. 745.

m Palgrave's " Parliamentary Writs," p. 296.   n Ibid. p. 297.   o Ibid. p. 65.

p Ibid. p. 314.   q Ibid. Digest. p. 745.   · r Ibid. pp. 102-3.   s Ed. 1810, p. 301.

, In the 35th Edw. I. thé King granted Monthermer the lands and dignity of the Earl of Athol in Scotland;[t] about which time, being engaged in the wars of that country, he was defeated by Robert Bruce, and was obliged to take refuge in the castle of Ayr, where he was besieged until Edward sent forces to relieve him. Early in that year Joan his Countess died, for orders were issued on the 1st April, 35 Edw. I. 1307, to the Bishop of London, to cause her obsequies to be celebrated, and her soul to be prayed for in his diocese.[u] Neither the title of Earl of Gloucester nor of Earl of Hertford was ever afterwards attributed to him, and from that time until the 2nd Edw. II. he is not recorded to have been summoned to parliament or to the field. This fact is a remarkable elucidation of the descent of earldoms in the fourteenth century, as it tends to show that they were considered to be attached tó the tenure of lands; and that the tenant *jure uxoris* of such lands was also entitled to the dignity. On the 4th March, 2 Edw. II. 1309, Monthermer was again summoned to parliament, but with the rank of a Baron only; and he continued to receive similar writs until the 30th October, 18 Edw. II. 1324;[x] during which period his name also occurs in the writs of service against the King's enemies in Scotland;[y] and on the 2nd August, 2 Edw. II. he obtained a license to hunt in all the royal forests on both sides of the Trent.[z] In the third year of his reign, Edward the Second granted the manor of Warblington in tail general "to his nephews, Thomas and Edward, sons of Ralph de Monthermer;"[a] and in the next year gave the said Ralph and his two sons the manor of Westenden.[b] The father received ccc marks in the 5th Edw. II. in reward of his services in Scotland, being part of DC marks which he was to have paid for the wardship of John ap Adam. He was taken prisoner at the battle of Bannockburn in the 7th Edw. II., when, Dugdale says, " he found favour in regard of former accidental familiarity with the King of Scots in the court of England, and was pardoned his fine for redemption; who thereupon returned, and brought the King's target which had been taken in that fight, but prohibited the use thereof." In the 8th Edw. II. 1315, he was appointed to hold an inquest in consequence of a petition from John Earl of Richmond relative to his claim to the

---

[t] Calend. Rot. Patent. p. 66 b; et Calend. Rot. Chart. p. 137 b, anno 34 Edw. I.

[u] Fœdera, N. E. vol. I. p. 1013; see also p. 1016.

[x] Appendix to the First Peerage Report. [y] Ibid.

[z] Fœdera, N. E. vol. II. p. 51. [a] Calend. Rot. Pat. p. 71 b. [b] Ibid. p. 72 b.

towns of Great Yarmouth and Gorleston.[c] With this notice all information respecting Monthermer terminates ; and it is supposed he died about the 18th Edw. II. though no inquisition appears to have been held on his decease. By the Countess of Gloucester he had issue a daughter, Mary, who married Duncan, twelfth Earl of Fife ;[d] and two sons, Thomas and Edward. The latter is presumed to have been the Edward de Monthermer who received writs of summons to parliament on the 23rd April and 21st June, 11th Edw. III. 1337, and who was commanded, from Sussex, to serve with horse and arms against the Scots, in December, 8 Edw. III. 1334.[e] Thomas de Monthermer, the eldest son, though never summoned to parliament, was a knight, and was partially distinguished in political affairs .for, by the appellation of the King's kinsman, he obtained pardon in the 1st Edw. III. for having been an adherent of the Earl of Lancaster.[f] He was enjoined to serve with horse and arms against the Scots by writ tested 21st March, 7 Edw. III. 1333,[g] and again on the 27th March, 9 Edw. III. 1335 ;[h] and was ordered to provide six armed men for the same purpose on the 6th October, 11 Edw. III. 1337.[i] Dugdale informs us that he was slain in the great sea-fight between the English and French in 1340. By Margaret his wife, who survived him until the 23rd of Edw. III., he left issue a daughter, Margaret, who was found to be ten years of age at her father's death, and twenty-one on that of her mother, and then the wife of Sir John de Montacute, second son of William first Earl of Salisbury. Sir John Montacute was summoned to parliament

---

[c] Rot. Parl. vol. I. p. 301 a.

[d] Permission was ordered to be asked of the Pope, by Edward the Second soon after his accession, for a dispensation for the marriage of Mary, who is expressly called " Mary de Monthermer, the King's niece," with Duncan Earl of Fife, notwithstanding their relationship. Fœdera, N. E. vol. II. pp. 5 and 6, but which was only a repetition of a similar request made by Edward the First in October 1306. Ibid. vol. I. pp. 1001-2. On the 22nd December, 8 Edw. II. 1314, a passport was granted to the said Duncan, at the instance of Ralph de Monthermer, his father-in-law, for leave to come into England, and to pass through it to parts beyond the sea. Ibid. vol. II. p. 258. According to Douglas's Peerage, the issue of the Earl of Fife and Mary de Monthermer was Duncan 13th Earl of Fife, whose only daughter and heiress, Isabel, though twice married, died s. p.

[e] Appendix to the First Peerage Report, p. 433.

[f] Calend. Rot. Patent. p. 107 a. See also Fœdera, N. E. vol. II. p. 796, where several notices occur relative to the wardship of his daughter.

[g] Appendix to the First Peerage Report, p. 421.   [h] Ibid. p. 443.   [i] Ibid. p. 488.

in the 31st Edw. III., and his son succeeded to the earldom of Salisbury, in which dignity the barony of Monthermer, created by the writ of 2 Edw. II., continued merged. It, however, became forfeited in 1400; was restored in 1421; and was finally forfeited by the attainder of Richard Neville, Earl of Warwick and Salisbury, on whom it had devolved, *jure matris*, in 1471.

After the death of the Countess of Gloucester Ralph de Monthermer married Isabel, the widow of John de Hastings, and sister and coheiress of Aymer de Valence, Earl of Pembroke; and in the 13th Edw. II. 1319, he received a pardon of the fine he had incurred for having done so without the King's license,[k] but by her he is not stated to have had any children. She survived him, and by his will he left her certain houses in the parish of St. Dunstan's in London.[l]

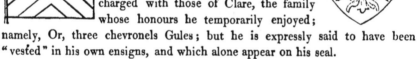

The arms of Monthermer were, Or, an eagle displayed Vert;[m] and a similar eagle appears from the seal of this Baron in 1301 to have been his crest.[n] It would seem that did not bear his own arms on his banner at Carlaverock, but that it was charged with those of Clare, the family whose honours he temporarily enjoyed; namely, Or, three chevronels Gules; but he is expressly said to have been "vested" in his own ensigns, and which alone appear on his seal.

---

[k] Fœdera, N. E. vol. II. p. 403.   [l] Calend. Inquisit. post mortem, vol. III. p. 327.

[m] Page 48; Cottonian MS. Caligula, A. xviii.; and the seal of Ralph de Monthermer in 1301.

[n] Archæologia, vol. XXI.

280

ROBERT DE LA WARD.

[PAGE 50.]

As the account given of this individual by Dugdale, commences with the 31st
year of Edw. I., and only fills four lines, nothing can, perhaps, be said of his parentage or birth. It is most probable that he was the Robert de la Ward who
complained of being unjustly imprisoned in the 18th Edw. I. 1290, by Ralph de
Hengham, one of the King's justices;[o] and who, on the 10th September, 23 Edw. I.
1295, obtained a remission of the tenth of his goods which had been granted to
the Crown.[p] In the 25th Edw. I. he was returned from the counties of Nottingham and Derby as holding lands or rents to the amount of £20 yearly value and
upwards, either *in capite* or otherwise; and as such was summoned to perform
military service in person with horse and arms in Scotland.[q] He was commanded
to serve in Flanders in the ensuing year;[r] and in the 27th Edw. I. 1299, was
summoned as a Baron to serve against the Scots.[s] La Ward received his first
writ of summons to parliament in 1300; in June in which year he was at Carlaverock, and he appears to have distinguished himself at the siege of the castle.[t]
On the 12th of the following February he was a party to the Letter from the
Barons to Pope Boniface, in which he is styled " Lord of Alba Aula."[u] He was
again in the Scottish wars in the 31st Edw. I.;[x] and in the 34th Edw. I. 1306,
was appointed steward of the King's household;[x] on the 24th of October in
which year he was present when James Steward of Scotland took the oath of
fealty to Edward at Lanercost;[y] after which time nothing seems to be known of
him. De la Ward was summoned to parliament from the 29th December, 28
Edw. I. 1299, to the 3rd of November, 34 Edw. I. 1306;[z] and died in the 35th
Edw. I. 1307;[a] leaving by Ida[b] his wife, who, according to some authorities, was

---

o Rot. Parl. vol. I. p. 52.   p Palgrave's " Parliamentary Writs," p. 391.
q Ibid. p. 288.   r Ibid. pp. 304, 306.   s Ibid. p. 318.
t Page 78 ante.   u Palgrave's " Parliamentary Writs," p. 103.   x Ibid. p. 366.
y Fœdera, N. E. vol. I. p. 1001.   z Palgrave's " Parliamentary Writs," Digest.
a Esch. eod. ann.   b Ida is said to have been his wife in the Escheat on his death.

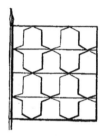

the daughter of Robert Lord Fitz Walter, a son, Simon de la Ward, who was summoned to parliament from the 18th Edw. II. to the 8th Edw. III. and died s. p.; and a daughter, Joane, who married Sir Hugh Meignill, knt. and became heir to her brother; and in whose descendants the representation of this barony is vested.[c]

The arms of De la Ward were, Vaire, Argent and Sable.[d]

JOHN DE ST. JOHN.

[PAGE 50.]

This Banneret was the son and heir apparent of the John de St. John, of whom a memoir has been given in a former page, and was born in 1274. Soon after he became of age he was summoned to the field, for, by the description of " John le St. John the son," he was ordered to serve in Flanders in November, 1297;[e] and by the appellation of a Baron was, in the 27th Edw. I. 1299, commanded to perform military service against the Scots.[f] In March, 28th Edw. I., he was summoned to parliament;[g] and was enjoined to be at Carlisle properly equipped with horse and arms on the 24th June following,[h] about which day he was at the siege of Carlaverock, when he must have been just twenty-six years of age. Some notice of him will be found in the extracts from the Wardrobe Accounts of the time relating to his father's retinue; and to which it is only necessary to refer.[i]

c MS. marked " Black Book," f. 438, in the College of Arms. See also the pedigree of Meignell in Nichols's Leicestershire; and in Dugdale's Warwickshire, where she is called the eldest daughter and heiress of Robert de la Ward, and is said to have been the second wife of Sir Hugh Meignell.

d Page 50; Cotton MSS. Caligula, A. xviii., where the name of Robert de la Ward has been added to the list of the names and arms " abatues" of great personages.

e Palgrave's " Parliamentary Writs," p. 304.   f Ibid. p. 318.   g Ibid. p. 82.
h Ibid. p. 347.   i Page 247 ante.

As has been already observed, it is by no means certain whether it was this Baron or his father who, by the title of " Lord of Hanak," was a party to the Letter from the Barons to the Pope in 1301; but most probably the former.[j] In the 31st Edw. I. he was again summoned to the Scottish wars;[k] and he succeeded his father in 1302, when, performing his homage, he had livery of his lands. In the 35th Edw. I. he petitioned the King to issue his precept to Hugh le Despenser, who was then Justice of the Forests, to permit him to enjoy his park at Shereburne, in the county of Southampton, which his father had made with the King's license; he was answered that any park which had been formed since the deforestation should be laid open.[l]

During the early part of the reign of Edward the Second this Baron was frequently enjoined to serve in the Scottish wars, but nothing memorable is recorded of him. Writs of summons to parliament were addressed to him from the 29th December, 28 Edw. I. 1299, to the 10th October, 19 Edw. II. 1325, though Sir William Dugdale cites an escheat to prove that he died on the 14th of May, 12 Edw. II. 1319. By Isabel, daughter of Hugh de Courtenay, he left issue Hugh his son and heir, then twenty-six years old, who, in the 5th Edw. III. " represented to the King by petition, that, whereas his father had served King Edward the Second in his wars both in Gascony and Scotland, according to the tenor of a certain indenture, whereby he was retained with that King as well in times of war as peace, upon certain wages then agreed upon for himself and those of his retinue, and to have recompense for as many horses as should be lost in such service; as also to receive in times of peace such wages as other bannerets of the King's household had; and moreover that divers sums of money due to him, both for his wages and loss of horses in those wars, were then in arrear; and did thereupon obtain the King's precept to the Lord Treasurer and the Barons of his Exchequer to account with him for the same, and to make satisfaction for what should be found in arrear."

The said Hugh de St. John died in 1337, without being summoned to parliament, and Edmund his only son dying at Calais on the 18th August, 21 Edw. III. 1347, s. p., Margaret and Isabel, sisters of Edmund, became his heirs; of

---

j Page 248 ante.   k Palgrave's " Parliamentary Writs," p. 366.
l Rot. Parl. vol. I. p. 201.

whom Margaret married John de St. Philibert, but left no issue that survived; and Isabel, married before the 23rd Edw. III. to her second husband, Lucas de Poynings, by whom she had a son and heir, Thomas de Poynings, who was called Lord St. John. Henry de Burghersh, the first husband of the said Isabel, died s. p.

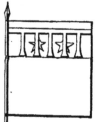

The arms of St. John were, Argent, on a chief Gules two mullets Or; but during the lifetime of his father this Baron bore a label Azure for difference.[m]

RICHARD FITZ ALAN, EARL OF ARUNDEL.

[PAGE 50.]

Notwithstanding that almost every writer on the subject has considered that both the father and the grandfather of this individual were Earls of Arundel, in consequence of the marriage of John Fitz Alan, the father of the latter, with Isabel, the second sister and coheiress of Hugh de Albini, Earl of Arundel, in whose right he acquired Arundel Castle, it has been satisfactorily proved by the Lords' Committees in their " First and Second Reports on the Dignity of a Peer of the Realm,"[n] that neither of them enjoyed that honour; but that the first Earl of Arundel of the family of Fitz Alan, was the person of whose life the following memoir will contain all which is known.

· On the antiquity of the house of Fitz Alan, or the achievements of the long line of peers who inherited the earldom of Arundel, it is not necessary to enlarge, for the former is known to every genealogist, and their deeds are matter of history.

Richard Fitz Alan was the son and heir of John Fitz Alan, by Isabel, daughter

---

[m] Page 50; Cotton MSS. Caligula, A. xviii.   [n] Page 410 et seq.

of Roger de Mortimer of Chirk; and succeeded his father in his lands in March, 1272, at which time he was just five years of age, having been born on the feast of St. Blaze, 3rd February, 1267.[o] The custody of his lands were, in the 1st Edw. I. 1273, committed to John de Oxinden, and his wardship to Roger de Mortimer; but in the 8th Edw. I. 1280, Isabel his mother, by the description of "Isabelle, que fuit uxor Johannis fil' Alani," obtained the custody of the castle and honour of Arundel during her son's minority,[p] though in the 10th Edw. I. Roger de Mortimer received a grant from the King of the custody of the castles of Arundel and Oswaldestre.[q] He became of full age in February, 11 Edw. I., 1283, and by the appellation of "Richard Fitz Alan" only, obtained a grant of a fair at his manor of Arundel in the 13th Edw. I.:[r] his bailiffs of "Blaunc Monster" and Clone were directed to raise foot soldiers to march against Resus filius Mereduci,[s] in July, 15 Edw. I. 1287: he was enjoined to reside on his demesnes and lordships in Wales, until the rebellion of the said Resus was quelled, by writ tested on the 14th November following:[t] he was ordered to give credence to William de Henley, Prior of the Hospital of St. John of Jerusalem, in matters which the Prior was to declare to him, in the 16th Edw. I. 1288:[u] and was again desired to reside on his lordships in Wales, for the purpose of defending them against Resus filius Mereduci, in November, 17 Edw. I. 1288.[x] In the 20th Edw. I., Fitz Alan was first styled "Earl of Arundel," by which title he was summoned by two different writs to answer to the King respecting the hundred of Pesseburn and other property in Shropshire; and it is justly inferred that he became Earl of Arundel between the 17th and 20th Edw. I. 1288 and 1291.[y] By writs tested at Westminster on the 18th and 27th October, 22 Edw. I. 1294, and addressed to him as "Richarl Earl of Arundel," he was appointed commander of the forces destined for the relief of the castle of Bere:[z] in the 23rd Edw. I. 1297, he was summoned to parliament;[a] and in the same·year he obtained a quietus for remission of the tenth charged upon his own proper

---

o Escheat cited in the First and Second Peerage Reports, p. 416.   p Ibid. p. 418.
q Dugdale, p. 315, on the authority of Pat. 10 Edw. I. m. 8.
r First and Second Peerage Reports, p. 420.
s Palgrave's "Parliamentary Writs," p. 251.   t Ibid. p. 252.   u Ibid. p. 254.
x Ibid. p. 255.   y Peerage Reports, I. and II. p. 420.
z Palgrave's "Parliamentary Writs," p. 264.   a Ibid. p. 29.

goods by virtue of the grant made by the laity of the kingdom.[b] In November following the Earl was ordered to perform military service in person in Gascony;[c] from which time until the 29th Edw. I., he was repeatedly commanded to serve in the wars either in Gascony or Scotland, and was summoned to every parliament that was held within that period.[d]

The Poem informs us that the Earl of Arundel, " a handsome and well beloved knight," was at the siege of Carlaverock in June, 1300; and in February, 1301, he was a party to the Letter from the Barons to Pope Boniface, in which he is styled " Earl of Arundel."[e] This was, however, perhaps the last public action of his life, as he died before the 9th of March, 1302, in the thirty-fifth year of his age.[f]

He married Alizon, the daughter of the Marquess of Saluces in Italy, by whom he had issue Edmond, the next Earl, who was sixteen years old at his father's death; and, according to Dugdale, two daughters, Maud, wife of Philip Lord Burnel, and Margaret, who married Philip Boteler of Wemme.

The arms of Fitz Alan are, Gules, a lion rampant Argent.[g]

ALAN LE ZOUCHE.

[PAGE 50.]

Alan le Zouche was the son and heir of Roger le Zouche, and succeeded to his father's lands at Ashby in Leicestershire in the 13th Edw. I. 1285, when he was eighteen years old. Dugdale states that having, on the feast of St. Dennis, 16th Edw. I. 9th October, 1288, about which time he became of age, offered

---

b Palgrave's " Parliamentary Writs," p. 391. c Ibid. p. 269.
d Ibid. Digest, p. 599. e Ibid. pp. 102-3 f Peerage Reports, I. and II. p. 421.
g Page 50; Cottonian MSS. Caligula, A. xviii.; and the seal of this Earl, in 1301.

his services to the King in Gascony, " he was courteously received," in consequence of which his homage was respited; and a special precept was immediately
sent to Walter de Lacy, the King's Escheator in Ireland, to deliver to him all
his lands there, which he had seized for neglecting to perform that essential
ceremony. In the 22nd Edw. I. 1294, he was excepted from the general summons of persons holding by military tenure or serjeantcy which was then issued
for the King's expedition into Gascony : [h] on the 7th July, 25 Edw. I. 1297, he
was ordered to serve with horse and arms in person beyond the sea : [i] in the
same year he was returned from the counties of Northampton, Sussex, and Surrey,
as being possessed of lands or rents to the amount of £20 yearly and upwards,
either *in capite* or otherwise; and as such was summoned under the general writ
to perform military service abroad.[k] About the same time he was commanded to
attend a great council before Edward the King's son, the Lieutenant of England,
at London, on the 30th of September, 1297 : [l] on the 24th November, he was
enjoined to serve in Flanders ; [m] and on the 6th December following against the
Scots.[n]

Zouche received his first writ to parliament in March, 1299 ; and on the 6th
of June in that year was summoned as a Baron to the Scottish wars ; [o] again on
the 12th of November ; [p] and to be at Carlisle, equipped for the field, on the 24th
June, 1300,[q] in which month we learn from the Poem that he was at the siege
of Carlaverock. The charges in his arms are there alluded to in a manner
which, if any thing was positively meant, would admit of the inference that he
was of a generous, or rather, profuse disposition ; for the writer adds," I know well
that he has spent more treasure than is suspended in his purse." He was at that
time thirty-three years of age. In February, 1301, Zouche was a party to the
memorable Letter from the Barons of this country to Pope Boniface the Eighth,
in which he is styled " Lord of Ashby :"[r] in the ensuing June he was commanded to serve in the wars of Scotland ; and again in the 31st and 34th Edw. I.,
1303 and 1306.[s] He was a manucaptor of William de Montacute, then a
prisoner in the Tower of London, in the 33rd Edw. I. 1305 ; [t] and on the acces-

h Palgrave's " Parliamentary Writs," p. 260.   i Ibid. p. 282.   k Ibid. pp. 288-294.
l Ibid. p. 56.   m Ibid. p. 304.   n Ibid. p. 302.   o Ibid. p. 318.
p Ibid. p. 324.   q Ibid. p. 327.   r Ibid. pp. 102-3.   s Ibid. Digest, p. 88.
t Rot. Parl. vol. I. p. 176 b.

sion of Edward the Second he was one of the peers summoned to attend that monarch's coronation.[u] In the 1st, 3rd, 4th, 5th, and 7th Edw. II. he served against the Scots :[u] in the 5th Edw. II. he was appointed Governor of Rockingham Castle in Northamptonshire, and Steward of that forest; and having been regularly summoned to parliament from the 6th February, 27 Edw. I. 1299, to the 26th November, 7 Edw. II. 1313, died in 1314, aged about forty-seven. By Eleanor his wife, but whose maiden name is not known, he left issue three daughters who were his coheirs ; namely, Elene, who was then twenty-six years old, and the wife of Nicholas St. Maur ; Maud, aged twenty-four, the wife of Robert de Holand ; and Elizabeth, then a nun at Brewode in Staffordshire, and twenty years of age. The said Elene married, secondly, before the 15th Edw. II. Alan le Cherleton.

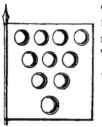

The arms of Zouche of Ashby were, Gules, Bezanté.[x]

---

[u] Appendix to the First Peerage Report.

[x] Page 50; the Cottonian MS. Caligula, A. xviii.; and the seal of this Baron in 1301, on which the shield appears suspended to the neck of a demi-lion rampant. It is also worthy of remark that round the shield six lions are placed, and which, there can be no doubt, alluded to his mother's arms, Ela, the daughter and coheiress of Stephen de Longespee, who bore six lions rampant. As a curious example of the manner in which arms were differenced in the early part of the fourteenth century, the following notice of the coats of Zouche, mentioned in the Roll in the Cottonian MS. just cited, may be acceptable.

BARONS.

Alan le Zouche,   Gules, besanté Or.

William le Zouche,   Idem.   a quarter Ermine.
[of Haryngworth, first cousin of Alan.]

KNIGHTS IN LEICESTERSHIRE.

Sir William Zouche,   Idem.   a label Azure.

Sir Oliver Zouche,   Idem.   a chevron Ermine.

Sir Amory Zouche,   Idem.   a bend Argent.

Sir Thomas Zouche,   Idem.   on a quarter Argent, a mullet Sable.

ANTHONY BEK, BISHOP OF DURHAM.

[PAGE 54.]

Although this eminent prelate was not present·at the siege of Carlaverock, he occupies so large a share of the Poet's attention, the eulogy on him is so striking, and the number of his retinue in the English army was so great, that it is necessary a brief notice should be given of his career. The task is comparatively an easy one, because his character has been pourtrayed in so masterly a manner by the Historian of Durham, that little else is required than to abridge his interesting memoir: thus the idle affectation will be avoided of trying to do better, what few could have performed so well.

Of the period of Bek's birth we have no precise information. He was a younger son of Walter Bek, Baron of Eresby; and in the 54th Hen. III. 1270, was signed with the cross on going to the Holy Land with Prince Edward,[y] who nominated him one of the executors of his will, which was dated at Acre in June, 1272.[z] In the 3rd Edw. I. 1275, being then a clerk, he was appointed Constable of the Tower of London;[a] and was constituted Archdeacon of Durham as early as 1273.[b] He was present in the parliament at Westminster at the feast of St. Michael, 6 Edw. I. 1278, when the King of Scotland did homage to Edward;[c] and on the 9th of July, 1283, was elected Bishop of Durham. The ceremony of his consecration was performed by the archbishop of York, in the presence of the King, on the 9th of January following; but at his enthronization at Durham on Christmas Eve, a dispute arose between the Official of the Archbishop of York and the Prior of Durham as to the right of performing the office, which the Bishop elect terminated by receiving the mitre from the hands of his brother, Thomas Bek, Bishop of St. David's: on the festival of St. John the Evangelist, he presented the church with two pieces of rich embroidery, wrought with the history of the Nativity.

---

y Dugdale's Baronage, vol. I. p. 426. In this memoir all the statements are taken from Surtees' History of Durham, excepting where other authorities are cited.

z Royal Wills, p. 18, and Testamenta Vetusta, p. 8.   a Dugdale's Baronage, vol. I. p. 426.

b Le Neve's Fasti Ecclesiæ Anglicanæ, p. 353.   c Rot. Parl. vol. I. p. 224.

It is impossible to state even the principal occasions on which Bishop Bek was conspicuous; it being perhaps sufficient to observe that scarcely a single event of any importance took place during the reign of Edward the First, whether of war or diplomacy, but in which he was concerned. Several facts might be mentioned which tend to prove the influence that he at one time possessed over the mind of his sovereign: according to Fordun it was by his advice that Edward supported the claim of Baliol instead of that of Bruce, in the competition for the crown of Scotland; and he was frequently a mediator, not only between the King and his Barons, but between his Majesty and his children.[c] The Prelate's ambition was equal to his resources; and both were evinced by the splendour of his equipage and the number of his followers. If his biographer,[d] from whom Mr. Surtees has derived great part of his statements, may be believed, the retinue with which he attended the King in his wars amounted to twenty-six standard bearers of his household,[e] one hundred and forty knights, and five hundred horse; and one thousand foot marched under the consecrated banner of St. Cuthbert, which was borne by Henry de Horncestre, a monk of Durham. The Bishop's wealth and power soon however excited the suspicion of the King; and the process of " quo warranto" was applied with the view of reducing them. His temporalities were seized, but he recovered them after an appeal to parliament; and his palatine rights were confirmed in the most ample manner by the Justices Itinerant in 1293. From the proceedings in parliament in the 21st Edw. I. it seems that on the Wednesday before the feast of St. James the Apostle, in the 20th Edw. I. namely, on the 23rd July, 1292, at Derlyngton, and afterwards at Alverton, and other places, the Archbishop of York had formerly excommunicated the Bishop of Durham, he being then engaged in the King's service in the North; for which offence the Archbishop was imprisoned, but pardoned on paying a fine of 4000 marks.[f] Bek's frequent quarrels with the Prior of Durham, whom he had of his own authority deprived and ejected, soon afforded a pretext for the royal interference; and a formidable attack was afterwards made upon his possessions. About the same time he espoused the popular cause, by joining

---

[c] See p. 275 ante.

[d] Robert de Gledstanes, who was elected Bishop of Durham in 1333, but was set aside by the Pope, and died soon afterwards. His labours are preserved in the Cottonian MS. Titus, A. ii.

[e] " Habuit de familia sua xxvj vexillarios"—*Bannerets* were most probably meant.

[f] Rot. Parl. vol. I. p. 102, et seq.

4 E

the Earl Marshal and the Earl of Hereford against the crown; and when charged
by the King with deserting his interests, he boldly replied, "that the Earls laboured
for the advantage and honour of the sovereign and his realm, and therefore he
stood with them, and not with the King against them." In the meanwhile he
obeyed a second citation to Rome for having deprived the Prior, where he appeared
with his usual magnificence, and triumphed over his adversaries by obtaining from
the Pontiff a confirmation of his visitorial superiority over the convent. By quitting
the realm without license he exposed himself to the enmity of the crown; and
his vassals availed themselves of his absence to urge their complaints. The
Palatinate was seized into the King's hands; and in July, 1301, the temporalities
of the See were committed to the custody of Robert de Clifford. In the parliament in the following year, having effected a reconciliation with his vassals and
submitted to the King, the Bishop obtained a restitution of his temporalities.
But Bek's intractable spirit soon involved him in fresh disputes with the Prior;
and being accused of having infringed on the dignity of the crown by some in-
struments which he had obtained from Rome, his temporalities were, in December
1305, once more seized; and the King seems to have used every exertion not
only to humiliate the haughty prelate, but to divest his See of some part of its
extensive territories. From this time until Edward's demise he continued under
the royal displeasure; but no sooner was Edward the Second on the throne than
he added to his power and titles by procuring the dignity of King of the Isle of
Man, together with ample restitution of what had been wrested from him by the
late monarch.

It is here, however, necessary to refer to the notice of the Bishop in the preceding Poem. Mr. Surtees has evidently adopted the translation given of it in
the "Antiquarian Repertory," where the words "uns plaitz," are rendered "a
wound;" as he says, "the Bishop of Durham is described in the Roll of Carlaverock as being absent from the siege on account of a wound," whereas the
passage is presumed to have meant that the Bishop was detained in England in
consequence of a treaty or some other public transaction. It appears that he then
sent the King one hundred and sixty men at arms; and at the battle of Falkirk
he is stated to have led the second division of the English army with thirty-nine
banners.[g] In the 35th Edw. I. being sent to Rome with other Bishops and

---

[g] This passage probably meant that among the Bishop's followers there were thirty-nine
Bannerets.

the Earl of Lincoln to present some vessels of gold to the Pope from the King, his Holiness conferred on him the title of Patriarch of Jerusalem.[h] Thus, Mr. Surtees remarks, on receiving the sovereignty of the isle of Man, " his haughty spirit was gratified by the accumulated dignities of Bishop, Count Palatine, Patriarch, and King." The last political transaction of his life was his union with the Earl of Lancaster against Piers de Gaveston in 1310; and on the 3rd of March following, 1310-11, he expired at his manor of Eltham in Kent.

The character of Anthony Bek is given with more elegance than truth in the Poem. " The mirror of Christianity" is an emphatic allusion to his piety and virtue; and his wisdom, eloquence, temperance, justice, and chastity, are as forcibly pointed out, as the total absence of pride, covetousness, and envy for which he is said to have been distinguished. But this is rather a brilliant painting than a true portrait; for if all the other qualities which are there ascribed to him be conceded, it is impossible to consider that humility formed any part of his merits. His latest biographer, Mr. Surtees, has however described him with so much discrimination and elegance, that his words are transferred to these pages, because they form the most appropriate conclusion of this sketch, and powerfully tend to redeem its many imperfections.

" The Palatine power reached its highest elevation under the splendid pontificate of Anthony Bek. Surrounded by his officers of state, or marching at the head of his troops, in peace or war, he appeared as the military chief of a powerful and independent franchise. The court of Durham exhibited all the appendages of royalty: nobles addressed the Palatine sovereign kneeling, and, instead of menial servants, knights waited in his presence chamber and at his table, bareheaded and standing. Impatient of control, whilst he asserted an oppressive superiority over the convent, and trampled on the rights of his vassals, he jealously guarded his own Palatine franchise, and resisted the encroachments of the crown when they trenched on the privileges of the aristocracy.[i] When his pride or his patriotism had provoked the displeasure of his sovereign, he met the storm with firmness; and had the fortune or the address to emerge from disgrace and difficulty with added rank and influence. His high birth gave him a

h Dugdale's Baronage, vol. I. p. 426.
i During one of Edward's progresses to Scotland, a palfrey belonging to the royal train threw and killed its rider, and Anthony seized the palfrey as a deodand: "dedeins sa fraunchise roiale."

natural claim to power, and he possessed every popular and splendid quality which could command obedience or excite admiration. His courage and constancy were shown in the service of his sovereign. His liberality knew no bounds; and he regarded no expense, however enormous, when placed in competition with any object of pleasure or magnificence.[k] Yet in the midst of apparent profusion he was too prudent ever to feel the embarrassment of want. Surrounded by habitual luxury, his personal temperance was as strict as it was singular; and his chastity was exemplary in an age of general corruption.[l] Not less an enemy to sloth[m] than to intemperance, his leisure was devoted either to splendid progresses[n] from one manor to another, or to the sports of the field;

---

[k] He gave 40s. for as many fresh herrings : ' Aliis magnatibus tunc in Parliamento ibi consistentibus pro nimiâ caristiâ emere non curantibus.' Grayst. c. 14. On another occaion, hearing one say ' this cloth is so dear that even Bishop Anthony would not venture to pay for it;' he immediately ordered it to be bought and cut up into horse cloths. Ibid.

[l] ' Castissimè vixit, vix mulierum faciem fixis oculis aspiciens ; unde in translatione S. Willelmi Eboracensis cum alii Episcopi ossa ejus timerent tangere, remordente eos conscientiâ de virginate amissâ, iste audacter manus imposuit ; et quod negotium poposcit reverenter egit.' Ibid.

[m] ' Quietis impatiens vix ultra unum somnum in lecto expectans, dixit illum non esse hominem, qui in lecto de latere in latus se verteret.' Ibid.

[n] ' In nullo loco mansurus, continuè circuibat de manerio in manerium, de austro in boream ; et equorum, canum et avium sector.' Ibid. And here one cannot avoid being reminded of the satirical lines of Piers Plowman :

' And piked a boute on palfrays : fro place to maners
Have an hepe of houndes at his ers : as he a Lord were.'

Bishop-Middleham, then a fortress of the first class, appears, from the date of several charters to have been Anthony Bek's chief residence within the county of Durham. The reasons which led to this preference are obvious : defended by a morass on two sides, and by broken ground to the north, the fortress presented an almost impregnable stronghold during the wars of the Border, whilst Auckland lay bare and defenceless, on the direct route of Scottish invasion. It is no wonder that in after-times Middleham was deserted for the green glades of Auckland.

The following lines are extracted, from an inedited poem on the ' Superstitions of the North :'

' There Valour bowed before the rood and book,
And kneeling Knighthood served a Prelate Lord ;
Yet little deigned he on such train to look,
Or glance of ruth or pity to afford.
There time has heard the peal rung out by night,
Has seen from every tower the cressets stream :
When the red balefire on yon western height,
Had roused the Warder from his fitful dream ;

and his activity and temperance preserved his faculties of mind and body vigorous under the approach of age and infirmity.

" In the munificence of his public works he rivalled the greatest of his prede-

---

Has seen old Durham's lion banner float
    O'er the proud bulwark, that, with giant pride,
And feet deep plunged amidst the circling moat,
    The efforts of the roving Scot defied.

" Long rolling years have swept those scenes away,
    And peace is on the mountain and the fell ;
And rosy dawn, and closing twilight gray,
    But hears the distant sheep-walk's tinkling bell.
And years have fled since last the gallant deer
    Sprung from yon covert at the thrilling horn
Yet still, when Autumn shakes the forest sear,
    Black Hugo's voice upon the blast is borne.
Woe to the wight who shall his ire provoke,
    When the stern huntsman stalks his nightly round,
By blasted ash, or lightning-shivered oak,
    And chears with surly voice his spectre hound."

Of this black Hugh take the following legendary account: ! Sir Anthon Bek, Busshop of Dureme in the tyme of King Eduarde, the son of King Henry, was the maist prowd and masterfull Busshop in all England, and it was com'only said that he was the prowdest Lord in Christienty. It chanced that emong other lewd persons, this Sir Anthon entertained at his court one Hugh de Pountchardon, that for his evill deeds and manifold robberies had been driven out of the Inglische Court, and had come from the southe to seek a little bread, and to live by stalynge. And to this Hughe, whom also he imployed to good purpose in the warr of Scotland, the Busshop gave the lande of Thikley, since of him caulid Thikley-Puntchardon, and also made him his chief huntsman. And after, this blake Hugh dyed afore the Busshop : and efter that the Busshop chasid the wild hart in Galtres forest, and sodainly ther met with him Hugh de Pontchardon that was afore deid, on a wythe horse ; and the said Hugh loked earnestly on the Busshop, and the Busshop said unto him, ' Hughe, what makethe thee here ?' and he spake never word, but lifte up his cloke, and then he shewed Sir Anton his ribbes set with bones, and nothing more ; and none other of the varlets saw him but the Busshop only ; and the saide Hughe went his way, and Sir Anton toke corage, and cheered the dogges ; and shortly efter he was made Patriarque of Hierusalem, and he sawe nothing no moe ; and this Hughe is him that the silly people in Galtres doe call Le gros Venour, and he was seen twice efter that by simple folk, afore that the forest was felled in the tyme of Henry, father of King Henry that now ys.'

4 F

cessors. Within the bishopric of Durham he founded the colleges of Chester and Lanchester, erected towers at Gainford and Coniscliff, and added to the buildings of Alnwick and Barnard Castles. He gave Evenwood manor to the convent, and appropriated the vicarage of Morpeth to the chapel which he had founded at Auckland.[o] In his native county of Lincoln he endowed Alvingham Priory, and built a castle at Somerton.[p] In Kent he erected the beautiful manor-house of Eltham, whose ruins still speak the taste and magnificence of its founder. Notwithstanding the vast expenses incurred in these and other works, in his contests with the crown and with his vassals, in his foreign journeys, and in the continued and excessive charges of his household, he died wealthier than any of his predecessors, leaving immense treasures in the riches of the age; gallant horses, costly robes, rich furniture, plate, and jewels.[q]

" Anthony Bek was the first prelate of Durham who was buried within the walls of the cathedral. His predecessors had been restrained from sepulture within the sacred edifice by a reverential awe for the body of the holy confessor;[r] and on this occasion, from some motive of superstition, the corpse was not allowed to enter the doors, although a passage was broken through the wall[s] for its reception, near the place of interment. The tomb was placed in the east transept, between the altars of St. Adrian and St. Michael, close to the holy shrine. A brass, long since destroyed, surrounded the ledge of the marble, and bore the following inscription :

---

[o] ' Sed ipso mortuo Radulphus filius Willielmi Dominus de Graystoke patronatum præfatæ Ecclesiæ per litem obtinuit; et presentato per ipsum per Episcopum admisso et instituto, capella indotata remansit.' Grayst. c. 22. The patronage still remains with the heir of Greystoke.

[p] "Castrum de Somerton curiosissimè ædificavit." Grayst. c. 22.   [q] Ibid.

[r] " Ante illum enim ob reverentiam corporis S. Cuthberti non est permissum corpus mortuum ingredi ecclesiam Dunelmensem." Anthony Bek was, therefore, the first who dared to bring

" A slovenly, unhandsome corse,
Betwixt the wind and his nobility."

[s] If, however, the funeral of the Patriarch Bishop was conducted with the same solemnities as that of his successor Cardinal Langley, the breaking an entrance through the wall was a matter of necessity rather than superstition, for Langley's hearse was drawn into the nave of the Cathedral by four stately black horses, which, with all their housings of velvet, became the official perquisite of the Sacrist.

" Presul magnanimus Antonius hic jacet imus
Jerusalem strenuus Patriarcha fuit, quod opimus
Annis vicenis regnabat sex et j plenis
Mille trecentenis Christo moritur quoque denis."

The Bishop's heirs were found, by the inquisition held after his decease, to be his nephew, Robert de Willoughby, son of Alice his eldest sister; and his nephew, John de Harcourt, son of his second sister, Margaret.

The personal arms of Bishop Bek were, Gules, a fer de moulin Ermine;[t] and which it appears were borne on his banner without any junction with those of his see, he being deemed merely a temporal Noble when in the field.

JOHN DE HASTINGS.

[PAGE 54.]

A eulogy better calculated to render the memory of man an object of respect could not have been devised than that which the Poet has bestowed on John de Hastings. His conduct, we are told, was uniformly honourable: that in the field he was distinguished as much by bravery, as in the hostel he was eminent for mildness, graciousness, and suavity of manners; whilst his love of equity was not even exceeded by that of either of the King's Justices Itinerant.

The individual thus recommended to our attention was the son and heir of Henry Baron Hastings, by Joan, the sister of George de Cantilupe, Baron of Abergavenny. He succeeded his father in the 53rd Hen. III., at which time he was a minor; but on the death of his maternal uncle, George de Cantilupe, in

---

t Page 54; and Cotton MSS. Caligula, A. xviii.

the 1st Edw. I., he was found to be one of his heirs, and was then of full age : hence he must have been born about the year 1251.

In the 12th Edw. I. he was in the expedition then made into Scotland; and in the 15th Edw. I. 1287, attended the Earl of Cornwall into Wales, in which year he was enjoined to reside on his lordships and demesnes, until the rebellion of Resus fil. Mereduci was quelled;[u] and in the following year he was ordered to defend them against that person.[x] He was present in parliament in May, 18 Edw. I. 1290, when the aid was granted for the marriage of the King's eldest daughter;[y] and about the same time was a party to the Letter addressed to the Pope on the behalf of the Earls, Barons, and " Proceres" of England, complaining of the attempt made to appropriate certain prebends of the cathedrals of York and Lincoln to the hospital of the Holy Ghost and the Basilica of St. Peter's of Rome;[z] and in the same year was one of the manucaptors of William de Duclas.[a] In the 20th Edw. I., Hastings obeyed the Kings mandate to attend at London relative to the disputes between the Earls of Hereford and Gloucester,[b] and became one of the manucaptors of the latter,[c] as well as a surety for his payment of the fine of 10,000 marks which was then imposed upon him.[d]

In the 21st Edw. I. John de Hastings was one of the claimants of the crown of Scotland,[e] in right of his grandmother, Ada, daughter of David Earl of Huntingdon, brother of William the Lion. In April, 22 Edw. I. 1294, he was at Dublin, and a plea was then held before the Earls of Gloucester and Ulster, himself, and other barons :[f] on the 1st September following he was commanded to perform military service in Gascony ;[g] and in the next year he was summoned to parliament. In the 25th Edw. I. he was ordered to raise one hundred men from his lordship of Abergavenny ;[h] and from that time until his demise continued to be summoned to nearly every parliament, and was commanded to serve in every expedition which occurred, but it is not necessary to mention the different occasions.[i]

---

u Palgrave's " Parliamentary Writs," vol. I. p. 253.   x Ibid. p. 255.

y Ibid. p. 20, and Rot. Parl. vol. I. p. 25.   z Palgrave's " Parliamentary Writs," vol. I. p. 20.

a Rot. Parl. vol. I. p. 34.   b Ibid. pp. 70, et seq.   c Ibid. pp. 75 b, 76 a.

d Ibid. p. 77.   e Ibid. p. 114 a.   f Ibid. p. 132.

g Palgrave's " Parliamentary Writs," p. 259.   h Ibid. p. 294.

i Ibid. See Digest, p. 659; and Appendix to the First Peerage Report, pp. 174, 226.

. Hastings was present at the siege of Carlaverock in June 1300, at which time he was about fifty years of age. Besides his own retinue he then commanded the men at arms furnished by the Bishop of Durham, with whom it is stated he was on terms of the greatest friendship; and in February, 1301, he was a party to the Letter from the Barons at Lincoln to Pope Boniface the Eighth, in which he is styled " Lord of Bergavenny."[k] In the 30th Edw. I. he was appointed the King's Lieutenant in the duchy of Acquitaine, to which circumstance Peter of Langtoft thus alludes:

> For perille of suilk gopnges, the kyng purveied to go,
> Sir Jon of Hastynges he was first of tho,
> And Sir Emery the Brette to Gascoyn ferto wende,
> To bide the terme sette, the treus how it suld ende.[l]

In the 33rd Edw. I. he was one of the English peers appointed to treat with the Scotch representatives concerning the government of Scotland; but he was prevented from attending by illness.[m] On James, Steward of Scotland, performing homage before the council at Lanercost on the 23rd October, 34 Edw. I. 1306, Hastings was one of the barons then present;[n] and in the same year he received a grant from the King of the whole county of Menteith in Scotland, with the isles, together with all the other lands of Alan late Earl of Menteith, who was declared a rebel. On the 30th September, 1st Edw. II. 1307, he was ordered to assist in repressing a rebellion in Scotland;[o] and on the 18th January following he was summoned to attend the King's coronation:[p] in the 3rd Edw. II. being constituted Seneschal of Acquitaine, he obtained the King's precept to the Constable of Dover Castle for license to transport himself and his family, plate, money, &c.; and letters were written to the King of France to give him safe conduct into that duchy.

Having been summoned to parliament from the 23rd June, 23 Edw. I. 1295, to the 22nd May, 9 Edw. II. 1313, this eminent soldier died in the 6th Edw. II. 1312-1313, aged about sixty-two. From the time he attained his majority

---

k Palgrave's " Parliamentary Writs," pp. 102-3.   l Ed. 1810, p. 318.
m Palgrave's " Parliamentary Writs," p. 161 ; and Rot. Parl. vol. I. p. 297.
n Ibid. p. 180 ; and Fœdera, N. E. vol. I. p. 1001.   o Fœdera, N. E. vol. II. p. 8.
P Appendix to the First Peerage Report, p. 176.

until his decease, a period of above forty years, he was distinguished by his constant devotion to the service of his country; and by his undeviating fidelity to his sovereign. However remarkable he may have been for the amiable qualities attributed to him, in the preceding Poem, the fact that he is not once recorded to have incurred the royal displeasure, speaks loudly in. favour of his prudence, his zeal, and his loyalty; and in considering him one of the brightest ornaments of the peerage in the fourteenth century, we probably shall not overrate his real merits, even if we do not implicitly believe in the correctness of the beautiful view which the Poet has presented of his character.

He was twice married: first to Isabel, daughter of William, and sister, and in her issue coheiress, of Aymer de Valence, Earl of Pembroke, by whom he had John; William[q] and Henry, who both died s. P.; Joane;[r] Margaret; and Elizabeth, who married Roger Baron Grey of Ruthyn. Hastings' second wife was Isabel, daughter of Hugh le Despencer, by whom he had Hugh, who is said to have been born before his mother's marriage, and Thomas. John, his eldest son, was twenty-six years old at his father's decease; succeeded him in his honours; and became the ancestor of the Hastings Earls of Pembroke; upon the extinction of

whom in 1389, his issue failed, when the descendants of Elizabeth de Grey, his sister, and of Hugh, his half brother, had the memorable contest for the right to the arms of Hastings, which was determined in favour of the former.[s] Isabel, the Baron's widow, remarried Ralph de Monthermer, whom she also survived.[t]

The arms of Hastings were, Or, a maunch Gules.[u]

---

q It would appear that this William was the eldest son, and either married, or was intended to marry, the daughter of William Martin: " 25 Edw. I. Maritagium inter Willielmum de Hastinges, filium et hæredem Johannis de Hastinges, Domini de Abergavenny, et Alienoram, filiam seniorem Willielmi Martin, Domini de Kamoys, ad Ed'dum, filium et hæredem dicti Willielmi, et Jonett', filiam seniorem dicti Johannis." Calend. Rot. Patent. p. 58 b.

r See the preceding note. She probably died young, and before the marriage was consummated.

s Placita, 14 Ric. II. whence the genealogical particulars here stated have been taken.

t Fœdera, N. E. vol. II. p. 403, and Calend. Inquisit. post Mortem, vol. III. p. 327. See also p. 279 ante, where however, on the authority of Dugdale, she is erroneously called the sister and coheiress of Aymer de Valence, Earl of Pembroke.

u Page 54; and Cotton MSS. Caligula, A. xviii. The extraordinary seal used by him to the

EDMUND DE HASTINGS.

[Page 56.]

Of Edmund de Hastings, a younger brother of the subject of the preceding memoir, very little is known ; and as the great biographer of the Peerage of England has merely mentioned his name, the few facts which are recorded of him have been almost entirely deduced from the invaluable collection of " Parliamentary Writs" lately printed.

As his elder brother was born about 1251, it may be inferred that his birth took place a few years afterwards; and hence that he did not become of age until the 5th or 6th Edw. I. 1276-7. The earliest notice which occurs of him is in June, 27 Edw. I. 1299, when he was commanded as a Baron to perform military service against the Scots ;[x] and in March following he received his first writ of summons to parliament.[y] In June, 1300, he was, we learn from the Poem, present at the siege of Carlaverock in his brother's retinue ; and from the notice of his character it is to be inferred that his zeal in the pursuit of honour was too ardent not to be attended by success.

Edmund de Hastings was a party to the Letter from the Barons to the Pontiff in February 1301, in which he is styled " Lord of Enchuneholmok," or " Enchimeholmok ;"[z] but where this place was has not been discovered. Though included in the general summons to parliament, dated on the 24th July, 1302,[a] he was commanded to remain in the King's service in Scotland by a special writ, tested at La Sele on the 11th September following ;[b] and from that time until his decease in the 7th Edw. II. he was frequently enjoined to serve in the field or to

---

Letter from the Barons to the Pope in 1301, is the subject of some remarks in the " Archæologia,'· vol. XXI. p. 205. On one side it contained a shield charged with a cross with five fleurs de lis between four fleurs de lis ; and on the other a shield with a cross similarly charged, between, 1st and 4th, a lion passant guardant, and, 2nd and 3rd, a lion rampant, all looking to the dexter.

x Palgrave's " Parliamentary Writs," vol. I. p. 318.　　　　y Ibid. p. 82.
z Ibid. p. 103.　　　　a Ibid. p. 114.　　　　b Ibid. p. 117.

attend parliament.[c] In the 5th Edw. II. he was appointed Custos of the town of Berwick;[d] and having been summoned to parliament from the 29th December, 28 Edw. I. 1299, to the 26th July, 7 Edw. II. 1313, he probably died about 1314, as no further notice occurs of him. Whether he was married and left issue is unknown, for no inquisition is recorded to have been held on his death; nor is anything stated on the subject in the pedigrees of his family.

The arms of Edmund de Hastings were those of his brother, Or, a maunch Gules, differenced by a label Vert or Sable.[e]

JOHN PAIGNEL.

[PAGE 56.]

Who can fail to be interested in an individual who is introduced to our notice as,

Un Bachelor jolif et cointe,
De amours et d'armes bien acointe;

qualities so very similar to those which an eminent living poet has described as necessary to ensure the esteem of a chieftain by his followers:

---

c Palgrave's " Parliamentary Writs," Digest, p. 658; and Appendix to the First Peerage Report.

d Calend. Rot. Patent. p. 73 b.

e In the Poem the label is stated · to have been " Noir," but in the Cotton MSS. Caligula, A. xviii. it is called " Vert." His seal to the Barons' Letter in 1301, however, contains a very different bearing, the shield being charged with barry wavy of six: the legend is, S. EDMUNDI HASTING COMITATU MENETEI. It is suggested in some remarks on the seals attached to that document in the " Archæologia," vol. XXI. p. 218, that the place of which Edmund Hastings described himself was probably St. David's in Wales.

They love a Captain to obey,
Boisterous as March yet fresh as May;
With open hand, and brow as free,
Lover of wine and minstrelsy;
Ever the first to scale a tower,
As venturous in a lady's bower.[f]

It unfortunately happens, however, that of this Banneret but few facts are recorded; and from the following circumstance it is extremely doubtful whether he can be identified with them. Dugdale takes no notice of any baron of this name, but from the "Parliamentary Writs" we learn that a John Paynel was summoned from the county of Suffolk to perform military service in person against the Scots on the 25th May, 1298; again for the same purpose as a Baron in June, 1299; to attend parliament in March, 1300; and to assemble at Carlisle against the Scots on the 24th June, 1300; hence it might be considered that all these circumstances related to the knight who in that month was present at the siege of Carlaverock, were it not that, in February, 1301, a John Paynel, who is styled "Lord of Otteleye," was a party to the Letter to the Pope, and to whom it is most probable that the greater part if not all of those records referred, and who could not possibly have been the person alluded to in the Poem, for the arms of the former, as they occur on his seal to the Barons' Letter, were two bars between eight martlets, whilst those of the latter were, Vert, a maunch Or.

Thus it is evident that there were two individuals of the same names,[g] and possessed of nearly the same rank, living in June, 1300; and as there are no possible means of identifying them, except by their seals which of course do not occur to the writs alluded to, or by their lands which were seldom mentioned, it would be worse than useless to do more than to remark that a John Paynell continued to be summoned to parliament from the 28th Edw. I. to the 12th Edw. II.; that in the 12th Edw. II. 1318, a John Paynell, who held lands in Sussex, Surrey, Southampton, and Wilts, died, leaving Maud his daughter, the wife of Nicholas de Upton, his heir;[h] and that in the 18th Edw. II. 1324, a person of those names, who was seised of lands in Dorsetshire, Berks, Lincoln, and Sussex, died, leaving two daughters his heirs; Elizabeth, then aged nine,

---

f "Scott's Marmion."

g Although the name is spelt "Paignel" in the Poem, it is written "Paynell" in the Roll of Arms in the Cottonian MS.   h Esch. 12 Edw. II.

4 H

 and the wife of John de Gastryk, and Margaret, who was at that time seven years old;[i] and that as a John Paynel, who bore Vert, a maunch Or, is mentioned in the Roll of Arms just cited, it is almost certain that the Knight who was at Carlaverock was living as late as the 10th or 12th Edw. H.[k]

The arms of the subject of this notice were, Vert, a maunch Or.[l]

---

[i] Esch. 18 Edw. II.

[k] A William Paynell, whose arms were also two bars between eight martlets, and who styled himself "Lord of Tracyngton," was likewise a party to the letter to the Pontiff in 1301. "Otteley," of which John Paynell described himself, was probably in Suffolk ; and it is somewhat remarkable that Lord Hastings, under whose immediate command John Paignel served at Carlaverock, held Ottley manor, and Lyttelton Paynel in Wiltshire. The escheats of Paynell, from the commencement of the reign of Edward the First to the end of that of Edward the Second, besides the one mentioned in the text, were,

4 Edw. I. John Paynell, who held the manor of Combe in Dorsetshire, and left John Paynell, his son, his heir, who was then æt. 14.

15 Edw. I. John Paynell, who held lands in Lincoln, York, and Dorset, and left Philip his brother, æt. 18, his heir.

25 Edw. I. Katherine Paynell, who held lands in Dorset and Wilts, and who left Philip Paynell, æt. 25, her son, her heir.

27 Edw. I. Philip Paynell, who held lands in Lincoln, York, and Dorset, and left John his son, æt. 1, his heir.

7 Edw. II. Thomas Paynell, who held lands in Southampton and Dorset, and who left William Paynell, æt. 60, his brother, his heir.

10 Edw. II. William Paynell, who held lands in Middlesex, Surrey, Wilts, and Sussex, and who left John, æt. 50, his brother, his heir,

11 Edw: II. Ralph Paynell (Joan his wife) who held lands in Bedfordshire, and left John, son of Baldwin Pygott, æt. 27, his cousin and heir.

17 Edw. II. Isabella, wife of John Paynell, who held lands in Kent, and left Maud, æt. 40, her daughter, her heir.

It is singular, however, that numerous as those escheats of Paynell are, neither the name of " Ottley" nor " Tracyngton," of which the Barons Paynell styled themselves " Lords" in the Letter to the Pontiff, once occur in them.   The

---

[l] Page 56 ; and Cotton MSS. Caligula, A. xviii.

EDMUND DEINCOURT.

[PAGE 56.]

As this individual was not present at the siege of Carlaverock, it is not necessary that much should be said of him; and, were it possible to collect the requisite particulars, this article ought rather to contain a memoir of those " two brave sons whom he sent in his stead," and to whom he entrusted his banner and his followers.

Unfortunately, however, the name of but one of them has reached us; and so utterly has the other been forgotten, that Dugdale considers Edmund Deincourt to have had only one son. That the Poet's statement is correct is singularly proved by a document lately printed among the " Parliamentary Writs," dated about a year after the siege of Carlaverock, namely, in April, 1301, by which the father was commanded to attend with horse and arms at Carlisle on the 24th of June following, or " to send his sons, with ' decenti comitiva.'" It is consequently certain not only that Deincourt had more than one son, but that he occasionally sent them to perform the services which he owed to the crown. He was, it is most likely, at that time an aged man, for though he lived until many years afterwards, he could not have been then less than about sixty-five, as he was in all probability of full age in the 42nd Hen. III. 1257-8 when he " answered £70 for twenty-five knights' fees, upon levying the scutage of Wales."

From the 5th Edw. I. to the 20th Edw. II., a period of half a century,

---

The following Knights of the name of Paynell occur in the Roll of Arms in the Cottonian MS. Caligula, A. xviii. :

BARONS.

Sir John Paynell, Vert, a maunch Or.

WILTSHIRE AND HAMPSHIRE.

Sir Thomas Paynell, Or, two bars Azure, between martlets Gules.
Sir William Paynell, Argent, two bars Sable, between martlets Gules as a border.

LEICESTER.

Sir John Paynel, Gules, a quatrefoil Argent.
Sir Ralph Paynel, Argent, a bend Sable.

Edmund Deincourt was almost uninterruptedly summoned to the field or to parliament,[1] but his career does not appear to have been distinguished by any peculiar incident. He was present in the parliament at Lincoln in February, 1301; and
was a party to the Letter to the Pope, in which he is styled " Lord of Thurgerton," and in 1305 he was appointed a Justice of Trailbaston;[m] but the most
remarkable fact of his life is his anxiety to preserve the importance of the male
line of his family; for in the 7th Edw. II. 1313-14, in consequence of his grand-
daughter being his heir apparent, he obtained the King's license to settle his lands
on whomsoever he pleased; and he accordingly entailed them on William[n] the son
of John Deincourt in tail general, with remainder to John Deincourt, the brother
of the said William, in like tail, with remainder to his own son Edmund in fee.[o]

The pedigree of Deincourt has never, and probably does not admit of, being
established by evidence; hence it has been variously stated. Dugdale does not
inform us whom Edmund Lord Deincourt married, and, as is before observed, says he had only one son, who was called Edmund, who had a daughter,
his heiress, named Isabel; nor does he attempt to explain in what manner the
Baron was related to the William and John Deincourt, on whom he settled
his lands in the 7th Edw. II. The late Mr. Blore, in his " History of
Rutland," bestowed considerable research on the subject, and he evidently
availed himself of every possible source of information, but which scarcely
proves all that he has asserted. According to that pedigree Edmund Lord Deincourt married Isabel, the daughter of Reginald Mohun, and by her had two

1 Palgrave's " Parliamentary Writs," and Appendix to the First Peerage Report.

m " Parliamentary Writs.".

n The following is the copy of the license in question in the Cottonian MS. Julius, C.vii. f. 244 b.
" Secunda p's Pat. ao 10 Edw. II. m^a 13. Rex, &c. Sciatis ut, cùm nuper pro eo quòd dilectus et
fidelis noster Edmundus Deincourt advertebat et conjecturabat quòd cognomen suum et eius arma
post mortem suam in p'sonam Isabellæ filiæ Edmundi Deincourt hæredis eius apparentis a memoriâ
deferentur, accorditer affectabat q'd cognomen, et arma sua post eius mortem in memoriâ in
posteru' haberent', ad requisic'o'em eiusdem Edmundi, et ob grata et laudabilia servitia quæ bonæ
memoriæ D'no Edward' quondam Regi Angliæ patri nostro, et nobis impendit, per l'ras n'ras
patentes concesserimus, et licentiam dederimus pro nobis et hæredibus quantu' in nobis est, eidem
Edmundo q'd ipse de omnib's manerijs terris et ten'tis, et quæ de nobis tenet in capite, feoffare
possit quemcumq' velit, habendum et tenendum sibi et hæredibus suis de nobis et hæredib's nostris
per servitia inde debita imperpetuu'."

o Calend. Rot. Patent. p. 77.

daughters: Margaret, who married Robert Lord Willoughby of Eresby, and Maud who was the wife of Sir William Fitz-William; and an only son, John, who died in vita patris, leaving, but by whom does not appear, three sons: namely 1. Edmund, who died in his grandfather's lifetime, leaving by Johanna, who in the 1st Edw. III. was the wife of Hamon de Massy, an only child, Isabel, who died before her great-grandfather without issue; 2. William, who was twenty-six years old in the 20th Edw. II. 1326, and who was then found cousin and heir to his grandfather, and from whom the subsequent Lords Deincourt descended; 3. Sir John Deincourt, Knight, ancestor of the family of Deincourt of Upminster in the county of Essex. From this statement it is to be inferred that the William and John Deincourt on whom the lands were settled in the 7th Edw. II. were the grandsons of Edmund Lord Deincourt; that their elder brother Edmund was then dead; that his daughter and heiress Isabel was at that time living; but that, from her uncle William being found heir to her great-grandfather on his demise in 1326, she had died issueless before that year.

The only part of this account which can be proved to be erroneous, is with respect to the sons of Edmund Lord Deincourt, as he had undoubtedly at least two sons; and it may be supposed that the John Deincourt mentioned in another part of the Poem as bearing a shield charged with the same arms, and as displaying much bravery in the assault of the castle,[p] was one of them.

Although the following notices[q] respecting individuals of the name of Deincourt afford but little positive information on the pedigree, they are useful to illustrate it.

Edmund Lord Deincourt received a variety of writs of summons, both to the field and to parliament, from the 5th Edw. I. 1277, to the 20th Edw. II. 1326; and as in 1300 two returns were made from the county of Lincoln that an Edmund Deincourt held lands of the yearly value of £40 and upwards, it has been conjectured[r] that one of them related to Edmund the son; and it is also presumed that the writ of summons to Edmund Deincourt from Northamptonshire, to serve against the Scots in June, 1300, referred to the latter. In 1295 a John Deincourt obtained a quietus for the remission of the tenth charged on his

---

[p] Page 82, ante.
[q] All of which are taken from Palgrave's " Parliamentary Writs," Digest, pp. 565-6.
[r] Ibid.

4 I

goods; in 1297 he was returned from the counties of Nottingham and Derby as holding lands there of £20 yearly value and upwards, and as such was enjoined to perform military service in Scotland : he was a Justice of Oyer and Terminer in Derbyshire in May, 1300 ; and in June, 1301, was impowered to inquire into the conduct of the bailiffs in that county. In 1301 a Ralph Deincourt was elected by the " communitas" of the county of. Cumberland to be an assessor and collector of the fifteenth, and held that office .in 1302. In·1282 Robert Deincourt performed military service due from his brother Edmund Lord Deincourt, the father of the knights who were at Carlaverock; and in 1295 a William Deincourt obtained a quietus for remission of the tenth charged on his property.

· If an opinion may be hazarded as to the real facts of the case, it would be observed that the. probability is that Edmund Lord Deincourt had two sons ; that the eldest was called Edmund, and died in his father's lifetime, leaving Isabel his daughter his heiress, and who it is most likely died before the 20th Edw. II. s. p. ; that Lord Deincourt's second son was named John, and was the individual alluded to in the account of the assault of Carlaverock Castle, and in the writs addressed to John Deincourt which have been just noticed ; and that he also died before his father, leaving two sons, the William and John on whom the Baron's lands were settled in the 7th Edw. II.

It is remarkable that only two individuals of the name of Deincourt should  be mentioned in the Roll of Arms in the. Cottonian Manuscript, namely, Sir John Deincourt among the peers, whose arms are said to have been, Azure, billetté and a dancette Or ; and Sir William Deincourt, of Yorkshire, who bore, Argent, the same charges Sable.

. . The arms of Edmund Lord Deincourt were, Azure, billetté surmounted by a dancette Or.[r]

---

r Page 56 ; and his seal in 1301.

JOHN FITZ MARMADUKE.

[PAGE 56.]

The little which can be said respecting Fitz Marmaduke, has been chiefly taken from the same source whence the greater part of the particulars of the Bishop of Durham were derived; and the accuracy and research of Mr. Surtees render his labours worthy of the utmost credit.

He was the eldest son of Marmaduke Fitz Geoffrey,[r] Lord of Hordene in the Bishoprick of Durham,[s] who in the 45th Hen. III. 1260-1 obtained the King's license to embattle his mansion-house there.[t] In August, 1282, John Fitz Marmaduke, with nine other knights, performed services due from the Bishop of Durham,[u] who styled him on another occasion, " nostre tres cher bachelier, Monsr Jehan le Fitz Marmaduk ;" but from that time nothing is recorded of him until February, 1301, when he was a party to the Letter from the Barons of this country to the Pontiff, in which he is called " Lord of Hordene,"[x] excepting that he was at the siege of Carlaverock in June, 1300, where his bravery was particularly conspicuous. He came, we are told, to assail the castle with a great and full troop

---

[r] ·The following is the pedigree of Fitz Geoffrey in the College of Arms, and which Mr. Surtees has partially proved by evidence :

Richard, to whom his uncle, Bishop Ralph Flambard, granted his manor of Ravensworth.=

Robert Fitz Richard.　　　　　　Geoffrey de Hordene.=

Geoffrey Fitz Geoffrey. =　　Emma.=Sir Roger de Epplingdene, Knt. he had with her in free marriage lands in Silkesworthe.

Marmaduke Fitz Geoffrey.=　　Richard Fitz Geoffry.　　William Fitz Geoffrey.

JOHN FITZ MARMADUKE.=　　Robert Fitz Mar-=Juliana.　　Cecilia.=John Fitz Richard maduke.　　　　　　　　de Parco.

John, fil. John de Parco.

[s] Surtees's Durham, vol. I. part 2, p. 24, from a pedigree in the College of Arms. ·
[t] Calend. Rot. Patent. p. 33.　　[u] Palgrave's " Parliamentary Writs," pp. 228, 235.
[x] Ibid. pp. 103-4.

of good and select bachelors,[y] and stood as firm as a post, and his banner received many a rent difficult to mend.[z]

It is most extraordinary that for nearly twenty years no notice can be found in the records of the time of an individual who, at the end of that period, was a party to an instrument from the Baronage of the realm; and it was from this circumstance, the similarity of their arms, and his surname, that he was confounded with Marmaduke de Thweng in the "Synopsis of the Peerage."[a]

In the 31st Edw. I. Fitz Marmaduke was commanded to appear before the King in the first Sunday in Lent, with full powers from the community of the bishoprick of Durham to accept his Majesty's mediation between them and the Bishop;[b] and in April in the same year he was appointed a Commissioner of Array.[c] On the 30th September, 1 Edw. II. 1307, he was ordered, with others, to proceed to Galloway to repress the rebellion of Robert de Brus;[d] and in October following he was commanded to serve with horse and arms against the Scots;[e] after which time his name does not occur among the writs of service. He continued in the wars of Scotland, "comme une estache;" and on the 21st June, 1308, was again enjoined to oppose the attempts of Bruce.[f] On the 16th February, 3 Edward II. 1310 he was authorised with others to treat with the Scots for a truce.[g] Fitz Marmaduke died in 1311, at which time he was Governor of St. John's Town of Perth;[h] and a very curious fact is recorded respecting his funeral. He particularly requested to be interred within the precincts of the cathedral of Durham, but as the state of the country prevented the removal of his corpse in the usual manner, his domestics adopted the expedient of dismembering the body, and then boiling the flesh from the bones; by which means they preserved his reliques until an opportunity offered of transmitting them with safety across the border. For this outrage against an ecclesiastical canon, which had been promulgated in consequence of the frequency of the practice, Cardinal Berengarius, Bishop of Jerusalem, imposed on the offenders the mild penance of

y Page 68, ante.   z Page 70, ante.

a Page 772. The arms of Marmaduke de Thweng were, Argent, a fess Gules between three popinjays Vert; but the colours of course could not be distinguished on his seal.

b Palgrave's "Parliamentary Writs," p. 405.   c Ibid. pp. 371-2.

d Fœdera, N. E. vol. II. p. 8.   e Appendix to the First Peerage Report, p. 175.

f Fœdera, N. E. vol. II. p. 52.   g Ibid. p. 104.   h Ibid. p. 108.

attending their master's obsequies in the cemetery of the cathedral of Durham, having first used the authority of the church to ensure the quiet transportation of his remains.[i]

Fitz Marmaduke was twice married: first, to Isabella, sister and heiress of Robert Brus, of Stanton, by whom he had Richard, his son and heir; and a daughter, Mary, who married —— Lumley; and, secondly, Ida, who survived him, and was living his widow in 1313. Richard Fitz Marmaduke was Seneschal of the bishoprick of Durham, and was slain in 1318 by his kinsman, Robert Neville, on the old bridge of Durham, as he was riding to hold the county court, which event is described as " a most strange and detestable action."[i] Though married to Alianora——, he died without children, when Mary his sister became

his heiress. She left issue Robert Lumley, of Ravensholm, who married Lucia, the daughter and coheiress of Marmaduke de Thweng. They had issue a son, Marmaduke Lumley, whose representative is the present Earl of Scarborough.[j]

The arms of Fitz Marmaduke were, Gules, a fess between three popinjays Argent;[k] his son, Sir Richard, bore the same coat, differenced by a baton Azure.[l]

i An old Chronicle quoted in Surtees' Durham.

j Harleian MSS. 294. That volume contains an exceedingly valuable collection of pedigrees, compiled from escheats and other records ; but as they are not indexed they are comparatively useless. It will be seen how erroneous is Collins's account of the early state of the Lumley pedigree, as he says that John Fitz Marmaduke, the subject of the memoir in the text, was descended from the common ancestor of the house of Lumley ; and some grounds exist for considering that his other statements respecting that family before the reign of Richard the Second are equally incorrect. Peerage, ed. 1779, vol. IV. p. 116.

k Page 56; Cotton MS. Caligula, A. xviii., where his name occurs among the Barons ; and his seal in 1301, which is inscribed with the motto CREDE MICHI. See " Archæologia," vol. XXI.

l Cotton MSS. Caligula, A. xviii.; where his name occurs under the counties of Northumberland and Cumberland.

4 K

MAURICE DE BERKELEY.

[PAGE 58.]

Maurice de Berkeley was the eldest son, and, when present at the siege of Carlaverock, the heir apparent of Thomas Baron Berkeley. He was born in 1281,[1] and is said to have displayed a disposition for military pursuits at a very early period of his life. He was present at the tournaments held at Doncaster, Dunstable, Stamford, Blithe, and Winchester; and in the 23rd Edw. I. 1294-5, he accompanied his father in the expedition into Wales: in the next year he was at the siege of Berwick; and in the 25th Edw. I., was again with his father in Flanders.

On the 7th July, 25 Edw. I. 1297, he was returned from the counties of Somerset and Dorset as holding lands or rents to the amount of £20 yearly value and upwards, either in capite or otherwise, and as such was summoned under the general writ to perform military service in parts beyond the sea.[m] For several years afterwards he was engaged in the wars of Scotland, apparently with his own retinue, for in the 28th Edw. I. 1300, he was commanded to serve with horse and arms, and to assemble at Carlisle on the 24th of June,[n] in which month we accordingly find him at the siege of Carlaverock. As in the case of Lord Deincourt, the father of Maurice de Berkeley was, in 1301, enjoined to attend at Berwick on Tweed with his followers, or to send his sons in his stead;[o] a circumstance which corroborates the line in the Poem in which the bravery of the " brothers Berkeley" is mentioned.[p] Of those brothers a few words will hereafter be said.

In the 35th Edw. I. 1306-7, he accompanied his father, who, with the Bishop of Worcester, were appointed ambassadors to the court of Rome, relative to some affairs between Edward and the King of France; and on the 16th of August, 2 Edw. II. 1308, he was summoned to parliament as a Baron.[q] On the 2nd Aug.

---

1 MS. note of the inquisition on the death of his father in the 15th Edw. II.

m Palgrave's " Parliamentary Writs," p. 292.   n Ibid. p. 337.   - o Ibid. p. 357.

p Page 82 ante.   q Appendix to the First Peerage Report, p. 185.

4 Edw. II. 1310, he was enjoined to serve in the Scottish wars;[r] and again in May following;[s] and in the 6th Edw. II. 1312-13, was made Governor of Gloucester; but was once more summoned to the wars in Scotland in the 7th Edw. II.[t] In April, 1315, he was appointed Governor of Berwick upon Tweed;[u] and was ordered to treat with Robert de Brus on the 12th Feb. 1316 :[v] in the 9th Edw. II. 1315-16, Berkeley was constituted Justice of South Wales,[w] having all the castles there entrusted to his custody; and in 1316 he was' present when Aymer Earl of Pembroke conferred the honour of knighthood on Richard de Rodney, and placed the spur on the young Chevalier's right foot :[x] in the 11th Edw. II. 1317, he and his two sons, Thomas and Maurice, formed part of the retinue of Roger de Mortimer, and marched with him into Scotland.

On the 28th February, 13 Edw. II. 1320, by the appellation of " dilectus consanguineus Regis," a title which was probably applied to him in consequence of his marriage with Isabel, the pretended sister and coheiress of Gilbert de Clare, Earl of Gloucester,[y] the King's nephew, Maurice de Berkeley was made Steward of Acquitaine, with an assignment of two thousand pounds tournois.[z] On the 28th March, 14 Edw. II. 1321, his father and himself, with five other peers, were ordered to attend at Gloucester on the 5th of April fol-, lowing, to devise how the insurrection in Wales might be suppressed;[a] and in July, 15 Edw. II. 1320, he succeeded his father in his lands, at which time a MS. note of the inquisition held on Thomas Lord Berkeley's decease, states that Maurice his son and heir was forty years of age. About the same period he joined the Earl of Lancaster in his attempt to reform the abuses of the government, and in harassing the Spencers; and he, with Roger de Mortimer and others, having burnt the town of Bridgenorth, the King issued a writ to the Constable of Bristol, commanding him to seize all his lands and goods ;[b] and part of the latter were conferred on Hugh le Despenser, junior.[c] Relying on letters of safe conduct, which were granted to him and his other con-

---

[r] Appendix to the First Peerage Report, p. 203.　　　　[s] Ibid. p. 206.

[t] Rot. Parl. vol. I. p. 396.　　[u] Rot. Scotiæ, vol. I. p. 145 ; and Fœdera, N. E. vol. II. p. 266.

[v] Fœdera, N. E. vol. II. p. 286.

[w] A writ was addressed to him by that title on the 20th Nov. 1316. Ibid. p. 301.

[x] Selden's Titles of Honour, p. 642, cited in " Anstis's Collections of Authorities on the Order of the Bath," p. 8.　　　　　　　　　　[y] See the next page.

[z] Fœdera, N. E. vol. II. p. 418.　　[a] Rot. Parl. vol. I. p. 455 b ; and Fœdera, N. E. vol. II. p. 445.

[b] Fœdera, N. E. vol. II. p. 471.　　　　　　[c] Calend. Rot. Patent. p. 91.

federates to go to the King for the purpose of conferring amicably with him, he was made prisoner, and conveyed to the castle of Wallingford,—an act of treachery which his sons revenged by laying waste the lands of the obnoxious favourites.

In the same year George de Brithmereston complained that Sir Maurice de Berkeley the father, and the son, by collusion with the Sheriff of Wiltshire, had seized on a manor which had belonged to him, whilst the petitioner was in confinement on a charge of felony; but he was answered that as Maurice was then in prison he must wait till he was released.[z]

Berkeley, however, died a prisoner; for although Sir John de Goldingham endeavoured to rescue him in 1325, the attempt failed, and on the 31st May, 1326, he departed this life in Wallingford Castle, and was buried in the south aisle of the conventual church of the abbey of St. Austin near Bristol, under the arch before the door of the quire.

He was twice married: first, to Eva, the daughter of Eudo la Zouch by Milisent sister and coheiress of George de Cantilupe, by whom, who died on the 5th December, 1314, he had issue, 1. Thomas, his successor in his honors; 2. Maurice, ancestor of the Berkeleys of Stoke Giffard in Gloucestershire, of Bruton in Somersetshire, and of Boycourt in Kent; 3. John, to whom it is necessary again to allude; 4. Eudo, rector of Lampredevaux in Wales; 5. Peter, a prebendary of the cathedral church of Wells; and a daughter, Isabel, who married, first, Robert Lord Clifford, and, secondly, Thomas Lord Musgrave.

The second wife of Maurice de Berkeley was Isabel, who claimed to be the sister and coheiress of Gilbert de Clare, Earl of Gloucester, but her pretensions were proved to be unfounded by the proceedings on the subject in the 9th Edw. II., though she was returned as one of the heirs of the Earl in the inquisitions held in several counties;[a] hence it is most probable that she was the natural sister of that nobleman. In the 1st Edw. III. 1327, by the description of " Isabel de Clare, who was the wife of Maurice de Berkeley, deceased," she petitioned for the recovery of the manors of Shipton and Barford, which she said had been granted to her by her brother Gilbert de Clare, late Earl of Gloucester;[b] and died without issue by Lord Berkeley in 1338.[c]

z Rot. Parl. vol. I. p. 396 a.   a Ibid. p. 353.   b Ibid. vol. II. p. 431.

c Collins's Peerage, ed. 1779, vol. V. p. 10. The name, however, of " Isabel de Clare, wife of Maurice de Berkeley," occurs in the Calendar of the Inquisitions post Mortem of the 1st Edw. III. Second Numbers, No. 10, vol. II. p. 10.

It is said by Dugdale that Thomas, Maurice, and John, the three elder sons of Maurice Lord Berkeley, were with their father in Scotland in the 28th, 29th, 31st, and 32nd Edw. I., and consequently that it was to them the Poet alludes; but that eminent genealogist must have been mistaken, for it is impossible that either of them could then have been sufficiently old. Thomas Lord Berkeley was found to be thirty years of age at the death of his father in the 9th Edw. I. 1280, hence his son Maurice could scarcely have been born before 1270, though the inquisition on the death of his father in the 15th Edw. II. states that he was then forty, which would make him to have been born in 1281. Allowing, however, that his birth occurred in 1270, his eldest child could not have been born long before 1290, so that in 1299, when he is stated to have had three sons in the wars of Scotland, neither of them could by any possibility have been above twelve years old; whilst, if the age attributed to him in the MS. note of the inquisition on the demise of Thomas Lord Berkeley in the 15th Edw. II. be correct, they must have been much younger. Thus it is almost certain that the John Berkeley whom Dugdale considers was the son of the subject of this article, was in fact his brother.

Thomas, the eldest son, succeeded to his father's honours, and became conspicuous by his connection with the murder of King Edward the Second: from him all the subsequent Barons and Earls of Berkeley are descended.

The arms of Berkeley are, Gules, crusilly of crosses patée, over all a chevron Argent; but when at Carlaverock those of this Baron were differenced by a label Azure, " because his father was alive."d

---

d Page 58; and Cottonian MSS. Caligula, A. xviii.

ALEXANDER DE ·BALIOL.

[PAGE 58.]

The brother and uncle of a King of Scotland claims more than usual attention from the biographer of the Knights who were at the siege of . Carlavcrock ; and considerable trouble has been therefore taken to collect every particular which is recorded of his life. .Though much has been found, when compared with what is said of him by Dugdale, .the facts which can be related are not more interesting than what have been stated in these pages of his contemporaries. It may excite our surprise that a witness of the splendid rank.which his brother possessed should have omitted to allude to it; but this can be explained by the circumstance of John de Baliol being then dethroned, and nothing could at that moment justify the expectation that his son would ever wield the Scottish sceptre. But it certainly is extraordinary that the.compilers of all the printed pedigrees of the royal families of Scotland, should have been so careless or so ignorant in their accounts of the house of Baliol, as entirely to pass over the subject of this memoir and the other members of his family. To supply those defects the following account of the immediate relatives of John Baliol, King of Scotland, is here submitted :

John de Baliol, the founder of Baliol College, Oxford, married Devorguila, the daughter and heiress of Alan Lord of Galloway, by Margaret, the daughter and coheiress of David Earl of Huntingdon, brother of William the Lion, King of Scotland, through which alliance his descendants derived their claim to the crown. Baliol died in 1269,[e] leaving, by the said Devorguila, who survived until the 16th Edw. I.: Alexander ;[f] John,[g] who became King of Scotland ; another Alex-

---

[e] Esch. 53 Hen. III. No. 43. It would be very desirable to ascertain who was found to be his heir by this inquisition.

[f] Esch. 6 Edw. I. and 16 Edw. I. Palgrave's " Parliamentary Writs," pp. 194, 209. He is stated in those writs to have been the son of a John de Baliol : his brother John was his heir in the 6th Edw. I. and was then about *twenty-one* years of age. On the death of Devorguil his (presumed) mother, in the 16th Edw. I. John her son was her heir, who was then *thirty* years old, which tends to identify him as the same John who was found heir to Alexander ten years before, as his age at the respective periods exactly agrees. Moreover, the Alexander who died in the 6th Edw. I. held two manors of which John de ·Baliol died seised in the 53d Hen. III.

[g] Esch. 6 Edw. I. See the last note.

ander;[h] and, according.to one pedigree,[i] .Alan, who died s. p.; Hugh, Lord of Bywell, who married Agnes, daughter of William de Valence, Earl of Pembroke,[k] but also died without children:[l] and four daughters, Margaret, Lady of Multon; Ada, who married William Lord Lindsey, and whose daughter and heiress, Christiana, was the wife of Ingelram de Guisnes; Cecilia, wife of John de Burgh, junior; and Mary, who married John Lord Comyn. Alexander, the eldest son, by the description of "Alexander, filius Johannis de Baliol," was summoned to perform military service against Llewellin Prince of Wales, in July, 5 Edw. I. 1277;[m] and in the 5th Edw. I. being then a knight, acknowledged the service of three knights' fees in Hache, Beyvelle, and Wodehorn, which was performed by himself and two knights, Ralph de Coton and John de Coton, in the expedition against the said Prince of Wales, on the 16th July in the same year.[n] He died issueless[o] in the 6th Edw. I.[p] leaving .John, his brother, his heir, and who was then twenty-one years old.[q]

Notwithstanding that it cannot perhaps be established by evidence that the Alexander de Baliol who served in Edward's army at Carlaverock was the brother of the King of Scotland, still, as it has been asserted by such respectable authority, and has remained wholly uncontradicted,—as no circumstance can be adduced to render it unlikely, but on the contrary as so many facts tend to support it,—that account of his birth will be assumed to be correct. The period when it took place can only however be surmised, but he was probably born about 1258, the year following his brother John, since he must have been

---

h No *evidence* has been discovered to establish that this Alexander was the brother of John King of Scotland, but not only is he so described by Dugdale, and in a pedigree in the College of Arms compiled by Glover, in a MS. entitled " Illorum Magnatum Stemmata quorum hæreditas, deficientibus masculis, ad fœminas devoluta est," Philpot, No. 4. 78. f. 41; but many facts render it highly probable, as they show that he was a man of considerable importance in Scotland, and for some years held the office of Chamberlain of Scotland.

i Glover's pedigree above cited.

k She was the widow of Maurice Fitz Gerald, and afterwards married John de Avenes. Glover. She was living in August, 1308. See infra.

l Glover states that Alexander was the brother and heir of this Hugh de Baliol.

m Palgrave's " Parliamentary Writs," vol..I. p. 194.   n Ibid. p. 209.

o Esch. 6 Edw. I. No. 5.   p Rot. Fin. 6 Edw. I. m. 2.

q Palgrave's " Parliamentary Writs," p. 194.

of full age when, by the style of " Alexander de Baliol, Lord of Chilham," he was commanded to serve against the Prince of Wales in July, 5th Edw. I. 1277, at which time he was married, as Chilham was part of the inheritance of his wife, Isabella, the daughter and heiress of Richard de Dovor;[r] and in the same month, by the designation of " Alexander de Baillol de Caures," he acknowledged the service of two knights' fees, " per Baroniam de Chilham," the inheritance of his wife, and one-third of two knights' fees for the manor of Beninton ; which services were performed by himself, and Henry de Baliol, and Nicholas de Rochford, Knights.[s]

In the 10th Edw. I. he was again enjoined to serve in person against the Welsh :[t] in the 19th Edw. I. 1290, he and Isabel his wife procured a grant of a market and fair at Chilham in Kent;[u] and in the 25th Edw. I. he served, Dugdale informs us, in the retinue of the Bishop of Durham in the expedition into Flanders; from which year until the 35th Edw. I. he received repeated writs to perform military service in the Scottish wars.[x]   On the 5th of February, 1284, he was one of the peers of Scotland who agreed to accept of Margaret, daughter of Eric King of Norway, as their sovereign.[y]   He was Chamberlain of Scotland as early as June, 1290, for in that year Alexander son of the Earl of Dunbar, acknowledged to have received XVIII marks from his hands,[z] and numerous documents are extant, from 1291 to 1292, in which that title is ascribed to him;[a] but

---

[r] Hasted, in his History of Kent, says she was the daughter of Richard Fitz Roy, natural son of King John, by Rose, daughter and heiress of Robert de Dovor ; whilst Dugdale states that Rose was the daughter and heir of Robert de Dovor, that she first married Richard Fitz Roy, but that she afterwards dissented, and married Richard de Chilham, by whom she had Isabel, the wife, first of the Earl of Atholl, and secondly of Alexander de Baliol. If Dugdale had not added that Chilham was also called Dovor, it might be inferred that there was some mistake in his account, since Baliol, in his petition to parliament in the 33rd Edw. I. relative to the manor of Hugham, which he held in her right by the laws of England, expressly calls her " Isabel de Dovor," Rot. Parl. vol. I. p. 166, and in a record in Thorne's Chronicle in the " Decem Scriptores," she is styled " Isabel de Dovor, Countess of Atholl, wife of Alexander de Baliol."

[s] Palgrave's " Parliamentary Writs," p. 209.   [t] Ibid. pp. 225, 232.
[u] Calend. Rot. Chartarum, p. 121.   [x] Palgrave's " Parliamentary Writs," Digest, p. 442.
[y] Fœdera, N. E. vol. I. p. 638.

[z] Ancient Charters in the British Museum, 43 B. 10.   The instrument marked 47 I. 28, is a similar acknowledgment of £xx. from Sir William Byssett, Knt. in 1292.

[a] Fœdera, p. 757, et seq. : and Rotuli Scotiæ.

they afford no materials for his biography. On the 18th of August, 1291, Edward ordered six deer to be allowed to him :[b] he was present at the convention relative to the crown of Scotland, on the 13th June, 1292 ;[c] and also when his brother did homage to the English monarch on the 20th November in that year :[d] in 1293 he was a witness to the demands of his brother John, respecting his manors and other property.[e]

About the 23rd Edw. I. 1295, Baliol incurred the royal displeasure, and all his lands were seized; but he was soon restored to favour, for in September, 1296, he obtained restitution of them ;[f] and on the 24th of June in the next year, a writ was addressed to the Earl of Surrey, Lieutenant of Scotland, stating that one hundred pounds had been assigned to Baliol in England, who was then about to go beyond the Trent and there to remain, for the support of himself, his children, and his household; and that, as he had asserted that fifty marks of that sum were then unpaid, the Earl was commanded to cause the same to be immediately delivered to him.[g]

In the 28th Edw. I. he was first summoned to parliament: in May, 1298, he received letters of protection, being then in the King's service ;[h] and he was commanded to attend at Carlisle with horse and arms on the 24th June, 1300,[i] in which month he was present at the siege of Carlaverock, when he must have been about forty-two years of age. Though summoned to the parliament which was to meet at London or Westminster at Michaelmas, 1302,[k] Baliol was specially ordered to remain in the King's service in Scotland.[l] About that period he, however, once more gave offence to Edward, and writs were addressed to the sheriffs of Kent, Hertford, and Roxburgh, tested on the 3rd February, 31 Edw. I. 1303, commanding them to seize his goods and chattels for divers transgressions; to arrest him ; and to bring him before the King, on the first Sunday in the ensuing Lent.[m] It is uncertain how long he continued in disgrace, but probably a very short time only, as on the 26th May following he was commanded to serve in Scotland ;[n] and in the same month he obtained letters of pro-

---

b Rot. Scot. p. 5.   c Fœdera, N. E. vol. I. p. 768.   d Ibid. p. 782 et seq.   e Ibid. p. 801.
f Rot. Scot. p. 30. On the 31st July in the same year, the Earl of Surrey was also ordered to restore to Baliol all the lands in Scotland, which were then in the King's hands. Ibid. p. 44.
g Ibid. p. 41.   h Ibid. p. 51 b.   i Palgrave's " Parliamentary Writs," p. 347.
k Ibid. p. 115.   l Ibid. p. 117.   m Fœdera, N. E. vol. I. p. 948.
n Palgrave's " Parliamentary Writs," p. 366·

4 M

tection in consequence of being so engaged.[o] Among the petitions on the Rolls
of Parliament, to which unfortunately no precise date can be assigned, is one
from Alexander de Baliol, " of Cauers," claiming the wardenship of Selkirk
forest, in which he states that the King had of his grace by his open letters
restored all his lands and tenements in England and Scotland, which had been
seized into his hands for divers causes ;[p] and in the 35th Edw. I. 1304, about a
year after the date of the writ to arrest him, he petitioned relative to the manor
of Hughan ;[q] hence, even if the first of those petitions referred to the pardon for
his transgressions in 1295, instead of for those in 1303, the latter tends to show that
he had ceased to be in disfavour before it was presented. After the accession of
Edward the Second Alexander de Baliol was never summoned to parliament ; but
on the 30th September, 1307, he was ordered to suppress the rebellion of Robert
de Brus in Scotland ;[r] and on the 30th of July, 3 Edw. II. 1309, 2nd August, 4
Edw. II. 1310, and on the 20th May, 4 Edw. II. 1311, he was commanded to
serve against the Scots.[s] On the 5th June, 1309, he obtained letters of protection in consequence of his being in the King's service ;[t] about which time Dugdale, on the authority of the Close Rolls,[u] states that his son Alexander was
imprisoned in the Tower of London ; "but upon security given by this Alexander
his father, and two of the Lindeseys, for his future fidelity to the King, he was
enlarged." On the 12th of August, 1308, Edward the Second confirmed to
John Earl of Richmond all the castles, towns, manors, lands, &c. that had
belonged to John de Baliol, and which had been granted to him by Edward
the First, and also bestowed on him all the lands and tenements which
Agnes de Valentia who was the wife of Hugh de Baliol, and Eleanor de Geneure
who was the wife of Alexander de Baliol, held in dower, of the inheritance of the
said John de Baliol, after the decease of the said Agnes and Eleanor.[x] That
record throws some doubt on the statement of Glover that the subject of these
pages married, secondly, Eleanor de Geneure, unless the words of the instrument,
" quæ Agnes de Valencia quæ fuit uxor Hugonis de Balliolo,[y] et Alianora de
Geneure, quæ fuit Alexandri de Balliolo, tenent in dotem," can receive any

---

o Rot. Scot. p. 52.   P Rot. Parl. vol. I. p. 470.   q Ibid. p. 166.
r Fœdera, N. E. vol. II. p. 8.   s Appendix to the First Peerage Report, pp. 193, 203, 206.
t Rot. Scot. p. 65 b.   u 3 Edw. II. m. 8.   x Fœdera, N. E. vol. II. p. 56.
y Widow of Hugh de Baliol, brother of Alexander.   See ante, p. 319.

other interpretation than that the said Eleanor was, on the 12th August, 1308, the *widow* of an Alexander de Baliol, for it is certain that the individual of whom she is said to have been the wife, was living on the 5th June, 1309, when he received letters of protection from the King, even which though possible is not very probable, if he was dead, in July, 1309, August, 1310, and May, 1311, when his name was included in the writs to perform military service in Scotland. These discrepancies, may however be reconciled either by considering that Eleanor de Geneure was the wife of the Alexander de Baliol who died in the 6th Edw. I. instead of the baron who was at Carlaverock; or by deeming that the words in the record do not mean that she was at that time a widow.

Alexander de Baliol was summoned to parliament from the 26th September, 28 Edw. I. 1300, to the 3rd November, 35 Edw. I. 1306. He is said to have been twice married; first, to Isabel, daughter and heiress of Robert de Dovor,[z] and widow of David de Strabolgie, Earl of Atholl, by whom she was mother of John Earl of Atholl who was hung for felony.[a] With her, Baliol acquired the manor of Chilham and some others in Kent, and they undoubtedly had issue, for he expressly states that he held the manor of Hugham in Kent by the law of England in her right;[b] and in the writ to the Earl of Surrey in June, 1296, his children are mentioned.[c] It appears from the Clause Roll cited by Dugdale that he had a son of his own names of full age in the 3rd Edw. II. 1309-10, but of

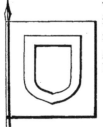

whom nothing more is known. Isabel de Dovor died in February, 1292;[d] and Baliol is considered to have remarried Eleanor de Geneure, who is alluded to in the grant to the Earl of Richmond in 1308, and who survived him; but by her he had no children.[e]

His arms were, Or, an orle Gules.[f]

---

z See note r, p. 320 ante.   a Calend. Rot. Patent. p. 70.   b Rot. Parl. vol. I. p. 166.
c See p. 321, ante.   d Hasted's Kent, vol. III. p. 127.
e Glover's pedigree in the MS. marked "Philpot, No. 4. 78," in the College of Arms; but see the preceding remarks on the subject.   f Page 58.

BERTRAM DE MONTBOUCHIER.

[PAGE 66.]

It will naturally be expected that, if materials for the lives of the Earls and Barons of the thirteenth century are extremely few and unsatisfactory, the particulars recorded of persons of lower rank must be still more limited both in extent and information; hence it is that of the Knights who never attained the honours of the peerage, it is in many instances impossible to say much.

Bertram de Montbouchier, who eminently distinguished himself in the attack of Carlaverock Castle, was, there can be little doubt, the son and heir of Bertram de Montbouchier, by Margaret, the daughter and heiress of Sir Richard Sutton, Knight,[g] and it may be conjectured that he was born about the year 1264.[h] The only circumstances which are mentioned of a person of those names, besides his being at the siege of Carlaverock in 1300, are, that in the 3rd Edw. II. 1309-10, he obtained a confirmation, in tail general, of the manors of Hamerden and Filsham, with all lands in Corley and Crotesby, in the county of Sussex, which had been granted to him by John de Bretagne, Earl of Richmond, by the service of a pair of gold spurs " ac per forinseca servitia ;"[i] that in the 10th Edw. II. 1316-17 the King bestowed on him for life the manor of Syhal in Northumberland, which belonged to Walter de Seleby, a rebel ;[k] and that on the 12th November, 18 Edw. II. 1234, being of the household of the Earl of Richmond, he was allowed to accompany him abroad, provided he did not engage in any war against this country.[l] He died in the 6th Edw. III., leaving by Joan, daughter and sole heiress of Sir Richard,[m] or of Guischard, de Charon, Lord of Beamish and Tan-

---

g Pedigree in the collection of Charles George Young, Esq. F. S. A. York Herald.

h Reginald de Montbouchier, his son and heir, was forty-seven years old in the 6th Edw. III. hence this calculation presumes that Bertram de Montbouchier was twenty-one years old in 1285, when his son was born.

i Calend. Rot. Patent. p. 72.   k Rot. Orig. p. 247.   l Fœdera, N. E. vol. II. p. 581.

m Pedigree cited in note g.

field, and of Sutton in Nottinghamshire, and who was Knight of the Shire in the 4th Edw. II., and afterwards sheriff of Northumberland, Reginald de Mont-bouchier, his son and heir, then forty-seven years of age.[n] The male line of this Reginald failed in the 4th Hen. VI., when the representation of the family devolved on the issue of Isabel his granddaughter, who married Robert Harbottle. Eleanor, the eldest daughter and coheiress of Sir Guischard Harbottle, their descendant, married Sir Thomas Percy, and is now represented by the Duke of Northumberland; and Mary, the second daughter and coheiress, became the wife of Sir Edward Fitton.[o]

Two facts only tend to render it possible that the Sir Bertram de Montbouchier who married Joan de Charon, and the knight who was at Carlaverock, were not the same individual. The arms of the former are considered to have been, Argent, three pots or pitchers Gules; whilst the latter bore those charges within a bordure Sable Bezanté; and in the Roll of Arms in the Cottonian MS. which is supposed to have been compiled about the 10th or 12th Edw. II. the name of

Sire Bertram de Montbouchier, whose arms were, " De Argent, a iij pos de Goules, od le bordure de Sable besanté de Or," is inserted among the names and arms " abatues de grand seignors."

The arms of Bertram de Montbouchier who was at Carlaverock, were, Argent, three pitchers Sable within a bordure of the Second Besanté.[p]

---

n Surtees' Durham, vol. II. p. 225.   o Ibid.
r Page 66; and Cottonian MSS. Caligula, A. xviii.

326

GERARD DE GOUNDRONVILLE.

[PAGE 66.]

As neither the contemporary historians, the Fœdera, the Rolls of Parliament,
the Calendars to the Patent Rolls, Charters, Inquisitiones Post Mortem, the Roll
of Arms in the Cottonian MS., the Appendix to the First Peerage Report, the
Parliamentary Writs, nor the publications of the Record Commission, once
mention this individual, it is of course impossible to say anything about
him. If, however, the following entry in the " Liber Quotidianus Contrarotulatoris Garderobæ," of the 28th Edw. I. related to him, and of which there
is not much doubt, it appears that he was a foreigner, and which explains the
omission of his name in contemporary records:

" Ciphus argenti, pond' IV marc', xv st. precij, xxIV *li.* v *s.* Datur per Regem
Domino Gerardo de Gaundrummillers, Militi Domini Johannis de Baar, in
recessu suo versus partes proprias, apud Karliolum xiij die
Novembris." P

Thus it seems that in November, 1300, five months
after the siege of Carlaverock, Goundronville returned to his
own country.

He was, the Poet says, an active and handsome bachelor,
and his arms were Vaire.

P Page 338.

ROBERT DE WILLOUGHBY.

[PAGE 68.]

Robert de Willoughby, who afterwards became a peer of the realm, was the eldest son of William de Willoughby, by Alice, daughter and coheiress of John Bek, Lord of Eresby; and was born in 1270.

Dugdale informs us that in the 25th Edw. I. he was in the expedition into Gascony; and in the 28th Edw. I. 1300, he was returned from the county of Lincoln, as holding lands or rents, either *in capite* or otherwise, to the amount of £40 yearly value and upwards, and as such was summoned under the general writ to perform military service against the Scots in June in that year,[q] at which time he was present at the siege of Carlaverock, and was wounded by a stone in his breast in the assault.[r] In the 33rd Edw. I. he obtained a grant of free warren in his manors of Eresby and Wyleghby in Lincolnshire,[s] and of a market and fair in his manors of Spillesby and Skidbroke in that county;[t] and in the following year was a manucaptor of John de Knytecote, one of the burgesses who were returned from Leicester, an office which he also performed for Ralph Noman in the 24th Edw. I.[u] On the 21st June, 1 Edw. II. 1308, Willoughby was ordered to attend at Carlisle with horse and arms to serve against the Scots:[x] in the 4th Edw. II. he was found to be one of the heirs of his maternal uncle, Anthony Bek, Bishop of Durham, when he is stated to have been forty years of age; and in the same year the manor of Lilleford in Northamptonshire was granted to him and his heirs.[y] On the 14th July, 5 Edw. II. 1311, he was again commanded to serve in the wars of Scotland;[z] and on the 26th June, 7 Edw. II. 1314, he received a writ of summons to parliament,[a] in consequence, Dugdale conjectures, of his services in Scotland, and his possessing the extensive property which had devolved upon him by the death of Bishop Bek. In the

---

q Palgrave's " Parliamentary Writs," p. 334, 355.   r Page 70, ante.

s Calend. Rot. Chart. p. 136.   t Ibid. p. 137.

u Palgrave's " Parliamentary Writs," pp. 44, 176.

x Appendix to the First Peerage Report, p. 181.   y Calend. Rot. Chart. p. 143.

z Appendix to the First Peerage Report, p. 207; and Fœdera, N. E. vol. II. p. 139.

a Appendix to the First Peerage Report, p. 231.

8th Edw. II. 1315, he was, with others, ordered to investigate the facts stated in the
petition of the Prior of Park Norton against Sir Philip Darcy;[b] and shortly afterwards to inquire into and determine a complaint of the inhabitants of Lincoln,
relative to divers robberies, murders, &c. in that county.[c]   On the 30th June,
8 Edw. II. 1315, Willoughby was for the last time commanded to serve in the
Scottish wars; and in the 10th Edw. II. 1317, according to Dugdale and Collins, he shared with Edmund de Somerville the manors of Orreby and other lands
in Lincoln which belonged to John de Orreby, clerk; but it would appear that
Orreby survived him, and that it was his son, John de Willoughby, who inherited
these possessions, for by the inquisition on the death of John de Orreby, in the 11th
Edw. II. Edmund de Somerville, æt. 40, Alvered de Sulny, æt. 30, and John, the son
of Robert de Willoughby, æt. 12, were found to be Orreby's cousins and heirs.
Having been summoned to parliament on the 26th July and 26th November, 7 Edw.
II. 1313, he died in 1316, aged about forty-six.   By Margaret his wife, the daughter of Lord Deincourt,[d] he left John, his son and heir, the second Lord Willoughby of Eresby, then fourteen years old.

The present representatives of Robert Lord Willoughby are Priscilla Barbara
Elizabeth, Baroness Willoughby of Eresby, in whose favour the abeyance of the
Barony was terminated on the 18th March, 1780; and her sister, Georgiana
Charlotte, Marchioness of Cholmondeley.

The arms borne by this Baron at Carlaverock, and which
are those of Willoughby of Eresby, were, Or, fretté
Azure;[e] but after the death of Bishop Bek in the 4th Edw. II.
he adopted the coat of Bek, for in the Roll of Arms in the
Cottonian MS. the arms of " Robert de Wylebi," whose name
is placed among the Barons, are described as, " de Goules, a
un fer de molin de Argent.[f]

b Rot. Parl. vol. I. p. 314.   c Ibid. p. 330.
d Pedigree by Glover in the Harl. MSS. 254.   e Page 68, ante.
f Cotton MSS. Caligula, A. xviii. Glover, however, assigns to him the arms of Willoughby
with a canton of Bek, Harl. MSS. 254, f. 88 and 94; and to his son, John de Willoughby, the
coat of Bek only; and which also occurs on the seal of Joan de Rosceline his wife, Harl. MSS.
254 f. 96. Robert third Lord Willoughby, on his seal in the 12th Ric. II. used a quarterly coat;
1st and 4th, Ufford; 2nd and 3rd, Bek.

ROBERT DE HAUMSART.

[PAGE 68.]

This Knight was, it is confidently presumed, the son of sir John Hamsard,[g] who was Lord of Evenwood in the Bishoprick of Durham in 1294, by Joan his wife, who had an assignment of dower in the 28th Edw. I. 1300.[h] Of the time of his birth no particulars are extant, and the earliest information which has been discovered of a person of similar names, and which probably related to him, is that a Robert Hansard was, in the 21st Edw. I., 1292-3, one of the mainpernors of John de Parles.[i] In the 28th Edw. I. 1300, he was returned from the county of Lincoln, and also from the wapentake between Ouse and Derwent in Yorkshire, as holding lands or rents, in capite or otherwise, to the amount of £40 yearly value and upwards; and as such summoned under the general writ to perform military service against the Scots in June, 1300,[k] in which month he was at the siege of Carlaverock. His impetuous bravery is commemorated in glowing terms: he conducted himself so nobly, the Poet says, that from his shield fragments might often be seen to fly in the air, for he and the followers of Richmont drove the stones upward as if the castle were rotten, whilst they received heavy blows upon their necks and heads from the besieged.[l]

In the 29th Edw. I. 1301, Hamsard was again summoned to the Scottish wars from the counties of Lincoln and York;[m] and on the 19th April, 31 Edw. I. 1303, he was appointed a Commissioner of Array in the county of Durham.[n]

---

g He was the son of Gilbert Hamsard, who was living in 1250 (Surtees' Durham, vol. III. p. 318); and who in the 1st of John, by the appellation of "Gilbert, the son of Gilbert Hamsard," obtained a charter of divers lands in Durham (Calend. Rot. Chart. p. 4). The said Gilbert was the son of Gilbert Hamsard, who was living in 1220, whose arms, as they occur on his seal, were a chief and bend, and who was the brother of Robert Fitz Maldred, Lord of Raby. Surtees' Durham, vol. III. p. 318.

h Surtees' History of Durham, vol. III. p. 318.   i Rot. Parl. vol. I. p. 95.

k Palgrave's "Parliamentary Writs," pp. 332—334.   l Pages 70, 71, ante.

m Palgrave's "Parliamentary Writs," pp. 355—356.   n Ibid. pp. 371—372.

On the 17th July, 4 Edw. II. 1310, by the description of " Knight," he obtained letters of protection in consequence of his being then engaged in the King's service;[o] and on the 30th June, 8 Edw. II. 1315, he was commanded to be at Newcastle with horse and arms on the feast of the Assumption of the Blessed Virgin to serve against the Scots.[p].

Here all notice of Sir Robert de Hamsard ceases, nor are we even informed of the date of his death. By Margaret his wife, who appears to have died in 1313, he had a son, Sir Gilbert Hamsard, who was under age at the death of his mother.[q]

William Hamsard, tenth in descent from Sir Robert who was at Car-laverock, left a daughter and heiress, Elizabeth, who married Sir Francis

Ayscough, of South Kelsey in Lincolnshire, and died in the 1st Eliz. 1558, leaving issue, and who consequently are the representatives of the elder line of the family; but there were several younger branches, of which a minute account is given in Mr. Surtees' " History of Durham."

The arms of Hamsard were, Gules, three mullets Argent.[r]

---

o Rot. Scot. p. 89.   p Appendix to the First Peerage Report, p. 249 ; and Rot. Scot. p. 146.
q Surtees' Durham, vol. III. p. 318.

r Page 68 ; and Cotton MSS. Caligula, A. xviii., where Sir Robert Hamsard's name occurs among the Knights of Westmoreland and Lancashire. The next name to Sir Robert's in that Roll is that of Sir John Haunsard, who bore " de Goules, a un bende e vj moles de Argent." Glover gives a sketch of a seal of Sir John Hamsard, but without assigning any date to it, with the arms of three mullets. Harl. MSS. 245, f. 12.

HENRY DE GRAHAM.

[PAGE 68.]

Of a person of these names only one fact has been discovered, although every probable source of information was consulted. On the 5th February, 12 Edw. I. 1283, a Henry de Graham, and who possibly was the individual that was at Carlaverock in June, 1300, was one of the peers of Scotland who agreed to receive Margaret of Norway for their sovereign.[s]

It appears that he evinced much bravery at the siege of the castle: the Poet says that those led by him did not escape, for there were not above two of his followers who returned unhurt, or brought back their shields entire.[t]

From his arms there can be little doubt that he was nearly allied to the house of Graham in Scotland; but Sir William Douglas takes no notice of him. He bore Gules, a saltire Argent; on a chief of the Second, three escallops of the First.[u]

---

[s] Fœdera, N. E. vol. I. p. 638.   [t] Page 73, ante.   [u] Page 68, ante.

THOMAS DE RICHMONT.

[PAGE 70.]

The first notice which has been discovered of this Knight, is that, by the description of " Dominus Thomas de Richmunde," he was returned from the liberty of Richmondshire in the county of York as holding lands or rents, either *in capite* or otherwise, to the amount of £40 yearly value and upwards; and was consequently summoned under the general writ to perform military service against the Scots, and to muster at Carlisle on the Nativity of St. John the Baptist, 24 June, 1300,[x] in which month he was present at the siege of Carlaverock. His followers were very conspicuous in the assault of the castle : they passed, the Poet tells us, quite to the bridge, and demanded entry; but they were answered only by ponderous stones and cornues;[y] and Richmont, assisted by Hamsard, behaved so bravely that they drove the stones of the castle up as if it had been rotten; whilst the besieged loaded their heads and necks with heavy blows.[z] In the 29th Edw. I. 1301 he was again summoned from the county of York to serve with horse and arms in the wars of Scotland;[a] and in the 30th Edw. I. he obtained a grant of free warren in his manors of Corkeby and Torcosseck in Cumberland.[b] Richmont was a manucaptor of William Olifant, a Scot, who was taken in the castle of Sterling by Edward the First, and for whose release from the Tower of London a writ was addressed to John de Cromwell, the Constable of that fortress, tested on the 24th May, 1 Edw. II. 1308.[c] On the 14th July and 9th October, 5 Edw. II. 1311, he was enjoined to serve against the Scots;[d] and on the 18th of the same month he was ordered to raise two hundred foot-soldiers in the neighbourhood of Richmond.[e] In the 8th Edw. II. 1314, he

---

[x] Palgrave's " Parliamentary Writs," p. 332.   [y] Page 70.   [z] Page 71, ante.

[a] Palgrave's " Parliamentary Writs," p. 356.   [b] Calend. Rot. Chart. p. 133.

[c] Fœdera, N. E. vol. II. p. 45.

[d] Appendix to the First Peerage Report, p. 207; Rot. Scot. p. 104; and Rot. Scot. p. 106.

[e] Rot. Scot. vol. I. p. 101.

received a grant of the castle and honour of Cockermouth for life;[f] and was again summoned to the Scottish wars on the 30th of June, 8 Edw. II. 1315;[g] after which year nothing is known of him.

Of the time of Richmont's birth or decease we are equally ignorant: nor are any particulars preserved of his family.

In a pedigree of Stapleton in one of the Harleian Manuscripts,[h] Nicholas Stapleton, of Richmondshire, the brother of Sir Gilbert Stapleton, whose descendant in the eighth generation died in the 27th Eliz. is said to have married Elizabeth, the daughter of a John Richmont; and in that of Andrew,[i] a Thomas Andrew is stated to have married Anna, daughter of —— Richmond, about the middle of the fifteenth century, and on whom the following observation is made, " cujus cognati maritam occiderunt." That pedigree is accompanied by some doggrel verses descriptive of the different alliances, and which is said to have been copied from a MS. of the reign of Edward the Fourth. The following relate to the marriage of Thomas Andrew :

Thomas Andrew an Richmond had to wyffe,
For the which mariage fell great stryffe,
On Andrew sore troubled, and in souch a casse,
That in a short tyme he ended his casse.

The arms of Thomas de Richmont were, Gules, two bars gemels, and a chief Or.[k]

---

[f] Rot. Orig. vol. I. p. 209.

[g] Appendix to the First Peerage Report, p. 249; and Rot. Scot. p. 145.

[h] Harl. MSS. 1487, f. 283, a copy of the Visitation of Yorkshire.

[i] MS. in the College of Arms marked " Vincent's Chaos," f. 50 b.   [k] Page 70, ante.

RALPH DE GORGES.

[PAGE 74.]

If it were not for the Poet's assertion that Ralph de Gorges was " a newly dubbed Knight," it would be at once concluded that he was the individual who is described by Dugdale as the son and heir of Ralph de Gorges who died in the 56th Hen. III. 1271-2 by Elene his wife, and who at her death in the 20th Edw. I. 1291-2 was thirty-six years of age, and inherited the lands of Bradepole, Yarde, Bedminster, and Redchore, in Dorsetshire; but that eminent writer informs us that the Ralph de Gorges alluded to was Marshal of the King's army in Gascony in the 21st Edw. I., 1292-3 when he must have been a knight of considerable reputation. It appears from the " Parliamentary Writs" that as early as the 5th Edw. I. 1277, a Ralph de Gorges was summoned to perform military service; and again in 1282, 1287, and 1294; that in 1297 a knight of those names was returned from the county of Northampton as holding lands there of the yearly value of £20; and in 1300 a Ralph de Gorges was returned from the counties of Somerset, Dorset, and Southampton, as possessing lands of. the annual value of £40, and as such was summoned under the general writ to perform military service against the Scots on the 24th June, 1300.[1] As in that month we find a Ralph de Gorges present at the siege of Carlaverock, there can be little doubt that he was the person mentioned in that writ; and that he was then seised of the lands in Dorsetshire of which Elene de Gorges died possessed in the 20th Edw. I.; but it is difficult to believe that her son Ralph, who was in that year thirty-six years old,[m] only received the honour of knighthood in 1300, when if living he must have been forty-four; hence it is most probable that he was the son of the said Ralph, and grandson of Elene de Gorges, though this conjecture is not supported by positive evidence. It is almost certain that the Ralph de Gorges who held lands in Northamptonshire was a distinct person from the subject of this article, though it was in all probability the former, who was ordered to perform military service in 1294. The editor of the

---

1 Digest, pp. 639-40.   m Esch. eod. ann.

" Parliamentary Writs" also observes, that " several individuals of this family appear to have been named Ralph ;" thus it would be useless to attempt to identify them; but it may perhaps be confidently assumed that the Knight who was at Carlaverock was then for the first time in the field after he received the accolade; and, as only one Ralph de Gorges is named in the Roll of Arms in the Cottonian MS. or in the writs of service during the reign of Edward the Second, every fact which is recorded of a man of those names from the 28th Edw. I. 1300, to the 17th Edw. II. 1323, when he is supposed to have died, will be here assigned to the Knight commemorated by the Poet.

Gorges' bravery during the assault is particularly mentioned : though more than once beaten to the ground by the enemies' stones, or thrown down by the crowd, he still maintained his post, disdaining to retire. In the 33rd Edw. I. 1304-5, he obtained a grant of a market and fair in his manor of Liditon in Dorsetshire, and of free warren in that of Staunton in Devon.[n] On the 4th March, 2 Edw. II. 1309, he received his first writ of summons to parliament; and on numerous occasions, from the 3rd to the 16th Edw. II. was enjoined to serve in the wars of Scotland with horse and arms; but it is sufficient to refer to the records of the writs without specifying their respective dates.[o] He solicited to be restored to the office of Bailiff of the forest of Whittlewood, which had been conferred upon him by Edward the First, in the 8th Edw. II. 1315; and Hugh le Despencer, the Justice of that forest, was ordered to state why he was removed :[p] in the same year he, with Peter de Evercy, petitioned for himself and all the inhabitants of the isle of Wight, relative to the levying of scutage there.[q] Gorges was appointed Justice of Ireland in the 14th Edw. II. 1320-1;[r] in which year he was involved in a dispute with Sir Henry Tyes, son of the Baron Tyes who was at the siege of Carlaverock, the Constable of Carisbrooke Castle, and " enprovour" of the isle of Wight, against whom he exhibited various charges.[s] On the 30th January, 14 Edw. II. 1321, he was with other peers forbidden to allow of any assembly, either secretly or openly, by themselves or others :[t] on the

---

[n] Calend. Rot. Chart. p. 136.

[o] Appendix to the First Peerage Report, pp. 194, 202, 206, 235, 251, 258, 283, 294, 295, 313, 247, 265, 271, 318, 330, 331, 337. See also Fœdera, N. E. vol. II. pp. 78, 239, 275, 296, 485, 512.

[p] Rot. Parl. vol. I. p. 321.   [q] Ibid. p. 323.   [r] Calend. Rot. Patent. p. 89.

[s] Rot. Parl. vol. I. p. 383.   [t] Fœdera, N. E. vol. II. p. 442.

21st April following he was directed to preserve the peace, and not to give credit
to false rumours;[u] and on the 12th November 15 Edw. II. 1321, he was
prohibited from attending a meeting with the Earl of Lancaster.[x]

Gorges was summoned to parliament from the 4th March, 2 Edw. II. 1309,
to the 18th September, 16 Edw. II. 1322;[y] and died in 1323;[z] leaving by
Eleanor his wife, who survived him, and in the 4th Edw. III. 1330, was the wife
of John Peche,[a] a son, Ralph de Gorges, who was sixteen years old at his father's
death.[b] He was never summoned to parliament, and appears to have died s. P,,
when his sisters, namely, 1st Elizabeth, who married —— Ashton, and left a son,
Sir Robert, who died s. P. in the 7th Ric.. II.; 2nd Eleanor, who was the wife of
Theobald Russell,[c] of Kingston Russell in Dorsetshire, by whom she had two
sons, Sir Ralph Russell, and Sir Theobald, who assumed the name of Gorges,[d]

---

[u] Fœdera, N. E. vol. II. p. 448.   [x] Ibid. p. 459.

[y] Appendix to the First Peerage Report.   [z] Esch. eod. ann.

[a] Rot. Parl. vol. II. p. 40. The late Mr. Townsend in his MS. collections from Dugdale's Baronage says she married, after Gorges' death, Sir Guy de Ferre, and who must have been her third
husband. It seems that she died in the 23rd Edw. III. Esch. eod ann.

[b] Esch. 17 Edw. II.   [c] He was twelve years old in the 4th Edw. II. Dugdalia.

[d] Of the assumption of the name and arms of Gorges, the following curious record is preserved
among the copies of documents of an heraldic nature in the Cottonian MS. Julius, C. vii. f. 239.

" Nous, Henry, Conte de Lancaster, de Derby, de Leicester, et Seneschall. d'Engleterre,
William de Clinton, Counte de Hontington, Renaud de Cobham, Gaultier Seigneur de Manny,
William Lovell, Steven de Cossinton, comis depar nostre Sire le Roy d'Engleterre et de
Fraunce, a oyer et tryer et juger toutes manieres debats d'Armes et Heaulmes dedans son oste
en son siege devant Calles, faisons sçavoir que come John, filz et heretier Mounsr John de War-
bleton, se plainct devant nous que Tibaud, filz Mounsr Tibaud Russell, come se appelle ung
surnom' de Gorges, porta ses armes, cestassavoir lozenge d'Or et d'Azure, plainement sans difference. Et pour ce que le dit Jehan et Tybaud jure et examines p'sonaillement devant nous, est
ouy le motyves et evidences si bien d'un p't come d'auter, trove fut si bien p' savy come p'
tesmoignage d'ancien Chivalers de leur pais que leur auncestres de dit Jehan, de auncester en
auncester du temps dont homme n'ay memoire, ont porte le ditz armes sauns changier, est un
Mounsr Rauf de Gorges ayle de cestuy Tibaud, susdict lessa ses armes, et print les armes
susdits de volunte. Et un de ses heires morut sanz heire masle, et fut le dict Tibaud, fitz de sa sœur.
Ad juge fait p' boun delib'ac'on, et avis par nous les dictes Armes au dict John heritablement. Et
nous avandictes Henry et Guillaume Countes, Reinauld et Gaultier Banerettes, et Guillaume et
Steven Ch'l'rs, susdicts a cestes lettres ouvertes avons fait mettre nous seaulx et in tesmoinage de
verite et de p'petuelle recorde. Donne en dit siege en la ville de St. Margaret, l'an de grace mill'
trois cens quarante sept. Ex ip'a charta sub sigillis nobiliu' infrascript in cutodia Ric'i Put-
tenham."

and from whom the family of Gorges of Wraxall in Somersetshire descended; and, 3rd, Joan, who was the second wife
of Sir William Cheney, by whom she had Sir Ralph Cheney,
and who is now represented by Lord Willoughby de
Broke; became the representatives of the subject of this
memoir.[e]

The arms of Gorges were, mascally Or and Azure.[f]

RICHARD DE ROKESLE.

[PAGE 74.]

Two persons called Richard de Rokesle, or Rokely, were living in the year
1300, but, as the Roll of Arms in the Cottonian MS. states that the Knight who
bore "mascally of Gules and Ermine" was of Suffolk, such facts as are related of
a person of those names who possessed lands in that county or in Norfolk, will
be attributed to the subject of this article, whilst the few notices which occur of
a Richard de Rokesle who cannot be identified, will be briefly mentioned, leaving
them to be applied to which of the parties the reader may think it most likely
they referred.

It is almost impossible to ascertain of whom Richard de Rokesly was the son,
the time of his birth or decease, or who were his heirs, for the Escheats present
nothing which can be safely considered to relate to him. All, however, that
has been discovered respecting the family of Rokesle of Norfolk and Suffolk will
be found in the note.[g]

---

[e] The late Francis Townsend, Esq. Windsor Herald, MS. Collections for Dugdale's Baronage,
marked " Dugdalia."

[f] Page 76; and Cottonian MSS. Caligula, A. xviii., where they are blazoned, Azure, six
mascles Or.

[g] Placita De Quo Warranto, p. 728, aº 14 Edw. I. In answer to a quo warranto Richard de

In 1296 a Richard.de la Rokely was enrolled, pursuant to the ordinance for the defence of the sea-coast, as a Knight holding lands in Essex, though non-resident in the county;[h] but, as the Rokesleys of Kent possessed lands in Essex, it does not seem likely that it related to those of.Suffolk: and on the 1st March in that year he was commanded to perform military service against the Scots.[i] On the 25th May, 1298, he was summoned from Norfolk for a similar purpose;[k] but neither he nor Richard de Rokesley of Kent were included in the writ to attend at Carlisle on the 24th June, 1300,[l] though the former was at that time present at the siege of Carlaverock, where he appears to have behaved with zeal and gallantry. In June, 29 Edw. I. 1301, he was summoned from the counties of Norfolk and Suffolk to serve in the wars of Scotland:[m] in 1302 he was elected a knight of the shire for Norfolk;[n] and obtained his writ *de expensis* for his attendance.[o] On the 10th May, 34 Edw. I. 1306, he was ordered to perform military service against the Scots, or to appear in the Exchequer to compound for his attendance.[p]

After that time he cannot be identified with a single record in which the name of Richard de Rokesly occurs: on the contrary it is almost certain that they referred to the Knight of those names in Kent, since the greater part relate to

---

Rokesley claimed to have frank pledge, &c. in Ryngeshale in Suffolk, from the record of which it appears that he was the son of Robert de Rokele.

Placita de Banco, term. Paschæ, aº 25 Edw. I. Norfolk. Richard, son of William de la Rokele, petitioned against Richard, son of Reginald de la Wade, relative to lands in Upeton, Helveston, and Berg near Helveston:

Richard de la Rokele.⊤

Reginald de la Rokele, ob. s. p.   William de la Rokele.⊤

Richard de la Rokele, petens.

Vincent's MS. in the College of Arms, marked " Picture of our Lady."

Escheats, 24 Edw. I. Ricardus de la Rokelee, Cecilia uxor assign' dot'	Ricardus, filius Ricardi de Rokele.	Colkirke et Gatelee in Co' Norfolk'.
32 Edw. I. Ricardus de la Rokelee, filius et heres Ricardi de la Rokelee. Margareta uxor.	Matildis soror. æt. 17.	Colkirke et Gatelee in Co' Norfolk'.

[h] Palgrave's " Parliamentary Writs," p. 273.   [i] Ibid. p. 276.   [k] Ibid. p. 311.
[l] Ibid. Digest.   [m] Ibid. p. 354.   [n] Ibid. p. 123.   [o] Ibid. p. 131.   [p] Ibid. p. 377.

that county.[q] Of those, however, which do not bear evidence of being addressed to that individual, and, however improbable, might have been directed to the person who was at Carlaverock, are, the appointment of Mons[r] de Rokeley to the office of " gardein" of the King's lands in Pontou and Monstroill, with special powers and directions to guard the same against all persons, on the 7th November, 1 Edw. II. 1307;[r] and who received several writs containing commands connected with that situation.[s] A Richard de Rokesley was summoned to the Scottish wars on the 30th June, 1311:[t] on the 3rd May, 6 Edw. II. 1313, he obtained letters of protection, being then about to accompany Nicholas de Segrave beyond the seas;[u] and an individual so called was ordered to receive some Cardinals at Dover on the 13th June, 10 Edw. II. 1317.[x] As two persons of that name were summoned to serve against the Scots in June, 1315,[y]

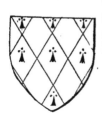 there can be no question that one of them was the Knight alluded to by the Poet. A Richard de la Rokele was also summoned to the Scottish wars on the 20th August, 10 Edw. II. 1316;[z] on the 20th March, 12 Edw. II. 1318;[a] and on the 22nd May, 12 Edw. II. 1319.[b]

The arms of Richard de Rokesle of Suffolk were, mascally Gules and Ermine.[c]

---

q Fœdera, N. E. vol. I. p. 945; vol. II. p. 191-2; vol. II. p. 31, which contains a writ summoning a Richard de Rokesley of Kent, and his wife, to attend the King's and Queen's coronation.

r Ibid. N. E. vol. II. p. 11.   s Ibid. pp. 39, 44.

t Rot. Scot. vol. I. p. 45.   u Fœdera, N. E. vol. II. p. 213.   x Ibid. p. 334.

y Appendix to the First Peerage Report, pp. 248, 250.   z Ibid. p. 262.   a Ibid. p. 294.

b Ibid. p. 296.   c Page 74; Cotton MS. Caligula, A. xviii.

ADAM DE LA FORD.

[PAGE 74.]

Very few circumstances are recorded of a person of these names; nor is it probable that all of them related to this individual. From the Roll of Arms in the Cottonian Manuscript it would appear that he held lands either in Wiltshire or Hampshire, as he is included among the knights of those counties.

There can be little hesitation in believing that he was the Adam de la Ford who, in the 26th Edw. I., 1297-8, obtained a grant for a market and fair in his manor of Wichford in Wiltshire;[d] and it is probable that he was the person mentioned in the following extract from the Calendar of the " Inquisitiones post Mortem:"

" 33 Edw. I. Adam de la Ford, pro capellano Beatæ Mariæ de la Ford, Stawelle unum messuag', l acr' terr', et iiij acr' prati, ib'm—Somerset'."[e]

In the 7th Edw. I. 1278-9, a man of these names held a virgate of land in the hundred of Ewelme, Oxfordshire;[f] and among the ancient charters in the British Museum, is one without date, to which an Adam de la Forde was a party.[g]

William Quintin, Forester of Grovele in the forest of Clarendon, complained in the 8th Edw. II. 1314-15, of a malicious information which Adam de la Forde and John Bonham had laid against him:[h] on the 30th June, 1315, an Adam atte Forde was summoned to serve with horse and arms against the Scots;[i] and in the 13th Edw. II. 1319-20, the King granted to John de Hanstede thirteen acres which Adam de Ford, deceased, held in the forest of Whittlewood.[j]

But the most important account which occurs of this Knight is in a MS. note of the escheat of the 19 Edw. II, 1325-6,[k] whence it appears that he died in or before that year, seised of De la Hale manor near Brommore in the county of Southampton, and of a moiety of the manor of Wichford Magna in Wiltshire; that by Christiana his wife, the daughter and heiress of Patrick Chaworth, he

---

d Calend. Rot. Chart. p. 128.   e No. 105, p. 200.   f Rot. Hundred, vol. II. p. 760.

g Marked 78 B. 20. It is without date or seal, nor is any place mentioned in it. The other names which occur in it are, Robert, son of Simon de la Forde, and Nicholas de la Forde. Other charters are preserved of Nicholas de la Forde, marked 78 B. 21 and 22.

h Rot. Parl. vol. I. p. 319.   i Appendix to the First Peerage Report, p. 248.

j Rot. Orig. p. 250.   k No. 46.

left Adam his son and heir then about thirty years of age. Christiana his widow died in the 3 Edw. III.[1] 1329.

Such are the few notices of persons of this name which are scattered through the numerous volumes that have been consulted for particulars relating to the Sir Adam de la Ford who, at the siege of Carlaverock, in June, 1300, " mined the walls as well as he could for the stones which were hurled about him, and by which many of his fellow soldiers were wounded."

He is therefore almost entirely indebted to the Poet for the preservation of his name ; and as no other notice has been discovered which can with certainty be applied to him, perhaps neither his ancestors nor his descendants can be traced.

His arms were, Azure, three lioncels rampant and crowned Or.[m]

THE BARON OF WIGTON.

[Page 75.]

The Baron of Wigton was John, the son and heir of Walter de Wigton, whom he succeeded in the 14th Edw. I. 1289, at which time he was twenty-two years of age;[n] and in the same year did homage for his lands.[o] His services in the field were, it will be seen, constant and distinguished; and he may be ranked among the most eminent soldiers of his time. The title of " Baron," by which the Poet describes him, is also attributed to him in a record that will be hereafter cited, and was one of the few instances of such an appellation being given to an individual, though in the remarks on the subject in the " Third Report on the dignity of a Peer of the Realm," no notice is taken of its having been assigned to him.

In the 15th Edw. I. 1287, John de Wigton was summoned to attend with

---

[1] Esch. eod. ann. No. 59.
[n] Esch. eod. ann.

[m] Page 74 ; and the Cottonian MS. Caligula, A. xviii.
[o] Rot. Orig. p. 51.

4 R

horses and arms at a military council at Gloucester before Edmund Earl of
Cornwall;[o] and in the 19th Edw. I. 1290-1, he was commanded to perform military
service against the Scots.[p]   He is mentioned in some pleadings about the wardship of the lands of Richard de Kirkbride in the 20th Edw. I.[q] 1291-2, which will
be more fully alluded to in the next article; and in that year answered a *quo warranto* respecting his right to a market and fair, and other privileges, in his manors
of Wygeton and Melborby;[r] but in the 28th Edw. I. 1299-1300, he obtained a
formal grant of those rights in Melborby.[s]   On the 26th June, 22 Edw. I. 1294,
he was commanded to join the expedition into Gascony;[t] and in the 25th Edw.
I. was ordered to proceed immediately to Scotland, to join the forces then under
the command of John Earl of Surrey.[u]   On the 14th January, 28 Edw. I. 1300,
he was appointed a commissioner to summon the knights of the county of Cumberland to meet the King for the purpose of serving against the Scots;[x] and by a
writ tested at St. Alban's on the 11th April following he was enjoined to enforce
the muster of the levies of the men at arms in that county, pursuant to the commission of the 14th January, and to return the names of the defaulters into the
Wardrobe.[y]   Wigton was nominated a Commissioner of Array in Cumberland on
the 30th April, 1300;[z] and in June in that year served at the siege of Carlaverock,
when he must have been about thirty-three years of age. His steadiness and valour
excited the Poet's admiration, and which no language can so well describe as his
own: " The good Baron of Wigton received such blows that it was the astonishment of all that he was not stunned, and, without excepting any Lord present,
none shewed a more resolute or unembarrassed countenance."   About that time
twelve foot-soldiers of his retinue were paid their wages for three days;[a] and in
the 29th Edw. I. 1300-1, he was returned a Knight of the Shire for the county
of Cumberland, and obtained his writ *de expensis* for attendance at the parliament at Lincoln in February, 1301:[b] on the 20th January, 1303, orders were

o Palgrave's " Parliamentary Writs," p. 250; and Fœdera, N. E. vol. 1. p. 675.
p Palgrave's " Parliamentary Writs," p. 256; and Fœdera, N. E. vol. I. p. 753.
q Placita de Quo Warranto, p. 115.   r Ibid. p. 116.
s Calend. Rot. Chart. p. 129; and Calend. Rot. Patent. 9 Edw. III. p. 124.
t Palgrave's " Parliamentary Writs," p. 259; and Fœdera, N. E. vol. I. p. 804.
u Palgrave's " Parliamentary Writs," p. 300.   x Ibid. p. 330.   y Ibid. p. 342.
z Ibid. p. 342.   a Liber Quotidianus Contrarotulatoris Gardarobæ, xxviij Edw. I. p. 261.
b Palgrave's " Parliamentary Writs," p. 102.

issued to him to place himself, with horses and arms, under the directions of John de Segrave, the King's Lieutenant in Scotland;[c] and in 1305 he was again a Knight of the Shire for, and in 1307 a Commissioner of Array in, Cumberland.[d] He was one of the manucaptors for Joan, the widow of John Wake, in the 35th Edw. I. 1306-7;[e] and obtained the custody of her lands in the 3rd Edw. II. 1309-10.[f] On the 30th September, 1 Edw. II. 1307, by the style of " John Baron of Wigton," he was enjoined to assist in repressing a rebellion in Galway with the men raised in the counties of Lancaster and Cumberland;[g] by writs tested on the 21st September, 2 Edw. II. 1308,[h] and 30th July, 3 Edw. II. 1309, in which he is called " John de Wigton" only, he was directed to serve with horse and arms in Scotland.[i] In consequence of his being so engaged he received letters of protection dated on the 20th June, 1309;[k] and on the 26th October in that year he was with others ordered to defend the marches near Carlisle against the Scots.[l] When the Earl of Lancaster opposed Piers de Gaveston, Wigton joined the Earl's party; and on the 16th October, 7 Edw. II. 1313, he obtained the King's pardon for his conduct on that occasion.[m] The last notice of him which has been found is in March, 1315, when a letter was addressed to him and others, desiring them to give credence to what Sir John de Benstede, Knight, and Robert de Wodehous, Clerk, should tell them.[n]

The Baron of Wigton died in the 8th Edw. II. 1315, leaving his wife Dionysia surviving.[o] It appears from some proceedings in Trinity term in the 13th Edw. II. 1320, that two inquisitions were held on his decease; and that it was doubtful whether his daughter Margaret, John Kirkbride, Joan, the daughter of John de Reygate, or Florence de Wigton, Margaret, and Elizabeth, his sisters, were his heirs, as the latter asserted that they were so, and that his daughter Margaret was a bastard.[p] A MS. note of one of these inquisitions states that Margaret, the wife of John de Crokedeke, was his heir; but it does not say in what

c Palgrave's " Parliamentary Writs," p. 370; and Fœdera, N. E. vol. I. p. 948.

d Palgrave's " Parliamentary Writs," pp. 156, 157, and 379.   e Rot. Parl. vol. I. p. 215.

f Rot. Orig. p. 168.   g Fœdera, N. E. vol. II. p. 8.   h Rot. Scot. vol. I. p. 57 b.

i Ibid. p. 78; and Appendix to the First Peerage Report, p. 194.

k Rot. Scot. vol. I. p. 66.   l Ibid. p. 77.   m Fœdera, N. E. vol. II. p. 230.

n Rot. Scot. vol. I. p. 140.   o Esch. eod ann. That he was dead in the 9th Edw. II. is also evident from the " Rotulorum Originalium Abbrevatio," p. 223.

p Placitorum in Domo, &c. p. 336.

manner she was related to him. It is nearly certain, however, that she was his daughter, but whether legitimate or not seems from the pleadings just noticed to be at least questionable.[p]

The arms of the Baron of Wigton were, we learn from the Poem, Sable, three estoils within a bordure indented Or;[q] but in the contemporary Roll,[r] where his name is inserted among the Barons, they are thus blazoned, " de Sable, a iij moles de Or, od la bordure endente de Or."

RICHARD DE KIRKBRIDE.

[PAGE 76.]

The individual who is described by the Poet as " he of Kirkbride," and to whose prowess he bears such honourable testimony, was Sir Richard Kirkbride, of Kirkbride in Cumberland.[s] It is said that he was the second son of Richard de Kirkbride, who died in or before the 4th Edw. I. 1275-6.[t] But became heir to his elder brother Robert, who died without issue in the 23rd Edw. I. 1294-5. Of the date of his birth no information is given; but it is evident from the proceedings in the 20th Edw. I. 1291-2, which are cited in the note, that he succeeded to his lands whilst he was a minor, and that he married before he became of age.[u]

P In the 12th Edw. II. a John de Wigton did homage for the lands of his mother, Cecily de Blida de Wigton. Placitorum in Domo, &c. p. 242.

q Page 76, ante.   r Cotton. MSS. Caligula, A. xviii.

s Nicholson and Burn's History of Westmoreland and Cumberland, vol. I. p. 211.

t Rot. Orig. p. 27.

u " Cumberland, 20 Edw. I. John, son and heir of Walter de Wygeton, Thomas de Normanvyl, late the King's Escheator, just before the last eyre seised into the King's hands all the lands and tenements which Richard de Kirkbride held, being a minor, of the King in capite, and his maritage belonged to the King. . Thomas afterwards committed the custody of Richard's lands to one Roger Mynyot with consent of the King, at an annual rent of £12. 16s. 9d. until the lawful age of

In the 24th Edw. I. he had, however, attained his majority, as on the 4th December, 1295, he was appointed assessor and collector in Cumberland of the eleventh and seventh granted in the parliament at Westminster on the 27th of November preceding.x We learn from the Poem that he was in the English army at the siege of Carlaverock in June, 1300; that many a heavy stone fell upon his followers during the assault of the castle; that they assailed the gate of it with such vehemence that it resembled the beating of a smith on his anvil, and that they were so hurt and exhausted by the severe wounds they received that it was with difficulty they were able to retire. That Kirkbride was present on the occasion· is further proved by an entry in the Wardrobe expenses of the 28th Edw. I. recording the payment of wages to ten of his foot-soldiers.y In March, 35th Edw. I. 1307, he was nominated a Commissioner of Array in Allersdale;z and on the 26th October, 3rd Edw. II. 1309, was with others commanded to defend the marches near Carlisle against the Scots;a and on the.17th July, 1310, received letters of protection.b On the 3rd February, 1316, a writ was addressed to him, stating that the King had appointed John de Castre, Constable of the castle of Carlisle, but that Andrew de Harcla would not deliver up the custody of it, and he and others were ordered upon pain of forfeiture to cause it to be rendered to Castre accordingly.c The Scots having committed various inroads, and destroyed the property of the inhabitants, Kirkbride with several other persons obtained a remission of the tax of one-eighteenth, in consequence of the losses they had sustained, by writ tested on the 25th November, 13 Edw. II.

Richard, and Roger transferred the same to Walter, father of John, who allowed Richard to marry under age without the license of the King. The marriage was valued last eyre at 100 marks, when Walter declared it to have occurred with license of the King, as John now says, who alleges the record. A writ was directed to the justices, 3rd December, anno 21, about referring their exaction of 100 marks to the next parliament. Upon inquiry by jury, it is reported that Richard's heritage came first to him on the part of his father, which was held of Walter, and afterwards fell to him, before he was married, on the part of his mother, a parcel of the barony of Levinton, held of the King in capite, whereby his marriage belonged at the time he was married to the King. —Placita de Quo Warranto, p. 115. Nicholson and Burn state that the parish of Kirkbride is part of the barony of Wigton, vol. I. p. 211.

x Palgrave's " Parliamentary Writs," p. 45, and Rot. Parl. vol. I. p. 227.

y Liber Quotidianus, &c. p. 261.   z Palgrave's " Parliamentary Writs," p. 380.

a Rot. Scot. p. 77.   b Ibid. p. 89.   c Ibid. p. 153.

4 s

1319;[d] and on the 8th May, 18 Edw. II. 1325, he was appointed to keep the
truce with the Scots.[e] After this time nothing more is recorded of him; and he
probably died in the 5th Edw. III. 1331, leaving Walter, his son and heir, then forty
years of age.[f] The name of his wife is not stated, but Nicholson and Burn assert
that he left a son called Walter, who was Knight of the Shire for Cumberland
in the 9th Edw. II., and " from whom male issue descended for several generations, who were lords of the manor of Kirkbride, until a coheir of George Kirkbride transferred a moiety of it to the Dalstons of Dalston Hall." For this very
vague statement a correct account of the family cannot perhaps be substituted;
but the following notices throw some light upon the descent.

In the Calendar of the Inquisitions " ad quod damnum," of the 12th Edw. II.[g]
is the following entry

" Walterus Kirkebride, Kirkeandres terr' ib'm. Eden Piscaria. Skelton maner'
3[tii] p's. Cumb'."

In the 1st Edw. III. a John Kirkbride died seised of lands in Cumberland,
and left Walter Kirkbride, his brother, his heir, then forty years old;[h] which John
and Walter were probably sons of the subject of this article.

The said Walter Kirkbride died in the 10th Edw. III., leaving Richard his
son, his heir, then twenty-two years of age.[i] Richard de Kirkbride died in the
23rd Edw. III. leaving Richard, his son and heir, one year old,[k] who, it may be
safely concluded, was the Sir Richard Kirkbride, husband of Johanna, who died
in the 22nd Ric. II., leaving Richard his son, his heir, nine years old.[l] In the
1st Hen. IV.,[m] however, an inquisition was held on the death of a Sir Richard
de Kirkbride, Knight, who held the same lands as were mentioned in the previous inquisition of the 22nd Ric. II., whose wife was called Agnes, and whose
son and heir was also named Richard, and then nine years old; hence it may be
inferred that these inquisitions related to the same person, that he was twice
married, and that his son Richard, who was a Knight, and made proof of his
age in the 1st Hen. IV.[n] was by his first wife Johanna.

In the 33rd Edw. I. a Richard de Kirkbride, of Laurencehelme in Cumber-

---

d Fœdera, N. E. vol. II. p. 409.   e Ibid. p. 598.   f Esch. 5 Edw. III. No. 74.
g Page 257.   h Esch. 1 Edw. III. No. 21.   i Esch. 20 Edw. III. No. 58.
k Esch. 23 Edw. III. No. 80.   l Esch. 22 Ric. II. No. 26.
m Esch. 1 Hen. IV. No. 68.   n Calend. Inq. post Mort. eod. ann.

land, died, leaving Johanna, the wife of John Smallwood, his heir;[o] and in the 23rd Edw. III. Richard, the son of Walter Kirkbride, junior, then æt. 21, was found heir to the lands in Cumberland of Margaret Wigton, the wife of Sir John Weston, Knight. She died seised of the lands which John Baron of Wigton held, and it may be supposed that she was his daughter; that she died without issue; and that the said Richard Kirkbride was descended from the John Kirkbride mentioned in the proceedings in the 13th Edw. II. relative to the Baron's heirs.[p] The Calendar of the Patent Rolls[q] contains the following entry in the 3rd Ric. II.: " Rex confirmavit Ricardo de Kirkebride in feodo consanguineo et hæredi Roberti Parvinge, Landam de Brathwaite infra forestam de Englewoode, pro feodifirma octo marcarum necnon licentiam assartandi quinquaginta acras parcell' ejusdem."

It has been already remarked that the male line of Kirkbride terminated with George Kirkbride, and that one of his daughters and coheirs married —— Dalston: Emma, another of these coheirs, appears to have been the wife of Robert Cliborne, of Westmoreland, whose great-great-grandson was five years old in 1585.[r]

The arms of Kirkbride are said in the Poem to have been, Argent, a cross engrailed Vert;[s] but in the Roll in the Cottonian MS.[t] Sir Richard de Kirkbride, whose name occurs among the knights of Northumberland and Cumberland, is stated to have borne, Argent, a saltire engrailed Vert; and which coat is also attributed by Vincent to George Kirkbride abovementioned.

---

o Esch. 33 Edw. I. No. 18.   P Esch. 23 Edw. III. No. 86.   q Page 203.
r Vincent's Yorkshire, f. 127 b.   s Page 76.   t Caligula, A. xviii.

348

BARTHOLOMEW DE BADLESMERE.

[PAGE 78.]

It is a singular coincidence that the career of the two knights, Badlesmere
and Cromwell, whom the Poet describes as having acted together at the siege of
Carlaverock Castle, should present such a striking resemblance. They became the most distinguished peers of the reign of Edward the Second, were
frequently selected to perform the same duties, and for a considerable time
equally deserved and enjoyed the confidence and esteem of their sovereign.

Bartholomew de Badlesmere was the son and heir of Sir Gunceline de Badlesmere, a knight of high reputation; and was born about the year 1275. In June,
22 Edw. I. 1294, he was excepted from the general summons of persons holding
by military tenure or serjeantcy which was then issued for the expedition into
Gascony. ᵘIn the 26th Edw. I. 1297-8, however, he was ordered by three writs to
perform military service in Flanders;ˣ and in June, 1300, he was at the siege of
Carlaverock. He and Cromwell were sent, the Poem states, by Lord Clifford to
the gate of the castle with that nobleman's banner, and behaved during the whole
day " well and bravely." The Wardrobe accounts of the time contain the following entries respecting Badlesmere and his father

Anno 28 Edw. 1299. " Domino Guncelino de Badelesmere, pro feodo suo
hiemali, per manus Bartholomei filii sui, apud Berewicum super Twedam, xxvij
die Decembr', vj*li.* xiij*s.* iiij*d.*"ʸ

" Domino Guncelino de Badelesmere, pro roba sua hiemali, per manus Bartholomei filii sui, apud Berewicum super Twedam, xxix die Decembr' v[i]ij marc."ᶻ

" Domino Bartho' de Badelesmere, pro roba sua hicmali, per manus proprias
apud Berewicum super Twedam, xxix die Decembr' iiij marc."ᵃ

In the following year his father, Sir Gunceline de Badlesmere, died, when
he was found to be his heir, at which time he was twenty-six years of age.ᵇ

ᵘ Palgrave's " Parliamentary Writs," p. 260.   ˣ Ibid. pp. 260, 304, 306.
ʸ Liber Quotidianus Contrarotulatoris Gardarobæ, 28 Edw. I. p. 188.
ᶻ Ibid. p. 310.   ᵃ Ibid. p. 311.   ᵇ Esch. 29 Edw. I.

According to Dugdale he was in the wars of Scotland in the 29th, 31st, 32nd, and 34th Edw.I.; and in the 35th Edw. I. 1306-7, he was a Knight of the Shire for the county of Kent, and obtained a writ *de expensis* for his attendance in parliament in that year at Carlisle.[c]

In the 1st Edw. II. 1307-8, Badlesmere was constituted Governor of Bristol Castle; and again in the 3rd Edw. II. 1309-10, when the custody of the town and barton were also entrusted to him. Through the influence of Gilbert Earl of Gloucester and Henry Earl of Lincoln he obtained a grant in that year of the castle and manor of Chilham in Kent, to hold for the life of himself and of Margaret his wife; and of several other manors. In November, 1308, at the request of Philip King of France, he was appointed a commissioner to grant a truce to the Scots;[d] and on the 3rd December following he was nominated Captain of the forces then sent into Scotland.[e] On the 26th October, 3 Edw. II. 1309, he received his first writ of summons to parliament as a Baron;[f] and on the 2nd August, 4 Edw. II. 1310, was enjoined to be at Berwick on Tweed, equipped for the field, to serve against the Scots.[g] As his life presents far more interesting objects of attention, it would be tiresome if not useless to state the date of every writ which he received to attend the King in his Scottish wars, it being sufficient to observe that his name appears on almost every occasion when an expedition was made into that country.

On the 17th of March, 1310, Badlesmere was appointed one of the peers to regulate the royal household;[h] and in the 5th Edw. II. 1312, he was constituted Governor of Leeds Castle: about that time he obtained a grant of various lands in Wiltshire; and on the 17th January and 16th August, 6 Edw. II. 1313, he was commanded, on pain of forfeiture of his possessions, not to attend a tournament which was proposed to be held at Newmarket.[i] He was, Dugdale says, again made Constable of the town, castle, and barton of Bristol, in the 6th Edw. II. 1312-13, which office he held in November, 1314;[k] and in March following he was Custos of Glamorganshire.[l] Badlesmere appears about that time involved in a

c Palgrave's " Parliamentary Writs," pp. 189, 190, 191.
d Rot. Scot. vol. I. p. 59.   e Ibid. p. 60.
f Appendix to the First Peerage Report, p. 198.   g Ibid. p. 202.
h Rot. Parl. vol. I. p. 443.   i Fœdera, N. E. vol. II. pp. 196 and 225.   k Ibid. p. 257.
l Ibid. p. 264.

dispute with the inhabitants of Bristol, a plea on the subject occurring on the rolls of parliament.[m]   He was present with.other peers in the 8th Edw. II. 1314-15, when the petition was heard from the Abbot and Convent of Rufford;[n] and attended the parliament when some proceedings took place with the ambassadors from Flanders.[o]   In the 9th Edw. II. 1315-6, he was present in parliament when the quarrel between the King and the Earl of Lancaster was settled;[p] and in the same year was one of the manucaptors of Theobald de Verdon.[q]   In February;. 9 Edw. II. 1316, he was sent to repress the rebellion of Llewellyn Prince of Wales;[r] and a few months afterwards he assisted at the ceremony of knighting Sir Richard de Rodney, and placed the spur on his left foot.[s]

Badlesmere was intended to have been dispatched to Scotland in August, 10 Edw. II. 1316, as letters of safe conduct were granted on the 28th of that month to Richard de la Lee, his clerk, Thomas de Eshe and Thomas de Chidecroft, his valets, who were sent to Newcastle upon Tyne to provide corn and other provisions against his arrival;[t] in December following the Bishops of Norwich and Ely, Earl of Pembroke, Otho de Grandison, and himself, were appointed ambassadors to Amadeus of Savoy;[u] and Dugdale asserts that in the 8th Edw. II. he and Grandison were sent in that capacity to the court of Rome.

In 1317 Edward the Second meditated a voyage to the Holy Land, and Badlesmere was, by writ tested on the 4th January in that year, directed to make the necessary preparations:[x] it was probably in relation to that object that he was appointed Ambassador to the Pontiff on the 8th January following;[y] from which time until July, many documents occur in the "Fœdera" connected with the Holy See; and in those negociations Badlesmere bore a very conspicuous part.[z]

His eminent services were in the 8th and 9th Edw. II. partially rewarded by a grant of the custody of Skipton Castle during the minority of Roger de Clifford; by an assignation of the proceeds out of the rents of the King's lands in

---

m Rot. Parl. vol. I. p. 359.   See also p. 434.   n Rot. Parl. vol. I. p. 298 b.
o Ibid. p. 359.   p Ibid. p. 351.   q Ibid. p. 353.   r Fœdera, N. E. vol. II. p. 283.
s Selden's Titles of Honour, p. 642, cited in Anstis's Collection of Authorities on the Order of the Bath, p. 8.   t Rot. Scot. vol. I. p. 162.
u Fœdera, N. E. vol. II. p. 302-3.   x Ibid. p. 309.   y Ibid. p. 311.
z Ibid. pp. 311, 335.

·Glamorgan and Morgansk; and by charters for free warren, markets, and fairs, in many of his lordships.

. In the 9th, 10th, and 11th Edw. II. he was in the Scottish wars; and in the latter year was once more appointed Constable of the Castles of Bristol and ·Leeds. He was sent to Northampton to treat with the Earl of Lancaster on the government of the realm; and on the 9th August, 12 Edw. II. 1318, was a party to the terms of agreement then determined on between the King and the Earl.[a]

Badlesmere became Steward of the King's household as early as November, 13 Edw. II. 1319;[b] and it is worthy of observation that in the various letters from Edward to the Pope, begging his Holiness to appoint Henry de Burghersh, Bishop of Lincoln, he constantly describes him as the nephew of Badlesmere:[c] this probably arose from the latter having become personally known to the Pontiff when an Ambassador at his court. On the 1st March, 13 Edw. II. 1319, he was appointed with Hugh le Despenser the younger, to reform the state of the Duchy of Acquitaine, and to remove all such officers there as were unfit to fulfil their duties:[d] on the 1st December in that year he was ordered to treat for a truce with the Scots;[e] and was present at the Friars Minors of York on the 23rd January, 13 Edw. II. 1320, when the King received the great seal from John Hotham, Bishop·of Ely, the Chancellor:[f] in March following he was appointed Ambassador to the King of France and to the Pope.[g] On the 19th January, 1321, he was sent with Aymer de Valence Earl of Pembroke, and many others, to treat for peace with Robert de Brus, at which time Badlesmere was still Steward of the Royal Household:[h] in the ensuing April he was Constable of Dover and of the Cinque Ports;[i] and on the 21st of that month commands

---

a Rot. Parl. vol. I. pp. 453, 454; and Fœdera, N. E. vol. II. p. 370.

· b Fœdera, N. E. vol. II. p. 405.

c Ibid. pp. 405, 406, 411, 412, 414, and others. Blore, in his " History of Rutland," states that Robert first Baron Burghersh married a sister of Bartholomew de Badlesmere, by whom he had the Bishop of Lincoln and his brother Bartholomew, who was probably named after his maternal uncle; and who was summoned to parliament from 1330 to 1354.

d Carte's Rot. Vasc. vol. I. p. 55. .   e Fœdera, N. E. vol. II. pp. 409-10.

f Ibid. p. 415.   g Ibid. pp. 419, 420.   h Ibid. p. 441.   i Ibid. p. 448.

were issued to him and several other peers to preserve the peace ; and they were
forbidden to give credence to false rumours.[k]

Lord Badlesmere obtained a release dated on the 20th August, 15 Edw. II.
1321, from all engagements contained in a writing by which he had bound himself to perform "plusurs choses,"[l] but of what nature they were does not appear.   From the date, this document seems to be the one which is referred to in
the Calendar of the Patent Rolls.[m]

Until this time Badlesmere's career was marked by uninterrupted success : his
talents and fidelity had been conspicuous both in the field and in diplomatic
affairs ; and he enjoyed in the highest degree the favour of his sovereign.   However
important his services were, and the simple statement of the occasions upon
which he was employed are sufficient evidence of the confidence which was reposed in him, his merits were amply rewarded.   He had been raised to the
peerage, and had received innumerable grants of lands ;[n] but more than all, as it
is unquestionable proof of Edward's regard, he was the Steward of his Household.   This brief review of the conduct of this Baron, and of the manner in
which he was treated by the king is material to the consideration of the causes
which could have induced an individual so deservedly honoured, to join a powerful rebellion against the royal dignity and authority ; for his conduct evinced
either the most exalted patriotism or the most despicable ingratitude.   Every
motive which is supposed to actuate the human heart must have bound Badlesmere to support the King, excepting those which ought to be paramount to all
others, a love of our country and of public and private liberty, and their insepa-
rable attendants, a hatred of injustice and oppression.   It argues, then, powerfully
against Edward that even his friends and the officers of his house deserted him ;
and instead of that desertion exciting our compassion for his situation, it only
tends to raise those who abandoned him in our good opinion ; since to have
submitted longer would have been to approve of the unhappy state into which
the realm was thrown by his weakness or his vices.

The fact, then, that Badlesmere joined the Earl of Lancaster and the other
Barons in the effort to produce a reform in the government can scarcely create
surprise, and ought not to be considered as a stain upon his character.   He

---

[k] Fœdera, N. E. vol. II. p. 448.   [l] Ibid. p. 454.   .   .   [m] Page 90 a.
[n] See Calendar to the Patent Rolls, pp. 69 b, 70, 73, 78, 82, 84, 84 b, 85.

forfeited, it is true, his fidelity to his sovereign, but it is at least doubtful if he did not thereby preserve his fidelity to his country. The first act of disobedience he committed was to go from Tilbury in Essex to Hengham in Kent, where being met by some of his adherents, and having taken part of his soldiers out of his castle of Leeds, he marched to Chilham, and thence to Canterbury, with nineteen knights; and visited the shrine of St. Thomas. At Canterbury he was joined by his wife and John de Cromwell, soon after which he proceeded to the Barons at Oxford. The King having sent the Queen to Leeds Castle, where she was denied admittance by the persons whom Badlesmere had left to guard it,[o] siege was immediately laid to the castle, and its owner having failed in persuading the confederated peers to march to its relief, it fell into the King's hands, when Margaret, the wife of Lord Badlesmere, and Giles his son and heir, were taken prisoners and conveyed to the Tower.

On the 26th December, 1321, a writ was issued to the Sheriff of Gloucester to arrest him, and to inquire by a jury, to whom he had given protection, for what time, and their names;[p] and he, with the other rebellious Barons, having entered and burnt Bridgenorth, they were declared to have forfeited all their lands.[q]

So inveterate was Edward's resentment against Badlesmere, that, when at the request of the Earls of Richmond, Pembroke, Arundel, and Warren, he gave Roger de Mortimore of Wigmore safe and sure conduct with any forty persons of condition whom he chose to select, to come from Belton le Strange to treat with those Earls, on the 17th January, 15 Edw. II. 1322,[r] this Baron was specially excepted from being one of the number. The following curious letter, which is translated from the copy in the " Fœdera," shows that Badlesmere was then at Pomfret. It was addressed to Ralph Lord Neville, and was sealed with the seal of James de Douglas: it was probably written early in 1322.

" Sire,—Know that the treaty which was to take place between us is nearly completed, as the Earl of Hereford, Monsr Roger Dammory, Monsr Hugh D'Audley, Monsr Bartholomew de Badlesmere, Monsr Roger de Clifford, Monsr John Giffard,. Monsr Henry Tyes, Monsr Thomas Maudyt, Monsr John de Wylington, and I, and all the others, are arrived at Pomfret, and ready to give

o Writs to the Sheriffs of several counties relative to this circumstance, tested October 1321, are preserved in the Fœdera, N. E. vol. II. p. 467-8.

p Ibid. p. 469.   q Ibid. p. 471.   r Ibid. p. 472.

you surety[s] if you will perform the things proposed, that is to say to come to
our assistance, and to accompany us into England and Wales. Moreover we
also entreat that you will appoint a day and place where we may meet you to
perform the things faithfully, and to live and die with us in our quarrel. And
we pray you to cause us to have safe conduct for thirty horsemen to go safely
into your parts."[t]

Badlesmere was summoned to parliament from the 26th October, 3 Edw. II.
1309, to the 5th August, 14 Edw. II. 1320;[u] but his long and, unless his junction with the discontented Barons be considered to tarnish his former merits,
honourable career, terminated in the most tragical manner. On the 11th March,
15 Edw. II. 1322,[x] writs were directed to the Earls of Kent and Surrey to arrest
the Earl of Lancaster, this Baron, and his other adherents. In obedience to the
royal mandate the Earls marched with a strong force against them; and, as is
well known, defeated them at Boroughbridge in Yorkshire on the 16th March,
1322. Badlesmere shared the fate of his leader, the Earl of Lancaster: being
taken prisoner he was immediately sent to Canterbury to be drawn and hanged,
which sentence was accordingly executed. He was hung on a gallows at Bleen,
and his head being cut off, it was set on a pole at Burgate.

Lord Badlesmere was about forty-seven years of age at his death, and left issue
by his wife Margaret, who was born in 1289, the daughter of Thomas de Clare,
grandson of Richard Earl of Gloucester, a son, Giles, and four daughters; 1.
Margery, who married William Lord Roos;[y] 2. Maud, who married John de
Vere, Earl of Oxford;[z] 3. Elizabeth, who was first the wife of Edmund Mortimer, and secondly of William Earl of Northampton;[z] and 4. Margaret, who
married John Lord Tibetot.[z]

Lady Badlesmere continued a prisoner in the Tower for several months; but at
the intercession of her son-in-law, Lord Roos, and others, who engaged for her appearance on receiving three weeks notice, she obtained her release, when she entered the convent of Minoresses without Aldgate; and two shillings per diem were
allowed for her support, which were to be paid by the Sheriff of Essex. She was

s " Faire seurte vers vous."   t Fœdera, N. E. vol. II. p. 474.
u Appendix to the First Peerage Report.   x Fœdera, N. E. vol. II. p. 477.
y Calend. Rot. Patent. p. 103.   z Ibid. p. 220.

the sister of Richard de Clare, and aunt and coheiress of Thomas de Clare; Maud, her sister, married Robert de Clifford, and her son Robert de Clifford was the other coheir of the said Thomas de Clare.[a] In the reign of Edward the Third she petitioned for the restitution of certain lands which had been enfeoffed to her and her late husband,[b] and also for the castle of Leeds or her manor of Aderle ; and succeeded in obtaining the latter :[c] other lands were also ordered to be restored to her.[d]

Giles second Lord Badlesmere was fourteen years old at his father's death, and his wardship was committed to his cousin-german, Henry de Burghersh, Bishop of Lincoln. He obtained a restitution of his father's lands[e] which had been declared forfeited, and part of which were conferred on Eleanor the King's niece, wife of Hugh le Despencer;[f] and was summoned to parliament from the 9th to the 11th Edw. III. 1336 to 1337, but died in 1338 without issue; when his sisters before-mentioned became his heirs.

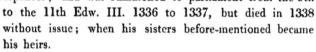

The arms of Badlesmere were, Argent, a fess between two bars gemells Gules ;[g] but when at Carlaverock the arms of Bartholomew de Badlesmere were differenced by a label Azure, his father being then living.

---

a Escheats, 14 Edw. II. No. 45, and 1 Edw. III.; and Calend. Rot. Patent. p. 147 b.

b Rot. Parl. vol. II. p. 430.   c Ibid. pp. 436, 437.   d Ibid. pp. 420, 422, 423.

e Calend. Rot. Patent. p. 103.   f Fœdera, N. E. vol. II. p. 491 ; and Calend. Rot. Patent. p. 91.

g Page 78, ante; and Cotton MSS. Caligula, A xviii.

JOHN DE CROMWELL.

[PAGE 78.]

Although Dugdale states that " there is notable mention in our public records of this family before any of them became Barons of the realm," he does not positively inform us who was the father of John de Cromwell, the first peer, but leaves it to be inferred that he was the son as well as successor of a Ralph de Cromwell who was living in the 35th Edw. I. It appears however from the inquisition on a Ralph de Cromwell, and who, it may be safely presumed, was the person mentioned by Dugdale, that he left Ralph his son his heir, and who was then only seven years of age.

Many reasons[h] could be adduced for believing that the subject of this article was not related to the Lords Cromwell of Tatshall; but as the pedigrees of that house are confused and contradictory, and as the usual sources of information, Inquisitiones post Mortem, relating to that family do not regularly occur, it is impossible to throw any light on the subject, without very considerable expense and labour.

The earliest occasion on which a John de Cromwell is mentioned in the reign of Edward the First is in 1292, when he was one of the manucaptors of Ralph de Cromwell, but it is doubtful if it was the same individual who was at the siege of Carlaverock in June, 1300.[i] He was then in the prime of life: we are told he was both brave and handsome, and that his shield was bruised and defaced by the stones that fell on it during the assault of the castle. In the 29th

---

h The arms of Cromwell, from whom the Lords of Tatshall descended, were, Argent, a chief Gules, over all a bend Azure, and which are attributed to "Le Seygnyer de Cromwell," in More's "Nomina et Insignia Gentilitia," though they do not occur on the Roll in the Cottonian MS. Caligula, A. xviii. The seal of Ralph Lord Cromwell, in December, 1370, to a charter in the British Museum, contains the same arms: that of Maud his wife, who styled herself " Lady of Tatshall," in November, 1417, (Ancient Charters, 49, A. 44,) and which is also annexed to the charter in 1370, contains four shields; the 1st, Tatshall; 2nd, Vaire, a fess; 3rd, Vaire, and a fess impaling a chief and a bend; 4th, three quintefoils and a canton.

i Rot. Parl. vol. I. p. 89.

Edw. I. he married Idonea, youngest daughter and coheiress of Robert de Vipount, hereditary Sheriff of Westmoreland, and widow of Roger de Leyburne; and on the 20th January, 31 Edw. I. 1303, he was ordered to place himself with horses and arms, and all his forces, under the command of John de Segrave, the King's Lieutenant in Scotland.[k] In the 33rd Edw. I. 1305, Cromwell became involved in a serious quarrel with Nicholas de Segrave, who had insulted him whilst in the King's service in Scotland; but as the dispute, the particulars of which are fully related on the Rolls of Parliament, has been alluded to in the memoir of that Baron, it is unnecessary to enlarge on the subject.[l]

As soon as Edward the Second ascended the throne, he loaded Cromwell with distinguished marks of his confidence and favour: on the 10th of March, I Edw. II. 1308, he caused him to be summoned to parliament as a Baron;[m] and in the same year he bestowed on him the castle of Hope in Flintshire, with the manor, for life, upon condition that he should rebuild that castle; he nominated him Governor of Striguil Castle; and also appointed him to the important situation of Constable of the Tower of London, an office which he held with but short intermissions during his life.[n] From the 1st Edw. II. to the 7th Edw. III. numerous writs were directed to him or to his seneschal, commanding him to raise from forty to sixty foot soldiers from the lands of Hope.[o] During the reign of Edward the Second, and in the early part of that of Edward the Third, he was repeatedly commanded to serve in the Scottish wars.[p] On the 17th March, 3 Edw. II. 1310, he was one of the peers appointed to reform the royal household;[q] and on the 8th March, 5 Edw. II. 1312, he was ordered to treat with other peers relative to certain ordinances which they had made.[r] In July, 1310, he was constituted Ambassador to the King of France:[s] on the 15th

---

k Palgrave's "Parliamentary Writs," p. 369; and Fœdera, N. E. vol. II. p. 948.

l See pp. 123, 124, ante, and Rolls of Parliament, vol. I. pp. 172, 174.

m Appendix to the First Peerage Report.

n In the 8th Edw. III. the year before that in which Cromwell is supposed to have died, the King granted the office of Keeper [Custos] of that fortress to William de Montacute, after the death of John de Cromwell " custodis ejusdem."

o Rot. Scot. vol. I. pp. 106, 120, 127, 159, 171, 176, 185, 231; and Fœdera, N. E. vol. II. pp. 857, 863.

p Appendix to the First Peerage Report.　　　q Rot. Parl. vol. I. p. 443 b.

r Fœdera, N. E. vol. II. p. 159; and Rot. Parl. vol. I. p. 447.　　s Fœdera, N. E. vol. II. p. 110.

4 x

April, 5 Edw. II. 1311, he was sent to Boulogne sur Mer to treat with certain persons sent there by that monarch ;[t] and in the 6th Edw. II. 1312, he was dispatched on the King's service into Gascony, and obtained a precept to the Constable of Bordeaux to pay him £50 sterling towards his expenses on the occasion. In January, 6 Edw. II. 1313, he was ordered to treat with some Cardinals ;[u] and in the 7th Edw. II. 1314, he was sent with Henry de Scrope into Wales, when he was allowed ten marks for his charges, which were to be paid by the Chamberlain of Caernarvon. He was commanded with three others to hear and determine all complaints against John de Segrave or his servants in the execution of his duties of Keeper of the Forests beyond the Trent, and of the castles of Nottingham and Derby, in the 8th Edw. II. 1314 ;[x] and also to inquire into the petition presented by the inhabitants of Nottingham relative to the state of the bridges and causeways in that county.[y]

In December, 10 Edw. II. 1316, Cromwell was sent with Badlesmere and others on an embassy to the Pontiff ;[z] and in the 11th Edw. II. 1317, he was made Governor of Tickhill Castle in Yorkshire: he received a grant of various lands in that year; again in the 11th,[a] 12th[b] and 15th Edw. II. ;[c] and in the 14th Edw. II. he was one of the manucaptors of Henry Tyes.[d]

Excepting that Cromwell's name appears among the Barons who were forbidden to attend the assembly which the Earl of Lancaster had appointed to meet at Doncaster on the 12th November, 15 Edw. II. 1324,[e] the evidence in favour of the opinion that he escaped the vicissitudes of fortune which attended the peerage in the reign of Edward the Second, was so strong, and the probability that he adhered under every circumstance to the cause of his sovereign, so great, that some remarks on the subject were actually written; but proof was afterwards discovered that he was connected with the rebellion of the Earl of Lancaster, as his estates were consequently forfeited, and he did not recover them until the 1st Edw. III., when commands were issued to the Sheriffs of York, Wiltshire, Nottingham, Warwick, Rutland, Bedford, Bucks, Northampton, and Lincoln, to restore to him his lands in those counties.[f]   But,

---

t Fœdera, N. E. vol. II. p. 166.   u Ibid. p. 197.   x Rot. Parl. vol. I. p. 325 a.

y Ibid. p. 333 a.   z Fœdera, N. E. vol. II. p. 303.   a Calend. Rot. Patent. p. 84 b.

b Ibid. p. 86 b.   c Ibid. p. 91.   d Rot. Parl. vol. I. p. 385.

e Fœdera, N. E. vol. II. p. 459.   f Rot. Parl. vol. II. p. 422 a.

though his territories were withheld from him, he evidently recovered Edward's favour,[g] for, in the 18th Edw. II. 1324, he was appointed Admiral of the King's fleet towards the Duchy of Gascony; and as Dugdale says that he attended Queen Isabel to France in that year, it may be inferred that he commanded the ships which escorted her across the channel.

On the accession of Edward the Third he was re-appointed Constable of the Tower of London; and was soon afterwards enjoined to serve in the wars of Scotland. Having been summoned to parliament from the 10th March, 1 Edw. II. 1308, to the 1st April, 9 Edw. III. 1335, he " departed this life soon after," according to Dugdale; but, as his name occurs among the Inquisitiones post Mortem in the 7th Edw. III., it is most probable that he died in that year.

His wife was, as has been before observed, Idonea,[h] the daughter and coheiress of Robert de Vipount; but the statement of Dugdale, that he was the ancessor of the Lords Cromwell of Tatshall is too doubtful to be repeated.

The arms borne by John Cromwell at Carlaverock, were, Azure, a lion rampant double queued Argent, crowned Or;[i] but, agreeably to the Roll of Arms in the Cottonian MS. he then used the coat of Vipount, Gules, six annulets Or,[k] of which family his wife was one of the coheiresses.

---

g In the 6th Edw. III. he and Idoigné his wife petitioned, stating that, by a statute made at Westminster soon after the coronation, the fines levied by Hugh le Despenser by force and constraint should be reversed at the suit of the parties, and, that as they had levied a fine to him by force and menace, and at peril of their lives, they prayed that they might not be disinherited by the effects of it, to the damnation of his soul. Rot. Parl. vol. II. p. 68.

h Blore, in his " History of Rutland," says she died s. p. before the 8th Edw. III.

i Page 78, ante.　　　　　　　　　k Caligula, A. xviii.

JOHN DE CRETING.

[PAGE 78.]

There are several reasons for believing that this Knight was the individual who many years afterwards was raised to the dignity of a Baron of the realm; but, notwithstanding that that circumstance occasioned him to be noticed by Sir William Dugdale, few facts can be stated of his life.

He was the son of Sir Adam de Creting, who died in the 24th Edw. I. 1296, seised of lands in the counties of Essex, Huntingdon, Suffolk, and Shropshire, and also in Wales.[1] Two inquisitions were held on his decease, one in the 24th Edw. I. and the other in the 27th Edw. I., by the former of which John his son and heir was found to be seventeen, and by the latter twenty-four years of age, a trifling discrepancy not uncommon in those records. The precise time of his birth cannot therefore be determined, but it evidently occurred between 1275 and 1279; and as he must have been of full age, if not a few years beyond it, when he was at the siege of Carlaverock, the first of those statements is the most likely to be correct. Dugdale asserts that he was born at Striguil in Wales, and that he accompanied his father in the expedition into Gascony in the 22nd Edw. I.; but this is not very probable, since he could not, according to either of the inquisitions just cited, have been then more than nineteen years old.

The manner in which Creting is spoken of by the Poet is not a little ambiguous; and, though the passage is translated that he was in danger of losing his horse by a person pricking it with an arrow, and that he used such haste to strike him that he did not appear to be dissembling, considerable doubt is entertained of the accuracy of the version. It is however certain that he rendered himself conspicuous in the assault of the Castle; and it is said that he was again in the wars of Scotland in the 34th Edw. I. 1305-6. Among the petitions on the Rolls of Parliament of the reigns of Edward the First and Second, but to which the exact date cannot be assigned, is one from John de Creting, stating that

---

[1] Esch. 24 Edw. I. No. 47, and 27 Edw. I. No. 25.

Adam de Creting his father had borrowed two hundred and twenty marks of the King's Wardrobe towards the war in Gascony, and which were now demanded of him; but as he had heard that the King had remitted the claim of others who were so situated, he prayed that he might also be pardoned the debt; and he was answered that the King " le pardone du tot."[m]

On the 30th June, 8 Edw. II. 1315, he was commanded to serve with horse and arms against the Scots;[n] and on the 20th February, 18 Edw. II. 1325, was summoned from the counties of Huntingdon and Cambridge to attend, similarly equipped, in Acquitaine.[o] In the 4th Edw. III. 1330, he obtained 'a charter for free warren in his manor of Stocton Magna in Huntingdonshire;[p] and on the 27th January, 20th July, 20th October, and 11th December, 6 Edw. III. 1325,[q] he was summoned to parliament as a Baron; after which time nothing is recorded of him.

Creting probably died about 1333 or 1334, when he must have been nearly sixty years of age, but no inquisition was held on his decease, nor has any pedigree been found. It is evident, that his lands were inherited by his family, for in the 7th Ric. II. 1383-4, Thomas de Cretings held the manor of Barwe in Suffolk;[r] and in the 22nd Ric.[!]II. 1398-9, Edward Creting was possessed of three parts of the manor of Fornham, and John Creting held Barwe and part of Fornham, in that county,[s] each of which manors became the property of John Baron Creting on the death of his father Sir Adam in the 24th Edw. I.; but whether the said Thomas, John, and Edward Creting were his immediate descendants has not been ascertained.

The other facts relating to this family which have been discovered, are, that Isabella is called the daughter and heiress of an Adam de Creting in a collection of notes from records, and apparently upon the authority of an inquisition, 24 Edw. I.;[t] that in 1307 Roger Bigot, Earl of Norfolk, held of John de Creting, in Romford in Essex, one capital messuage, 180 acres of arable and five of meadow, 100 of pasture called Layes, and 54s. rent, by the service of one penny

---

m Rot. Parl. vol. I. p. 462.   n Rot. Scot. vol. I. p. 146.
o Fœdera, N. E. vol. II. p. 591.   p Calend. Rot. Chart. p. 164.
q Appendix to the First Peerage Report, pp. 410, 413, 417, 419.
r Calend. Inquisit. post Mortem, Esch. 7 Ric. II. vol. III. p. 63.   s Ibid. pp. 241-2.
t Cotton. MSS. Claudius, A. viii., the references cited are, " R. I. 24 Edw. I. r. 6."

per annum;[u] that on the 3rd October, 11 Edw. III. 1337, and on the 23rd May, 12 Edw. III. 1338, an Edmund de Cretyng[x] received letters of protection, he being then about to accompany the Earl of Northampton beyond the sea;[y] and that in the 38th Edw. III. 1364, Margaret, the daughter of Richard Creting, released to John de Montpiliers and Joan his wife, divers lands in Suffolk.[z]

The arms of Creting were, Argent, a chevron between three mullets Gules;[a] but in the contemporary Roll of Arms, where the name of "Sir Johan de Cretinge" occurs among the knights of Suffolk, they are thus blazoned, " de Argent, a un cheveron e iij rouwels de Goules.[b]

---

u Inq. 35 Edw. I. cited in Morant's Essex, vol. I. p. 64.

x The following abstract of a deed of Edm' de Creting, occurs in the Cottonian MS. Julius, C. vii. f. 175, with a drawing of the beautiful seal which was attached to it, which contains a shield charged with a chevron between three mullets, surmounted by a helmet, on which is an armed leg with a spur affixed, the foot uppermost, issuing from a ducal coronet.

"Edm' de Creting, Ch'l'r, conc' Joh'n' de Abindon, pisc'io London', terr' in manerio de Stock. ton, et ij p'tes advocac'o'is eccl'iæ de Stockton, in com' Hunt', Hawisia uxor ejusdem Joh'is, test', Johannes D'engayne, Will'us Moyne, Ric'us de Baiocis, Guido de S'to Claro, Joh'es de Papworth, Milites; Hugo de Croft, Nic' de Stukle, &c. Dat' ib'm xvj Maij, aᵒ 22 Edw. III." 1348.

y Fœdera, N. E. vol. II. p. 997 and p. 1037.

z Extracts from the Clause Rolls in the Harleian MS. 1176, f. 3.

a Page 81, ante.   b Cotton. MSS. Caligula, A. xviii.

Every thing which has been ascertained of this Knight will be found in the account of Edmund Lord Deincourt in a former page, where it is conjectured that he was a younger son of that Baron.

His arms, the Poet informs us, were, Azure, billetée and a fess dancette Or.

"THE BROTHERS BASSET."

[PAGE 83.]

Barren as many of the memoirs of the Knights who were at the siege of Carlaverock are, not only of interest, but of facts of any kind, the attempt to collect particulars of their lives has never proved more fruitless than with respect to "the brothers Basset."

We may conclude, from the Roll of Arms which has been so useful in identifying many of the individuals who have been noticed in these memoirs, that their names were Sir Edmund Basset and Sir John Basset, and that they were knights of the county of Gloucester. It might have been inferred from their being mentioned in that Roll that they were both living in the 10th or 12th Edw. II., when it is presumed to have been compiled; but an Edmund Bassett, of Gloucestershire, is recorded as " deceased" in the 4th Edw. II. 1310-11[c]; and according to the inquisition held on his death, he was possessed of lands in Gloucestershire and Somersetshire, and left his three sisters, Isabel, the wife of John Pinchardine; Margaret, the wife of Nicholas Valeirs; and Katherine, the wife of John Bisset; his heirs.[d]

A John Bassett was elected by the community of the county of Rutland to be one of the assessors or collectors of the fifteenth in the 29th Edw. I. 1300 ;[e] and was Sheriff of that county in 1302.[e] If the Edmund Basset who died in the 4th Edw. II. was at Carlaverock, the inquisition tends to raise a doubt as to whether the word "frere" does not mean " brother" in a military sense rather than in the common acceptation of the word ; because if the " brother" who was with him at that siege survived him, his sisters would not have been his heirs. The slight difference between their arms, however, supports the idea of their relationship.

Notwithstanding that it has been suggested that the names of the " brothers Bassett" were Edmund and John, some grounds exist for supposing that one of them was called Robert; for immediately after speaking of them, the Poet says, the " brother Robert" cast numerous stones from the Robinet; and in 1297 a

---

[c] Rot. Orig. p. 174, et seq.

[d] Esch. 4 Edw. II. No. 41. The following pedigree of Bassett, which occurs in the Harleian MS. 1041, f. 20, is cited in Fosbroke's " History of Gloucestershire."

Sir Aunselme Bassett, Knt.=Margaret, daughter to .... Lemahen.

| Sir Edmond Bassett, ob. s. p. [Esch. 4 Edw. II.] John Bassett, ob. s. p. | Isabel, sister and co-heiress. | =[John] Pyncharde [Pinchardin]. | Margaret, mar. [Nicholas] Valiers[is]. | Katherine, [mar. John Bisset.] |

Elizabeth, 1st wife.=Symon Pynchard.=Maud, 2nd wife.

| Elizabeth, 1st wife. | =John Pynchard.=Isabel. | Edmond Pynchard,=Margery. alias Bassett. | Mary, died before her father. |

Margaret, ob. s. p.   Sir Simon Bassett.=Maud, dau. and heir of Sir John Bytton.

A quo the Bassetts of Yewley in Gloucestershire.

The arms there attributed to the family of Bassett of Yewley are, Quarterly, 1st and 4th, Ermine, on a canton Gules a mullet pierced Or ; 2nd, Ermine, a fess Gules ; 3rd, Gules, a bend between six cross crosslets Or.

[e] Palgrave's " Parliamentary Writs," Digest, p. 449.

Robert Basset was returned from the counties of Nottingham and Derby as holding lands there, and was consequently summoned to the Scottish wars in July, 1297,[f] and on the 24th June, 1301 ;[f] and another Robert Basset, who is described as of Rushton, and an Esquire, was similarly summoned from Northamptonshire in the former of those years.[f] It is possible, however, that the Robert who conducted the robinet was Robert de Tony, and if it was any other person than a Robert Basset, the doubt which has just been expressed as to the meaning of the word "frere" is confirmed. But the name of Basset is too common to pursue the inquiry upon such uncertain evidence as the Poem affords.

The arms of the eldest of the brothers Basset, were, Ermine, on a chief indented Gules three mullets Or ;[g] and which, in the Roll of Arms, are assigned to Sir Edmund Basset.[h]

And of the other brother, Ermine, on a chief indented Gules three escallops Or,[g] and which are ascribed in that Roll to Sir John Basset.[h]

---

f Palgrave's " Parliamentary Writs," Digest, p. 450.

g Page 83, ante.

h Cottonian MSS. Caligula, A. xviii.

NOTES.

Page 2, line 12. *Cotes et Surcos.* Dr. Meyrick observes, " Cotes is here introduced merely for the sake of the metre, for strictly speaking it is the *juste au corps* which was worn when the person was out of armour. It was never at this period emblazoned, and therefore must in the present instance be considered as synonymous with Surcos. The surcoat, which had been adopted by the crusaders in the thirteenth century to prevent their mail armour from being heated by the sun's rays, a mode still continued by the Mamelukes of Egypt, was at first of merely variegated pattern, but soon became embellished with the same armorial bearings as the shield: hence the expression " coat of arms." It was a long loose dress without sleeves, open before and behind for the convenience of riding, and girted round the waist by the cingulum militare or belt. It was put on over the hauberk, and reached to the neck, and when the hood was placed on the head it was covered by it as far as the shoulders. The front and back were emblazoned alike."

Page 4, line 5. *Eschieles.* " Although this word has been translated ' squadrons,' it must not be understood in the modern confined sense of the word, any more than ' battalion' for *battaile.* The latter is equivalent to our word *line* or *column,* and the former to a *division of an army.* It is from the same source as the present term echellon, from representing the steps of a ladder, which would be the appearance of the four eschieles moved from one line a little in advance of each other, without the diagonal direction now given to this kind of march." Dr. Meyrick.

Page 5, line 2. del. " and sacks of."

Ibid. line 11. Read, " Henry, the good Earl of Lincoln, who was clasped and embraced by prowess, and who hath it sovereign in his heart, leading the first squadron, has," &c.

Page 11, line 4. For " He was with the Count," read " He belonged to the Earl."

Page 12, line 28. *Bacheliers.* " This word is contracted from two,—*bas-chevaliers,* and means the class generally termed poor knights. A further confusion was afterwards occasioned by the expression knights-bachelors." Dr. Meyrick.

Page 13, line 10. Perhaps the following is a preferable translation of the last sentence : ".I cannot recollect what other Bannerets were there ; but, if I sum up the truth thereof for you, there were full a hundred good bachelors there, not one of whom ever alighted at quarters till they had searched the suspected passes. 'Along with them rode every day the Marshal, the harbinger, who assigned quarters to those who were to be lodged."

Page 15, line 16. The translation should have been, "He had in his company Henry de Percy, his grandson, who seemed to have made a vow to disperse [or put to rout] the Scots."

Page 17, line 1. The sentence ought to have stood thus : " Walter de Moncy was joined to this company," &c.

Ibid. line 8. " Burele," or " burlee," has been translated, upon the authority of Roquefort, " stuff," but it undoubtedly meant " barry." In a Roll of Arms of the reign of Edward the Second, in a contemporary MS. in the British Museum, Caligula, A. xviii., the word often occurs in that sense, thus :

" Le Counte de Penbroc, *burele* de argent e de azure, od les merelos de goules."

" Sire Robert de Estoteville, *burlee* de argent e de goules a un lion rampand de sable," &c.

Ibid. line 11. " Of great fame," the following words of the original would have been better rendered, " whose feats had many a time appeared in wood and plain."

Page 18, line 2. The omission of two words in the translation is important, since, as has been noticed in the Preface, they perhaps afford a clue to the author of the Poem. The whole should have stood :

" Guy Earl of Warwick, as is said in my rhyme of Guy," &c.

Page 19, line 9. It has been suggested that this sentence ought to have been thus rendered : " We have drawn that of Tatteshal with them for his valour, of gold and red, chequered, with a chief ermine."

Ibid. last line. The word "him" ought perhaps to have been omitted.

Page 20, line 9. *Prestes a luscier les ventailles.* " At the end of the reign of Edward the First, the skull-cap had been pretty generally laid aside for the superior protection which the bascinet afforded. The helmet was then but seldom used except in tournaments, when it was put over it, and reached almost to the shoulders. For war, as being lighter, the ventaille, which covered the face, was fitted in the bascinet, and made to move on a pivot at each side. These words therefore mean that the knights were ' ready to let down (or lower) their ventailles,' which, to admit a greater freedom of breathing, had been pushed up. One of the equestrian figures on the monument of Aymer de Valence affords a good specimen of the bascinet with its ventaille at this period." Dr. Meyrick.

Page 21, line 6. A material variation has been suggested from the translation there given : " John de Beauchamp bore handsomely a banner of vair to the gentle weather and south-west breeze." A rhythmical version might in this instance have been easily attained :

" Handsomely bore his banner of vair,
To the gentle weather and south-west air."

Page 23. After the words " at a little distance," the following version is preferable : " and managed the order of march so closely and ably that no one was separated from the others. In his banner were three leopards of fine gold set on red, cruel, fierce, and haughty, thus placed to signify that like them the King is dreadful, fierce, and proud to his enemies, for his bite is slight to none who are envenomed by it; not but his kindness is soon rekindled when they seek his friendship again, and are willing to return to his peace. Such a Prince must be well suited to be the chieftain of noble personages."

Page 27, line 6. Instead of " He had a long," &c. read, " He had a long and broad banner of good silk, not of cloth," &c.

Ibid. p. 15. The account of Lord Clifford has been also thus rendered : " Robert the Lord of Clifford, to whom reason gives assurance of overcoming his enemies as often as he can call to mind his noble lineage, taketh Scotland to witness that it hath its rise well and nobly, as he that is of the seed of the noble Earl Marshal, who beyond Constantinople," &c. but Dr. Meyrick observes on the word *confort*, " that it must be considered rather as implying exhortation or excitement. When Odo, in the Bayeux tapestry, is represented as urging on a body of troops, the explanation is ' Hic Odo confortat pueros ;' *i. e.* Here Odo gives renewed energy to the lads. The word ' confort' in this sense is one of those engraved on the blade of the sword of James IVth of Scotland, still preserved in the Heralds' College." Lord Clifford's descent from the Earl Marshal has been shown in the memoir of his life.

Page 31, line 6. " Ki va prouesse reclamant," may mean " whose cry of war is ' Prowess.' "

Page 33, line 1. " He who hath a heart disposed to do good," is a preferable translation.

Page 35, line 4. Read, " That of the Earl of Lennox I knew to be red with a white lion, and the border was white with roses of the field."

Ibid. line 7. For " Count," read " Earl."

Ibid. line 10. For " Suwart," read " Siward."

Page 41, line 1. Read, " Also I recognised John de Grey there, who had his banner borne before him, inlaid barry of silver and blue with a red bend engrailed."

Page 42, line 20. *Blanche cote et blanche alettes.* " In the latter part of the reign of Edward I. were introduced those fanciful ornaments, placed on the shoulders capriciously, in the front, behind, or at the sides, which from their position were called Ailettes, or little wings. It is not clear whether, like the passguards at the beginning of the sixteenth century, they were designed to turn off the lance and protect the throat from the stroke of the sword. They were generally of an oblong shape, though sometimes pentagonal, and, as well as the surcoat, were emblazoned with the arms of the wearer. The effigy of Sir Roger de Trumpington, in brass, of this period, is a good example. The fashion continued until the commencement of the reign of Edward the Third." Dr. Meyrick.

Page 43, line 23. *Who well evinces that he is a Knight of the Swan.* As has been observed in the memoir of Robert de Tony, it is extremely difficult to explain the meaning of this allusion. According to the popular romance of the 𝔎𝔫𝔦𝔤𝔥𝔱 𝔬𝔣 𝔱𝔥𝔢 𝔖𝔴𝔞𝔫, the Counts of Boulogne were lineally descended from that fabulous personage, and genealogists of former ages have pretended to trace the pedigree of the houses of Beauchamp Earls of Warwick,

5 A

Bohun Earls of Hereford, and Stafford Earls of Stafford and Dukes of Buckingham, from the same source, whence they say they derived their respective crests.[a] It would not perhaps be difficult to deduce the descent of Robert de Tony from the Counts of Boulogne, and the accurate knowledge of genealogy which the Poet has displayed in his account of Lord Clifford,[b] justifies the idea that he referred to Tony's pedigree, an opinion which is further supported by the fact of the shield, on his seal affixed to the Barons' letter to the Pope in the year 1301, being surrounded by lions and *swans* alternately. But it must not be forgotten that a custom then prevailed for Knights to make their vows of arms " before the swan." " The ceremony of conferring knighthood upon Edward Prince of Wales in 1306," Mr. Palgrave observes,[c] " was performed with great splendour. Whilst they were sitting at the feast, the minstrel entered, gaily attired, and required of the knights, but principally the younger ones, to make their vows of arms before the swan;" or, to preserve the words of the original, " Eodem die cum sedisset Rex in mensa, novis militibus circumdatus, ingressa menestrellorum multitudo, portantium multiplici ornatu amictum, ut milites, præcipuè novos, invitarent et inducerent ad vovendum factum armorum aliquod coram Cygno." *Trivetus*, p. 342.

Although Tony might on a former occasion have made his vows " before the swan," it does not explain why he only of the Poet's heroes should have been described as a " Knight of the Swan," and still less why he should have assumed that badge on his seal, since the ceremony must have been common to the whole of the chivalry of the period. As Guy de Beauchamp, Earl of Warwick, married Alice, the sister and heiress of Robert de Tony, that family became doubly descended from the " Knights of the Swan," if the invaluable distinction was possessed by the Baron.

Page 47, line 1. Instead of the translation there given the following has been suggested : " He takes his way with the others, for he and the before named were appointed to conduct and guard the reind of the King's son. But as I reckon them, St. John [and] Latimer were first given him for the arrangement of his squadron, as those," &c.

Ibid. line 14. The sons of " my Lord Edmond, the best beloved brother of the King, whom I ever heard so called."

Page 49, line 9. For " He by whom," &c.. " He whose love was well supported and brought to an end, after great doubts and fears until it pleased God he should be delivered therefrom, endured for a long time great sufferings for the Countess of Gloucester. He had a banner," &c.

Page 51, line 11. The difficult passage relating to Alan le Zouche has been also rendered, " Alan le Zouch, to signify [to show by a sign or type] that he was a squanderer of treasure, bore bezants on his red banner, for I know well that he has spent more treasure than he hung in his purse."

---

[a] Ashmole's MSS. Dugdale, G. 2.   [b] See page 186.   [c] Parliamentary Writs, p. 71, note.
[d] *i. e.* to be his counsellors and guardians in battle.

Page 53, line 4. A different translation of the account of the Bishop of Durham has been suggested : " With them were joined, both in company and affection, the followers of the noble Bishop of Durham, the most vigilant clerk in the kingdom, yea, verily, of Christendom. I will tell you truly why, if you will attend to me. Wise he was and well spoken, temperate, just, and chaste. You never came near a rich man who better regulated his life. Pride, covetousness, and envy he had quite cast out. Not but that he carried a lofty heart for the maintenance of his rights, so that he suffered not tamely any conspiracy of his enemies, for so strongly was he influenced by a just conscience, that it was the astonishment of every one. He had been in all the King's wars in noble array, [attended by] great persons and at great charges. But owing to some outrage, whereof a suit was set on foot against him, he was kept in England, so that he came not into Scotland. However, he so well remembered that the King undertook the expedition, that," &c.

Page 55, line 9. Rather perhaps, " He who all honour teaches, John de Hastings is his name, was to be leader there on his account, for he had continued with him the most intimate," &c.

Page 59, line 10. Instead of, " To those last named," &c. this translation has been given : " In addition to the last named I have reckoned, not including attendants, eighty-seven banners, which quite filled the roads to the castle of Carlaverock, which will not be taken by check of rook," &c. Although the Poet says there were only eighty-*seven* banners, he had already described eighty-*eight*.

Page 61, line 2. Another version of this passage is, " Curlaverock was so strong a castle that it did not fear a siege before the King came there. For it had never been its fate to surrender; but was in its own power [maintained its own right]. Stored it was, when need thereof should come, with men," &c.

Page 63, line 17. Instead of " Consequently those of the castle," &c. a better version appears to be, " Wherefore I well believe that those of the castle might then divine that they were never in such peril. Which they might call to mind when they saw us arrive, drawn up as we were. We were lodged by the Marshals, and all assigned in every place, and then might be seen," &c.

Page 65, line 15. For " quarreaus," read " quarrels." " They were so called from their heads being quarrée, or square-sided, and were arrows, short in reference to their thickness, shot either from cross-bows, or the machines resembling them." Dr. Meyrick.

Ibid. line 18. For, " In one short hour," read, " In a short time."

Page 66, line 8. *Chapeaus et heaumes.* " The chapelle de fer, or iron hat, had a rim and a convex crown, and was worn over the capuchon or hood. One of the equestrian figures which ornament the canopy of the monument of Aymer de Valence has been already noticed; the other exhibits him wearing the chapelle de fer. The heaume or helmet was in shape a cone, swelling out in the middle. It was ornamented in front with a cross fleury, the transverse bar of which was pierced with occularia or openings for the sight. After being placed on the head it was kept from turning round, when struck, by cords, with which it was fastened to the shoulders. The effigy of Sir Roger de Trumpington not only gives its form, but shows that it was sometimes held to the body by means of a chain." Dr. Meyrick.

Ibid. line 9. *Escus et targes.* "The shield of the time of Edward I. differed from that of the preceding reign by having the curve at top so lowered as to form angles at the sides. The targe or target was, as well as the buckler, flat and circular, yet differed not only in being larger, but in its handle not extending quite across to the circumference. Both were held at arm's length." Dr. Meyrick.

Page 67, line 4. "Then might there," &c. is not so spirited a version as, "Then might there be seen stones fall as thick as if one must be covered with them, caps and helmets broken, shields and targets dashed in pieces, for to kill," &c.

Page 68, line 15. *Les enarmes.* "An examination of the monumental effigy of one of the Vere family, at Hatfield Broad-oak, certainly sculptured in the time of Edward I. although referred to an antecedent period, proves that the shield was not only furnished with a gig, as it was termed, for suspending it from the neck of the warrior, but two other straps for the arm and hand. These last were the 'enarmes,' and Skelton's engraved illustrations of armour, &c. show that this fashion for targets continued in the middle of the sixteenth century." Dr. Meyrick.

Page 70, line 14. *De grosses pieres et cornues.* "Great stones, during a siege, were hurled not only by machines, but with the hand. Over the doorway of the town-hall at Ratisbonne are two figures in armour, of the time of Edward IV., represented in the act of defending the entrance; one is hurling a great stone, the other holding the cornue. This weapon, sometimes termed besague, *i. e.* bis-acutum, was a staff with two horns of iron, formed in imitation of a pick-axe, though the broad end, or axe, was omitted for a pointed one." Dr. Meyrick.

Page 71, line 10. For, "Those of Richmont," read, "He of Richmont."

Page 72, line 24. *Meint riche gamboison.* "This dress, so called from its protection of the womb or abdomen, was of German origin, and, though often considered as sufficient armour itself, was generally, as in the passage quoted, worn under the hauberk. It was, according to an anonymous ancient writer, 'de rebus bellicis notitiæ Imperii,' put on before the hauberk, to prevent it from chafing the body, and it may be observed just beneath it in all monumental effigies of this period. It was externally garnie de soie, ornamented with silk, and stuffed with tow and cotton, stitched down in parallel lines, itself being of leather or cloth." Dr. Meyrick.

Page 73, line 1. After "Fly in the air," the following has been deemed the correct version; "For he and he of Richmont gather stones as they advance as though they were vieing with each other, whilst those within, in defiance, loaded their heads," &c.

Ibid. line 6 *et seq.* Nothing can be more opposite than the translation and one which has been suggested: "He of Graham did not escape; the whole of the shield that he shall carry off when he shall retire will not be worth two baked apples" [pommes cuites]. One of the MSS. reads " pomes quites," the other "promes quites."

Ibid. line 10. For, " Then you might hear," &c. " Do you hear? When the tumult began, a crowd of the King's people," &c. The interrogation being addressed to the reader or listener of the poem.

Page 75, line 15. The following version of the account of Ford and Wigton has been suggested, but it does not appear probable that such was the Poet's meaning : " Adam de la Forde mined the walls as well as he could : as thick as rain rains his stones fly within and without, whereby the gold of three lioncels rampant, natives of Ind, that he bore, was much injured. [As for the] good Baron of Wigtown, it is marvellous that he is not quite stunned by the blows that he receives, for though he is come hither without a lord, unattended, [or as a volunteer, without any immediate commander or retinue of his own] yet hath he not any the more on that account a countenance of alarm or fear." But this conjecture is proved to be erroneous, for an account of the payment of the wages of his retinue is preserved. See the memoir of this individual, page 342 ante.

Page 77, line 16. For " but as soon as," read, " but before," &c.

Ibid. line 20. " Et tant come bien le ai convoie," has been thought to refer to the writer himself, thus: " And (as I rightly take it) accompanied [i. e. Clifford's banner] by Bartholomew de Badlesmere, John de Cromwell made his attempt there as well as he could."

Page 80, line I. *Espringaut.* " The Espringalle, springal, springald, or springarde, as it was indifferently called, was a machine formed in imitation of the cross-bow, in order to eject quarrels of an immense size. Hence William Guiart, under the year 1304, says,

> Et font l'espringale gieter
> Li garros.
> And they made an espringale to cast
> Quarrels."
>   . Dr. Meyrick.

Page 81, line 1. This sentence has been considered to mean, " And shoot from their espringalls, and keep themselves quite a match both in casting and shooting."

Ibid. line 8. After the word " arms," the following translation is perhaps more correct : " Those who defended the gate very soon shelter their company, for no one else had assailed them so furiously before. However, they did not at all fail to give any one who came nigh a share of what they had to bestow, before he went away, till the sample was more than enough."

Ibid. line 17. After the word " horse," " When one came down upon it goading it with arrows, but he did not seem to be dissembling, he used such haste to get at the business. On his white," &c. is perhaps a preferable translation ; but the original is obscure.

Page 82, line 26. *Meint piere par robinet.* " The Robinet was one of that class of machines which threw stones ; but though the peculiarities of the onager and trepied may be pointed out, it is difficult to distinguish this from the matafunda, mate-griffon, bricolle, trebuchet, and others." Dr. Meyrick. The robinet used on this occasion is thus mentioned in the " Liber Quotidianus Contrarotulatoris Garderobæ," 28 Edw. I.: " Domino Thome de Bikenore, pro uno corio equino empto per ipsum ad lengas et alia necessaria inde facienda apud Carlaverok, pro ingenio Reg' quod dicitur Robinettus, per manus Ade Sellar' recipient' denariis apud Kirkudbright xxij die Julij—v *s.* vj *d.*" p. 65.

Page 83, line 10. After " three shells," has been suggested, " If those within had now sallied forth they would have found the passage straitened," &c. for the version there given.

Page 173. Upon the authority of Dugdale[d] it is said that in the 1st Edw. III. the Earl of Richmond obtained the King's license to grant the earldom of Richmond to his brother, *Arthur* Duke of Brittany, but that personage died before the 5th Edw. II. The remark in p. 174 upon the arms of the Earl has been also made by Nesbit.

Page 181. The extract from the Chronicle of Lanercost, which is inserted in page xiv, ought to have been noticed in the memoir of Hugh de Vere.

Page 324, line 10. Bertram de Montbourchier did not marry the heiress of Sir Richard Sutton. See Thoroton's Nottinghamshire. The Sir Richard or Guischard de Charon mentioned in line 23, is said in that work to have been a son of Guischard de Charon by a *second* wife, his *first* wife having been one of the coheirs of Sir Richard de Sutton, upon which Guischard or Richard, his father, with the consent of Stephen, his son by Mary de Sutton, settled the manor of Sutton.

Page 333. The following pedigree, for which the author is indebted to Thomas Stapleton, jun[r]. Esq. proves the remark, that no particulars are preserved of the family of Thomas de Richmont, to be erroneous :

...... Musard.

Hascoit Musard, held in demesne Keddington and Chilworth, co. Oxon, and Saintbury, co. Gloucester; he was also a tenant in capite in Derbyshire, Berks, and Bucks, at the time of the general survey.

Emsant Musard, also called in Domesday Enisan and Ernesi, first Constable of Richmond, under Alan Fergaunt, first Earl, Lord of Burton, Aldborough, Barningham, Easby, Stapleton upon Teys, Croft, Coldwell, Cleasby, Brompton, Thorp, Stanwick, Newton, Bolton, Kiplin, Brough, Hipswell, Hudswell, Masham, Middleton Quernhow, and Stratford, co. Ebor. of the fee of Earl Alan ; and of Eyford, Aston, Somerville, Siddington, St. Peter, and Miserden, co Glouc. of the fee of Hascoitt Musard at the time of the general survey, ob. s. p.

Richard Musard, son and heir according to Dugdale, vivens tempore Hen. I.

2. Roald Fitz Hascoit, second Constable of Richmond, under Stephen, third Earl; Lord of Burton, Aldborough, and most of the lands of his uncle the first Constable, by grant of Earl Stephen ; he founded an abbey on his manor of Easby in honour of St. Agatha, A. D. 1152, 17 Stephen, obiit .... buried at St. Agatha's.[e]

Graciana, daughter of ...... buried at St. Agatha's.

Isabella Musard.

Elias Giffard, Lord of Brimsfield, co. Glouc. Dugdale,vol. I. p. 501.

a   b

[d] Baronage, vol. I. p. 52.

[e] " Stephanus Comes Britanniæ omnibus Baronibus suis et hominibus suis de Anglia, Francigenis et Anglicis, salutem. Sciatis me dedisse et concessisse Roaudo filio Hariscodi Conestabulario meo et heredibus suis Bernincheham (Barningham), scilicet sex carucatas terræ in feudo et hereditate quemadmodum Herveus fi. Morini eas melius tenuit, et præcipio quòd bene et in pace et honorifice teneat. Testibus, Comitissa, Rogero Dapifero, Radulfo fi. Ribani, Akario, Scollando, Rogero de Sacel, Roberto Camerario, Alano Pincerno, Hugone fi. Iorn, Garnero fi. Guihomari Dapiferi, Roscelino fi. Ricardi." Madox's Baronia Anglica. The original is in the treasury of the Church of Westminster.

a   *b*

Alan Fitzroald de Richmond,[f] or de— | 2. William de | Elias Giffard, Lord of Brimsfield,
Burton, Constable of Richmond during | Burton. | co. Glouc.
the reigns of Henry II. Richard I. and | | Conan, son of Elias, Lord of Kirkby-
John; obiit .... [g] | | Fletcham, co. Ebor. temp. Ric. I.

Roald Fitzalan de Burton, or de Richmont,[h] Constable of Richmond temp.— | Amfeliza, uxor
Hen. III.; Lord of Burton, Aldborough, Caldwell, &c.; in the 32nd Hen. | Jollani de Neville,
III. 1248, sold his manor of Aldborough to the King; he rendered ward to | Lord of Rolles-
Richmond castle for 13 knights' fees; obiit temp. Hen. III. | ton, co. Notts.

Roald Fitz Roald, Lord of Burton, Caldwell, Croft, &c. at the time of Kirkby's Inquest, taken—
15 Edw. I. 1287, where he is generally styled Roald de Richmond, obiit temp. Edw. I.

Thomas de Richmont, or de Burton, Lord of Burton, Caldwell, Croft, &c.; sold Burton Con-—
stable to Geoffrey le Scrope, of Masham; PRESENT AT THE SIEGE OF CARLAVEROCK; he
was slain at Lintalee in the forest of Jedburgh in a personal rencounter with the famous James
Earl of Douglas, where the Earl of Arundel was defeated, A. D. 1316.[i]

Thomas, son of Thomas de Richmond, Lord of | John de Richmond, had lands in Cald-—
Caldwell, &c. released all his right in Burton to | well, for which he paid a fine to Sir
Geoffrey le Scrope, 6 Edw. III. A. D. 1333; sold all | Richard le Scrope, of Bolton, " pro re-
his lands to Henry le Scrope, of Bolton; ob. s. p. | laxanda secla curiæ ;" ob. ....

Isabella,[k] bur. in Drax=Sir Nicholas de Stapleton, Knight and Baron,=Elizabeth de Richmont,[l]
Priory, in Yorkshire, | Lord of Carlton by Snaith, co. Ebor. obiit 17 | daughter and sole heir-
1st wife. | Edw. III. 1343. | ess, 2nd wife.

Sir Miles de Stapleton, of Carlton, Knt.=Isabella, daughter of Sir Henry Vavasour, of
son and heir. | Hazlewood, co. Ebor.

Thomas de Stapleton, ob. s. p. | Elizabeth, sister and=Sir Thomas Metham, of
47 Edw. III. | sole heiress. | Metham, co. York.

---

[f] " Alanus filius Rualdi reddet compotum de c. et quater xx et x marcis pro habenda custodia Castelli de Richemunt cum Constabulatu in Thesauro xx marcas. Et debet c et lxx marcas. Mag. Rot. 5 Ric. I. Rot. 5. Everwichœc." Madox's History of the Exchequer, p. 317.

[g] This family are sometimes named from their office, as Roaldus Constabularius; sometimes also from their hereditary place, as Roaldus de Burton, or Roaldus de Richmond. Burton still retains the name of Constable affixed to it, now the seat of Marmaduke Wyvill, Esq. Conan, the son of Elias, was a witness to a deed of Alan the Constable to Jullanus de Neville, and to a grant of Lisiard, son of Robert to Helewise, widow of Robert, son of Ralph of Middleham. Helewise, who was a daughter of Ralph de Glanville, died A. D. 1195, 6 Ric. I.

[h] " Roaldus filius Alani debet c marcas et iii palfridos pro habenda carta Regis de quietancia sibi et heredibus suis et tenementis suis et omnibus militibus et libere tenentibus suis de Sectis Comitatûs et hundredorum et wapentac et treinges in perpetuum. Mag. Rot. 6 John, 14 his a." Madox.

[i] Leland's Collectanea, vol. I. p. 547, and Redpath's Border History, p. 253.

[k] Sir Nicholas de Stapleton released the Canons of Drax Priory from all services, rents, &c. for their premises in Camelsford, for the good of the soul of Isabel his wife, buried in Drax Priory." Burton's Monasticon Eboracense.

[l] Harleian MSS. 1487, f. 283, a copy of the Visitation of Yorkshire.

The following extracts from the contemporary copy of the Romance of " Guy Earl of Warwick," by Walter of Exeter, in the Harleian MSS. 3775, are here introduced as specimens of that production. The copy in the College of Arms, however, differs materially from them in many places.

It begins with a commendation of those authentic compositions whereby the noble and virtuous deeds of the " ancients, that have lived since the birth of our Lord and the diffusion of Christianity," are brought to light ; and states that the present narrative was about " an Earl who performed many laudable deeds; a good, valiant, and faithful Seneschal ; his daughter, a gentle and fair damsel; and how he loved a very beautiful girl, who was daughter to the Earl ;" to which follow,

En Engleterre un qens esteit
En Warewike la Cite manept
Riches ert de grant pouer
Copntes sages de grant saber
Riches dor et de argent
De dras de sepe et de nesselement
De fors chastels de Riche Citez
Par tut le Regne ert mult dotez
Habeit hom en tote la tere
Qi vers lui ogat prendre guere
Qi par force togt nel preit
E en sa chartre le meist
Bons chibalers mout ama
Riche dons sovent dona
Pur ceo fust creme et dote
Et par tut la Regne preise
Quens esteit de grant pris
Sires ert de top le pais
De Oxeneforte tote le honour
Sone esteit a icel iour
De Bokinham tut le counte
Sires esteit en cel tens clame
Li quens Roalt ont anoun
Mult par ert noble baroun
Une fille ont de sa moiller
Sa grant beaute ne sap counter

Pur la plu bele lout chopsie
Ore est resun qe ie vous die
Un petit de sa beaute
Le vis ont blanc et colore
Long treicis et abenant
Bele bouche nes ben seant
Les eols vers et le chef blop
De li ber vous semblat pop.
Ben fest de cors de beal estature
Tant par douce la regardure
Dortapse ert et ensegnee
De touz ars endoctrinee
Se mestres esteint venuz
De coulette touz blanc chaunuz
Qi la aparbepnt de astronomie
De arsmetrike et de jeometrie
Mult par ert fere de corage
Pur ceo qi eole esteit tant sage
Durz et countes le requereint
De mute teres pur lup benepnt
Mes nul de eus aber no boleit
Pur ceo qe tant noble osteit
Felice fu eole apelee
Pur sa beaute fu mult ame
De totes beautes ert eole la flur
Tant bele ne fust a cel iour

Qe tote teres adunqe cerchat   Qe tote sa beaute countercit

Une tant bele ne trobat   Trop grant domorance il freit.

The following lines are taken from the account of a battle, occasioned by the Emperor's anger at Guy's uniting in rebellion with the Duke Otho:

Quant Gi beit Heraut benir

E del fort estur eisser

Sun healme par lus quasse

E son esqu de terenche

E soun chibal qi naufre esteit

En fer estur este abeit

En haute bois se signe escrie

Al duc ad fest une en bope

Le compagnus Heraut ad rescus

E des seons pres et retenuz

Ou kil beit le Duc Otoun

Ferement le mostre sa raisoun

Duc pur qei me feites trair

E mes homes adel morir

Al pas del forest del pleins

Si bait deus et le seapns

Qe ieo des ore bous defi

Cum mon mortel enemi

A nul iour heite ne serreie

Si ieo de bous benge ne soie

Le chefs tresturnent de destrers

Enter ferir sen bont le bers

Grant coupes de glenbes trenchant

Les escuz ne lur bailut un ganz

Le Duc primer G. feri

Soun escu a or defendi .

Li hauberk fu bon ne se fausa

Qar trestut le gleibe depessa

Gi ad le duc feru

Parmi le cors dun espe molu

Pups unt tretes les espces

Entre ferir sen bont dure coles

G' lust ia le chef tolu

Quant socours li est abenu

De tels mil chibalers

Qi tous sunt pruz et legers

A Gi alerunt tuz ferir

De li occire unt grant desir

Mes G. cum leon se defent

Qui qil fert mort labate senglat

Sil unt pris pur lour segnour

Naufre le portut del estour

G sen segne et crie sobent

Ben ferir amoneste sa gent

Pups enter ferir se bont

Tant bons chibalers mourrunt

Emz qi le iour seit bien passe

Qar Gi sest durement pene

De Lumbars prendre et detrencher

Del deuc se bodra benger

Qua li fist la felonie

Dunt meint homo ad perdu la bie

Qi beid dunc Gi. tant bien ferir

E ses enemis si feire morir

E ses compaingnons tut ensement

Qi mult iferunt hardiement

Des espees de launces de tren-

schant dars

Occis en unt mult de Lumbars

5 c

Par lur: bon fet sunt descunfiz
Mors retenu et occis
Il sen vont G. les enchase
Repliz de mors en est la place
Gi les enchace et al sen vont
Cum cil qi discumfiz sunt
A tant. estevous le Duc Regner

E li conestable Walder
Quens lur Riches com
A un val unt G. encor
Mult lunt ferement es
Gi se retreit a une ple
Ensemble ou lui sa bo

The letter M. indicates the pages in which the Biographical Memoirs occur, and the references in *italics* are to the Notes.

Ailettes, 369.
Arundel, Richard Earl of, 50. M. 283.

Bachelor, 367.
Badlesmere, Bartholomew,78. M.348.
Baliol, Alexander de, 58. M.318.
Bardolf, Hugh, 6. M. 103.
Barr, John de, 24. M. 174.
Bassett, "the brothers," 82. M. 363.
Beauchamp, Guy; see Warwick.
————— John, 20. M. 168.
————— Walter, 30. M. 200.
Bek, Bp. Anthony, 54, 371. M. 288.
Berkeley, Maurice, 58, 80. M. 314.
Bohun; see Hereford.
Botetourte, 32. M. 202.
Brette; see La Brett.
Brittany, John of, 22, 80. M. 171.
Burton; see Richmont.

Carew, Nicholas, 16. M. 154.
Cantilupe, William, 40. M. 237.
Chapelle de fer, 371.
Clavering, John, 10. M. 117.
Clifford, Robert, 27, 28, 76, 86. M. 185.
Cornue, 372.
Courtenay, Hugh, 30. M. 193.
Creon, Maurice, 26. M. 184.
Creting, John, 78. M. 360.
Cromwell, John, 78. M. 356.

Dunbar, Patrick, 8th Earl of, 34. M. 210.
————, ————, 9th ————, 34. M. 211.
Daubeney, Elias, 24. M. 177.
Deincourt, Edmund, 56. M. 303.
————— John, 82. M. 363.
De la Ford, Adam, 74. M. 340.
De la Mare, John, 38. M. 231.

De la Ward, Robert, 50, 78. M. 280.
De la Warr; see La Ware.
Despenser, Hugh le, 28. M. 190.
Durham, Bishop of; see Bek.

Edward, the King, 2, 22, 86. M. 170.
Edward, Prince of Wales, 42, 46, 72. M. 243.
Enarmes, 372.
Engaine, John, 30. M. 199.
Eschiele, 367.
Espringal, 373.
EXETER, WALTER OF, v.

Ferrers, William de, 48. M. 273.
Fitz Alan, Brian, 36. M. 221.
————— Richard; see Arundel.
Fitz Marmaduke, John, 56, 68, 70. M. 307.
Fitz Payne, Robert, 14. M. 142.
Fitz Roger, Robert, 10. M. 115.
Fitz Walter, Robert, 4. M. 99.
Fitz William, Ralph, 18. M. 162.
Ford; see De la Ford.
Frescl, Simon, 36. M. 216.
Furnival, Thomas, 38. M. 228.

Gamboison, 372.
Gloucester, Countess of, 48; see Monthermer.
Gorges, Ralph, 74. M. 334.
Goundronville, Gerard, 66. M. 326.
Graham, Henry, 68, 72. M. 331.
Grandison, William, 24. M. 175.
Grey, Henry, 6. M. 106.
————— John, 40, 78. M. 235.

Hacche, Eustace, 32. M. 204.
Hastings, Edmund, 56. M. 299.
————— John, 54, 80. M. 295.
Haumsart, Robert, 68, 70. M. 329.

Helmet, 371.
Hereford, Humphrey Earl of, 86. M. 119.
Hodleston, John, 10. M. 114.
Huntercombe, Walter, 36. M. 9

Kirkbride, Richard, 76. M. 344.
Kyme, Philip de, 6. M. 104.

La Brett, Eurmenions, 26. M. 1
Lacy; see Lincoln.
Lancaster, John de, 8. M. 111.
————— Thos. Earl of, 46. M.
————— Henry de (afterwards of) 48. M. 270.
Latimer, William, 44, 46. M. 25
La Ware, Roger, 16. M. 155.
Lincoln, Henry Earl of, 4. M. 9
Lennox: see Dunbar.
Leybourne, William, 44. M. 257

Mare; see De la Mare.
Marshal, William le, 6. M. 101.
MAXWELL, pedigree of, xix.
Mohun, John, 18. M. 159.
Montacute, Simon, 40. M. 240.
Montalt, Robert, 6. M. 107.
Montbouchier, Bertram, 66. M. 374.
Monthermer, Ralph, 48. M. 275
Mortaigne, Roger, 36. M. 224.
Mortimer, Hugh, 40. M. 238.
————— Roger, 44. M. 259.
Mouncy, Walter de, 16. M. 143.
Multon, Thomas de, 8. M. 109.

Nithsdale; see Maxwell.

Paignel, John, 56. M. 300.
Pembroke, Aymer Earl of, 16. 145.
Pointz, Hugh, 20, 36. M. 167.

Quarrels, 371.

Richmont, Thomas, 70, 72. M. 332, 374.
Ridre, William, 38. M. 227.
Rivers, John, 26. M. 182.
Robinet, 373.
Rokesle, Richard, 74. M. 337.
Roos, William de, 20. M. 164.

St. Amand, Almaric, 30. M. 197.
St. John, John, 42, 46. M. 244.
————, —— jun. 50. M. 281.
Scales, Robert, 32. M. 208.

Segrave, John, 12, 86. M. 125.
———— Nicholas, 12. M. 122.
Shield, 372.
Siward, Richard, 34. M. 214.
Strange, John le, 38. M. 233.
Surcoat, 367.
Swan, Knight of the, 369.

Target, 372.
Tateshall, Robert, 18. M. 161.
Tony, Robert, 42, 74. M. 244.
Touches, Emlam, 34. M. 209.
Tyes, Henry, 44. M. 251.

Valence; see Pembroke.
Vavasour, William, 8. M. 113.
Ventaille, 368.
Vere, Hugh de, 26. M. 181.

Wales, Prince of; see Edward
Ward; see De la Ward.
Warren, John Earl, 14. M. 13
Warwick, Guy Earl of, 16. M.
Welles, Adam, 32. M. 206.
Wigton, John Baron, 75. M. 3
Willoughby, Robert, 68, 70. M

Zouche, Alan le, 50. M. 285.

PRINTED BY J. B. NICHOLS AND SON, 25, PARLIAMENT STREET.